The South West to AD 1000

A Regional History of England

General Editors: Barry Cunliffe and David Hey
For full details of the series, see pp. xiv–xv.

The South West to AD 1000

Malcolm Todd
(with a contribution by Andrew Fleming)

Longman
London and New York

Longman Group UK Limited
Longman House, Burnt Mill, Harlow
Essex CM20 2JE, England
Associated companies throughout the world

Published in the United States of America
by Longman Inc., New York

First published 1987

British Library Cataloguing in Publication Data
Todd, Malcolm, *1939–*
 The South-West to AD 1000. – (A Regional
 history of England)
 1. Man, Prehistoric – England – West
 country 2. West Country (England) –
 History 3. Great Britain – History – To
 1066
 I. Title II. Fleming, Andrew III. Series
 942.301   DA670.W49
 ISBN 0-582-49273-4 CSD
 ISBN 0-582-49274-2 PPR

Library of Congress Cataloging-in-Publication Data
Todd, Malcolm, FSA.
 The South-West to AD 1000.

 (A Regional history of England)
 Bibliography: p.
 Includes index.
 1. Great Britain – History – To 1066. 2. England –
Antiquities. I. Fleming, Andrew. II. Title.
III. Series.
DA135.T63 1987   941.01   86–18553
ISBN 0-582-49273-4
ISBN 0-582-49274-2 (pbk.)

Set in Linotron 202 10/12 pt Sabon Roman
Produced by Longman Singapore Publishers (Pte) Ltd.
Printed in Singapore.

Contents

List of plates

List of figures

List of tables

Acknowledgements

The Publishers would like to thank the following for their permission to reproduce plates in the text: Andrew Fleming (5.2a *and* b, and 5.3a *and* b); Exeter Museum (10.2); The Royal Commission on the Historical Monuments of England: Air Photographs. Crown copyright reserved (5.4 and 5.5); The Woolf-Greenham Collection (5.1, 5.6, 6.1, 6.2, 6.3, 8.1, 9.1 and 10.1).

Preface

The archaeology and early history of south-western Britain have been the subject of two outstanding works of synthesis: Hugh Hencken's *Archaeology of Cornwall and Scilly* of 1932 and Aileen Fox's *South West England*, first published in 1964. Having attempted to write a general work in the shadow of these two great achievements, all that I feel able to claim, in extenuation of shortcomings that will be all too evident, is that my geographical coverage is wider than the one and my chronological range longer than the other. A book of this kind, which begins with the first detectable human activity in Britain and ends in the relatively recent eleventh century AD, is bound to reveal some unevenness of treatment. That means there are gaps, and no one is more aware of them than the author. The South West is outstandingly rich in visible archaeological remains, especially in its upland areas, providing at once an encouragement and a deterrent. That richness cannot be fully displayed in a book which must of necessity present themes and processes in some consecutive way. If this volume provides a framework within which research can develop for a time without undue distortion, then something will have been achieved.

Many friends and colleagues have helped in the writing of this book, not always knowingly. I am particularly indebted to the following for information and advice. I hope that none will feel traduced by mention here.

John Allan, Nick Balaam, Katherine Barker, Neil Beagrie, Peter Berridge, Richard Bradley, Andrew Brown, Pat Carlyon, Chris Caseldine, Barry Cunliffe, Les Douch, Andrew Fleming, Aileen Fox, Cynthia Gaskell-Brown, Joyce Greenham, Tom Greeves, Sean Goddard, Daphne Harris, Chris Henderson, Robert Higham, Mary Irwin, Nicholas Johnson, Michelle Lawson, David Lloyd, Valerie Maxfield, Roger Mercer, Bryony Orme, Roger Penhallurick, Ann Preston-Jones, Henrietta Quinnell, Ralegh Radford, William Ravenhill, Alison Roberts, Peter Rose, Mike Rouillard, Win Scutt, Shirley Simpson, George Smith, Charles Thomas, Geoffrey Wainwright.

May 1985

General preface

England cannot be divided satisfactorily into recognizable regions based on former kingdoms or principalities in the manner of France, Germany or Italy. Few of the Anglo-Saxon tribal divisions had much meaning in later times and from the eleventh century onwards England was a united country. English regional identities are imprecise and no firm boundaries can be drawn. In planning this series we have recognized that any attempt to define a region must be somewhat arbitrary, particularly in the Midlands, and that boundaries must be flexible. Even the South-West, which is surrounded on three sides by the sea, has no agreed border on the remaining side and in many ways, historically and culturally, the River Tamar divides the area into two. Likewise, the Pennines present a formidable barrier between the eastern and western counties on the Northern Borders; contrasts as much as similarities need to be emphasized here.

The concept of a region does not imply that the inhabitants had a similar experience of life, nor that they were all inward-looking. A Hull merchant might have more in common with his Dutch trading partner than with his fellow Yorkshireman who farmed a Pennine smallholding: a Roman soldier stationed for years on Hadrian's Wall probably had very different ethnic origins from a native farmer living on the Durham boulder clay. To differing degrees, everyone moved in an international climate of belief and opinion with common working practices and standards of living.

Yet regional differences were nonetheless real; even today a Yorkshireman may be readily distinguished from someone from the South East. Life in Lancashire and Cheshire has always been different from life in the Thames Valley. Even the East Midlands has a character that is subtly different from that of the West Midlands. People still feel that they belong to a particular region within England as a whole.

In writing these histories we have become aware how much regional identities may vary over time; moreover how a farming region, say, may not coincide with a region defined by its building styles or its dialect. We have dwelt upon the diversity that can be found within a region as well as upon common characteristics in order to illustrate the local peculiarities of provincial life. Yet, despite all these problems of definition, we feel that the time is ripe to attempt an ambitious scheme outlining the history of England's regions in 21 volumes. London has not been included – except for demonstrating the many ways in which it has influenced the provinces – for its history has been very different from that of the towns and rural parishes that are our principal concern.

In recent years an enormous amount of local research both historical and archaeological has deepened our understanding of the former concerns of ordinary men and women and has altered our perception of everyday life in the past in many significant ways, yet the results of this work are not widely known even within the regions themselves.

This series offers a synthesis of this new work from authors who have themselves been actively involved in local research and who are present or former residents of the regions they describe.

Each region will be covered in two linked but independent volumes, the first covering the period up to AD 1000 and necessarily relying heavily on archaeological data, and the second bringing the story up to the present day. Only by taking a wide time-span and by studying continuity and change over many centuries do distinctive regional characteristics become clear.

This series portrays life as it was experienced by the great majority of the people of South Britain or England as it was to become. The 21 volumes will – it is hoped – substantially enrich our understanding of English history.

Barry Cunliffe
David Hey

A Regional History of England

General Editors: Barry Cunliffe (to AD 1000) and David Hey (from AD 1000)

The regionalization used in this series is illustrated on the map opposite.

*already published

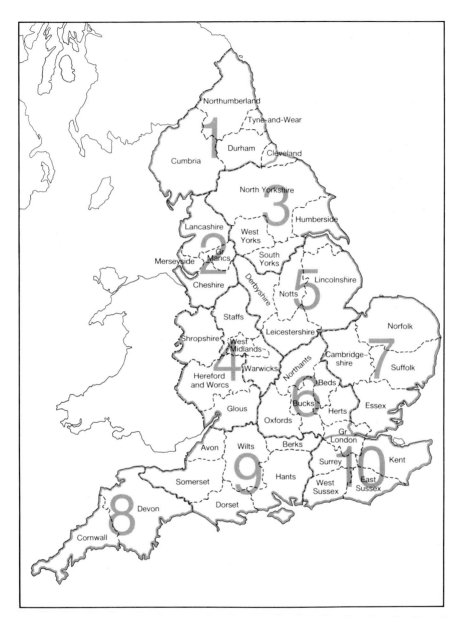

1. The Northern Counties
2. The Lancashire/Cheshire Region
3. Yorkshire
4. The Severn Valley and
   West Midlands
5. The East Midlands
6. The South Midlands and
   the Upper Thames
7. The Eastern Counties
8. The South West
9. Wessex
10. The South East

Chapter 1

The Land and the Study of the Past

The Land and the Sea

The briefest and most cursory acquaintance with the south-western peninsula of England is enough to convince the visitor that the most powerful influence upon the region is the sea. At no point in Devon is the sea more than 40 km away: for Cornwall the figure is scarcely more than 25. The long winding estuaries and the drowned valleys of the south coast carry sight and smell of the sea deep inland. In no other part of England are sea and land so intimately bound together. There are profound effects on much more than landscape. The traveller here soon discovers that he has come to one of the wetter parts of Britain. He may find comfort in the mild winters bestowed by a maritime climate, but the cooler summers than much of southern Britain enjoys may be an unwelcome surprise. It is easier to describe the land than it is the sea. But the sea is always present in the South West and human affairs have been subtly moulded by it since Britain became an island. It is not chance that the best known natives of the peninsula are Raleigh and Drake, and that the first south-westerner whom we can name was a sailor (below, p. 235).

This is an Atlantic peninsula, like Brittany, with which it has much else in common. Just as Brittany is like no other part of France, so the South West, especially west of the Exe, is like no other region of England. This is not merely due to the fact that it is an exceptionally long peninsula, with a coastline of 800 km and a land border of only 50 km. The South West *is* different, in its geology, its landscapes, its climate, and in the tenor of its life. There is nothing quite like high Dartmoor, or the salty moors of West Penwith, or the warm red land of Devon, in any other part of Britain. Just as sea and land are mingled together, so there is an un-English promiscuity of upland and lowland defying the ruling of Sir Cyril Fox that this is part of his Highland Zone (Fox 1938). There are no mountains in the South West and, except on the remoter heights of Dartmoor and Bodmin Moor, one is never far from sheltered and amenable ground. The areas of higher ground, however, do have the effect of shutting off considerable expanses of lowland, making them difficult of access and shield-

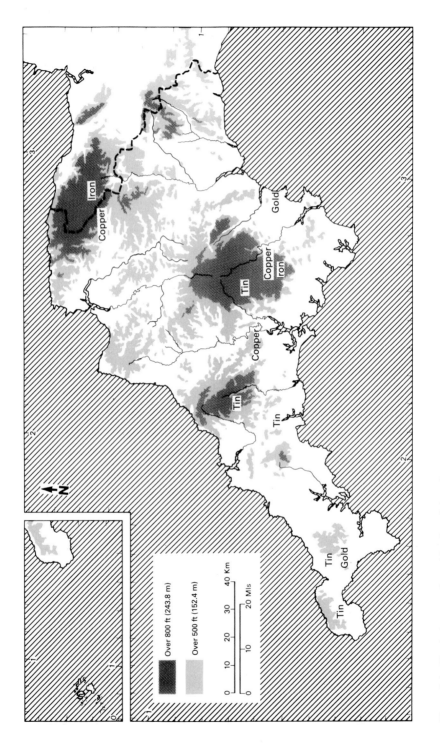

Figure 1.1 Physical geography, with mineral deposits

ing them from outside influence. This is often quoted of Cornwall. It is equally true of large areas of Devon. Diversity within the peninsula is still one of its distinctive characteristics as well as its principal attraction. It is a characteristic that is evident throughout its past.

Geology and Landscape

From the point of view of its geological history (Edmonds, McKeown and Williams 1975), the Cornubian peninsula forms a distinct entity, the main exception being the south-eastern corner of Devon where Greensand and clay country, and even a small fragment of Chalk, introduce an area closely related to Wessex. Stated simply, the peninsula falls into three major regions; a broad, low-lying trough lying between the Devonian rocks of Exmoor and the granite masses to the south-west. The central depression is floored by Carboniferous shales and sandstones which are subject to erosion; in south Devon, notably in the South Hams, there are found rather soft Devonian slates. The dominant feature is, of course, the series of granite uplands which diminish in height from Dartmoor (650 m on High Willhayes) across Bodmin Moor (430 m on Brown Willy), Hensbarrow (300 m), Carn Menellis (260 m), Lands End (260 m) to the Scillies (50 m) (Exley and Stone 1966). It is now accepted that this series of granite bosses or cupolas arise from a huge intrusive batholith, the form of which has been outlined by magnetic and gravity surveys. This batholith rises steeply along its southern side, extending southwards as a sheet some 10 km thick below Dartmoor, and terminating suddenly to form the eastern side of the moor. The massive tors of grey granite (Linton 1955) which are the most characteristic feature of Dartmoor and Bodmin Moor are the result of weathering and denudation of the cupolas over many millions of years, a process which first removed the covering of sedimentary rocks, exposed the solid, coarse-grained granite and etched upon its rounded slopes the radial pattern of drainage now followed by the main streams. The huge lozenge-shaped blocks of granite which often balance precariously on the tors display a varied range of the results of weathering, including temperature change, chemical processes, the slow attrition of small rock particles trapped in cracks and cavities, and above all the ceaseless action of the wind and rain. Below the tors the millennia of weathering have strewn the slopes with a clutter of granite boulders over which soil and vegetation is very slow to form. The erosion of the granite uplands and the development of the drainage pattern has been a long and complex process, best seen on Dartmoor. Early rivers played a part in eroding the rock to produce flood-plains and the broader valleys. The later uplifting of Dartmoor compelled the rivers to carve new valleys within the old producing a

3

well-defined series of terraces or erosion surfaces. The sea has also played its part. On the lower slopes of the moor, there is abundant evidence of a gradually falling sea-level in a series of flat platforms and steeper slopes which represent early shore-lines and cliffs. The highest levels at which these can be traced is just below 220 m OD (e.g. on Roborough Down and Green Down).

The same processes in Permo-Carboniferous times that led to the intrusion of the granite mass also bestowed upon the peninsula its mineral wealth (Scrivenor 1982). While the granite was still being crystallized, the remnant magma sent out hot volatile gases into fissures in the hardening granite and the adjacent deposits. This in turn led to the formation of mineral lodes within the granite and along the lines of weakness. Tin and copper were the principal minerals produced in this way and the 'strike' of their lodes is generally east–west, on the same alignment as the great batholith itself. Crossing these lodes from north to south, and of later date, is another series, containing lead, silver, iron and zinc. The later industrial history of Cornwall in particular is dominated by tin-mining but it is as well to note the presence of a much wider range of metal ores, including copper. Even the occasional nugget of gold has been picked up in west Cornwall. But the potential significance of tin in the prehistory of the South West may not be ignored and the subject will recur later in this account (below, p. 109). Tin-bearing gravels were deposited in valley-bottoms, in the west of Cornwall in particular, when the cassiterite ore-bodies were weathered under periglacial conditions in the Pleistocene. This stream-tin was frequently buried under alluvial deposits so that the early 'streamers', like their successors in recent times, were compelled to follow the buried river channels in their prospection, often to considerable depths.

Following the emplacement of the granite batholith, the region was severely denuded, apparently in very hot, arid conditions (Durrance and Laming 1982: 148–78). Huge screes collected on the slopes of hills to form breccias and conglomerates, while sandstones and marls were deposited in fresh water. Finer detritus was swept down the rivers and laid down at the mouths of valleys. The famous red soils of east Devon are the main visible result of these processes. These extend to both sides of the present Exe valley, northward in a narrowing belt into north Devon and similarly westward along the Creedy valley to the Okement. This is the rich heartland of Devon today, fertile and sheltered from frost and the western winds. Immediately to the east lies the narrow escarpment formed by the Pebble Beds. The most distinctive landscape feature produced by this is the area of commons between the Exe estuary and the River Otter, generally known as Woodbury Common, but including also Bicton, Colaton Raleigh and Lympstone Commons. To the east of the escarpment, the cliffs of the Devon coast reveal splendid exposures of Bunter and Keuper Formations, especially of the coarse red sandstones between the Otter and the Sid.

The Blackdown Hills and their outliers to the south and west have nothing in common with the landscapes of the South West proper. These are outcrops of Cretaceous rocks, Gault clay, Greensand and Chalk, in which the Greensand is dominant, producing long, narrow flat-topped ridges. The Haldon ridge to the west of the Exe is an outlier of these strata, in which the Greensand is capped by flint gravels. The Chalk outcrops are now limited to a few locations in the extreme east of Devon, the most striking being that at Beer Head where the Chalk contains bands of high quality black and grey flint exploited by Neolithic and Bronze Age man in particular (Macalpine Woods 1929). The chert which occurs in bands in the Greensand was similarly exploited.

The remaining area of high ground is Exmoor. Although lacking the bare wildness of Dartmoor, this is a considerable upland, more than half the size of Dartmoor and rising to a height of 550 m on Dunkery Beacon. Exmoor and the Brendon Hills to the east consist of Devonian rocks, the complicated sequence of which is far beyond the scope of this survey. Exmoor itself is a rounded upland deeply scored by narrow, twisting valleys and falling steeply to the sea on its northern flank. The soils tend to be both wet and acidic, and peat cover is now extensive. There are extensive mineral deposits on Exmoor and the Brendons, though how much these were exploited in antiquity is unknown, Iron lodes are close to the surface on the Brendons, while lead, copper and iron all outcrop on Exmoor.

The least attractive part of the region, from several points of view, is the great depression which lies between Exmoor and the Tamar valley. This broad vale of 2,000 km^2 is underlain by Carboniferous rocks generally known as the Culm Measures after the local occurrence in them of a soft, sooty coal for which the Devon name is *culm*. These rocks are chiefly the result of riverine deposition of sand and limy mud and are thus mainly sandstones and shales. They yield a range of soils which are heavy, wet and acidic, generally difficult to work but by no means devoid of early settlement. Indeed, in the early mediaeval centuries this was one of the richest and most populated areas of the peninsula.

The geology and landscapes of south Devon have much in common with those of north and east Cornwall. Middle and Lower Devonian rocks extend, in a broad band broken only by the lower Tamar valley, across the peninsula from the Atlantic coast across Cornwall and the South Hams to Tor Bay and Start Bay. These rocks were laid down in mainly deep-sea conditions and thus consist principally of sedimentary slates, mudstones, grits, sandstones and limestones. Their sequence is extremely complicated and need not concern us here. Of particular interest to the archaeologist are the Middle Devonian limestones around Tor Bay and immediately to the south of Dartmoor with their numerous caves and fissures (below, p. 37), and the Lower Devonian sedimentary rocks which impart to much of central Cornwall and the South Hams their open, rolling landscapes.

The igneous rocks of the Lizard are probably of Pre-Cambrian age and are thus the most ancient of the whole peninsula. The Lizard complex is an outstandingly complicated mass of intrusions in which serpentine, gneiss, schists and granite are to the fore. A major intrusion of gabbro, with associated dykes of the same mineral, on the eastern side of the sub-peninsula around and to the south of St Keverne, has been endowed with peculiar significance in certain archaeological contexts (below pp. 84–5). Gneisses and schists also make up the extreme tip of the South Hams, but these are most probably altered Devonian rocks.

The island of Lundy, 20 km north-west of Hartland Point in the Bristol Channel, is a plateau largely composed of Tertiary granite, the south-eastern promontory alone being of sedimentary Devonian rocks. This granite outcrop is the result of a brief period of volcanic activity in the Eocene and is thus related to the igneous rocks of Northern Ireland and Western Scotland and not to the granite of the South West (Durrance and Laming 1982: 238–48).

Glacial and Periglacial Conditions

It has long been appreciated that the Pleistocene ice-sheets at their greatest extent covered only small parts of the south-western peninsula of England. Together with the lower Severn Valley and much of South Wales, Devon and Cornwall, along with the rest of southern England, lay within a periglacial zone and were thus subject to the rigours of a very cold climate, and in particular to the effects of freeze–thaw processes (Kidson 1971). The results are clearly displayed in the landscape today: in the tors of the granite uplands, in the two-storied cliffs on the coasts, in the deep deposits of glacial 'head', and in the remains of frost-cracks and ice-wedges. Although it is probable that the region was largely free of permafrost, except on the highest ground, the effects of the major glaciations have done much to mould the land into its present form. The high moorlands in particular owe many of their distinctive features to the periglacial environment: the clutter of boulders below the tors, the terraces of rubble-drift, the buttresses on the valley sides. The coasts are another rich repository of evidence testifying to the influence of periglacial conditions, as was recognized early on by Borlase and De La Beche (Borlase 1758; De La Beche 1839).

Although much valuable work has been carried out on such matters as changing sea-levels in the Quaternary, the origins and age of south-western planation surfaces, the alternation of climate and the resultant effects on the landscape, many aspects are still imperfectly understood, or even inadequately recorded (Durrance and Laming 1982: 249–90). This brief summary must therefore be regarded as open to substantial revision. The development and disintegration of the vast ice-sheets to the north of the region were inevitably accompanied by major changes in sea-level, high levels corresponding to the interglacials, the lower to glacial phases. It is widely, though not universally, accepted that at the beginning of the Pleistocene, sea-level stood some 210 m higher than it does today. Indications of this fall have been identified in many locations, for instance in the Exe valley, where marine-cut platforms have been distinguished at nine different levels, and at a further series of six levels in west Cornwall. During warmer phases, when sea-level was fairly stable, erosion was largely linear. Lowering of sea-level led to dissection of valley-floors, the remains being left behind as benches or river-terraces. Although plainly evident in the South West, relatively little work has been devoted to these, particularly to the chronology of the stages which they represent.

Three main types of deposit directly resulting from the Pleistocene glaciations may conveniently be distinguished: glacial deposits (very few and limited in effect), periglacial deposits (very extensive in almost all areas), and deposits related to the interglacial phases. Glacial deposits, few though they are in number, are of particular significance for the establishment of a chronology. The glacial till at Fremington near Barnstaple, first described in 1864, appears to belong to the penultimate (Wolstonian) glaciation, as does a deposit of till on the northern shores of the Scilly Isles, most clearly revealed on St Martin's. The results of the same glaciation may also be in evidence at Trevetherick Point in north Cornwall. Still earlier glaciations appear to be represented by the occurrence of erratic boulders at many coastal locations, notably in Barnstaple Bay and in west Cornwall (Gregory 1969: 35). At Porthleven, for example, a 50-ton block of gneiss lies on a raised rock platform. These erratics were probably deposited on the coasts of the peninsula by rafts of ice which broke off from the ice-sheets to the north. The rock platforms on which they lie appear to date to the early Pleistocene, but much detailed study is needed to work out their detailed chronology.

Periglacial deposits are very widespread in the South West, not only on the coasts (where they are very much to the fore), but inland also. The commonest of these are the so-called 'head' deposits, angular fragments of rock embedded in a finer matrix, produced in cold climatic conditions and thus subject to congelifluction. Two distinct 'head' deposits have been identified on Dartmoor, Exmoor and in east Devon, both probably dating from the Devensian glacial or later. On Bodmin Moor, too, two deposits separated by a layer of peat have been distinguished, the later of which may date to the latest glaciation. Many features in the modern landscape are attributable to periglacial conditions of erosion and deposition, among them the terraces of rubble-drift on the granite uplands, the deep, dry valleys of north Devon, and the stepped slopes of Exmoor and the land around Dartmoor. In many points of detail, too, the succession of cold periglacial and warmer interglacial climates has left its mark on the land. In cold phases, the 'head' tended to accumulate on valley floors. When the climate ameliorated and sea-level fell after 12000 bc, the rivers began to excavate the 'head', a process which still continues on the Greensand uplands of east Devon. The fall in sea-level was also responsible for the creation of numerous dry valleys, especially in Devon.

In the lower Axe valley a prominent gravel terrace can be traced from Chard Junction southward to Broom and on to the coast at Seaton. Exposures in gravel-pits reveal this terrace to be composed of coarse gravels and sand, capped by a thin deposit of silt (Shakesby and Stephens 1984). Erratics derived from Palaeozoic rocks occur in the gravels, borne down by river channels in post-Glacial times. The Axe valley terrace also contains Palaeolithic implements of flint and chert, as has been revealed at Broom and Chard Junction, finds which are examined in greater detail below (p. 40).

The Coasts

This summary of the south-western landscape may not end without some reference to the 800 km of coast, in all its geomorphological variety. From the early survey of De La Beche in 1839, coastal studies have, understandably, attracted a great deal of attention (Kidson 1964, 1977). Studies of the raised beaches in particular have demonstrated that the present coastline is broadly a legacy from the Middle and Upper Pleistocene, a period when the level of the sea was only slightly above that of the present day (Orme 1960). Except in north Cornwall, there has been relatively little erosion since that time. For considerable distances, the ancient and the present coastlines can be seen to be either coincident or to run parallel to each other.

As early as 1758, Borlase described the raised beach at Porth Nanven. More than twenty instances had been identified by the time of De La Beche's *Memoir* of 1839, including the famous examples on Plymouth Hoe. Most of the beaches lie between present High Water Mark and 20 m OD, though related features occur up to 46 m OD. The southern coast from Dawlish to the Land's End reveals many exposures and the Atlantic coast of Cornwall offers others as far east as the estuary of the Camel.

The raised beach most visibly in evidence is the so-called 'preglacial' beach, or, as it is now commonly termed, the *Patella* beach. This is now held to be interglacial in origin. It is particularly visible between Prawle Point and Start Point, and inland from Mount's Bay where it occurs up to 700 m from the present shore. The beach deposits range from sand to boulders and may be up to 7 m thick. They are commonly overlain by debris carried downhill by solifluction in periglacial conditions.

Towards the end of the glacial period, as the volume and force of rivers diminished, the alluvium which had formerly been largely swept away was deposited in greater quantity on the coastal lowlands and estuaries. Over these deposits of fine, fertile earth a forest cover developed. Later, the lower lying vegetation was subject to submergence as the level of the sea rose. The result is one of the best known phenomena of peninsular geology, the 'submerged forests', of which the most extensive remains lie off the south coasts (Johnson and David 1982: 95). As early as 1818 a large area of buried vegetation was recorded in Mount's Bay between Penzance and Marazion, leaves and trunks of oak, hazel and birch being found in a peaty layer over a metre thick. Gales and high seas have revealed many other remains of this kind, for example at Falmouth, Perranporth, Porthleven, Hayle, Fowey, Looe and Bude, and in Devon in Start Bay, Salcombe and Sidmouth. Tin-streaming in valleys has also uncovered buried horizons of vegetation, in some cases containing remains of insects, molluscs, animals and, occasionally, humans. Unfortunately, few of the latter finds have been adequately recorded and subjected to detailed examination. Several of the early accounts are emphatic about the suddenness with which these wooded areas were overwhelmed and it is possible that in some cases at least submergence was due to a sweeping deluge driven inland by huge gales. Such massive storm-floods are quite well recorded in recent times.

Later, infilling of the lower reaches of valleys and estuaries continued. This process is still proceeding, though at a steadily diminishing rate, and has in recorded time drastically altered several estuaries. The Fowey, for example, was navigable up to Lostwithiel in the nineteenth century, the Fal to Tregoney until about 1600. The tide once reached St Blazey and St Erth, and even Grampound may have been accessible from the sea in the seventeenth century. Several major estuaries have been partially blocked by sand and shingle bars, including the Camel by Doom Bar and the Exe by Dawlish Warren. Others have been wholly dammed like the Cober river, a circumstance which has sealed off the former port of Helston from the sea. The freshwater pools which often form behind these bars, as at Slapton Ley and Marazion, in due course become choked with sediment and are turned into marshes.

Another feature of relatively recent time to leave its mark on the Cornish coast in particular is sand borne inland by south-westerly winds to form extensive dunes, commonly known as 'towans'. The largest of these are found on the north coast of Cornwall, at Perranporth, Padstow and on St Ives Bay between Gwithian and Hayle. So huge are the masses of sand carried inland (the dunes at Perranporth are 70 m above the rock) that considerable areas of land earlier settled and cultivated have been buried. In this way numerous settlements, cemeteries and even entire buildings have been overwhelmed (below, p. 291) and occasionally uncovered again by subsequent gales. The most dramatic case is that of the two successive churches of St Piran on Perranporth sands, but there are many others, including Lelant church on the Hayle estuary, the Iron Age cemetery at Harlyn Bay and the early medieval settlement at Mawgan Porth (below, p. 305).

The processes of marine transgression and submergence have left their

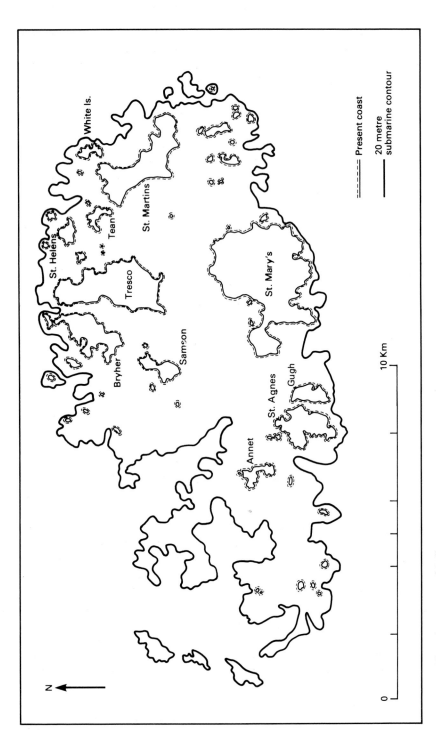

Figure 1.2 The submergence of Scilly

mark on one part of the region in particular, the Isles of Scilly. Borlase first drew attention to the 'great alterations which the Islands of Sylley have undergone' and later observers, including Crawford (1927), recorded some of the evidence for submergence of areas once occupied and cultivated, notably on Samson Flats. Briefly, this evidence consists of field-walls and other boundaries, huts, cists and other structures occurring about or below High Water Mark. Most of these remains are located in or adjacent to the internal waters of the island group and to some extent owe their preservation to their positions in these fairly shallow, sheltered waters. We cannot yet begin to discuss in detail the chronology of this submergence. But the conclusions of the latest and most comprehensive field-work in the islands (Ashbee 1974; Fowler and Thomas 1979: Thomas 1985) are that much of Scilly was once a single island, measuring roughly 8 km from east to west and 6 km north to south, with outliers to the south-west, and that this was so during much, if not all, of the Roman period. References in Roman writers to a single island, *Sillina*, are thus entirely explicable (below, p. 217). The main period of transgression may have begun in the later Roman period, intensified in the following centuries, finally producing the existing archipelago by the late medieval period. The level of the sea continues to rise, at a slight but measurable rate. There are important implications here for the study of the past of Scilly and probably also of Cornwall.

The Discovery of the Past

The discovery of the south-western past, in common with that of much of southern Britain, began as the Middle Ages drew to a close. The earliest journey in the South West of which a substantial record survives is that made in 1478 by William Worcestre (or William Bottoner as he often called himself), a forerunner of that distinguished school of British topographers which flourished in the sixteenth century (Harvey 1969). Worcestre's *Itineraries* were an account in Latin of a single journey which took him from Norwich to St Michael's Mount. He entered Devon from Somerset, passing through the centre of the county of Okehampton. On 13 September he arrived at Launceston and spent the next week in Cornwall, visiting Bodmin, Truro, Marazion, St Michael's Mount, Lostwithiel, Liskeard and Fowey. The account of this rapid tour is chiefly of interest to us for its architectural and archaeological detail. William was not, however, an outstanding observer. He was a great hagiographer rather than a topographer, a traveller, not a professional scholar. What is remarkable about his journey is the fact that he penetrated so far west in the late fifteenth century.

The substance of Worcestre's work is a series of brief observations, in no

11

particular order, on the topography, natural features, buildings and documents which he came across. As befits a traveller's notebook, distances are faithfully recorded, as are the major rivers, roads and bridges. Antiquities of great age are not prominent in the account. Visible structures, including great churches and castles, engaged his attention far more readily. Under the heading of castles and fortified houses, he did include hill-forts, cliff castles and other defensive enclosures. Some of the well-known Cornish Iron Age enclosed sites, including Castle Dore and Caerloggas, are here mentioned for the first time. Brief and disorderly as Worcestre's notes are, his *Itineraries* initiate that great tradition of topography from which in due course field archaeology was to grow. Its greatest exponents were John Leland (*c* 1506–52) and William Camden.

The work of these two illustrious figures needs no extensive comment here. Leland, in Kendrick's words 'a boastful, bigoted, and extremely touchy patriot' (Kendrick 1950: 49), stands at the end of the medieval tradition; Camden, who had drunk deeper of the Renaissance spirit, at the beginning of an enquiry which, in more developed form, still continues today. There is much in Leland which is reminiscent of William Worcestre's work, notably the attention paid to roads, rivers, bridges and castles. Earthworks receive mention but are not fully described or their significance discussed. Camden's majestic *Britannia* (1586), astonishingly the work of a man of only thirty-five, reveals a new approach to antiquity and to visible antiquities (Piggott 1957). Firmly based upon a sound knowledge of the ancient sources for Britain, his account of the 'Danmonii' presents in a few pages a lively picture of Cornwall and Devon in the late sixteenth century, with the theme of 'antiquitie' skilfully woven into the text. Sensibly, Camden relied upon the knowledge of at least one resident of the South West, Richard Carew of Antony in Cornwall. But the brilliant organization of the *Britannia* is Camden's own and succeeding editions merely underlined how decisive a break with the past the edition of 1586 really was. No single work published since the *Britannia* has had so decisive an effect.

Other contributions from Tudor antiquaries were less constructive. John Twyne, headmaster of King's School, Canterbury in the later sixteenth century, seems to have been the first to suggest that the Phoenicians, drawn on by the lure of Cornish tin, colonized Britain (Kendrick 1950: 105–8). He thus started a hare whose elusive shade is still hunted on the wilder shores of archaeological romance.

The most considerable of the early writers on the region, and the only one of south-western stock, was Richard Carew of Antony (Halliday 1953). His *Survey of Cornwall*, published in 1602 and dedicated to Sir Walter Raleigh, is a brilliant and intimate portrait of his native county. It is probably the most readable of the county surveys of the period, owing much of its charm to the multitude of discussions offered to the reader on Cornish customs, language, saints, mining, pastimes and houses. It contains also much that is historically and archaeologically valuable, as is to be expected of a writer who had contributed much on his county to the great *Britannia* of Camden. He had, indeed, been an Oxford contemporary of Camden and had immersed himself in the new antiquarian learning which is one of the jewels of later sixteenth-century scholarship. Thus we read of the drowned land of Lyonesse, the remarkable ruins of Tintagel Castle, the stone circles of the Hurlers, the Doniert stone and the Magdalene at Launceston. His love of the remoter past is evident from his fascination with the British history and the story of Arthur. So much, he felt, would be lost if man were to 'shake the irrefrangable authoritie of the round tables Romants'. Carew's *Survey* is a product of a particular and necessary phase in the development of British topography. It was to be followed by more substantial works of scholarship, but none possessed the literary qualities of the *Survey*. Devon is the poorer for having no comparable work of the period devoted to it. There were several attempts at a topographical account but none succeeded in finding a publisher. The most promising of these is John Hooker's *Synopsis Chorographical of Devonshire*, which was written about 1600. This survives as a manuscript volume of 171 pages in the British Museum. Hooker, who was Chamberlain at Exeter, was a very competent antiquary and his book deserves a printing. Later topographers used it as a quarry, but without constructing anything useful with the material. A somewhat later collection of manuscripts on the history and antiquities of Devon was compiled by Sir William Pole, but the project was incomplete on his death in 1635 and much of the material was a victim of the Civil War. The surviving remains were eventually published in 1791.

In the strictly topographical record of the South West, the contribution of the map-maker and surveyor John Norden must rank very high, if not at the very summit (Ravenhill 1972). Apart from the fact that he was born in Somerset, little is known of Norden's early life before he went to Oxford in 1564. He appears to have been of a somewhat melancholy disposition, a devout writer of religious treatises. In his early career, he made his way in the world by various services to landed families, which in turn led him into the survey of estates and later of counties. Norden's *Description of Cornwall* was completed about 1610, a manuscript copy being presented to King James. In it, much is described in impressive detail, including prehistoric cremation burials, megalithic burial monuments and fogous (or googoos, as Norden called them). But it is his use of illustrations which is chiefly remarkable and innovatory. In the illustrations of Trethevy Quoit and the Doniert stone, and no less of Launceston Castle, we can observe the beginnings of accurate archaeological draughtsmanship. Norden cannot lay claim to the fame of Camden, but he was at the least a worthy colleague.

Antiquarian studies did not make much headway in the South West in the long period from 1610 to about 1720. No work of real quality was published and some of the mediocre compilations of the period appeared long after their modest usefulness had been exhausted. This was the fate of Thomas Westcote's *View of Devonshire in 1630*, eventually published in 1845, and of Tristram Risdon's *Chorographical Description or Survey of the County of Devon*, finished in 1630 but not finally issued until 1714. This period of torpor was experienced in other regions of England, though in the South West it was prolonged into what was elsewhere manifest as the great age of antiquarianism. Edward Lhwyd's visit to Cornwall late in 1700 was primarily stimulated by his interest in the Cornish language. But he also had an eye for monuments and inscriptions, and twelve letters from him to Thomas Tonkin on Cornish subjects were included in William Pryce's *Archaeologia Cornu-Britannica* of 1790 and a number of his drawings of antiquities and inscriptions survive in the British Museum.

A friend of Lhwyd, and of John Aubrey, was John Anstis, a Cornishman who became Garter King of Arms in the early eighteenth century. He interested himself in the antiquities of his native county and compiled notes and drawings on them, though these did not become widely known in his own lifetime. Anstis was deeply involved in contemporary affairs and in 1715 was imprisoned for complicity in the rebellion of that year. His career as an antiquary did not prosper thereafter and he is now best known as the transcriber of Lhwyd's notes on field monuments.

Collection of materials for parochial histories of Cornwall was continued from the late seventeenth century until well into the eighteenth by two men, William Hals and Thomas Tonkin, neither of whom was able to bring his work to publication. Hals was a member of a Devonshire family who had settled at St Michael Penkevil. From about 1685 to 1736 he assembled a mass of material for his history, of very varying quality and overweighted by an emphasis on legends of the Cornish saints. On his death in 1739 the work was close to completion and about 1750 publication was begun by Andrew Brice, a Truro printer. Seventy-two parishes were treated in ten folio numbers, in alphabetical sequence from Advent to Helston. This publication is now a great rarity as purchasers were so few that publication was brought to a halt. There may have been a reluctance among leading families to subscribe to an account which contained so many discreditable anecdotes about their forbears. There is much of value in Hals, particularly on Cornish families and their properties. But he is not an authority of the first rank and the non-appearance of his work in its intended form was not a major calamity. In 1838, Davies Gilbert brought out a parochial history of Cornwall based on Hals's manuscripts and on those of a contemporary, Thomas Tonkin (Gilbert 1838). Tonkin, a member of an old Cornish family and Member of Parliament for Helston for a time, began his collection in 1702, at first being in touch with Hals and having access to his material. After thirty-five years of work he felt able to announce plans for publication. But financial difficulties intervened and he died in 1742 without any part of the work in print. Tonkin was a cooler scholar than Hals and his notes on topography, buildings and sites are of more lasting value. His manuscripts survive in their entirety.

The outstanding contribution to antiquarian studies in the eighteenth century was provided by the Cornishman William Borlase, born in 1695 the son of a Member of Parliament for St Ives [1].After Oxford, he was ordained in 1719 and returned to Cornwall in 1722 to take up the living at Ludgvan in West Penwith which he was to hold for half a century until his death in 1772. Although a devoted Churchman (and opponent of Wesley), Borlase found time for extensive scientific and archaeological studies. The isolation of Cornwall compelled him to concentrate on the far west, which for Borlase included the Isles of Scilly. Like many other early antiquaries he was interested in geology and it was for his work in this field that he was elected to the Royal Society in 1750. He began his field-work at the time when Stukeley and Horsley were revealing how rich the British countryside really was in visible antiquities and how much those antiquities could contribute to the whole picture of the past, prehistoric as well as historic. In Cornwall and Scilly, Borlase had a region outstandingly rich in monuments above the ground and he exploited it to the full. The standards of his field-work were high, as high as those of Stukeley and thus well in advance of most of his contemporaries. Although his draughtsmanship was not outstanding, it seems as if he may have been the first to publish a true archaeological section-drawing. Like Stukeley, whom he much admired (Pool 1966), Borlase introduced the Druids to explain certain monuments, notably the stone circles and chambered tombs, but included also as 'Druidic' were a number of phenomena of natural origin, such as 'Rock-basons'. Given the intellectual framework for British prehistory within which both Borlase and Stukeley worked, such deduction was not as naive as it now seems.

Borlase's literary output was immense, though he did not begin to write until he was over fifty. His best known book *Observations on the Antiquities . . . of . . . Cornwall*, appeared in 1754. This was quickly followed in 1756 by *Observations on the Ancient and Present State of the Islands of Scilly*. The equally impressive *The Natural History of Cornwall* came hard on its heels in 1758, to be followed by a pardonable lull until 1769, when *Antiquities, Historical and Monumental, of the County of Cornwall* was published. Scarcely another antiquary of the period matched this outpouring of substantial works, much of them based upon the writer's original scholarship. In his later years he worked at a *Parochial History of Cornwall* which was never finished, along with several works of theology (Borlase 1872). Happily his correspondence and many of his field-notebooks survive and are preserved in Penzance Library and the Royal Institution of Cornwall.

Unlike Stukeley and most of his contemporaries, Borlase was responsible for a number of excavations, notably on St Mary's in Scilly. The quality of his observation may be judged from the following extract from his account (1753) of the excavation at two barrows on Buzza Hill, St Mary's in 1752.

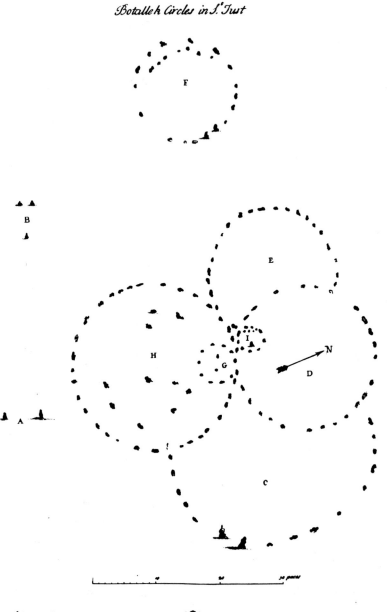

Figure 1.3 William Borlase's drawing of the Botalleck circles

We pitch'd upon a hill, where there are many of these *Barrows* and, as the common story goes, *Giants* were buried, with a design to search them, and on *Wednesday*, June the third, having hired some soldiers proceed to them.

In the first we found no bones, nor urns, but some strong unctuous earth which smelt cadaverous. In the middle of the *Barrow* was a large cavity full of earth: there was a passage into it at the Eastern end one foot eight inches wide, betwixt two stones set on end; the cavity was four feet eight inches wide in the middle, the length of it twenty two feet, it was walled on each side with masonry and mortar, the walls or sides four feet ten inches high; at the Western end it had a large flat stone on its edge which terminated the cavity; its length bore East and by North, and it was covered from end to end with large flat stones several of which we removed, and others had been carried off before for building the new *Pier*.

Forty two feet distant to the North, we opened another Barrow of the same kind, the Cave [chamber] was less in all respects, the length fourteen feet, bearing North-east by East, the walled sides two feet high; where narrowest, one foot eight inches, in the middle, four feet wide; in the floor was a small round cell dug deeper than the rest. In this we found some earths of different colours from the natural one, but nothing decisive. It was covered with stones like the former.

These appear to be the earliest recorded excavations in the South West which were in any sense systematic and in the quality of their record they were hardly surpassed for a century.

Borlase's illustrations give a fair idea of the range of his interests: stone circles, the Men an Tol, pottery from Beaker and later Bronze Age graves, the Iron Age coins from Carn Brea (an excellent engraving), various bronzes, hill-forts, early Christian memorials and carved crosses, medieval castles. As a tailpiece he added a Cornish–English vocabulary. Borlase's two major books are among the finest products of eighteenth-century antiquarian scholarship and are not yet as widely known as they deserve. It was to be nearly two centuries before another scholar attempted a major work of synthesis on the antiquities of Cornwall and Scilly.

The antiquities of Devon found no such exponent as Borlase in the eighteenth century. No one was inspired by the immense richness of the antiquities of Dartmoor to examine, or record them, in detail. The most eminent antiquary of the later eighteenth century with Devonian connections was Jeremiah Milles, Dean of Exeter from 1762 (Evans 1956: 124–5). He was well-connected and had enjoyed a very comfortable early career in a number of good livings. His reputation as an antiquary in the wider world was high, as his election to the Presidency of the Society of Antiquaries in 1769 indicates. But

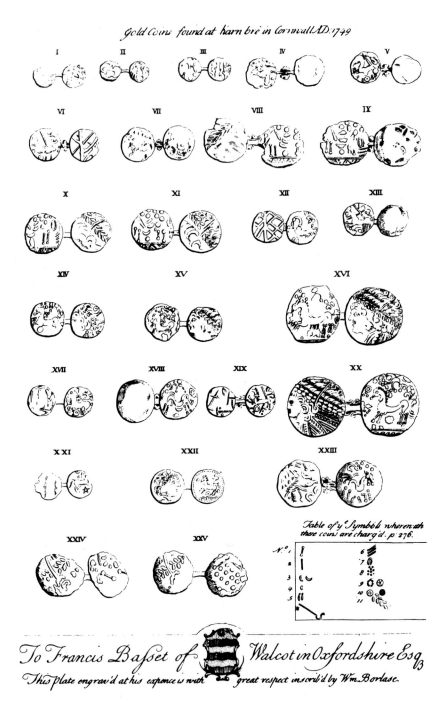

Figure 1.4 William Borlase's drawing of the Iron Age gold coins from Carn Brea

he published very little on Devon and his chief claim to our attention resides in a remarkable collection of information, which was never published, gathered by him by means of a printed questionnaire which was sent to all incumbents of Devon parishes and certain other residents. The replies which Milles received amount to a rich source for Devon history, antiquities and rural life, a source not yet fully exploited. These manuscripts now reside in the Bodleian Library in Oxford [2].

Devon remained without a county history until the very end of the century and when it finally appeared it fell short of the required standards. The Reverend Richard Polwhele's *History of Devonshire*, published in three volumes between 1793 and 1806, is a work of no great value, historically unreliable and indifferently written. The parochial descriptions in volumes 2 and 3 are the only parts of any use today and even these are incomplete.

The improvement in roads and thus in travel during the eighteenth century led to more intensive topographical study of the region, as of other hitherto remote parts of Britain. Of topographers with antiquarian interests one of the most effective was John Swete (born John Tripe, of Ashburton). He travelled widely, especially in north Devon, in the years 1792–1802 and produced a manuscript volume recording his tours. From his base at Kenton he also indulged in fieldwork on Haldon, a little of which found its way into print (below, p. 147).

If Devon lacked a capable antiquary in the mid-eighteenth century, at least it found a competent cartographer. Benjamin Donn, born of a Bideford family, produced a map of Devon in 1765, the original stimulus for which had come from a proposal put forward by William Borlase to 'employ proper Persons every year, from actual Surveys, to make accurate Maps of Districts, till the whole island is regularly surveyed'. This was a far-sighted suggestion and it was fortunate that the newly formed Society for the Encouragement of Arts, Manufacturers and Commerce (since 1847 known as the Royal Society of Arts) saw its merit and eventually established a fund for its financial support. In due course Donn was granted £100 for 'his actual and accurate survey of the County of Devon'. The essential field-work took up four or five summers and the drawing was completed in 1763. Two years later the map was published, in twelve sheets and to a scale of one inch to the mile (Ravenhill 1965).

Donn's map is now chiefly of interest to the historian as revealing the social and economic geography of the county in the mid-eighteenth century. Antiquities were not his prime concern, although some notable earthworks such as Woodbury Castle and Hembury, and an occasional prehistoric monument such as Spinster's Rock ('A Druid Cromlech'), were shown. Some medieval structures were included, chiefly castles and churches, and the rural seats of the gentry were carefully distinguished by small pictorial miniatures. Inset plans of Exeter and Plymouth were included, both of these important views of mid-eighteenth-century urban topography. In the case of Plymouth a surprising amount of detail was included on the naval installations. Finally, Donn's map includes an excellent picture of the roads of Devon, not comprehensive but representing the most complete survey of roads which had been attempted to that date.

Devon finally acquired a county history worthy of the name in 1822 when Daniel Lysons, working on alone after his brother Samuel's death, produced *Devonshire* as volume six of the brothers' *Magna Britannia*. Although devoted largely to medieval and later Devon, to the nobility and their seats, to ecclesiastical matters and to natural history, it also includes sound, critical accounts of some of the principal ancient sites. There is a particularly interesting section on ancient roads and trackways, which is not entirely vitiated by the fact that the writer, in this case a correspondent, was partly relying on Bertram's forged *Itinerary* of Richard of Cirencester. Following the appearance of Lysons' *Devonshire*, there was a perceptible quickening of the pace of research in several fields, and a steady improvement in the quality of publication. The new epoch was opened by an unlikely figure. John MacEnery was a Roman Catholic priest who came to Devon as Chaplain to the Cary family at Torre Abbey in 1822 (Alexander 1964). He was only 26 and there is no evidence of any earlier acquaintance with learned pursuits in the young man's career. By chance, according to MacEnery's own account, his attention was drawn to Kent's Cavern (then known as Kent's Hole) and he began digging there late in 1825. Professor Buckland had worked there earlier in the same year, but MacEnery was operating independently of the great geologist and indeed of anyone else. He found Anstey's Cave in the same year and carried out some digging there with the assistance of a Mrs Cazalet. A second visit to Kent's Cavern followed, this time in the company of Buckland and Thomas Northmore, in the course of which, MacEnery later claimed, he found the first flint knife ever recovered from a cave. Early in 1826 he found five teeth of a sabre-toothed cat (*Machairodus latidens*), though the true identification was not made until well after MacEnery's death.

Work in Kent's Cavern continued intermittently until 1829, when MacEnery suffered a serious accident in the cave and was nearly suffocated. He never fully recovered his health and was compelled to abandon his excavations. He died in 1841.

MacEnery's accounts of his work and his discoveries were far from meticulously recorded, but it is sufficiently clear that by 1827 he was seriously considering the possibility that flint implements might occur in the same deposits as the fossil remains of extinct animal species. Unfortunately, he himself did not publish any account of his conclusions and it was not until 1859 that any version of his manuscripts saw the light of day, and then only in a severely edited form. He found no support for his startling inferences from the Kent's Cavern evidence forthcoming from Buckland or the other orthodox Catastrophists of the day. Apparently deferring to Buckland's immense authority, and possibly his forceful personality, MacEnery did not press on with his project for publication and his major discoveries remained largely unknown for several decades (Daniel 1975: 57–67).

MacEnery is a touching figure. He was not a brilliantly original scholar and his methods of work were as crude as those which largely prevailed in the eighteenth century. But he was no mere collector. To read the pages of his manuscript is to observe a man wrestling with evidence which it was beyond the science of the day to interpret. That the effort was in vain is hardly surprising: it would have been astounding if he had been able to bring the mass of his data, geological, palaeontological and archaeological, into some sort of order. Whether or not the tendencies of his thinking about the contemporaneity of man and extinct animals raised any theological problems for him remains uncertain. It is difficult to believe that no mental tensions were aroused in this unpretentious man by his discoveries. Perhaps such tensions and uncertainties were ultimately responsible for the non-appearance of his projected *Cavern Researches*. Had MacEnery begun his work thirty years later, his achievement would have been much the greater and his name as celebrated as that of Boucher de Perthes.

The mapping of the peninsula made significant progress in the first years of the nineteenth century. Devon and Cornwall were among the first counties to be mapped by the recently established Ordnance Survey and a quarter of a century later they were the scene of major pioneering studies in geological cartography. The link with geological survey was to be an important one and its origins are not far to seek. The long tradition of mining in the South West had naturally stimulated an informed interest in geology and already before the nineteenth century much useful work had been done. A major impetus to co-ordinated study and record was provided by the work of one man, the forceful Henry De La Beche, who had spent part of his early life in Devon, returning after 1830 to devote most of his time to geological research (De La Beche 1839). Within a few years he was instrumental in setting up a geological survey on a semi-official basis and later succeeded in integrating the operations in Cornwall into the Ordnance Survey. The early Ordnance Survey maps for Devon (1813) and Cornwall (1809) although they possessed some of the limitations of eighteenth-century surveys, marked an important stage in the record of the peninsula, a tradition upheld by their successors until very recent times.

Geological research in the peninsula also made great progress in the late eighteenth and early nineteenth century, laying the essential foundation for some of the most significant archaeological discoveries of the following decades. Borlase's *Natural History of Cornwall* had already provided a good overall account of the rocks and minerals of that county, to which W. Pryce added much of value in his *Mineralogia Cornubiensis* of 1778. A little over twenty years later, the Royal Geological Society of Cornwall began to publish its annual *Transactions*, in which several notable works, on the mineral ores in particular, were to appear. The first major classifications of the rocks of the peninsula were attempted in the same period, by J. J. Conybeare in 1823. The Geological Survey carried out some of its first work in Devon and Cornwall and its first Director, De La Beche, was instrumental in the production of the classic *Report on the Geology of Cornwall, Devon and West Somerset,* in 1839.

These geological studies and surveys were considerably enlarged and made known to a wider public by the work of an extraordinary man, William Pengelly. This Cornishman of humble origins spent his later boyhood at sea and his interest in geology appears first to have been aroused by seeing fossils revealed in the classic beds at Lyme Regis. His life was a model of self-education and immense industry. Beginning as a village teacher in Looe, he trained himself in mathematics and natural sciences. In the 1830s he moved to Torquay and established himself there as a teacher and private tutor. His geological interests now came to the fore, and did so at a timely moment. Sedgwick and Murchison had recently established the outline of the Devonian system and further work was in progress by Godwin-Austen and De La Beche. For the next sixty years Pengelly worked, from his base in Torquay, on the rocks of Devon and Cornwall, with major diversions into palaeolithic archaeology arising from his exploration of the south Devon caves.

In 1844, Pengelly took a leading part in the foundation of the Torquay Natural History Society. Within two years a committee had been formed to prosecute further work in Kent's Cavern. This was directed by Pengelly himself and it was soon clear that the conclusions of MacEnery and Godwin-Austen on the remote antiquity of the man-made artifacts from the cave were correctly based. Pengelly, a devout Christian, apparently experienced no difficulty in accepting the implications of the Kent's Cavern evidence for the antiquity of mankind. But public opinion was not yet prepared to accept that Holy Writ could be revised by a study of the stratigraphy of caves. Not until the 1860s did the Kent's Cavern finds begin to win wide acceptance, and this was after another discovery in Devon had established the contemporaneity of man and extinct animals. In 1858 the Windmill Hill Cave at Brixham was discovered, offering the chance of examining entirely undisturbed deposits (Pengelly 1874). The latter point was of crucial importance, for one of the main criticisms levelled at the earlier work in Kent's Cavern centred on the allegation that the relevant deposits had been disturbed and confused by later activity. A committee of the Royal Society and the Geological Society entrusted the investigation of the new cave to Pengelly. In Pengelly's own words, flint implements were found in the cave earth, 'on which lay a sheet of stalagmite from three to eight inches thick; and having within it and on it relics of lion, hyaena, bear, mammoth, rhinoceros and reindeer'. The year that saw the publication of *The Origin of Species* thus also saw the true beginning of palaeolithic archaeology in Britain.

Pengelly's work was far from over. From 1884 he was back at work in Kent's Cavern and the reporting of the finds from this rich site was to absorb much of his time in the next thirty years. The mid-nineteenth century saw the foundation of many county societies for the advancement of various branches of learning. It is scarcely surprising that when the Devonshire Association for the Advancement of Science, Literature and Art was founded, a little tardily, in 1862, Pengelly was a founder member, and probably the instigator of the whole scheme. By now he was a scholar of national repute and his election to the Royal Society in 1867 was an honour richly earned. (One wonders how many of the contemporary Fellows of that body were self-taught.)

The Devonshire Association quickly began important work in preserving and recording sites and monuments in that county. In 1876 a standing committee, The Dartmoor Committee, was appointed to obtain and report information on many aspects of the Moor. Its expressed aims have a modern ring and would be accepted by any present-day Sites and Monuments official.

> The antiquities of this county are gradually decreasing from various causes. Those on Dartmoor are not less liable to destruction than others, and within the last few years some of the most interesting have been injured or removed. Among those that have been destroyed may be mentioned the quoit that covered the cromlech at Merrivale Bridge. A fine cairn that once stood near it was removed to make a road. Near Plym-head a barrow has been destroyed within the last year or two. It is therefore suggested that all known remains should be recorded and their position on the Moor identified with accuracy, and their size and form entered in a register kept for that purpose. If at any time one should be destroyed that fact should be recorded, as well as the manner and cause of destruction, together with the observation of any objects discovered during its removal
>
> (Collier 1877).

The same spirit led to the foundation of a Barrows Committee in 1879 and these two bodies continued to make useful reports until well on in the following century. The secretary of the Barrows Committee was Richard Nicholls Worth, another remarkable scholar in the mould of Pengelly. Born in 1837, Worth made his career as a journalist, mainly in the South West. Like Pengelly, he was largely self-educated having left school at fourteen. He came from a moorland family and his deep love of the Moor inspired his most important work. As a compiler of information, notably on Dartmoor geology and antiquities, he is without rival for he was as meticulous in recording detail as he was energetic in covering the whole expanse of the Moor. His scholarly method, too, was of a very high order, in sharp contrast to that of many of his contemporaries. Between 1869 and his death in 1896, he contributed more than 140 papers to local and national journals, most of them records of outstanding clarity, as well as writing several books, of which *History of the Town and Borough of Devonport* (1870) and *History of Plymouth* (1871) are the most notable. To gain a true impression of his labours we must read his annual reports published in the *Transactions* of the Devonshire Association.

Another of the leading figures in the Dartmoor Exploration Committee was Sabine Baring-Gould, whose greater fame resides in his hymns, novels and theological writings. Fired by his boyhood discovery of a Roman villa at Pau in France, Baring-Gould turned his attention to Dartmoor's antiquities during his family's residence at Tavistock about 1851. After taking Holy Orders, he eventually settled as the squarson at Lew Trenchard in west Devon and from that base carried out extensive surveys of Dartmoor and the eastern Cornish moors. He was not an exact and meticulous recorder of what he saw, but his boundless enthusiasm and energy did much to bring the archaeological wealth and importance of Dartmoor to general attention. He had his critics. Worth, for example, was not impressed by Baring-Gould's accuracy, nor, one suspects, by his imaginative approach to the reconstruction of the past. And he may not always have been entirely scrupulous in his claims to original discoveries. In his *Early Reminiscences* he claimed to have been the first to demonstrate that the stone monuments of Dartmoor had nothing to do with the 'Celtic' or 'Druidic' past but were relics of the Bronze Age. Baring-Gould was one of those formidable Victorians whose expertise and achievements in many fields now seem superhuman. But among his numerous interests Dartmoor was his love, his obsession, and the *Transactions* of the Devonshire Association from 1878 to 1896 reveal him at his most content.

There had been earlier work of importance on Dartmoor. The first accounts of the famous reaves appeared shortly after 1825 in the form of correspondence in *Besley's Exeter News* between Thomas Northmore, the Revd. J. H. Mason and the Revd. J. P. Jones. Mason and Jones recognized that the reaves were early land boundaries, though some later writers, including Rowe, introduced confusion by identifying some of the broader reaves as trackways. The Egyptologist, Sir J. Gardner Wilkinson made several useful contributions to the study of Dartmoor's antiquities, affirming, among much else, that the reaves were indeed boundaries. Curiously, later observers lost sight of this elementary fact. R. N. Worth, for example, thought that the great central reave was a Romano–British road continuing the line of the Fosse Way across the moor, while his son had little to say about reaves and nothing that was new. It was left to William Crossing to reaffirm their true significance in his great *Guide to Dartmoor* of 1906. The many hut circles and pounds on Dartmoor naturally gained much attention. The Chagford antiquary G. W. Ormerod recorded a number of sites on the eastern side of the moor in the 1850s and 1860s, as did Gardner Wilkinson at the same time. There seems, however, to have been little organized excavation before the formation of the Dartmoor Committee of the Devonshire Association.

Field-work in east Devon was in the hands of a different group of workers. The Revd. Richard Kirwan excavated and published three of the barrows in the Broad Down necropolis, unfortunately to poor standards (Kirwan 1867–8; 1869). Peter Orlando Hutchinson was active in the Sidmouth and Honiton area, recording and surveying sites rather than excavating. A major part of his work survives in an unpublished manuscript (Linehan 1983).

Some field-work carried out in Devon in the first half of the nineteenth century failed to reach publication. In the 1820s, Henry Woollcombe, a friend of Samuel Rowe, drew and described a number of the megalithic monuments of the South West, occasionally including plans. These records, along with similar observations on monuments in other parts of Britain, France, Scandinavia and Spain, were included in a manuscript volume bequeathed to Rowe and now housed in the Devon and Exeter Institution. Later, Wollcombe turned his attention to hill-forts in Devon, compiling a similar manuscript volume before 1839, *Some Account of the Fortified Hills in the County of Devon, whether British, Roman, Anglo-Saxon, or Danish with Plans of Many of Them.* This is not an outstandingly critical work and some of the plans are grotesquely inaccurate. But it was an enterprising first essay at a major task, unfortunately not taken up by others and still far from complete.

The most prolific of the east Devon antiquaries was James Davidson, the son of a wealthy London stationer, who bought the small estate of Secktor near Axminster while still a young man and lived there for the rest of his life, devoting much of his time to antiquities and local history. An early product of his studies was *The British and Roman Remains in the Vicinity of Axminster* (1833), still a useful source for the topography of that town, followed by *The History of Axminster Church* (1835) and *The History of Newenham Abbey* (1843). Thereafter, Davidson widened his scope to include all of Devonshire, publishing his most enduring work, *Bibliotheca Devoniensis*, a major work of bibliography, in 1852, and *Notes on the Antiquities of Devonshire* in 1861. Apart from this impressive range of publications he left behind him a manuscript of collected notes on the parishes of Devon based on his travels in the county. Davidson appears to have had little contact with other Devon antiquaries and field-workers in the mid-nineteenth century and as a result his work has suffered an undue neglect. Although not in the first rank, most of his output is still worth study, while his *Bibliotheca* is a major compilation on the past of Devon.

Before the middle of the century, the study of Roman Exeter gained considerably through the activities of a former army officer who settled in the city. The leisured W. P. T. Shortt devoted much of his time to rescuing coins, pottery and other fragments as they were turned up in the building operations then proceeding apace (Goodchild 1947). He was essentially a collector who went further than most of his kind in recording and publishing his acquisitions in a reasonably systematic way and speculating upon their significance. Coins were his principal interest and, largely thanks to his searches, the list of such finds from nineteenth-century Exeter is much more impressive than from any other Romano–British city at that date. Samian ware he also found worthy of record, including the potters' stamps as well as the designs on figured vessels. In Shortt's own copy of his little book *Sylva Antiqua Iscana*, now in the Westcountry Studies Library in Exeter, there is a handwritten note and a sketch relating to the discovery of a die used in the production of samian ware, found at Lesoux in the Auvergne, 'upon the site of an anct. manufty. of pottery', suggesting that Shortt attempted to keep up with relevant finds elsewhere. But he was no historian, nor did he carry out excavations of his own in Exeter. His literary output was confined to local newspapers, his two little books *Sylva Antiqua Iscana* and *Collectanea Curiosa Antique Dunmonia*, both of which appeared in 1841, being merely collections of what had already been issued in that medium. Nevertheless, Shortt's work must not be belittled. He represents that down-to-earth nineteenth-century attitude towards the past which fostered so many of the local and county societies which have performed so invaluable a service in the development of British archaeology. Unfortunately, Shortt played no role in the development of such an institution in Devon, for he left Exeter for family reasons in 1855 and settled in Germany.

Perhaps the most important work carried out in Cornwall during the first half of the century was the field observation of the relatively ill-known Richard Thomas of Falmouth. Thomas was an engineer and surveyor with special concern for tramways and railways, whose interests also embraced topography and local history. In 1815 he produced his *Falmouth Guide*, perhaps the first reasonably systematic account of a Cornish town. This was followed, in 1827, by a *History of Falmouth*. But his most remarkable work was never published in final form. From December 1850 to June 1852, *The West Briton* printed a series of fifty-five articles, the latter thirty-five of which were devoted to a detailed description of field monuments, notably in west and central Cornwall, many of them visited and recorded during his professional duties. No less than 490 barrows and 180 miscellaneous earthworks were dealt with in these articles. Thomas was very conscious of the increasing rate of destruction of these works and of the need to record as much of them as possible. Fortunately he made maps and plans illustrating his surveys and a substantial number of these survive in the Penzance Museum. They, together with the rest of Thomas' work, deserve a more permanent record.

In 1879, the Revd. W. C. Lukis, a member of a distinguished antiquarian family and at that time Rector of Wath in Yorkshire, worked on a wide range of prehistoric monuments in Devon and Cornwall, in the latter county alongside W. C. Borlase. The Society of Antiquaries of London supported the work with grants of money and in 1880 the Society undertook the publication of a series of volumes on prehistoric monuments, of which

Lukis's work in Cornwall was to be the first (Lukis 1885). It was duly published in 1885. But it was the only volume to be issued. In 1884 the drawings and most of the lithographs which had been prepared were lost in a fire. Lukis's monograph is an excellent and somewhat neglected work. His descriptions of monuments are brief but sensible. The surveys and drawings are vastly better than anything else being produced at the time, with the sole exception of Pitt-Rivers's work in Cranbourne Chase. Apart from being of a high standard of accuracy, they are most attractively presented and coloured. Much of the credit for them must apparently go to Borlase and he must be honoured for the best drawings of some of these Cornish monuments which have ever been published. Had the whole project come to fruition, there is little doubt that Lukis would have taken his rightful place among the leading archaeologists of the nineteenth century. His insistence upon the compilation of a clear and objective record is fully in accord with the aims of Pitt Rivers himself. Lukis must be regarded as a worthy peer of the great general.

Important pioneer work on several kinds of antiquities was carried out by J. T. Blight in the period 1855–80, though not all of it eventually found its way into print. Blight is best known for his good illustrated accounts of churches in west Cornwall and for the first serious attempt at a description of the many stone crosses across the county (Blight 1858; 1861). But his interests were very much wider, as is revealed by the contents of an album of his drawings, brought together by W. C. Borlase and now in the possession of the Society of Antiquaries. Here are drawings of flint and pottery artifacts as well as buildings, monuments, Roman milestones and later memorial inscriptions. Blight had in mind a volume on the 'Cromlechs of Cornwall' and his surviving drawings of the principal monuments are particularly worthy of attention a century later, when their condition has been altered in various ways. He had political aspirations, too, and achieved minor office under Gladstone. But a scandal, followed by financial ruin, brought him down. Later, Blight suffered a mental illness and resided in the Asylum at Bodmin, where at least he had the good fortune to be looked after by the chaplain William Iago. Iago was himself no mean antiquary and observer, though he seems not to have embarked on any major work intended for publication.

Discoveries in other parts of the South West were being made in these same decades and the more striking were becoming known to a wider public. The Rillaton gold cup was found in a barrow in Linkinhorne parish in 1837, finding its way thence to Buckingham Palace and, much later, into the British Museum. The Harlyn Bay gold lunulae were discovered in 1864, the notable Iron Age graves in the Stamford Hill, Plymouth, cemetery in the following year. Monuments in the field were also being recorded, not always outstandingly well. The fogou at Halligye was described in 1866, the barrows at Trevelgue in 1873, the Holcombe villa in 1880. No single figure was pre-eminent in these field researches in the way that Pengelly dominated his chosen field. Charles Tucker, secretary of the Royal Archaeological Institute,

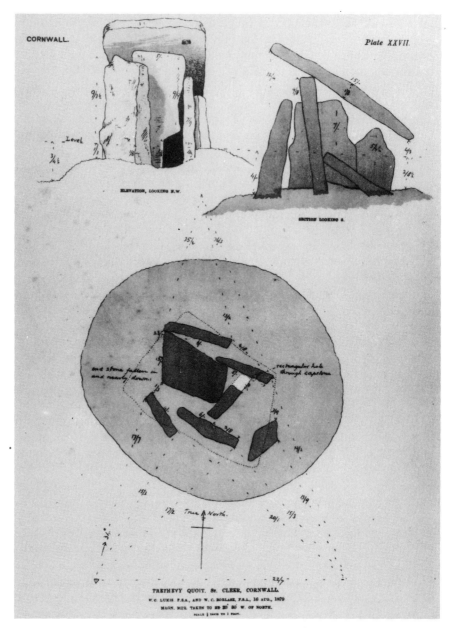

Figure 1.5a   W. C. Lukis's drawing of Trethevy Quoit

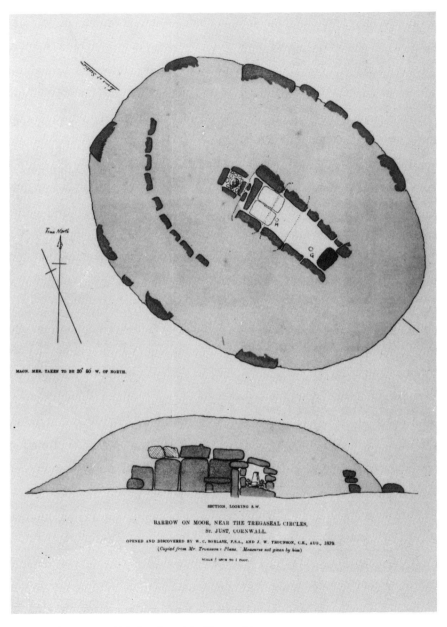

Figure 1.5b W. C. Lukis's drawing of the Tregaseal barrow

was resident in Exeter in this period and made several contributions on finds of Bronze Age metalwork in Devon during the 1860s. In Cornwall, W. C. Borlase, a descendant of the eighteenth-century scholar, was examining barrows and producing the first detailed plans of their internal arrangement. In 1872 he brought out his *Naenia Cornubiae*, a useful though hardly inspired collection of the results of his excavation and field observation. The abundant field monuments of the Isles of Scilly had also caught the attention of Borlase and of others. The redoubtable proprietor of Scilly, Augustus Smith, opened at least one barrow on Samson in 1862 for a 'select party of Cambrian archaeologists' and, at the very end of the century G. Bonsor excavated and recorded a number of chambered tombs on St Mary's and Gugh (Hencken 1933a; Ashbee 1974: 105–12). Bonsor's work was of a high standard, but was unfortunately not published for another thirty years.

Bonsor had settled in Spain in 1879 and there quickly became interested in excavation, inaugurating work on the great Roman cemetery at Carmona in 1880. It may have been the chambered monuments of the Iberian peninsula which first impelled him to visit Scilly and record there some of the burials which are now among the most famous of the islands' antiquities. He spent at least three seasons in these pursuits in 1899, 1900 and 1901, excavating with a care that was well in advance of the time and recording the burials in beautifully detailed plans and sections which show him to have been a significant, if rather isolated, figure in the development of recording in the field. That he has not been recognized as such is due to the fact that his admirable excavations were never published. Not until his drawings and notes were used by Hencken when compiling his *Archaeology of Cornwall and Scilly* of 1932 did the quality of Bonsor's work become apparent (Hencken 1932: 20–9).

Thus at the end of the nineteenth century, and for an appreciable time into the twentieth, archaeological studies in the South West, in common with most regions of Britain, had registered modest advances from the age of antiquarianism. The avenues opened up by William Borlase a century and a half earlier still lay open, beckoning the field-worker into a rich, unexplored territory. What was needed above all else in the earlier twentieth century was a fresh, major work of synthesis to lay a firm foundation for broad schemes of research. Such a work eventually came, for the further South West, in 1932 and it is a classic of its genre: H. O'N. Hencken's *The Archaeology of Cornwall and Scilly*. This arose directly out of Hencken's dissertation presented for his PhD at Cambridge on the Bronze and Iron Ages in Devon and Cornwall. The subject had originally been suggested by O. G. S. Crawford and several other scholars of the day assisted the young American author. But the final achievement was Hencken's own and this one book effectively brought the study of Cornish and Scillonian antiquity into the twentieth century. The range of the book is enviable and most of the periods covered, and especially those of later prehistoric time, bear the impress of

Hencken's own field-work. It was also well written, not the least of the reasons for its durability. It remains, after half a century, a handbook on western pre- and proto-history which is not to be ignored.

The 1930s saw the first modern excavations in the peninsula, notably Miss D. M. Liddell at Hembury in 1930–5, C. A. R. Radford at Castle Dore in 1936–7 and at Tintagel in 1933–4, and B. H. St. J. O'Neil at Magor in 1931. In the same period came further development of locally based societies with special archaeological interests. The Devon Archaeological Exploration Society (now the Devon Archaeological Society) was founded as an offshoot of the Devonshire Association in 1929, the West Cornwall Field Club, which formed the nucleus for the present Cornwall Archaeological Society, in 1935. The Second World War brought most field-work to a close and retarded the publication of several projects of the 1930s. Immediately after the war, fresh challenges faced archaeologists, especially in the shattered urban centres of Plymouth and Exeter. Lady Aileen Fox's work in the centre of Exeter in 1945–7 was among the earliest of such enterprises in war-damaged cities and, given the straitened circumstances of the day, it achieved important results (Fox 1952c). Lady Fox's subsequent work in Devon and Cornwall placed our knowledge of south-western prehistory in particular on a new and secure basis. The first careful excavation of settlements on Dartmoor took place under her direction in the 1950s, to be followed by outstanding field studies of distinctive forms of Iron Age hill-forts. The Roman conquest of the peninsula was also illumined by her excavation, with W. L. Ravenhill, of the fort at Nanstallon, near Bodmin and of the north Devon coastal fortlets of Old Burrow and Martinhoe. Her admirable summary of the state of research, *South West England*, first published in 1964, ranks among the best of regional archaeologies and takes its place alongside Hencken on any shelf of 'essential' books on the peninsula.

We can now summarize the present state of archaeological research in the peninsula, with particular attention to those aspects of the subject in which development has been slow, or which still present major challenges. The extraordinary richness in visible sites and structures of several areas has imposed its own peculiar influence on the progress of research. The outstanding degree of survival of ancient landscapes as well as settlement sites, burial and ritual monuments on Dartmoor has long, probably for too long, dominated work, especially in the prehistoric field. In the past decade it has been made clear that large areas of relict landscapes also survive on Bodmin Moor and in the uplands of West Penwith. Full study and assessment of these will take many years of work. For the present, the basic record has still to be assembled. The obvious attractions of working in an area as abundant as Dartmoor has inevitably meant that many areas of Devon and Cornwall have not received their full due of attention by field-workers. Thus, much of east Cornwall has been badly neglected, as has Devon south of Dartmoor. East of the Exe, much basic field-work has yet to be carried out on land which was probably very attractive to early settlers. Exmoor, too, has seen too little detailed field-work until very recently.

In all parts of the peninsula too few excavations have been carried out on anything like an adequate scale. Outside Exeter itself, indeed, very little truly extensive excavation of any one site over a number of years has been attempted. There has been too much nibbling away at such sites as Iron Age hill-forts, mounds, barrows and other burial monuments, groups of hut circles, Neolithic settlements, too much inadequate sampling of sites to enable any reliable conclusions to emerge. The large-scale programme of work at Shaugh Moor, in which the full range of available techniques was deployed, stands out among the rest and, although operations on this scale may not always be possible, they must always be the goal of the excavator. If anything has been learnt from the expansion of archaeological fieldwork in the 1960s and 1970s it surely is that small-scale excavation with sampling as its objective adds little to knowledge while squandering vital resources of money and expertise.

This point is made simply to explain why the present state of knowledge on the archaeology of settlement is, in most periods, still poor. To take only the common type of later prehistoric enclosed settlement, the round, of which hundreds exist, not one has yet been fully excavated and the few that have been scientifically excavated have all been examined on too small a scale for us to know what their internal planning was really like, still less what was the path of their detailed history. The larger Iron Age settlements, hill-forts and hill-slopes enclosures, are in an even worse case. Not one has been examined on the appropriate scale and few have even been excavated with a view of elucidating the history of their defences. Of most of them, no large-scale and up to date plans exist. Matters are little better in the Roman centuries. We are still woefully ignorant about the forms of rural settlement and the changes in morphology, economy and society which should be registered in them.

In urban archaeology, there has at least been excellent work in Exeter since 1945, and, on a smaller scale and illumining generally later periods of time, in Plymouth. But the beginnings of urbanism (if it may be so described) in the early medieval period are still extremely obscure and are likely to remain so for some time to come. This applies equally to post-Roman Exeter, to the new *burhs* in Devon and Cornwall, and to other embryonic towns. Most of the fundamental work remains to be done. It is probably in the early medieval field that the greatest advances will one day be made. With the exception of Gwithian, and Castle Dore, it is difficult to point to the controlled excavation of any early medieval (i.e. pre-English) settlement. Early ecclesiastical sites also present an open field, indeed with the removal of Tintagel an uncomfortably empty one (below, p. 262).

Within all these areas where major contributions are still to be made, there are deep-seated needs for larger programmes of environmental study. Aside from notable studies on Dartmoor and Bodmin Moor, techniques for reconstructing past environments have not been employed on a systematic basis and for many areas in the peninsula virtually nothing is known on this vital subject. The problems this poses for our understanding of early prehistoric periods are immense, but the need for major field-work projects in the Roman and medieval centuries is also pressing. In so many respects, we are at the beginning of our studies, nowhere near the end.

Notes

1. A forthcoming book by Mr P. A. S. Pool studies Borlase's contacts with other antiquaries of the time through his correspondence.
2. Milles conducted more field-work than is often realized, especially on Dartmoor. His activities deserve a thorough study.

Chapter 2

The First Endeavours: Palaeolithic Man in the South West

Lower Palaeolithic

The area of Europe of which Britain is a part lay at the north-western extremity of the Palaeolithic world. It is, in truth, both difficult and misleading to use the term 'Britain' at all within the confines of this immensely long period, for at times the land with which we are now familiar formed part of a large peninsula of the European land-mass, considerable parts of what is now the North Sea and the English Channel being dry land, while at others it was an island or a group of islands. Again, for long periods ice-sheets covered most of northern and midland Britain and extremely cold periglacial conditions obtained in the south. In other periods, the land lay in a sub-tropical zone and was the home of flora and fauna which are now to be found in latitudes three thousand miles to the south. All this has a bearing not only on the way the subject is studied but also, and more profoundly, on the survival of the evidence.

The student of the Palaeolithic is dealing not only with an extremely remote time, but one for which the surviving traces are excessively rare. The massively destructive forces of glaciation, erosion and deposition (to say nothing of Man's increasingly damaging intrusions into the Earth's surface) have undoubtedly removed most of those traces of the activities of Palaeolithic man which the archaeologist would expect to recover. Of the thousands of stone implements surviving from the Palaeolithic in Britain, only a minute proportion has been found *in situ*, and of these in turn only a fraction in controlled excavations. Sites (in the sense in which archaeologists of later periods use the term) which can be studied by the established methods of field-work and excavation are extremely difficult to identify, much less to examine. Skeletal remains, whether *in situ* or not, are relatively scarce and few indeed come from deliberate burials. Much more serious for the all-round picture of material which it is the prime aim of the archaeologist to reconstruct, the failure of such perishable materials as wood, fibre and even bone to survive in quantities which might represent their original importance is a major disadvantage. For the Lower and Middle Palaeolithic in particular we must regard the firm evidence we do possess as tiny pinpoints of light in an all-enveloping darkness. No one could hope to light his way with them.

Study of the Palaeolithic can be given shape only by reference to the Pleistocene sequence of glacials and interglacials. These component stages must not be looked upon as precisely defined periods of cold and warm conditions, their beginnings and ends accurately fixed by palaeomagnetic or potassium-argon dating. Within each stage there were considerable fluctuations of temperature and of other climatic conditions. The following table showing the divisions of the British Pleistocene must therefore be only a general guide to the changing environment in which Palaeolithic man found himself.

Table 1 Distribution of Palaeolithic sites during the Pleistocene period

	Devon	*Cornwall*	*Somerset/Dorset*
Cromerian			Westbury sub Mendip
Anglian		Porthleven (Erratic)	
Hoxnian	Fremington	Trebetherick	
	Raised Beach	(Raised Beach)	
	Tornewton Cave	Godfrey (Raised	
	(Laminated Clays)	Beach and Dunes)	
Wolstonian	Fremington Till		
	Tornewton Cave		
	('Glutton' Stratum)		Broom Gravels
	Kent's Cavern		
Ipswichian	Westward Ho!		
	Raised Beach		
	Plymouth Hoe	Porth Nanven	
	(Raised Beach)	(Raised Beach)	
	Joint Mitnor Cave		
	Tornewton Cave		
	(Hyaena Den)		
	Honiton Bypass Site		
	Kent's Cavern		
Devensian	Tornewton Cave	Hawks Tor (Peat)	
	(Reindeer Stratum)	Godrevy	
	Kent's Cavern	(Upper Head)	
Flandrian	Westward Ho!		
	(Peat and Clay)		
	Barnstaple Bay		
	(Submerged Forest)		

At present only two sites yielding Lower Palaeolithic artefacts have been scientifically examined in the South West, both of them caves in South Devon. Another site a little to the east, at Westbury sub Mendip in Somerset, has recently been added to this meagre total and as this site has been examined by controlled excavation it requires brief mention before the Devon evidence is discussed.

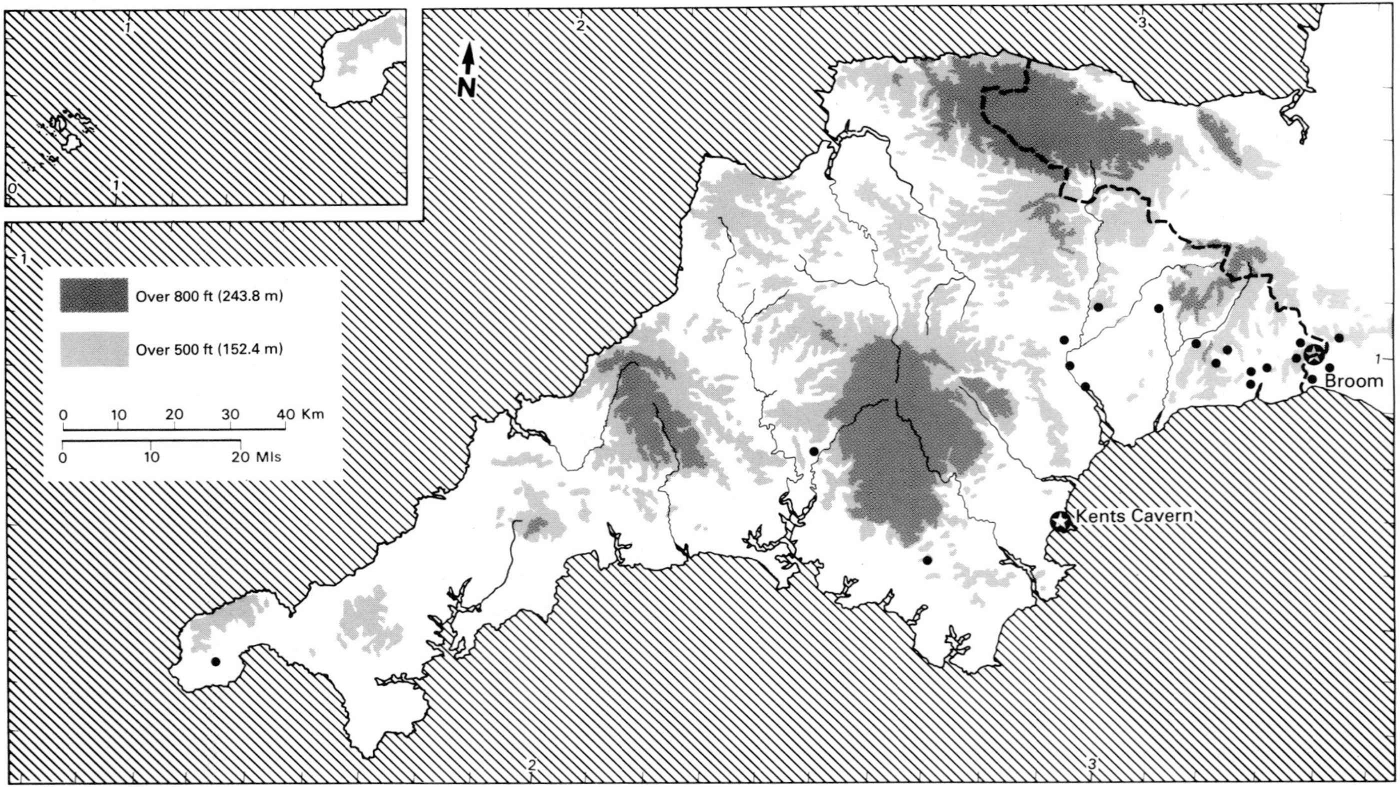

Figure 2.1 Distribution of Lower and Middle Palaeolithic material

The deposits at Westbury sub Mendip lay in a large fissure in the Carboniferous Limestone, probably originally part of a larger cavern system. The upper sediments, which are calcareous in character, contained a rich series of faunal remains, including species characteristic of the Cromerian, such as bear (*Ursus deningeri*), horse (*Equus mosbachensis*), rhinoceros (*Dicerorhinus etruscus*), wolf (*Canis lupus mosbachensis*) and sabre-toothed cat (*Homotherium latidens*). The smaller animals present in the calcareous deposits, notably from an earthy layer given the name Rodent Earth, support the ascription to the Cromerian interglacial or, less probably, to some warmer phase of the Anglian glaciation [1]. Undoubted artefacts from the fissure are few, but they include at least two bifacially worked flints, probably choppers rather than true handaxes. The very presence of flint objects is of interest as the material does not occur locally. Charcoal fragments from the sediments may indicate the use of fire in a habitation site at or near the cave-mouth, though this is not certain.

The importance of the Westbury sub Mendip cave is that it provides a clear association between a small group of Lower and Middle Palaeolithic (possibly Acheulian) tools and a probable Cromerian (and certainly pre-Hoxnian) fauna. Further study of the samples from the cave may define the date-range more closely, but for the time being there seems little doubt that this cave has produced the earliest evidence of human occupation in Britain.

Two of the most important Lower Palaeolithic sites in Britain lie on what is now the sweep of Torbay. These are the two caves, Kent's Cavern at Torquay and Windmill Hill cave at Brixham. The importance of Kent's Cavern as a major Palaeolithic site was revealed, as has already been noted, by the work of MacEnery, Buckland, Godwin-Austen and Pengelly in the nineteenth century (Roe 1981: 97–103). Modern studies of the material from both caves have demonstrated the presence of Lower Palaeolithic artefacts.

Kent's Cavern

The cavern lies on the western side of the Ilsham valley in limestone of the Middle to Upper Devonian, a formation which has undergone considerable dislocation, leaving shale and grit at higher levels on the adjacent hills. The limestone is bounded to the south and west by faults and is cracked by joints and fissures, some of which have been further enlarged by solution and erosion into large chambers and galleries. The system is actually a large and complex series of cavities, produced by dissolution of the Devonian limestone, linked together by fairly narrow fissures. The network of fissures follows two approximately parallel fault-lines which are linked by joints. Where faults intersect, large chambers have been formed. The fault lines are marked by high, rather narrow galleries. A further system of galleries lies beneath the main cavern, but this appears not to have been entered by Palaeolithic man. Before examining the earliest occupation material from this outstandingly rich site, the stratigraphy of the main deposits must be presented in outline. It will be recalled that by far the greatest amount of excavation in Kent's Cavern was carried out in the nineteenth century and that there has been no extensive digging which measures up to the best of modern standards. Fortunately, Pengelly's work was most meticulously recorded, even though it cannot satisfy all the demands of modern scholarship (Pengelly 1873).

The main components of the stratigraphy within the cavern are as follows, using Pengelly's terminology (Campbell and Sampson 1971: 7–10). Naturally, not all the elements are present in every cavity.

Black Mould   This contained a rich series of artifacts dating from the Mesolithic to the Medieval period: up to 30 cm thick.

Granular Stalagmite   This contained Mesolithic and Neolithic objects: up to 1.5 m thick.

Stony Cave Earth   Reddish sand and silt containing angular limestone fragments. Late Upper Palaeolithic artifacts and hearths, the latter in the Vestibule: up to 2 m thick.

Loamy Cave Earth   Light red silty sand containing limestone fragments. Early Upper and Middle Palaeolithic artifacts, the former occurring only in the topmost deposit: up to 10 m thick.

Crystalline Stalagmite   Patches of flowstone in the Gallery and South-West Chamber: up to 4 m thick.

Breccia   Limestone fragments cemented in a matrix of sand and silt. Very rich in faunal remains. Lower Palaeolithic artifacts: up to 3 m thick.

Red Sand   Apparently washed into the cave from the exterior. Very few artifacts and other remains: up to 1 m thick.

Older Crystalline Stalagmite
and
Laminated Silts   Lying over the bedrock of Devonian limestone.

The deposit which particularly concerns us for the moment is the breccia. Although the fact has often been overlooked by later commentators on the material from Kent's Cavern, Pengelly made it quite clear in his notes that artifacts were indeed found in the breccia, that is securely stratified below the deposits containing Upper and Middle Palaeolithic artifacts. Other observers have accepted the presence of man-made objects in the breccia but have mistakenly believed them to have been transported into the cave system by the forces of nature. The condition of the objects in question gives no ground for this. They are contemporary with the breccia and are thus stratigraphically earlier than the Middle Palaeolithic material in the Loamy Cave Earth above. What of the technology of the objects themselves?

Pengelly reported the finding of 116 artifacts in the breccia, of which only 29 can now be identified with certainty (Campbell and Sampson 1971: 17–23; Roe 1981: 99). Fourteen of these are handaxes, one a chopper, one a cleaver, one a uniface chopping tool, one a core and nine flakes. Although a small group of implements, this assemblage is tolerably coherent. The handaxes are rather crudely flaked and asymmetrical in shape. No attempt has been made to give them any kind of finish. Typologically, they are to be compared to Early Acheulian industries in Western Europe and Africa. The chopper, too, finds its closest counterparts on Early Acheulian sites. Crucial to the extreme antiquity of these objects is the age of the breccia from which they are derived. Its position in the geological sequence indicates that it is much older than the Cave Earth which contained both Upper and Middle Palaeolithic artifacts, without of course providing any pointer to its absolute age. The faunal remains from the breccia are more helpful in this respect. Bones of bear (*Ursus deningeri*) dominate this material, enormous quantities of bones of newly born individuals being present as well as those of mature animals. The sabre-toothed cat (*Homotherium latidens*) is also present, as are a number of rodent species. In its sum, the faunal evidence resembles that from the Westbury sub Mendip cave and must be assigned to the Cromerian, perhaps late in that period, or to a warmer phase of the Anglian [2]. It is greatly to be hoped that more of the breccia can be excavated by modern techniques of recovery in the future. For the present, Pengelly's careful records enable us to be certain that Kent's Cavern was visited, if not inhabited, by Lower Palaeolithic man.

The enormous accumulation of bones of bear, amounting to 90 per cent of the total of faunal remains, in the breccia stratum requires some attempt at explanation, as this is an unparalleled concentration of the bones of one species in one spot (Campbell and Sampson 1971: 23). It is, of course, possible that bears in hibernation or simply sheltering in the cavern had been trapped there or had met their deaths by natural causes. Since female bears give birth during the period of hibernation, the presence of the bones of very young animals could thus be accounted for. But this hypothesis does not adequately explain the unusual concentration of bear remains in this large deposit. There must be at least the suspicion that these animals met their deaths at the hands of Acheulian hunters, who took advantage of the vulnerability of bears in hibernation (cf. Green 1984). If this could be demonstrated by fuller study of the bones from this stratum, interesting light would be thrown on one aspect of Lower Palaeolithic hunting during the winter. It would also seem to imply mastery of some form of illumination to enable the hunters to locate animals hidden deep in the many recesses of the cavern, and therefore of the use of fire.

The implications for a general revision of the hunting strategies of Lower Palaeolithic man are thus considerable.

Several caves in the limestone at Brixham have produced fossil animal bone. The Ash Hole Cavern contained reindeer bones, as well as those of small predators, while the Bench Bone cave yielded up a particularly rich collection of bones, especially of hyaena. In neither case, however, were human bones or artifacts noted (Pengelly 1870–1: 73–7). The largest of the Brixham caves is Windmill Hill Cavern, a system of narrow, intersecting fissures and one large chamber. This was the scene of a major excavation by Pengelly in 1859 on behalf of a distinguished committee which included both Prestwich and Lyell. More was expected of the cave deposits than was actually revealed. About 36 flint implements, mostly now lost or mislaid, were found, in direct association with the bones of hyaena, cave-bear and rhinoceros, the most important being a crude, bifacial tool similar to those from the breccia at Kent's Cavern (Pengelly 1874; Evans 1860: 282–3). The most recent commentator on this implement does not commit himself to an acceptance of a Lower or Middle Palaeolithic date, pointing out, correctly, that the stratigraphy may have been more complex than Pengelly realized and that the lapse of time involved in the formation of the cave deposits was probably very long (Roe 1981, 103). The Windmill Hill cave is thus of considerable, though still unproven, potential, and further work is needed to clarify the significance of the artifacts [3].

Deposits of alluvial gravel are comparatively limited in the South West so that examination of classic alluvial deposits like those at Swanscombe and Hoxne has not been possible. In at least one instance, however, there are clear indications that a major Lower Palaeolithic site existed on the river gravels. This is in the Axe valley at Broom, near Axminster, on the Devon/Dorset border (Reid Moir 1936). Gravel extraction over more than a century has extensively disturbed the deposits containing the Palaeolithic implements, thereby producing thousands of specimens of which virtually none has any clearly defined stratigraphical or archaeological context. Many fine handaxes from Broom are preserved in Exeter Museum and in the British Museum. Unfortunately, the less impressive implements and flakes, and no doubt the less attractive handaxes, have largely been ignored or discarded so that a balanced view of the material is not possible. Further, since there has been no archaeological examination of the Broom deposits, the effects of periglacial conditions on the positions of the artifacts, in so far as these are recorded at all, are quite unknown. The potential importance of the Broom gravels remains high, however, despite these limitations and a thorough study of the lower Axe valley is a major desideratum. The recent discovery of a series of Lower Palaeolithic handaxes in gravels at Kilmington, near Axminster, is a further indication of the potential significance of the Axe valley for the study of this period.

An excellent and abundant raw material for handaxes and other implements was available to Palaeolithic man in the form of Greensand chert, a tough medium but workable without undue effort. The Axe valley chert is highly distinctive, greenish-brown shading to medium brown in colour and usually with a dull sheen when the implement has not been weathered or rolled. It is unknown how many Lower Palaeolithic implements have been recovered from the Broom gravels but the total must run into thousands. More than one thousand are represented in a single private collection.

Only one section of the Broom gravels has been published, by J. Reid Moir in 1936. This records a thick deposit of tumbled gravel to a depth of 25 ft below the modern surface. This contained a number of displaced implements. Below this lay the most interesting layers, incorporating a sequence of old ground-surfaces with interleaves of stratified gravels. These layers yielded a number of implements, apparently *in situ* and suggestive of working surfaces visited over a long period of time. Below these surfaces in turn lay a further 17 ft of gravel and sand, probably laid by glacial melt-water over the bedrock of Gault clay.

Use of sites like these at Broom and elsewhere can be given a little more substance by reference to continental sites in similar latitudes. At Salzgitter-Lebenstedt, near Brunswick, for example, an open summer encampment has produced a radiocarbon estimate of 55600 bp (Tode *et al.* 1953). In considerably cooler climatic conditions than those of today, the midsummer temperature being at least 5°C lower than at present, a wide range of animals was hunted as the herds moved northwards into the tundra in the warm season: mammoth, reindeer, bison, horse and woolly rhinoceros. The stone tools included late hand-axe forms but were mainly Mousterian flake tools. The working of bone and horn was common, notable items being barbed and plain points, and antler clubs. The hunting band which used this place may have numbered forty or fifty, suggesting well co-ordinated activity within some elementary 'command-structure'.

Since no other Lower or Middle Palaeolithic sites have been examined – scientifically or otherwise – only the distribution pattern of recorded handaxes and other implements, important and limited though this evidence is, provides any guide to the areas visited by Lower Palaeolithic man and to individual sites which might have been of particular significance in the cycle of hunting and subsistence (Roe 1981: 131–5). The distribution centres upon east Devon, notably upon the valleys of the Exe, Culm, Otter and Axe. For the most part, only finds of single artifacts have been noted. In three cases, however, interesting groups of several handaxes have been recorded from a single findspot, all of these close to a major stream. At Seaton Junction, close to the Lower Axe, six handaxes have come from the river-gravels, while others have occurred nearby at Colyton, Beer and Seaton. Among several sites in the Exe valley, that at Halberton, near Tiverton, has produced at least eight handaxes, as yet unpublished. The most westerly concentration occurs at Tavistock, where a site has yielded eleven handaxes and at least two flakes. Among these implements is a handaxe of Greensand chert, probably from the Axe valley area. Another, from Upton Pyne in the lower Exe valley, suggests either long-range hunting parties or possibly an elementary means of exchange. A third Greensand chert handaxe was reported from the Lizard in the nineteenth century, though unfortunately without precise details of its discovery and exact location. This may well be a modern import into Cornwall, though the possibility of its loss in the Lower Palaeolithic does still remain. Only one handaxe has been recorded so far west, from St Buryan. It is perhaps worth note, even though the total sample is relatively small, that no implements have been recorded from the Dartmoor upland, although a few are known from the fringes of the Moor.

A few finds of Lower Palaeolithic implements around Exmoor and the Quantocks indicate at least limited activity in this period. Some twenty-five handaxes have come from the gravels at Doniford near Watchet, some of these apparently composed of Blackdown chert. Isolated finds have been reported from Porlock Bay and from a number of sites in the Tone valley near Taunton. This west Somerset material probably represents activities similar to those in evidence around Broom to the south and thus more of these implements may reasonably be expected to turn up between the Blackdowns and the Bristol Channel (Grinsell 1970: 13–14). The occasional find of Broom chert has been reported outside the region, for example at Knowle Farm, Savernake in Wiltshire (now in Devizes Museum).

It has already been remarked that the South West lay on the fringes of the world ranged over by Lower and Middle Palaeolithic hunters. To the west and north of the region, in Ireland and western Scotland, there is no evidence of human presence during the Pleistocene. The distribution of the major known sites visited by Lower and Middle Palaeolithic man is mainly to the east, in southern and south-eastern England. Broom stands out as the most prolific site on the western fringe of this territory. Further west, little has been recorded. Since Britain was a peninsula of western Europe for lengthy periods, and since the total human population was very small, it must be regarded as certain that even in favourable climatic conditions it was a peripheral zone, to which groups of people came with relative infrequency (Roe 1981: 135). In no respect was it a region of innovation from which new ideas and modes of life were dispersed. The immediate contacts between the South West and the wider world were most probably with Atlantic Europe. Apart from the obvious geographical reasons, the typology of the Acheulian handaxes from south-western sites suggests as much. But links with northern Europe via south-eastern Britain are by no means disbarred.

The Earlier Upper Palaeolithic

Those developments which are generally taken to signify the beginning of a new stage in material culture, the earlier Upper Palaeolithic, manifest themselves in south Britain, as in western Europe generally, as regional deviations from Middle Palaeolithic traditions but with the possible impress of cultures from east and central Europe. The general context of this emergence of new industries and working traditions was the earlier phase of the Upton Warren interstadial, between 40,000 and 30,000 radiocarbon years bp. The earliest radiocarbon date yet obtained for this stage is one of 38,270 radiocarbon years, this from a horse bone from Kent's Cavern. Later dates from other samples from the same caves centre on 28,000–27,000 years bp. The total time-range of this cultural phase was not longer than 20,000 years at most, the later stages being accompanied by the onset of a glaciation which, about 20000 bp or somewhat later, brought human settlement in Britain to a close for several millennia. Even before this, migration in winter from Britain was probably the norm for a lengthy period.

The basis for our knowledge of the earlier Upper Palaeolithic is still slender. Only some forty sites producing roughly 6,000 artifacts are known from Britain as a whole, most of these cave sites or unstratified open sites. Four

Figure 2.2   Plan of Kent's Cavern

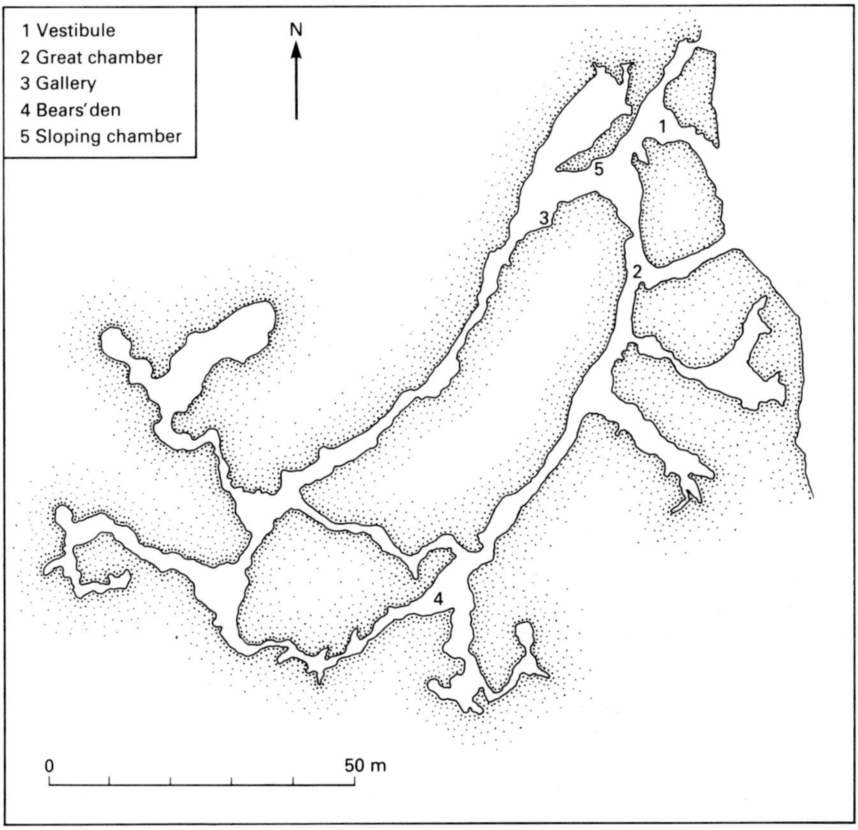

such sites are so far known in Devon, the record again being dominated by the material from Kent's Cavern, one of the most prolific Upper Palaeolithic sites in Britain (Campbell 1977: 3–4, 7). Two of the Devon sites, however, Tornewton Cave and Cow Cave, may not be included in the list with total certainty, although the evidence of their stratigraphy indicates that they might have been occupied in the appropriate period. Most of the Kent's Cavern artifacts were found by Pengelly in the deposit known as the loamy Cave Earth. Originally, about a thousand objects were recovered, of which only a few more than thirty can now be identified. All told, 112 implements of early Upper Palaeolithic types are now available from the Cavern. Numerically, the scrapers are predominant, accounting for 41 per cent of the total. 24 per cent of saws or notched blades, 10 per cent retouched flakes or blades, 10 per cent leaf-points and 7 per cent burins. Most of these tools are of flint, the remainder being of Greensand chert. Only the Paviland Cave in South Wales has thus far produced a comparably large sample of early Upper Palaeolithic tool-forms, so that it is impossible to assess how typical the Kent's Cavern assemblage might be. It is notable, however, that both of these sites include a substantial proportion of scrapers in their total equipment, although at Kent's Cavern the predominant forms were side- and end scrapers as against rounded scrapers at Paviland.

The most distinctive artifacts in the assemblage are the finely worked leaf-points of which seven unifacial and one bifacial instances survive. Where their find-spots are known, these implements lay in the southern part of the Cavern, in the Great Chamber, the Gallery and the South-West Chamber, whereas other forms were more generally distributed. This limited evidence might suggest that the final stages of butchering were carried out in and near the Great Chamber, following preliminary selection from the carcase at the kill-site. Scraping, cutting and chopping, by contrast, seem to have been carried on in most areas of the Cavern. Several of the leaf-points have radiocarbon estimates derived from associated material. The bifacial point from the Gallery is estimated at 28720 ± 450 bp, a unifacial point from the Great Chamber at 28160 ± 435 bp. The earliest radiocarbon estimate from Kent's Cavern is for a deposit in the Great Chamber which included two further unifacial points. These objects are among very few of the early Upper Palaeolithic in Britain for which reasonably convincing radiocarbon determinations have been obtained.

For our knowledge of the mammalian remains of the period, we depend largely upon Pengelly's careful record of what he found in the loamy Cave Earth, particularly in the Great Chamber. The commonest mammals were horse and hyaena, the presence of the latter being no doubt due to the species' predilection for sheltering in caves. Among the remainder, the following are well represented: cave lion, wolf, wolverine, red deer, bison, mammoth, *coelodonta*, *megaloceras* and reindeer. Red deer and *coelodonta* were notably commoner than the others. The bone-sample from the Cave Earth is large enough to make it certain that the commonness of the wild horse is not due to chance. This animal was clearly sought out by Upper Palaeolithic hunters and its presence further suggests that expanses of steppe-grassland existed in the vicinity, as well as a tundra-like environment on which reindeer grazed. There is a remarkable similarity here with late Glacial Scandinavia, where herds of reindeer, wild horse, bison and giant deer were hunted by man. In both regions, it was the larger herbivorous mammals that were of the greatest significance to man as sources of food, and those mammals were directly linked with particular forms of vegetation, notably tundra and steppe-grassland.

At least one cave in the group of limestone caves in the Torbryan valley, near Denbury in south Devon, has yielded evidence for occupation by Upper Palaeolithic man. This is Tornewton Cave, first examined by J. L. Widger (along with other caves on the western side of this valley) at about the same time as Pengelly's later investigations in Kent's Cavern. The two men knew each other but there appears to have been no collaboration between them. Desultory excavations in the late 1930s were followed by an organized programme of work supervised by A. J. Sutcliffe and F. E. Zeuner. The results of this important excavation were never published in full, but a summary account reveals one of the longest stratified sequences of deposits of the Pleistocene ever discovered in Britain (Sutcliffe and Zeuner 1957–8).

The main chamber of Tornewton Cave is in reality a deep pot-hole rather than a cave. Its great depth, more than 12 m, combined with a very slow process of sedimentation, has led to the build-up of a remarkably long series of deposits, which remained undisturbed by erosion or other agencies until Widger's exploration in the nineteenth century. The deposits in the main chamber were effectively protected from erosion by a mass of limestone against which the talus accumulated. Though of immense value in ensuring that the deposits in the main chamber remained intact, this circumstance makes it difficult to relate the stratigraphy of the chamber with that of the talus. Nevertheless, the carefully observed excavation of Sutcliffe and Zeuner, allied with study of the environmental sequence, has made of the Tornewton Cave a most revealing source of information on the later episodes of the Ice Age.

The lowest deposit, water-laid laminated clay, contained no faunal remains and thus its climatic context cannot be determined. A layer of stalagmite had formed over the clay, probably in moist, temperate conditions, and over this in turn lay a thick mixed deposit of earth, boulders and shattered stalagmite, the last-named indicating the agency of frost under extremely cold conditions. Two distinct layers were distinguished in this deposit, a lower named the Glutton stratum on the strength of the bones of glutton or wolverine (*Gulo gulo*), the upper being designated the Bear stratum, bones of *Ursus arctos* being abundant in the entire deposit. Cave lion, fox and wolf were also represented, along with horse, rhino and reindeer. A cold, but not arctic, climate is indicated by this faunal assemblage, and the most probable period is that of the Wolstonian glaciation.

The most remarkable deposit at Tornewton lay over a layer of stalagmite which sealed off the Bear stratum. This was a deposit of earth and coprolites

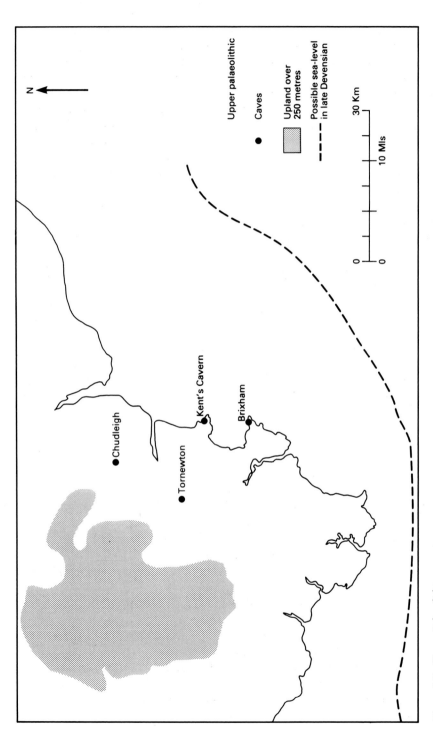

Figure 2.3 Upper Palaeolithic cave sites

Upper palaeolithic

● Caves

Upland over 250 metres

Possible sea-level in late Devensian

30 Km

10 Mls

Chudleigh

Tornewton

Kent's Cavern

Brixham

N

over a metre thick, containing immense numbers of hyaena bones and teeth (*Crocuta crocuta*). Over a very long period, the cave had clearly been taken over as a hyaena den, visited occasionally by other carnivores such as the wolf and the fox. The bones of other species in the deposit may have been carried in by the carnivores and as these included specimens of the southern rhino and the hippopotamus, a fairly warm interglacial stage may be safely assumed. Colder conditions are indicated by the later deposits, perhaps even permafrost. This phase fairly certainly is to be placed within the Devensian glaciation.

The first certain evidence of human activity within the cave occurs in the deposits which follow: the Elk stratum and the Reindeer stratum. The fauna in evidence in these layers are characteristic of the cool climate and open land-scapes of an interstadial and the Reindeer stratum contains a small number of flint artifacts, suggesting that man was using the cave on occasions. More interesting is the presence of more than 400 fragments of reindeer antler, as against a small sample of bone and teeth (Sutcliffe and Zeuner 1957–8: 138–41). The antler fragments are mainly bases (of naturally shed antlers) and other irregularly shaped pieces, suggesting strongly that straight lengths of antler beam were removed by man. Remains of bovids pointed to the same conclusion. These included nearly a hundred rib fragments, breakage having occurred when the bones were still fresh. This evidence for the selection of bone and antler clearly demonstrates human activity at Tornewton and the presence of man in this phase is proven by the presence of a human incisor, as well as a few flint tools. These include two blades without retouch, a pointed flake with two notches, and a backed point. Two bone artifacts were found in this same layer, a grooved fragment of antler and a rounded spatula. The evidence for human working of the site is thus greater than that for human occupation and the possibility that use of the cave in this period was seasonal must be enter-tained. There is support for this idea in the fact that the reindeer antlers are those of females and young animals, not mature males. Whereas males shed their antlers in winter, females and young reindeer do so in spring and early summer so that the total absence of the former indicates either that the cave was not in use by man in winter or that reindeer were not in the area at that season of the year.

Seasonal occupation of the Tornewton Cave by reindeer hunters is fully in line with evidence from other parts of north-western Europe in the Upper Palaeolithic. Several open sites on the north German plain, for example, indicate a similar pattern of reindeer-hunting in spring and early summer, accompanied by working of bone and antler and then followed by abandon-ment for the remainder of the year. The environmental evidence from Tor-newton suggests that the winters were too severe for reindeer to maintain themselves in this part of Britain and thus that the herds migrated south to the Continent when the short summer was over. This reconstruction of the relationship between man and large herds of herbivores is of considerable im-portance for an understanding of the life-style of Upper Palaeolithic man in the harsh environment of the Devensian glaciation. As has been noted, it accords well with evidence from broadly contemporary sites in western Europe. It also fits into the shadowy picture presented by other earlier Upper Palaeolithic sites in southern England and, more locally, may be related to the occupation of Kent's Cavern in late glacial times.

Campbell has plausibly argued that the south Devon cave-sites within 12 km of Kent's Cavern may have been used by Upper Palaeolithic hunters whose main base was Kent's Cavern itself (Campbell and Sampson 1971: 29). These groups could have been active in the valleys of the Teign and the Dart, as well as in the lowland plain now covered by the English Channel. The outlying caves would have lain within an arctic tundra environment, visited only in summer, as the Tornewton evidence suggests. What is sorely needed for further advance in this field is an intact series of deposits in a cave, preferably supplemented by examination of an open site on which the artifacts occur *in situ*. No certain instance of the latter dating from the earlier Upper Palaeolithic has yet been identified in Devon or Cornwall, though an area immediately north-west of Beer on the east Devon coast presents a possible candidate. Elsewhere in the peninsula, surface finds of flint and stone artifacts seem more probably to date from the later phases of the Palaeolithic. This is true of a number of sites on the Greensand of east Devon from which chert implements have been obtained.

Excavation in another of the Torbryan caves, Three Holes Cave, has yielded a little evidence to suggest the presence of Upper Palaeolithic man, in the form of a few backed blades and a number of roughly flaked tools in a vesicular lava. Unfortunately, the deposits from which this material came were very extensively excavated by J. L. Widger and little, if anything, remains of the original context (Rosenfeld 1964).

A life-style based upon similar hunting practices has been reconstructed for other areas of Europe in the Upper Palaeolithic. A study of particular relevance to Kent's Cavern is that undertaken by Sturdy (Sturdy 1975) on the Magdalenian hunter-bands which ranged over Germany and Switzerland, setting up temporary camps close to the limits of reindeer migration. During the winter the bands were resident in the north German plain. As the reindeer moved south in summer towards the Alps or north into the Scandinavian uplands, the hunters followed. In one of the summer camps, the cave of the Brillenhöhle in south Germany, the age-structure of the reindeer remains indicated that the animals had been killed in the summer months only. In winter the cave had not apparently been occupied by man. The analogy with Kent's Cavern may be close, although the Brillenhöhle is a much smaller cave, probably occupied by not more than ten people at a time.

Reindeer offer enormous advantages to hunter-groups. First, virtually all of the carcase could be consumed; meat, viscera, fat and even the stomach-contents which are rich in vitamins derived from the plants grazed by the animal. Their skins could be used for clothing and shelters, their sinews for

48

sewing and binding. The antlers, borne by both sexes were invaluable for many forms of implement. Secondly, the habits of reindeer make them easier to hunt than many large herd animals. Their migratory movements usually follow determined paths so that hunters have little difficulty in predicting where the herds are to be found. The herds are so large that, once located, it is easy to bring down one or a number of animals simply by firing into their midst. On the other hand, hunters largely dependent on reindeer needed to be mobile and prepared to operate far from any home base. The herds moved far and fast, up to 40 km an hour when trotting, making close pursuit impossible for any but a lightly equipped, unencumbered hunting band. Such a band might thus be away from its base for some time and may well have needed to establish temporary camps at or near kill-sites. Such constraints imply that the hunting of large herbivores such as reindeer and wild horse was organized on a seasonal basis, and for this there is compelling evidence from the north German plain in late Glacial times. Reindeer bone assemblages at Stellmoor and Meiendorf indicate that slaughter was seasonal, the bones of animals at certain stages of growth being entirely absent. In that area of northern Europe at least, the main kill of reindeer appears to have occurred in the autumn, as the herds moved north to their wintering grounds, with a smaller kill in the spring as they moved in the other direction. Whether or not a similar pattern of exploitation was followed in south-western Britain cannot yet be determined. It is, however, an entirely sensible procedure, the main kill being designed to provide enough food for the winter (when cold conditions would allow the storage of a surplus of meat), the smaller spring kill being all that was necessary to supply basic needs at a season when other forms of food were more accessible.

If a subsistence-system analogous to that outlined for northern Europe was followed by Upper Palaeolithic man in south-western Britain, it is likely that the entire peninsula and adjacent areas to the south were included in one social territory.

It is possible that a number of caves in the Devonian limestone in the Plymouth area were also used by Palaeolithic man. One of these was discovered at Stonehouse as early as 1776, but of this no record appears to survive. Quarrying of limestone at Oreston early in the nineteenth century revealed important cave deposits (Pengelly 1872). In them were found remains of extinct mammals; including cave lion, bear and woolly rhinoceros, as well as human bones. The latter may well have been in the same deposits as the extinct fauna, but were subsequently thrown away as being out of a credible context. Another interesting cave was found in a quarry at Cattedown in 1886, in the estuary of the Plym. The entrance of this cave had been sealed below sea-level, possibly since the final glaciation. Fortunately, this discovery was recorded fairly fully by R. N. Worth and may be regarded as reliable (Worth, R. N. 1887). A deposit of cave-earth 15 ft thick made up the bulk of the filling of the cave, this being sealed by a limestone concretion. Over this lay a mass of breccia some 5 ft thick. In all, the remains of at least fifteen human beings were found in these deposits, in direct association with bones of cave lion, rhinoceros and hyaena. Only one implement was certainly identified, a lump of flint from which flakes had been struck, though three horn splinters may also have been produced by man. No reliable dating can be applied to this cave and, as it has now been completely destroyed, no further data will be forthcoming. On balance, a date in the Middle Palaeolithic is likely, or perhaps early in the Upper Palaeolithic. Other potentially important deposits were reported from a cave on the south side of Battery Hill in 1879. A narrow fissure, partly filled with cave earth, contained a rich fauna, including wild horse, rhinoceros, reindeer, bear, hyaena, wolf, fox, ox and red deer. No stratigraphical record was made, but the range of species suggests that the cave was open during late Glacial times, while the presence of horse and reindeer raises the possibility of human use of the cave. At the very least, then, these meagre records of discoveries near Plymouth are a reminder that the numerous small caves in this limestone district may have served as shelters for Palaeolithic man and that the celebrated Torbay caves did not stand alone.

The Later Upper Palaeolithic

During the very severe conditions of the full Devensian glaciation which lasted from about 18000 to 15000 bp, it is reasonably certain that the south-western peninsula, like the rest of Britain, was unpopulated and probably unvisited by man. From about 15000 bp, or possibly somewhat earlier, the ice-sheet, which had extended southward to South Wales and the Bristol Channel, steadily receded and a fairly rapid amelioration of living conditions allowed human settlement once more. It was, however, still a harsh environment so that caves and rock-shelters were still favoured as major bases. The most extensive and reliable record of environmental change in later Devensian times thus far obtained comes from Bodmin Moor. Studies by A. P. Brown, notably at Hawks Tor and Parsons Park, have produced the earliest known organic deposits following the retreat of the ice (Brown 1977). The evidence of pollen indicates the existence of open grassland which must be earlier than 13000 bp, and probably appreciably earlier. The earliest radiocarbon date from Hawks Tor is of 13138 ± 300 bp, and is likely to be later than the pollen record. Further amelioration in climate allowed the growth of juniper scrub by about 12000 bp and sporadic patches of birch woodland, mainly in the valleys, before 11000 bp. It is known from other parts of Britain that considerably colder conditions followed and on the south-western uplands this phase of periglaciation appears to begin about 11000 bp on the radiocarbon evidence from Hawks

Tor. It is unfortunate that our information on this vital subject relates almost exclusively to the uplands, and specifically to Bodmin Moor. There is an obvious need to seek evidence from the valleys and the lower ground, since such areas are likelier to have offered man a wider variety of game and vegetable food. This work is yet to begin.

The animal population had altered too, though not profoundly. Large herbivores were present in abundance, especially the wild horse and the reindeer, to a lesser extent giant deer, red deer and bison. Woolly rhinoceros is also attested in the South West, though not elsewhere. Among carnivores, brown bear, fox, wolf and lynx were dominant, the hyaena no longer common. Lion and mammoth appear to have vanished by this phase.

One large limestone cave in the Buckfastleigh area has produced important evidence for Pleistocene mammalian fauna. This is the Joint Mitnor Cave near Buckfastleigh Church, which has yielded the richest deposits of faunal remains related to an interglacial phase ever located in Britain, amounting to over 4,000 bones and teeth. The most prevalent species were bison, hippopotamus, rhinoceros, hyaena, cave lion and red deer. Fox, badger, wild cat, pig, straight-tusked elephant, bear and giant deer were also represented in small numbers (Sutcliffe 1960).

The remains appear to be broadly contemporary and the range of species clearly indicates the warm climate of an interglacial. This receives further support from the complete absence of animals tolerant of cold conditions such as the horse, reindeer and wolverine. It is reasonably certain that the final interglacial is in question, on the analogy of the Upper Floodplain terrace of the Thames. A further site in Devon, on the outskirts of Honiton, has produced a similar, though more limited, fauna and may be related to the same interglacial. This was a peat-filled depression in the Trias in which lay many remains of hippopotamus (especially of old and very young animals), and smaller quantities of straight-tusked elephant, red deer and giant ox. These animals had apparently died at or near a water-hole or spring. Finally, the fauna of the Eastern Torrs Cave near Yealmpton seems to belong to the same warm phase since it includes hippopotamus, rhinoceros and elephant.

Kent's Cavern

Kent's Cavern was again occupied by Upper Palaeolithic hunters after the severe phase of the Devensian glaciation was over and again it is due to Pengelly's careful record that their occupation can be distinguished from those of other periods. Pengelly identified and excavated a deposit which he named the Black Band, which was largely restricted to the Vestibule and the adjacent

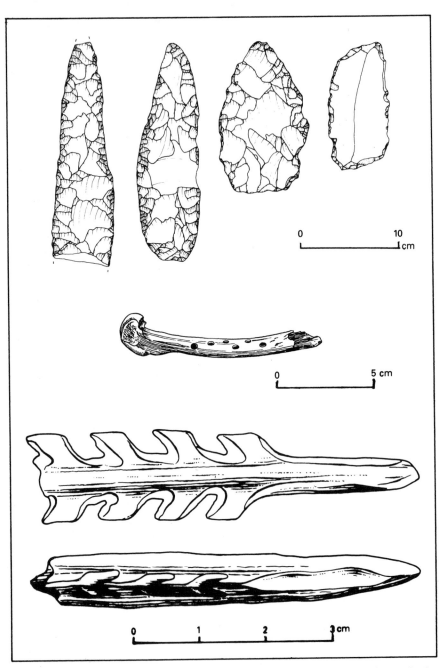

Figure 2.4 Upper Palaeolithic material from Kent's Cavern: flint implements; bone whistle; antler harpoon

Sloping Chamber, North Entrance and North-East Gallery. He recovered more than 500 artifacts from this deposit, of which Campbell has been able to trace 144 (Campbell 1977: 161–2). Prominent among these are five points characteristic of the industry in evidence at Creswell Crags on the Derbyshire/Nottinghamshire border and thus usually referred to as Creswell points. Backed blades and burins were also present, along with various forms of scraper, a saw and an awl. A small group of bone and antler tools was also associated with the Black Band. This comprised an eyed needle, an awl, two uniserial and one biserial harpoons of antler. Campbell has suggested that two clusters of implements are to be distinguished within the Black Band, one in the Vestibule, the other at the North Entrance, and that these may be discrete in time, the group at the North Entrance being somewhat earlier in date. Most of the bone and antler objects lay at the eastern edge of the Black Band, suggesting specialized activities (including sewing) in that area. Burins also tended to occur near the eastern side of the deposit. Scrapers, on the other hand, were fairly evenly distributed throughout the Black Band as might befit their many-sided functions.

The significant radiocarbon estimates have been obtained from this deposit. The find-spot on the eastern edge which contained a uniserial harpoon and a group of backed blades has produced an estimate of 14275 ± 120 bp, while material associated with the biserial harpoon to the north-west of the Black Band has an estimated age of 12180 ± 100 bp. These estimates of date are among very few so far obtained for the late Upper Palaeolithic in Britain.

Although not large in size, the material assemblage from the Black Band is of great interest. The backed blade is the dominant tool-form, the most distinctive element being the Creswell point. This was an obliquely pointed blade, backed down one edge and occasionally around the end of the blade. The fine leaf-points of the early Upper Palaeolithic have now disappeared, but fine flint-working is in evidence on the burins, scrapers and shouldered blades in particular. The bone and antler artifacts naturally catch the attention. These are well-made, the biserially barbed harpoon outstandingly so. The small needle and the awl hint at fairly advanced sewing techniques employed on clothing and perhaps other coverings. The barbed harpoons in particular are generally comparable with objects found on many Magdalenian sites in continental Europe: indeed Garrod believed them to be Magdalenian. The Kent's Cavern assemblage as a whole, however, is closer to that evinced by the final glaciation cultures of north-west Europe, notably the Tjongerian and 'Federmesser'-groups of that region.

The main animal of prey was still the wild horse, followed by giant deer and cave bear (Campbell and Sampson 1977: 13–16). Reindeer played a much reduced role in the meal diet. Probably there was a greater emphasis upon the snaring and catching of birds and small mammals. Among the bird bones represented are those of geese, swan, grouse and ptarmigan. Bones of fish are extremely uncommon finds, but this may be largely due to the inability of earlier excavators to recognize them. The harpoons clearly suggest that the catching of fish and sea mammals was practised.

The views of Upper Palaeolithic man himself on life and death, what might be termed his psychic needs, can only be glimpsed in evidence from other parts of Europe. The advanced Palaeolithic cultures have bequeathed to us the earliest considerable body of art, from the brilliant engraving and painting in French and Spanish caves and the female figurines of the Gravettian to the less ambitious, but still evocative, engravings and designs on pieces of bone or ivory. The South West has produced no certain example of decorative art of this period, though an engraving on bone of a human figure from Pin Hole Cave in Derbyshire and a careful series of notches on a bone from Gough's Cave in the Mendips (perhaps a tally) reveal that representational art and perhaps even an elementary numeracy were known to the later Palaeolithic inhabitants of the peninsula.

That not all of Upper Palaeolithic man's energies were absorbed in finding sustenance is well established. At least one object from Kent's Cavern hints at some form of imaginative recreation. This is the hollow long bone of a hare, perforated by six neat holes and thus forming a whistle or a primitive flute.

We may be sure, too, that burial of the dead was carried out, in at least some cases with formal ceremony. Again, the South West has produced no certain evidence bearing on this aspect of human affairs, but across the Bristol Channel the careful burial of a young man in the Paviland Cave, the body having been sprinkled with red ochure, exemplified a rite practised by advanced Palaeolithic cultures in other parts of Europe. It appears to be generally true that no attempt was made to separate the dead from the living and given them a resting-place at some distance from settlements. Numerous cases are recorded of graves being dug in occupation deposits within caves, while open settlements in eastern and central Europe frequently include graves in the midst of occupation debris. Grave-goods were frequently provided, usually in the form of ornaments for the person. Evidence from France and northern Italy suggests that some of the dead were buried fully clothed as well as decked with necklaces and amulets. All this provides leads as to where the Palaeolithic dead may be sought in the South West and how they might be disposed.

Notes

1. i.e. about 500000–400000 BC

2. Between 450000 and 350000 BC

3. The recent excavation of the Pontnewydd cave near St Asaph in North Wales is a most significant addition to Lower Palaeolithic studies: Green 1984.

Chapter 3

Mesolithic Cultures: Interlude or Prelude?

The conventional division between the advanced Palaeolithic and early Mesolithic cultures, marked in the record of material equipment by major changes occurring after the middle of the ninth millennium BC, is an issue which has long stimulated debate and disagreement among European prehistorians. Not all archaeologists of the twentieth century have been willing to accept the independent existence of an intermediate phase between the advanced hunter-gatherer cultures and the first farmers, with a more or less decisive break occurring at the beginning of Flandrian times. Gordon Childe consented to a very limited use of the term 'Mesolithic' to cover material assemblages which plainly fell between the Upper Palaeolithic and the Neolithic. More recent scholarship, notably in Eastern Europe but increasingly in the West, takes a more elevated view of the significance of the cultures which held sway in early post-Glacial Europe. The Mesolithic has in the past few decades emerged as a vital stage in social and economic development. J. G. D. Clark expresses the view succinctly: 'The time is now ripe to expound and justify the proposition that the Mesolithic, so far from being a dead end, was in fact an essential prelude to fundamental advance in the development of culture' (Clark 1981: 7). As early as the 1950s, some scholars were viewing the Mesolithic as a period in which the first signs of much that emerged into the full light of day in the early Neolithic became visible. There are no breaks in prehistory (still less is there place for a hiatus) and it is from this standpoint that the archaeological record of the early post-Glacial period is to be regarded.

It is easier to define a break between the late Pleistocene and early post-Glacial in southern Britain on environmental evidence than to distinguish clearly the emergence of recognizable Mesolithic cultures. On the present meagre evidence of a few radiocarbon estimates, the earlier Mesolithic commenced some time after 8500 bc, though the continuance of fundamentally late Upper Palaeolithic subsistence economies could well have persisted until considerably later in many regions, including the South West, overlapping and merging with the newer strategies of food collection. There is general agreement that the shift to different patterns of subsistence was essentially the product of marked environmental change from about 10000 to 8500 bc. Extensive areas of tundra and cold steppe grassland were steadily replaced by scrub woodland and denser forest. The enlargement of the oceans altered the configuration of the north-western European coastlands, while the warmer waters allowed a much wider range of fish and molluscs to thrive. On land, the most formative change was the increase of woodland game at the expense of the great herds of larger mammals which had ranged over the inter-glacial landscape. Tactics and equipment for hunting the smaller woodland species, as well as deer and aurochs, had to evolve, the new emphasis being on projectiles, either thrown by hand or shot from a bow. Above all else, the greater variety of food resources now available to man, on land and in the sea, encouraged a greater variety of subsistence-forms, in some of which a more marked degree of sedentarism developed as climatic and other conditions continued to improve or at least to stabilize. The picture of 'Mesolithic plenty' which some prehistorians have conjured up may be somewhat overdrawn, but the food-quest pursued by a still small population of Mesolithic hunter/gatherers was vastly more rewarding than that which had confronted their Upper Palaeolithic forebears. Increasingly, modern scholarship has begun to regard the cultures which developed in Britain between 8000 and 5000 bc as major contributors to the emergence of settled, food-producing societies and the Mesolithic therefore as an essential and formative stage in the cultural history of Europe.

As has already been stated, the South West offered as wide a range of food-resources to the hunter/gatherer as any part of Britain, and wider than many (Jacobi 1979: 76–86). Within the peninsula it is possible to distinguish several types of environment offering resources which were diverse in richness as well as in kind. By considering these different types of locale it may be possible to define the bounds of the food-quest more precisely and gain some insight into how it was pursued. The most productive localities will have been the many large estuaries with their combination of marine, coastal, riverine and terrestrial food-supplies. Unlike other resource-areas, estuaries might provide sustenance virtually throughout the year, a fact which probably assumed greater significance in the later Mesolithic. After estuaries, the inland river valleys and the adjacent upland offered the most productive and varied of resources in the form of forest game, fish and plants. These would obviously be present in greatest abundance in the period from Spring to late Autumn, though some game and fish might be available throughout the year. These inland localities are unlikely to have been outstandingly attractive to foragers in the early Flandrian, as the force and content of rivers will have been inimical to exploitation and even to movement. But from about 7000 bc, as climate and ground conditions ameliorated, their advantages must have steadily increased. Dense woodland and scrub offered much more restricted opportunities, except in summer and early autumn. Probably most limited of all were locations on the open coasts away from estuaries. These did offer opportunities, some of them requiring special skills such as off-shore navigation, sea-fishing and seal-hunting, but these were limited to relatively short seasons only. Nevertheless, as in other parts of north-western Europe, the marine resources of the South West were tapped from camp-sites on and near the coast, illustrating the all-embracing nature of Mesolithic food-collection.

Change in the Environment

The five-thousand-year epoch from 10000 to 5000 bp saw drastic changes in the level of the sea (and thus in the form of Britain), in climate, in fauna, and in the relationship between man and the natural environment. The significance of many developments in human activity during this formative period, often underestimated or even ignored by earlier prehistorians, among them Gordon Childe, has come into clearer focus in recent decades, not least as a result of a growing awareness of the direct impact of human groups on their habitat and of increased sophistication in the techniques which allow that impact to be measured and assessed. We must begin with the questions of sea-level and climate.

In the early post-Glacial period, two main factors stimulated changes in the relationship of sea to the land mass. The one was the release of an immense volume of water from the melting of the ice-sheets, affecting not only north-west Europe but most of the world. The other was the rise of the level of land as the weight of immense bodies of ice was reduced and finally removed. This isostatic movement was probably fairly rapid at first and thereafter slowing down considerably. It was not, however, a uniform process since the load of ice was not evenly distributed. Accurate measurement of its course is thus not yet possible, though important advances have recently been made. Studies of sea-level in north-west England indicate considerable oscillations in the post-Glacial, with a major rise of the sea from about 7800 to 7000 bp followed by a fall and then in turn by a series of rises and falls to about 5000 bp. Such oscillations can only have profoundly influenced the environment of the south-west peninsula and the economy of its human habitants.

The change in climate was equally profound. By about 8000 bc, the ice-sheets had disappeared and a rapid amelioration of climate took place, a stable period of relatively high temperatures being reached about 6000 bc. There was a further increase to a maximum average of over 16° C in summer, one which may have been maintained into the fifth millennium bc and thus down to the origins of agriculture. The separation of Britain from the continent about 5800 bc tended to raise winter temperatures, so that from this time to the early Neolithic average temperatures were some 2° C higher in winter and 1° C in summer than today. The onset of an Atlantic climate following separation from Europe also brought an increase in rainfall and possibly in high winds. The figures quoted above refer to southern Britain as a whole. Regional differences have not been defined to any notable extent.

The record of environmental change in the early Flandrian is sketchy, the best results being again provided by work on Bodmin Moor. The earliest radiocarbon date from a Post-glacial deposit has been obtained from peat at Hawks Tor (9654 ± 190 bp) (Brown 1977). The pollen evidence of this time indicates the presence of a heathland with juniper scrub. From other parts of southern England, however, there is clear evidence of birch woodland and this is likely to have been growing at lower altitudes in the South West. The climatic improvement already mentioned allowed the growth of ivy by about 9000 bp and a little later hazel, which requires somewhat higher temperatures. At about the same time oak was established and thereafter oak and hazel fairly rapidly became the dominant tree-species, notably on lower ground and in sheltered areas. Other trees, such as elm and pine, had a much more restricted distribution.

The Earlier Mesolithic

The sea, its relation with the land and its resources assume great importance in the period of early post-glacial settlement. Changing coastline levels cannot be mapped with any certainty over the millennia after 8500 bc, but down to about 6500 bc it is likely that the South West was separated from the European land-mass by a channel no more than 120 km wide. Britain remained attached to the Low Countries, Denmark and northern France by a low-lying, marshy region until about 5800 bc when separation finally occurred. It has been argued (Jacobi 1973: 245–6) that this extensive tract now beneath the eastern Channel was a particularly attractive food-source for early Mesolithic man and that its final loss to the sea forced hunting-groups west and east in search of fresh territories. Whether or not this was the case, it does seem certain that the separation of Britain from the Continent did stimulate a more systematic and intensive exploitation of the food-resources found in the island. In these the South West was as rich as any other part of Britain. The isolation of Britain is here adopted as marking the end of the earlier Mesolithic, partly following convention, but mainly because of the quickening pace of cultural development discernible after that event, in southern Britain in particular.

Across much of north-western Europe in the earlier Mesolithic there is a striking degree of uniformity underlying the types of flint and stone equipment, by far the greatest mass of surviving material. As defined by German, Scandinavian and increasingly by British archaeologists, this earlier *facies* is dominated by non-geometric microliths, limited in their range of forms and generally executed on broad blades. The common forms are obliquely blunted points, trapezoidal blades and roughly isosceles triangles, well suited to the tipping of arrows or throwing-spears, or for use in fish-spears and other multiple-pointed implements. Burins, awls and scrapers are also in evidence, though not to the fore. Flint axes and adzes were in use, suggesting attempts at large scale tree-felling, and thus at least some woodland clearance, and perhaps working in timber. Equipment in organic materials, especially bone, antler, wood and plant-fibres, is still poorly recorded in Britain, but the rich variety of these materials on Maglemosan camp-sites in Denmark is a reminder of their enormous importance to Mesolithic man (Jensen 1982: 33–53).

Few sites in south-western Britain have yet produced artifacts which can convincingly be assigned to the earlier phase of the Mesolithic. All that we can point to at present are a few scatters of microliths and other lithic material from relatively limited areas. From large tracts of the peninsula nothing has been recorded so far, including Dartmoor and its fringes, Exmoor and the Quantocks, the Blackdowns, the major inland valleys and coastal lowlands such as the South Hams. On no site has it been possible to identify and excavate stratified remains or deposits which might give some impression of how the place was used by its occupants. On the analogy of evidence from northern Europe and from the classic eastern English camp at Star Carr (Clark 1954), periods of use ranging from the occasional to the seasonal seem probable. Repeated use, on a seasonal basis, of the same locality is hinted at in one or two cases. On no site, however, have signs of structures or temporary shelters been noted and no burial remains are recorded for certain.

The distribution of known Mesolithic finds in the South West cannot be used as an indicator of the areas or locations particularly favoured by hunting bands. Potentially attractive localities now lie beneath the sea and have thus produced nothing. Equally liable to distort the record is the fact that collectors of flint-artifacts and other field-workers have tended to concentrate their attention on coastal and estuarine areas, where the yield of material is easier to come by. This will sufficiently explain why most of the recorded early Mesolithic find-spots occur in Cornwall and close to the modern coast-line. Just as the earliest studies in southern Scandinavia tended to emphasize exploitation of coastal resources at the expense of those of the interior, so there is a danger that the abundant marine resources of the South West may tempt us to underrate those of the inland valleys and uplands. Due allowance must be made for what lies buried beneath the valley alluvium, the estuaries and the peat-cover of the granite masses.

The most substantive evidence for an earlier Mesolithic site has come from around Dozmary Pool, a small lake at a height of 275 m OD near the Jamaica Inn on Bodmin Moor (Jacobi 1979: 51–4). The largest collection of

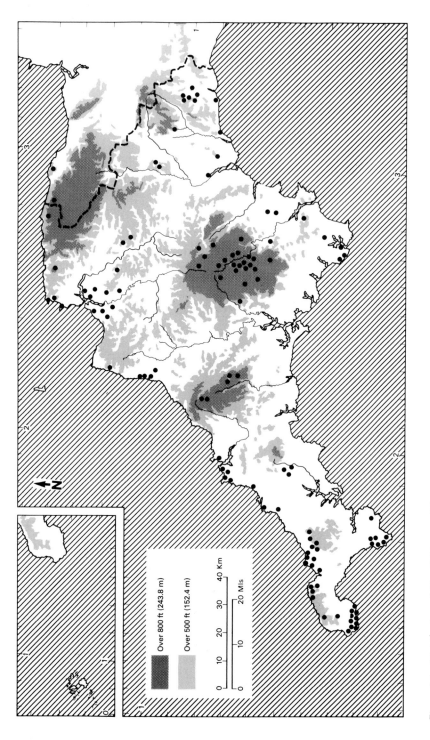

Figure 3.1 Distribution of Mesolithic material

early flint artifacts so far known in the peninsula was recovered from the pool during the drought of 1866 and later collections have been amassed from sites around its margins.

The microliths from Dozmary Pool are characterized by obliquely back-ed pieces, as are the assemblages from the better known sites at Thatcham in Berkshire, for which radiocarbon estimates suggest dates in the first half of the eighth century bc. Scrapers worked on the ends of rather long flints are also present in quantity, again suggesting an early date. The flint used here is mainly translucent material derived from the beaches. Little, if any, of the fine flint or Greensand chert of east Devon was used.

There are other indications of early Mesolithic camp-sites on the Bodmin Moor granite, notably from the area of the Crowdy Reservoir. On the rocky cliffs of the present north coast of Cornwall is recorded a further series of sites whose artifact assemblages seem to place them in the early Mesolithic. These include Trevose Head, Dinas Head, Stepper Point, Penhale, and North Cliff near Camborne. There is then little doubt that the contemporary Atlantic shore was frequented by early Flandrian hunters, at least at certain seasons.

The most striking group of early sites has been identified in the vicinity of Trevose Head, Booby's Bay and Constantine Bay (Johnson and David 1982). One such site, close to Trevose Head itself, has produced a fairly large sample of tools from systematic field-work (though not from excavation), including scrapers and other forms as well as microliths. A considerable proportion of the microliths tend towards the broad forms with oblique or straight retouch in evidence at Dozmary Pool, though narrower, possibly later, forms are also present. The broader forms are present in several of the collections from the Trevose Head area, suggesting a nucleus of early Flandrian activity. Scrapers form the commonest category of implement at Trevose, a number of end-scrapers on flakes and blades giving an indication of early Mesolithic activity. Awls, backed blades and possibly serrated blades are the most notable forms among the remainder of the early assemblage. Several of the other flint-scatters from Trevose Head include typologically early tool-forms, especially broad microliths.

The pebble ridge of Woodbury Common immediately east of the Exe estuary is the only location in Devon where early Mesolithic material has so far been found. The best-known site lies on Black Hill, on the western side of the Common overlooking the estuary. This has produced a small number of broad-bladed microliths and a few scrapers, as well as *petit-tranchet* arrowheads (Smith 1956: 118–21). Other sites on this upland have yielded broad-bladed implements (as yet unpublished) and it is quite possible that the well drained sandy soil supported scrub and light woodland which afforded a favoured habitat for small game, and perhaps deer. The nearness of the Exe estuary may also be remarked. Not surprisingly the flint used for the Woodbury Common implements was derived either directly from the chalk at Beer, 20 km to the east, or from the nearby beaches on which high-grade flint occurs in pebble form. There are objects of Greensand chert as well, suggesting that the early hunting bands were familiar with the Greensand ridges flanking the Otter valley immediately to the east and perhaps the Blackdown plateau itself.

The Later Mesolithic

After the period in which Britain was finally separated from the Continent there are evident changes in the archaeological record. Sites occupied or otherwise employed become much more common. There are clearer signs of regional variation in the patterns of exploitation. The common types of artifact undergo marked change, particularly the microlithic implements. Narrow-bladed forms now begin to dominate the assemblages, often to the virtual exclusion of broader forms. So narrow and delicately flaked are some microliths that their use as single points or blades seems impossible. More probably, they were mounted in series in wooden hafts and used as harpoons or fish-spears, or perhaps in some cases set in armatures and used in the processing of vegetable foods.

One of the few carefully excavated Mesolithic sites is that at Poldowrian, close to the present shore near the end of the Lizard peninsula (Smith and Harris 1982). Here, the characteristically later Mesolithic assemblage of narrow-blade microliths was dominated by convex-backed and lanceolate points. A small number of scrapers, on flakes and pebbles, was present, as was a smaller number of awls and borers. No structures, or indeed any certainly Mesolithic features, could be identified, but the great density of flint and stone artifacts, and waste material, in a limited area demonstrates use as a camp-site for some time. The site lay not far from the contemporary shore-line, perhaps in the interests of shelter from cold winds. The relatively large amount of waste material suggests a working area in use over some time. If there were associated structures, they could have lain at a little distance, beyond the excavated area. Aside from the familiar microlithic component of the assemblage, there were present numerous 'chopping-tools' formed from beach pebbles and a series of elongated slate pebbles, most of which were bevelled at one end, a few being facetted or chipped. Such implements are known from sites elsewhere in western and northern Britain and are often identified as hammers for detaching limpets from rocks. For this purpose their form is well suited, but the wear pattern produced on them suggests rather a rubbing or smoothing process, perhaps on skins. The presence of seal-colonies on this coast may be relevant here.

Poldowrian lay within easy walking distance of the late Mesolithic shore and may therefore have been a base used for limited seasons in spring or autumn. The latter is suggested by the presence of hazelnut shells and the fact that certain forms of mollusc would be at their most palatable at that time. Other late Mesolithic flint scatters in the Lizard indicate the activity of small bands, perhaps paying brief visits to locations near the coast.

The uplands and coasts of north Devon have produced enough later Mesolithic material to indicate the potential for further work here. Most of the sites have yielded rather small numbers of implements, but at Hawkcombe Head, nearly 400 m above sea level behind Porlock Bay, a site near a stream-head has produced a rich series of microliths, points, cores and a stone object with an hourglass perforation (Grinsell 1970: 21). Other sites on the high ground, at West Anstey, Georgeham and Quaking House near Milverton, reveal the attraction of greater Exmoor for the later Mesolithic hunter. But there are sites in low lying positions, too, one of the most interesting being at Bishop's Hull near the river Tone. From here has come an unusually varied range of tools, including scrapers, saws, points and a possible tranchet axe as well as microliths. Beach pebble flint was employed for implements in this region, but considerable quantities of chert from the Blackdowns also found its way into north Devon.

Several interesting sites are known on the present coast, notably at Northam Burrows near Bideford, at Woolacombe Sands, Yelland and at the submerged site also covered by peat at Westward Ho! (Rogers 1946). There are several references from the seventeenth century onward to submerged woodland in this area and in the 1860s a large deposit of the shells of oyster, limpet and mussel was reported here, in which lay flint implements and waste pieces. Animal bones were present in quantity, chiefly deer and ox, with wild boar, wolf and sheep or goat also represented. These deposits had subsequently been buried by a layer of peat. There were signs, too, of timber structures or fences. Pointed stakes had been thrust into the subsoil, some in a semicircle, others in a curve up to 16 m in length (Townsend Hall *c.* 1864). More recent examination of this site, by Mr N. Balaam, shows that the peat deposit and the middens have been much eroded by the sea, but radiocarbon estimates have been obtained from the middens indicating a date towards the close of the Mesolithic (6000–6500 bp), and from the peat of 5700 bp. Some of the timber stakes remained *in situ* and a date of 4800 bp was obtained for one of them. It would seem, then, that the Westward Ho! area was frequented at the end of the hunter period and probably continued to be visited, if not occupied, in the succeeding early farming stage. Some of the plant remains suggest the existence of coastal marshland which might have attracted a wide range of wild fowl, always an acceptable addition to the diet, even after the advent of agriculture.

On Dartmoor Mesolithic material has not been forthcoming in great quantity, but it exists and points to more than occasional use of the moor and quite possibly to areas from which the vegetation cover had been cleared. The highest site from which Mesolithic flints have been recovered is that on

Gidleigh Common, at over 400 m (Russell Collection in Torquay Museum), the most prolific that at Batworthy near the head of the North Teign, where several thousand flints of Mesolithic and Neolithic character have been reported (unpublished private collection). Microliths and cores are known in quantity from a site at Ringhill near Postbridge and from Runnage nearby, while occasional finds are reported from a scatter of other sites in central and eastern Dartmoor. It is certain that over most of the moor Mesolithic sites will in due course come to light. For the present they lie deeply buried under peat and blanket bog.

Some of the limestone caves of Devon were used by Mesolithic man, though none has yet produced evidence of intensive occupation. Three Holes Cave, Torbryan, at least occasionally housed late Mesolithic visitors, who left behind small numbers of narrow-blade microliths. These were mixed up in the same deposits with plainly Neolithic material, so that they may represent continued hunting and food-collection by early agriculturalists, or even the activities of a remnant forager-group. But it is also likely that the stratigraphy within the cave may have been disturbed during the Neolithic, thus accounting for the mixture of artifacts (Rosenfeld 1964: 10–13).

There is still much to learn about the contemporary vegetation and landscape of the later Mesolithic. In particular, more accurate knowledge of the extent of woodland would be helpful. The height of the tree-line on the south-western uplands is virtually unknown (Caseldine 1980: 10). There appears to be no climatic bar to its reaching up to 900 m in highland Britain at large, though there is no clear evidence that there was a continuous spread of woodland above about 600 m in any one region. To the birch woods established early in the Flandrian, hazel and oak were added, especially at lower altitudes. Both pine and elm were more restricted in their spread. Oak and hazel woods occupied the valleys and the coastal lowlands, while the vegetation of the uplands may already have been mainly grassland and heather (Caseldine 1980: 10, on Bodmin Moor). The importance of the margins of woodland for the grazing of wild herbivores will be obvious and such areas would clearly be a draw to hunters. But there is a growing body of evidence from several parts of Europe, from France, Switzerland and Denmark in particular, to suggest that by this latest phase of the Mesolithic man was not merely hunting herbivores such as cattle and sheep but exploiting them and their products on a more regular pattern. This did not amount to full domestication, but it represented an important step in the development of animal husbandry. These activities may in turn have led to profound effects on the woodland cover. The felling of trees had for long been well within the power of Mesolithic man. The deliberate clearance of large areas of woodland to provide open grazing could have followed in natural sequence, stimulated perhaps by destruction of wooded areas by accidental fires and the subsequent regeneration of scrub and grassland. Thus equipped with the means of controlling and modifying the vegetation cover in his own interests, man had made a significant advance towards a limited form of pastoralism. There are a few signs of this in the pollen record, tree-clearance being the most obvious (Simmons 1964: 1969). Possibly of related significance is the appearance of ivy pollen in the late Mesolithic record, for example at Westward Ho!, the result perhaps of the plant being used as winter feed for herbivores such as cattle and red deer (Simmons and Dimbleby 1974).

Hunter-Gatherer Society

Archaeology throws little light on the character of hunter/gatherer society in the South West and it may therefore seem wise to pass over the subject in silence. But some essay at the likely structure of Mesolithic society may be allowable, relying on discreet reference to foraging societies in comparable environments recorded in recent times. Although on points of detail the picture cannot be relied on, even a sketch will be better than nothing.

A constant feature of foraging societies is the small, mobile group of people commonly termed the band. This is known to have existed in most continents under remarkably varied pre-agricultural conditions and it appears to have been the most adaptable social group for a small foraging population. Its wide distribution and clear affinity with other higher primate groups have led social anthropologists to identify the band as the most primitive element in human society, perhaps extending back into the Upper Palaeolithic or even earlier. The size of the band was variable but 8–10 men was common, making the total number of persons 30–40. Each band was self-sufficient in basic foodstuffs for much of the year, but often food and other commodities were shared or exchanged with other groups. Internal distinctions within the band were minimal, except that major decisions were left to the leading males. Accumulation of property scarcely occurred so that any degree of status acquired by an individual was not automatically passed on.

Relations between hunting bands existed on several levels and served various purposes. Exchange of resources has already been mentioned. Exchange of women might rank as more important still, for the marriage of a woman into another band might bring access to a wider range of resources as well as otherwise stabilizing relations between groups. In many environments, bands came together to form interlinked groups of several hundred individuals who might overwinter in the same base-camp, breaking up again into their original bands at the onset of spring. Such larger groups might command a distinct social territory covering hundreds of square kilometres.

The limited evidence for the contemporary environment and for the sparseness of human activity in the Mesolithic indicates, so far as such evidence can, the presence of a very small population down to about 6000 bc. The vegetation cover over most of the peninsula is unlikely to have been generous before that time and thus animals will not have been plentiful enough to satisfy the needs of a sizeable hunting population. It can be little more than a guess, but it seems reasonable in the present state of our knowledge that only two or three bands, as defined above, p. 65), that is, about a hundred people in all, were able to support themselves off the resources of the peninsula in this earlier phase. Even if we allow for the richness of marine food-sources at certain times of the year, it is difficult to see how a larger number of foraging groups could subsist on a permanent basis. In most foraging societies, hunting bands are dispersed in the spring and come together in the late autumn or early winter, usually within the same broad territory. The entire south-western peninsula might, therefore, have been exploited as a unitary territory by a foraging group about a hundred strong. This rests on a slender foundation, underpinned by general probability and analogy rather than by firm evidence. For the late Mesolithic, the grounds for identifying a distinct social territory in the peninsula are somewhat stronger (Jacobi 1979: 56), but they are by no means compelling.

Study of the microlithic component of flint assemblages from southern Britain and the adjacent parts of northern Europe reveals the existence of a regional pattern within this basic equipment (Palmer 1977: 181–93; Jacobi 1979: 56–71). Thus in the South West assemblages tend to be dominated by convex-backed and lanceolate forms, these characteristics being typical on later Mesolithic sites as far to the east as a line from the Quantocks to Portland Bill. Further east still, the microlith components are present in quite different proportions (Jacobi 1979: 63–4). The total number of well recorded assemblages is still small but the available evidence gives general support to this notion of the South West as a distinct territory, at least in the late Mesolithic. But from about 4500 BC the region will have been increasingly open to external influence, and perhaps intrusion, as new means of subsistence began to spread from the Continent. The long history of life by foraging was drawing to its close.

Chapter 4

The Opening-up of the Land

It was suggested in the previous chapter (above, p. 64) that during the latter phases of the Mesolithic, probably after about 5000 BC, the economic relationship between man and certain large herbivorous animals underwent an important change, which was eventually to lead to full domestication. After 4000 BC that process, in southern Britain at least, was complete and about 3500 BC a new dimension was added to the food-quest when the cycle of deliberate cultivation and harvesting of food-plants was instituted. Precisely how this method of producing food from the land was transmitted from the Continent is beyond our knowledge at present and is in any case outside the scope of this book. What does concern us is the certainty that the South West shared in the early development of agriculture in southern Britain and thus in the growth of stable communities which depended increasingly upon settled agrarian practice for their sustenance. No doubt hunting, gathering and fishing continued to play a part in providing food for the inhabitants of the peninsula. In certain areas, including Scilly and several coastal regions of Devon and Cornwall, such activities may have endured for many centuries as staple providers of food, indeed still did so down to the modern period. But the introduction of agriculture radically altered man's relations with the natural world and had profound effects on human society, effects which are still with us in this industrial age. The beginnings of the social order which we know, and of which the history is to be traced in the rest of this book, lie in the middle of the fourth millennium BC.

Enclosures and Settlements

A site which has occupied the dominant position in studies of the south-western Neolithic is Hembury, which lies 6 km west of Honiton. A series of

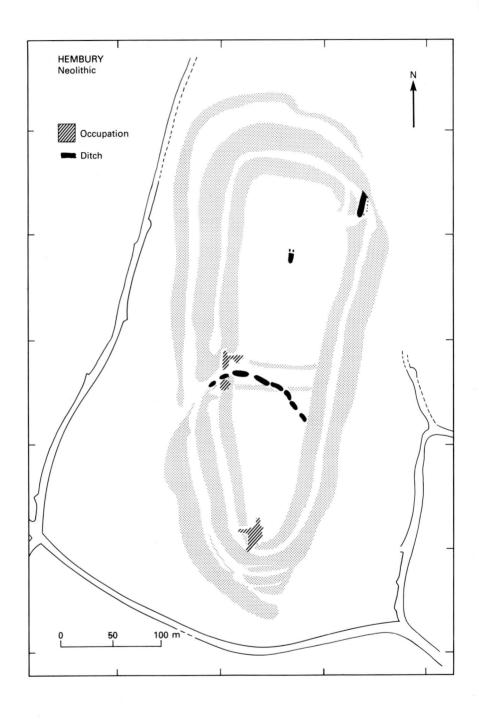

Figure 4.1 The Neolithic complex at Hembury

narrow, flat-topped Greensand ridges extends southward from the Blackdown Hills towards the coast. Hembury occupies the extreme tip of one of these, rising high above the valleys of the Otter and the Culm and giving distant views of the Exe valley, the Haldon ridge and Dartmoor. The site was the scene of major excavations from 1930 to 1935, a programme of work which was originally designed to elucidate the history of the great hill-fortress of later prehistoric times which is still so prominent a feature of the landscape (Liddell 1930, 1931, 1932, 1935). The direction of the work was entrusted to Miss Dorothy Liddell, who had earlier worked with her brother-in-law Alexander Keiller at Windmill Hill in Wiltshire, an experience which was to stand her in good stead as work at Hembury proceeded.

By the second season of work it was already plain that a major Neolithic settlement lay below the Iron Age hill-fort and examination of parts of this site occupied a considerable proportion of the excavation. Interim reports on the progress of work were diligently issued but, sadly, the excavation was never to be definitively published. In 1938 Miss Liddell died at a prematurely early age and no one took up the formidable task of compiling the final report.

A major earthwork was found to cross the spur, cutting off about 1.2 ha (3 acres) of the southern tip (Liddell 1935: 137–41). The principal surviving element in this work was a curving, discontinuous line of ditch, comprising at least eight separate lengths parted by causeways of varying widths. The ditch-lengths themselves varied from 7 m to about 15 m. Their depth and profiles were also various. The remains of a bank were observed on the south side of the ditch, but this was not systematically sectioned, except on the western side where an entrance was identified at one of the causeways. Little of the interior of the enclosure thus formed was examined. A small area immediately within the entrance was cleared and the remains of an oval or sub-rectangular timber building defined. At the southern tip of the spur, another small area was excavated and a trench over 30 m long dug into the interior. The rest of the enclosed area lies largely intact for future study.

A second substantial earthwork of Neolithic date was noted about 200 m to the north of the first (Liddell 1935: 148–54; Todd 1984). This took the form of a flat-bottomed ditch nearly 5 m wide and 2 m deep, running north–south, and with a bank 6.5 m wide on its western side. Outside the ditch, a number of large post-holes was interpreted as the remains of an external timber palisade. A butt-end to the ditch was defined at the south end of the excavation. From that point, however, an uninterrupted length of ditch was traced for some 25 m. The further course of this earthwork remains unknown.

Along the entire length of the causewayed ditch, Miss Liddell recorded a deposit of silt which, in this sandy subsoil, is likely to have accumulated in a very brief space of time. Over the silt at many points lay a thick deposit of burnt matter, much of which had been fired *in situ*, as was shown by the staining of the ditch-sides, and of the overlying deposits. A high proportion of the burnt debris comprised wood charcoal, especially of oak, ash and hazel, the remainder consisting mainly of wood-ash and burnt stones. Over this deposit, which had plainly entered the ditch in one episode, a thick mass of earth, clay and stone had slid or been pushed, fairly certainly from the bank on the inner side. It has been suggested (Smith 1971), that recutting of the ditch took place at a later stage, and that the stony areas which figure on Miss Liddell's section-drawings close to the outer edge of the ditch represent the subsequent filling of the recut ditch. That is probably to read too much into what are, after all, less than realistic drawings. So far as it can now be reconstructed, after initial silting, possibly interspersed with periodic cleaning of the ditch-bottom, an episode which involved the burning of large quantities of timber accounted for much of the filling in the centre of the ditch, this being followed by the descent of material from the rampart, either at one time or within a relatively brief interval, into the upper ditch-space. This sequence can be best explained as the result of a destruction of the rampart and its attendant works in timber, whether by accident or in some conflict. The wood charcoals represented in the burnt deposit, oak, ash and hazel, are suggestive of wattling attached to a stout timber frame of the type noted at Hambledon Hill by Mr Mercer. The burning seems to have extended to the gate-structure near the west side of the enclosure, where the burning had penetrated deep into the post-holes, and to a timber structure immediately inside the gate (Miss Liddell's 'Guard House'), in which a pile of wood ash was found, over which lay two large lengths of charred oak.

The area immediately within the enclosing bank and ditch was not examined by Miss Liddell. At the southern tip of the promontory, however, an area of about 800 sq m was fully excavated and in it abundant traces of intensive Neolithic occupation recorded (Liddell 1932: 172–4). The most striking feature of the published plan is the number of pits, some ('fire-pits') seemingly housing hearths, others, deeper and steep-sided, probably used for storage. Substantial post-holes, too, were recognized, though no coherent plans of structure were identified. From the pits and other deposits in this area there came a quantity of seed remains, subsequently studied by Helbaek (Helbaek 1952), who observed in them a clear predominance of wheat over barley. Emmer was the principal component, but spelt was also present in one or two of the deeper pits. This is so far the only instance of this type of grain on a Neolithic site in Britain and for that reason the stratigraphical position of these grains at Hembury has been called into question. There seems inadequate reason for this. Miss Liddell's record of the contents and stratigraphy of pits and other features appears to have been meticulous and, though the possibility of much later intrusion into a Neolithic deposit is ever-present, the assumption that it did occur is unwarranted. It might also be noted that spelt wheat was cultivated by later Neolithic communities in central Europe, so that a Neolithic date for the Hembury grains cannot be lightly discounted. The apparent dominance of wheat over barley is interesting and might be explained (as by Dennell 1976), by reference to the cultivation of heavier soils in the vicinity of Hembury than existed, for example, close to Windmill Hill and Maiden Castle, where barley was more favoured. But it must also be pointed out that the Hembury evidence is largely a single sample from one pit, which may not be representative of all the cultivated grains.

The highly acidic soils of the Upper Greensand do not permit the survival of bone, so that no assessment can be attempted of the role of animal husbandry in the local economy. The flint assemblage, however, is dominated by various forms of scraper, so that the processing of animal products could have been of major importance, even though the archaeological remains may never allow this to be determined in detail.

At many points in the areas investigated, a layer of burnt material was encountered. Some of the post-holes still held charred stumps of timbers and elsewhere burnt fragments of daub lay scattered about, apparently where they had fallen. The conflagration seems to have been general and it seems to mark the close of this phase of occupation. It is, of course, tempting to link this evidence of abrupt termination of settlement with the obliteration of the defences already described above (p. 69), itself apparently a final act, and on present evidence this seems most probable [1]. But the circumstances surrounding the ending of the occupation are difficult to define further than this. No later Neolithic material has been recorded from the hill and, although sporadic use of the tip of the promontory is attested in the early Bronze Age, there is no evidence for a further major phase of occupation until the mid-first millennium BC (below, p. 157).

The flint assemblage has not yet been studied in its entirety, but preliminary examination of what has been recovered in the excavations of 1980–83 suggests major differences between it and the material found by Miss Liddell in the promontory work. First, leaf arrowheads are much less prominent: 15 as against over 120 from Miss Liddell's excavation, most of those from around the probable entrance through the earthwork barrier. Scrapers are to the fore from both the excavated areas, though finely worked discoidal scrapers are much more common in the promontory work. Far more waste flint seems to occur in the areas recently excavated, though it is not certain whether or not such material was discarded by the excavators of the 1930s. The vast bulk of the flint was, of course, brought only a few miles to Hembury from Beer Head and the sweep of Lyme Bay immediately to the west, the grey, white and translucent flint probably deriving from the cliffs about Salcombe Regis. The significance and wide distribution of Beer flint in the south-western peninsula area are now well established, but there is much more work to be done on these and related topics. How far to the east and in what quantities was this high quality material carried? In what ways, if at all, was its distribution associated with that of stone axes from west Cornwall? Was any control on its extraction exercised at Beer itself? This is a large subject and one in urgent need of attention. The much less tractable local Greensand chert was also worked at Hembury, though in small quantity, and even smaller amounts of chert reached the site from Portland, 60 km to the east.

Hembury was for long considered to be a member of that class of earthwork site known as causewayed camps, partly on the grounds that it possessed a causewayed ditch cutting off a promontory, partly because the material from the site was so similar in character and composition to that from the classic causewayed camp of Windmill Hill in Wiltshire. The enlargement of knowledge on Neolithic settlement in southern Britain, and in the adjacent parts of western Europe, over the past twenty years has revealed the existence of several types of major enclosures apart from causewayed camps of which Windmill Hill and Whitehawk in Sussex are familiar representatives. In particular, the presence of enclosures which may fairly be described as fortified has been clearly demonstrated, as at Carn Brea (below, p. 73), Crickley Hill (Gloucestershire) and Hambledon (Dorset). As it is at present known, the promontory enclosure at Hembury seems to belong in this company. The natural defences provided by the steep slopes of the hill are themselves powerful. The ditch-lengths which cut off the tip of the promontory are deep and could have provided material for a substantial internal bank of stone and earth. All this suggests analogy with the promontory work at Crickley Hill. There are many other similar works in France, notably the *éperon barrée* of the centre and the east, of which excavation is now beginning to demonstrate early and middle Neolithic date. In Germany and Denmark, too, strongly protected settlements of the fourth and third millennia BC are beginning to emerge (Röder 1951: Schlette 1964: Madsen 1978).

Part of a third Neolithic earthwork has recently been traced, running north–south along the centre of the Hembury ridge (Todd 1984: 255–6). The surviving remains comprise a ditch up to 4 m wide and 1 m deep, flat-bottomed and steep-sided. This had not long remained open, the refilling being carried out with great care. Flint objects apart, nothing was found in the 5 m length of ditch excavated and its purpose is obscure. A utilitarian function seems unlikely and this impression is reinforced by the character of a number of shallow scoops and pits in the same area. These did not contain domestic debris and may have served specialized purposes outside those of daily routines.

The site at Hembury begins to emerge as a nexus of enclosures, as yet only partially known. We are not yet in a position to determine the probable functions of the various elements, or even to define clearly their chronological and spatial relationship. Provisionally, it may be suggested that the enclosure at the southern end of the promontory was a defended site, occurring at the end of the sequence of occupation. After its final abandonment, the focus of settlement shifted elsewhere. The other earthworks are more difficult to characterize. That at the northern end of the site appears to be a work of purposeful enclosure. The other, in the centre of the ridge, may have more to do with less mundane matters, with ritual and/or the disposal of the dead. At all events, Hembury can no longer be labelled as simply the westernmost instance of a causewayed camp. Its complexity of remains and of purpose is manifest and facile solutions to the problems presented by the site will no longer suffice.

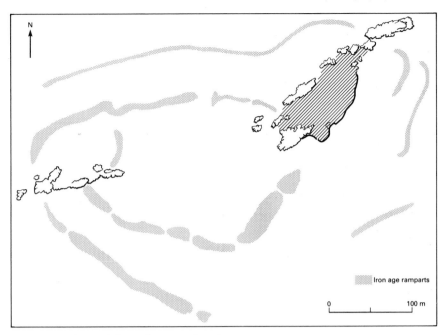

Figure 4.2   The Neolithic enclosure at Carn Brea

The most extensively examined of the Neolithic hill-top settlements is that on the elongated hill of Carn Brea near Redruth in west Cornwall (Mercer 1981). This eminence rises to three summits linked by two broad saddles. The easternmost summit is surrounded by a massive stone wall running between outcrops of granite, a work of such strength that it was long thought to form part of the defences of an Iron Age hill-fort. Excavation in the late nineteenth century had already revealed that this end of the hill had been the focus of much Neolithic activity and the work carried out in 1970–3 confirmed the importance of the site in the third millennium BC (Mercer 1981). The most striking surviving feature of the settlement is the massive enclosing wall, 2 m wide at the base and containing many huge boulders weighing up to 3 tons. It surrounded an area of about 7,200 sq m (*c.* 2 acres). The defensive purpose of this obstacle is patent and beyond doubt. It was raised not merely to mark off the bounds of the settlement or to keep out wild animals, but to deter or ward off attacks by man. Carn Brea thus falls into that small, but growing, number of Neolithic settlements which must be counted as strongholds, generically related to the hill-forts of later prehistoric times. Outside the enclosure on the eastern summit lay a complex of larger enclosures embracing in all over 3.5 ha of ground within strong ramparts of stone. These works are also of Neolithic date and within them areas of contemporary cultivation have been identified. The degree of organization and co-operative effort needed to erect works of this scale should not be underestimated. Construction of the wall around the eastern summit, with all that entailed in moving granite boulders, 'trigging' them into position, collecting smaller stones for the core, digging the accompanying ditch, is likely to have taken fifty or sixty men five to six months of continuous labour. The settlement may have been considerably less well manned than that, so that the task may have required a year's work or even longer. When the more extensive outworks are taken into account, this estimate must be substantially increased, though naturally their construction may have been carried out in separate operations spanning a long period of time [2].

It is certain then that the enclosed site was the work of a community organized at a fairly high level. It is also clear that a considerable number of buildings lay within the enclosure. Several of these are represented by small stake-holes driven into the subsoil, but others had more substantial timber uprights set in foundation slots and held in place by stone packing. In the case of the latter structures, the walling may have consisted of vertical planking held or pinned against horizontal timbers linked with the uprights. At least one building was solidly built, while two others appear to have been long lean-to's abutting the enclosure wall. The material associated with these buildings suggests domestic functions for them, perhaps with variation in the activities carried out from building to building.

The artefact record at Carn Brea reveals a community able to tap many channels of exchange. Stone artefacts from Cornish sources are naturally to the fore, notably stone axes of Groups I, IV, XVI and XVIII (below, p. 83). But lithic supplies from much further afield were also reaching Carn Brea. Dark grey and black flint probably from Beer in east Devon was present and had apparently been imported in the form of nodules rather than finished implements. Chert from Portland in Dorset and probably from Broom on the Devon/Dorset border was also brought to the site, again possibly as raw material. Some of the pottery from Carn Brea contained gabbroic inclusions, indicating an origin in the clays of the eastern Lizard peninsula, 30 km to the south. The settlement thus shared in the same widespread distribution network of artefacts which linked other sites in the South West: contacts with Wessex are thus not surprising.

The artefact assemblage, although large, has been retrieved from a relatively small number of stratified contexts and thus provides only a general picture of the material equipment of the Carn Brea community (Mercer 1981: 101–52). The flint objects include more than 700 leaf-shaped arrowheads, an exceptionally large proportion of the total assemblage when comparison is made with, for example, Windmill Hill and Hembury. Many of these were broken and numbers were recovered from the stones of the enclosing rampart, suggesting the possibility that the site had witnessed conflict on at least one occasion. Indications of burning of the structures within the defences may also find their explanation here. British prehistorians have been curiously reluctant to discuss the likely role of warfare in Neolithic society. A period in which land was being actively colonized for the first time and in which competition for natural resources of many kinds is bound to have developed must surely have known clashes of interest which burst forth into open conflict. The development of communities like that at Carn Brea and the appearance of strongholds in the landscape is at once an effect of and stimulant to conflict. What can be visualized on *a priori* grounds now has its archaeological testimony, notably at Crickley Hill in Gloucestershire and probably, too, here at Carn Brea.

In so large a sample the relative scarcity of certain categories of implement is worth note. Scrapers are noticeably fewer than at other south-western sites such as Hembury and Hazard Hill. This might seem to suggest that animals and their products played a less than prominent part in the local economy, since scrapers are commonly associated by archaeologists with the cutting of meat and the treatment of animal products such as skins and hides. But the latter hypothesis rests on assumption, not demonstrable fact, and until micro-wear studies have made much greater progress than they have hitherto, it will be safer to defer judgement. Serrated flakes, too, a common implement type at other Neolithic settlements, are markedly less common at Carn Brea, though edge-trimmed flakes are present in abundance.

The evidence for conflict at Carn Brea (and at Hambledon and Crickley Hill) is an important indicator of warfare which went beyond mere redress of wrongs or the personal feud. Rather it suggests that competition existed between communities, either for prestige or for wealth or natural resources. It does not necessarily follow that it is an indicator of 'stress' in Neolithic society or that natural resources were in short supply. The latter would seem an unlikely eventuality, since the total population of the peninsula is unlikely to have numbered more than a few thousand at most before 2000 BC and large tracts of land still lay open for the taking. Stress has been invoked as an all too convenient explanation for change in prehistoric societies. Rarely can it be demonstrated in any convincing way. Much more probably, what we are beginning to witness in these Neolithic enclosed communities is the growth of a consciousness of identity, natural enough as dominance over the local environment was steadily achieved, and thus of separateness from neighbours. Rivalry need not imply that what was being competed for was finite, never to be expanded. Rather, the emergence of competition suggests that a significant stage had been reached in social development, one in which relations both peaceable and hostile had to be maintained between different communities. Those relations extended beyond the rights and obligations of mere kinship towards those of more developed social organisms. Recourse to violence to settle an issue can scarcely arouse surprise. It is a constant theme in the earliest literature of most European societies.

Although no hill-top sites closely resembling Carn Brea have yet been *excavated* in the South West, there is a number of sites whose surface features suggest that they are akin, and from which material suggestive of substantive

Neolithic occupation has been recovered. The most compelling instance is that of Helman Tor, Lanlivery, 6 km south of Bodmin. On the summit of this isolated hill, a position resembling that of Carn Brea, lies an enclosure of about 1 ha in extent, surrounded by a wall of large granite orthostats linking natural rock outcrops. Inside a number of terraces are evident, again recalling the remains at Carn Brea. Helman Tor has never been excavated, but ploughing and other activities have brought to the surface considerable quantities of flint and stone implements on the slopes of the hill. These include two stone axes, one of Group I, the other of Group XVI (below, p. 83), and a polished flint axe. Objects likely to date from later periods of time have not been recorded from the hill. Interestingly, one of the survivors of the notoriously decrepit chambered tombs of the South West, Lesquite or Lanivet Quoit, lies only 1 km from Helman Tor. This tomb is so badly destroyed that the recovery of dating evidence from it would seem a forlorn hope. But the possibility of a link between settlement and burial monument must be seriously entertained.

Two further sites in Cornwall appear to belong to the same category. One is Trencrom Hill, on which a wall of large boulders running between natural outcrops encloses an area of about 1 ha. Here, too, two stone axes have been reported from the hill. The other is the remarkable site of Roughtor, above Camelford on the north-western side of Bodmin Moor. Again a wall of large orthostats and outcrops of granite are used to enclose a hill-top, here of about 3 ha in area, and a number of terraces are visible within the boundary. There has been no excavation here and no chance finds seem to have been reported.

A small number of enclosures on Dartmoor and Bodmin Moor fall outside the categories of 'hill-fort' and 'pound' or 'enclosed settlement' as commonly defined, and might be considered here. These include Whittor and the Dewerstone on Dartmoor and Stowe's Pound on Bodmin Moor (Silvester 1979). All are sited on prominent granite outcrops and tend to use natural outcrops in their enclosing walls. The latter may be massive in their width but their generally loose construction would not have allowed them to reach any great height. Hut-circles and other settlement remains do not occur within them in numbers and those that do exist may not be of the same date as the enclosing walls. There has been little excavation of any of these curious sites and dating evidence for them will probably always remain slight. That on Whittor on west Dartmoor was examined by the Dartmoor Exploration Committee in 1898–9 without producing more than a few flint flakes (Baring-Gould *et al.* 1899). Even the large boulder-cairn built into the south side yielded no finds. Two hut-circles on the north side were likewise barren of artifacts. Roughtor and the Dewerstone, both unexcavated, share the double enclosure wall evident around much of the perimeter at Whittor. Stowe's Pound is a much more complex work. A small acropolis at the south end is girt by rubble walls up to 4 m thick. Abutting this is a larger oval enclosure surrounded by one continuous wall pierced by two gates and by two outer lengths of walling on the northern side. A small rectilinear enclosure was attached to the western side, covering one of the gates, and this entire complex of works was encompassed by a narrow wall enclosing in all about 18 ha of the hill-top. Stowe's Pound further differs from the others in having some thirty hut-circles within the oval enclosure, along with a series of cleared platforms which could have been occupied by other structures. In the absence of dating evidence provided by orderly excavation it is rash to guess at the date of this unusual site. The oval enclosure, however, does resemble Bronze Age settlements on Dartmoor, in form though not in its exposed siting. The massively walled acropolis may well be of much earlier date, perhaps even a contemporary of the walled hill-tops of Carn Brea and Helman Tor, and thus may go back to the early days of colonization of this upland area. The same may be true, of course, of Whittor, Roughtor and the Dewerstone and in that case the detailed examination of one of them would be a useful project.

Although study of sites like these is still in its infancy and many fundamental matters are wholly unclear, it is steadily becoming apparent that enclosed hill-top settlement was an important element in the Neolithic settlement-pattern and that some enclosures at least were strongly defended (Mercer 1980). Plainly, this has been inadequately appreciated in Britain, where hill-top strongholds have with too great facility been associated primarily with later prehistoric periods. Yet Neolithic fortifications around high places have long been familiar to archaeologists in central Europe, in the Rhineland and in France. Following the clear demonstration that defended settlements existed in southern Britain, and that their construction was occasioned by the very real possibility of warfare between groups of people, radical revision of the nature and tenor of Neolithic society becomes necessary. Until very recently there was very little for the archaeologist to work on if he wished to study how Neolithic society in Britain ordered itself and what kinds of settlement it brought into being. Thirty years ago, Piggott wrote, 'In the extremely incomplete state of our knowledge it is almost impossible to estimate any settlement unit likely to have been common to British Neolithic communities' (Piggott 1954: 366). This situation has been slow to change and the important results of recent work at Crickley Hill, Hambledon and Carn Brea must be seen as initiating a new phase in the enquiry, and not as the final word.

The high ground to the west of the Exe also had its Neolithic settlements. Close to the Belvedere Tower on the Haldon ridge, part of an extensive site was examined by E. H. Willock in 1935–37 (Willock 1936; 1937). This included one structure interpreted as a sub-rectangular hut 7 m long and 3.5 m wide, along with other possible traces of timber buildings. Among other features excavated, a number of stone settings were prominent. Pits were few and rather small. The material assemblage had much in

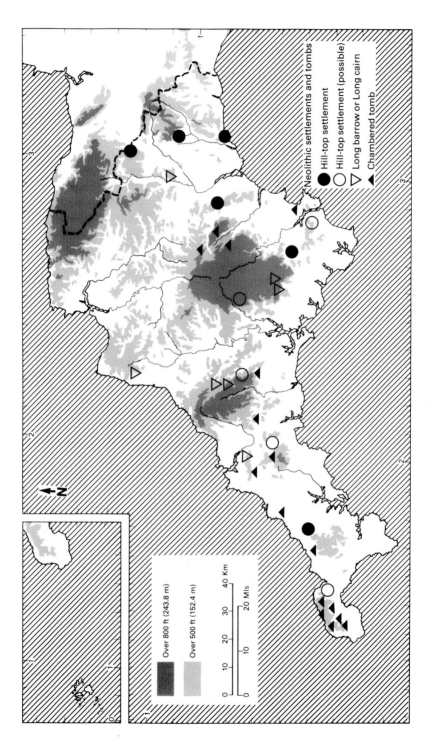

Figure 4.3 Neolithic settlements and tombs

common with that from Hembury. The same pottery forms are present, notably the deep, round-based vessels with solid lugs. Much of the flint had been brought from Beer, though a substantial proportion of the implements are of the less tractable white and grey flint from Haldon itself. In a rather small sample, arrowheads are to the fore, as are round scrapers like those from Hembury. The quality of the Haldon excavation, and its record, cannot be regarded as high. But at the very least the finds are a further indicator of the attraction which these hill-top locations had for earlier Neolithic settlers. Too little of the site was examined to reveal its complete character. It is often quoted as an example of an open settlement, but there could well have been an enclosing work which has not yet been located, or even looked for. One object suggests the possibility of occupation in a phase later than that associated with the Hembury ware. This is a small flat-bottomed bowl decorated with two zones of incised vertical lines. This has much in common with the Grooved Ware of later Neolithic Wessex both in its form and in its incised ornament. Such vessels are extremely rare in the South West, the only other examples in Devon being recorded from the Three Holes Cave at Torbryan and Topsham.

The South Hams between Dartmoor and the sea have also produced evidence of widespread settlement in the Neolithic, including sites on hill-tops. Hazard Hill is a steep-sided eminence 5 km south-west of Totnes above the Harbourne river (Houlder 1963). Over much of the 2 ha (*c.* 5 acres) on the hill-top Neolithic debris has been recorded and limited excavation has revealed settlement remains similar to those recorded at Haldon and within the enclosure of Hembury. Air photographs indicate ditched enclosures on the hill-top and field survey here suggests that there may also have been a large enclosing earthwork, not yet tested by excavation. The features which were revealed in excavation include shallow, irregular pits and depressions, somewhat deeper pits which may have served for storage of grain and other commodities, pits which contained quantities of burnt debris, hearths situated on an old land surface and a number of post-holes. Two of the post-holes had held substantial timbers, clearly part of sizeable structures which only extensive area excavation could adequately uncover. Thus, most of the remains which had penetrated the subsoil are closely comparable with those identified at Hembury. The material assemblage also has the same constitution as that from Hembury and Carn Brea. The pottery forms are mainly open bowls, some with trumpet-lugs, upright jars with incurved rims, and straight-sided vessels – all well attested in the south-western *facies*. The thirteen stone axes include examples of Groups I, IV and XVII, as at Hembury and Carn Brea. The flint implements are mainly of Beer flint, derived from small nodules, supplemented by brown and white flint from beach pebbles. Leaf-shaped arrowheads are very much to the fore with 140 examples and a wide variety of forms. But the total assemblage is dominated by scrapers, of which there were more than 320. By contrast, edge-trimmed flakes, awls and other implements are sparsely represented at Hazard Hill.

North Devon, Exmoor and the Quantocks have so far produced slight evidence for Neolithic settlement. Small concentrations of Neolithic material have been noted at Orleigh Court near Bideford, on Kentisbury Down, at Bathealton in west Somerset and at a number of locations in the hills between Porlock and Minehead (Grinsell 1970: 24–5). Virtually nothing likely to date from the fourth and third millennia BC has been reported from High Exmoor and little from the Quantocks. Small scatters of Neolithic flint artifacts indicate at least limited exploitation of the Quantock hills. The most notable of these are on Cothelstone Hill, at a height of 300 m, Thorncombe Hill, and Shapnoller Farm. Beer flint, Greensand chert and Portland chert are all represented in the range of objects found. The lower land between the Brendon Hills and the Quantocks is more likely to have attracted early farming settlements, though the evidence has yet to be assembled. It is, of course, possible that major settlements like those in south Devon and in Cornwall may exist undetected in the north Devon and Somerset hills. One such site probably occupies a flat-topped hill 2 km west of Milverton (Somerset), in a commanding position overlooking the Vale of Taunton. Surface collection has produced 98 leaf-arrowheads, a polished flint axe and fragments of a further 14, and a range of scrapers, edge flakes, blades and saws, some in Beer flint and Blackdown chert. All this is scattered over about 6 ha and excavation here might well reveal another sizeable, and perhaps enclosed, hill-top settlement.

Although no major settlements have yet been identified and examined, the distribution of Neolithic flint and stone implements makes it abundantly plain that Dartmoor was at least partially settled in the middle and later Neolithic. The maps show the main occurrences of distinctively Neolithic material, notably leaf-shaped arrowheads and certain scraper-forms, the main bias of distribution being towards the eastern and southern fringes of the moor, and the central valleys of the Dart rivers. The stone axes and other implements tell much the same story, though there is a suggestive number of these on the western side too. It must be stressed that the pattern is probably distorted by the presence of deep peat deposits in the central and northern parts of the moor. As it stands, however, the available evidence suggests widespread but not intensive settlement in the late fourth and third millennia. The main exploitation of the moor was not to come for another thousand years (below, p. 111).

The importance of the eastern and southern fringes in the early settlement history of Dartmoor is underlined by the siting of the major chambered tombs (below, p. 86). These fall into two groups, one on the southern edge (Butterdon Hill, Cuckoo Ball, Coringdon Ball) and the other on the east (Spinster's Rock, Buttern Hill and Meacombe). To the latter group belongs the structure described as a 'cromlech', the Bradstone, which stood at Christow until it was destroyed in 1817 (Davidson 1861: 23).

The landscape and vegetation of Dartmoor over this period cannot yet be reconstructed in detail but it seems likely that it was much more varied than the moorland of later prehistory. Trees probably did not exist above about 400 m, though oak, pine, hazel and alder were growing lower down in suitable positions. Grasses, sedges and heathers were the dominant taxa on the high ground by the beginning of the Neolithic and probably before that (Simmons 1964; Caseldine and Maguire 1981).

After the abundance of sites which can be assigned to the later fourth and earlier third millennia, the dearth of later Neolithic sites and assemblages comes as a surprise. The decorated wares of the later Neolithic are conspicuous by their rarity in the South West. None was found at Hembury, or at Carn Brea, or in the less extensive excavations at Hazard Hill. Grooved ware, current somewhat before and after 2000 BC has been found on occasion, for instance at Topsham (Jarvis and Maxfield 1975: 250–1), Three Holes Cave, Torbryan (Rosenfeld 1964, Pl. 1b) and notably in the form of a small flat-bottomed bowl from Haldon, with two zones of decoration on the body (Willock 1937: 43). Further excavation in some of the larger ceremonial monuments might reveal more of this pottery, but at present it seems as if it was not current in the peninsula in great quantity.

The Peterborough pottery tradition is also sparsely represented, making distinction of a later Neolithic cultural horizon difficult, indeed impossible. After the relative cultural unity presented by the earlier Neolithic communities at sites like Hembury and Carn Brea, those of later times (after about 2500 BC) seem fragmented and incoherent. This may mean that smaller, more dispersed social groups had emerged as the colonization of land proceeded, and that the settlement pattern underwent radical reordering during the mid- and late third millennium, perhaps as a result of the demands of an increasing population. A shift in the emphasis of settlement towards the valleys and lowlands may have been one consequence and it is in these localities that field-work and excavation has yet to make much impact. Some such shift is hinted at by the distribution of Neolithic/early Bronze Age flint scatters, the majority of which lie on lower slopes, on valley floors or on coastal lowlands (Miles 1976). Recent survey in the Exe valley and the South Hams shows the promise of these locations for the eventual identification of settlements of this period.

Material Culture

There has been no full study of flint sources in the South West, even of the principal single source of dark grey and black flint found in the chalk at Beer

Head (Macalpine Woods 1929). It is, however, clear that this source of high-quality flint was extensively exploited in the Neolithic and that the raw material was exported to many parts of the peninsula. It is not surprising that the vast bulk of the flint employed at Neolithic Hembury came from Beer, only 20 km away. A substantial proportion of the flint found at East Week on the north-east flank of Dartmoor, rather more than 30 per cent, came from Beer, 60 km distant (Grieg and Rankine 1953). Along the south Devon coast, too, Beer flint is fairly consistently found, some of it probably derived from beach pebbles, but by no means all. A site at Dittisham, near Dartmouth, has produced large nodules of Beer flint, clearly carried there by man, not by the agency of the sea. Farther west, small quantities of this distinctive material have appeared in Cornwall, some of this probably collected from beaches. But the large flint assemblage at Carn Brea is largely composed of material which is likely to have come from Beer, about 150 km by sea and considerably more overland, so that considerable quantities of this high-grade flint must have been carried westward in the opposite direction to the Cornish stone axes (Mercer 1981: 108). Its export northward, into north Devon, is less certain, but small quantities have been recorded on sites in the Taw valley.

Chert from the Greensand uplands of east Devon was transported westward in small quantities, mainly into south and central Devon. Occasional chert implements have turned up in Cornwall, for instance at Carn Brea, though it is not clear whether they are the result of reworking imported artifacts or limited exchange in this material. The dark grey or black chert from Portland in Dorset continued to be traded westwards and has appeared at most of the larger Neolithic settlements in the peninsula.

The dispersal of implements, mainly axes, made from igneous rocks over considerable distances from a number of sources is one of the most remarkable aspects of the material culture of the Neolithic. Most of the rock-sources lie in western Britain, including Cornwall. The implements are usually ground and polished, occasionally flaked, and are ovoid in section with a rounded or tapering butt. There is considerable variation in size but most are between 5 cm and 20 cm in length. These ground axes were much more resilient and therefore more versatile than implements of flint. How they were used is a matter for debate. Commonly it is assumed that they were employed in tree-felling and scrub-clearance and no doubt they could have been used for such purposes. But they may principally have been designed for wood-working, for the preparation of planks and other lengths of timber. Beyond their utilitarian functions, however, axes may have been potent symbols of power and prestige, may even have possessed magical or totemic significance as they have for so many primitive and early societies. The fact that axes were carried for immense distances by some combination of social and economic agencies suggests that these implements were endowed with supra-mundane significance by early farming communities in Britain and the same applies to much of Europe. The high quality of the finishing applied to some implements and the evident care with which some were deposited are other pointers to the peculiar significance they carried (Bradley 1984: 53–7).

At least six distinct groups of axes from separate sources have so far been identified in the South West. The largest of these (Group 1) comprises axes made of greenstone occurring in the Mount's Bay area of west Cornwall. The distribution pattern of these objects is remarkable and matched by none of the other groups. A number occur in Cornwall and Devon but the great majority have been reported from Wessex and south-eastern England (Evens, Smith and Wallis 1972; Cummins 1979, Fig. 7a) and clearly achieved an exceptional reputation either for their peculiar qualities or perhaps for the very fact that they were exotics and therefore desirable items for their own sake. Axes of this group were in use at Carn Brea and thus were being made in the earlier third millennium. Outside the South West, those occurring in datable contexts indicate a date around 2000 BC and not much later. Several of these finds have been made in ceremonial monuments in Wessex and association with Grooved Ware elsewhere (Evens, Smith and Wallis 1972: 253). In this connexion it is worth noting that as many as eight 'mace-heads', all found outside Cornwall, have also been ascribed to this group.

The smaller groups have distributions which centre on the South West itself. Group IVa is represented by axes at Hembury, Hazard Hill and Maiden Castle, and its production range is thus to be placed in the centuries to either side of 3000 BC. Group IV may be somewhat later in origin and could have continued down to 2000 BC. Another series which was being made by 3000 BC is that comprised in Group XVI, mainly represented by Cornish finds. The same may be true of Group XVII and this too may have provided axes over a long period.

Axes and other implements were coming to the South West from other regions, from Wales, from the Midlands, even from the Lake District. Several jadeite objects reached the region, one a small axe in pristine condition from a barrow at Kingswear in Devon (Rogers 1947), another an axe-fragment found at High Peak. Other specimens in jadeite come from Newquay, Falmouth, and Hayle in Cornwall and from Bovey Tracey in Devon. The origins of these fine implements are still obscure but they are more likely to lie on the Continent than in Britain. The Alpine region and Brittany seem the best candidates. Like so many of the other beautifully finished axes they can scarcely have been used for any workaday purpose: several have plainly seen no wear before their deposition. The probability is that many of the axes were produced first and foremost not as tools but as items for use in cycles of gift-exchange that may have embraced other commodities which leave no archaeological trace behind them (skins, furs, brides). Exchange relations as an important function of social systems is a relatively recent study, given considerable impetus by the work of Polanyi (Polanyi, Arensberg and Pearson 1957 for early statements), though in early European societies a full understanding of how they operated has not yet been achieved. The main interest of the axes, then, resides not so much in the production of efficient and handsome woodworking implements, but rather in the glimpse they provide of wide-ranging exchange-networks and contacts between far-flung communities in the fourth and third millennia, for the most part at an elevated level. They are an important witness, too, to the prolonged stability of such contacts and of the society which found them necessary. For over a thousand years these objects helped to forge and symbolize bonds between groups of people, perhaps between polities on a small scale, and to play their part in ritual observance at monuments and at the water's edge. The nature of that observance is elusive: its strength is patent (Bradley 1984: 46–57).

Pottery

The pottery found in the earlier Neolithic sites is characterized by deep, bag-shaped pots and carinated bowls, usually with round bases and often with lugs or cordons on the shoulder. Decoration occurs very rarely and when it does it is of the simplest. These vessel forms are found across the entire region and have been generally accepted for some time as forming a distinct south-western style which extended eastwards into Dorset, Somerset and Wiltshire (Whittle 1977: 77). These vessels had certainly developed by the later fourth millennium BC as the Hembury evidence reveals and they continued in currency throughout much of the following thousand years. The craftsmanship evident in a proportion of the pots is high and specialized production of these is very probable. A few were carefully finished with a black slip or paint, as at Carn Brea and Hembury.

The production of this pottery has provoked a great deal of attention in view of the hypothesis advanced by Peacock (1969a) that the origin of the clay used for many vessels lay in the gabbroic rocks of the Lizard peninsula about St Keverne. The basis for this argument needs to be widened before it can be regarded as proven. Local production is suggested at Carn Brea (Mercer 1981, 179) and at Hembury, where Greensand chert and possibly granitic inclusions appear in the fabrics. The overall pattern of production is still not clear and more analytical work is clearly called for. The Hembury evidence, for instance, suggests that most of the pottery was produced on the site or nearby.

Apart from indicating a shared ceramic tradition across the peninsula, these vessels tell us little about the cultural affinities of the communities that produced them. The forms are simple, decorative schemes limited. The trumpet-lugs which earlier generations saw as diagnostic of imported items now seem to owe nothing to external influence. Throughout the Neolithic, influence from outside, so far as this can be assessed from ceramic evidence, was minor.

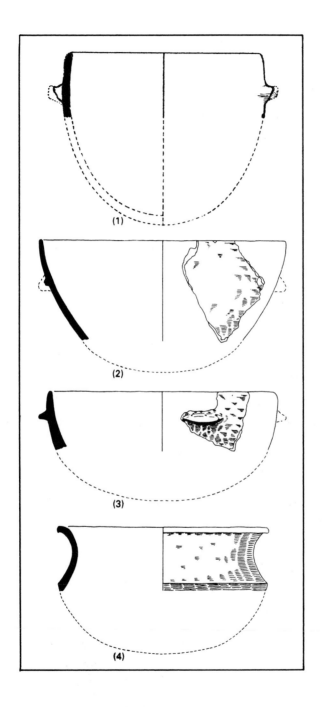

Figure 4.4 The main forms of Neolithic pottery: (1) Hembury; (2)–(4) Carn Brea

Ceremonial Monuments: the Living and the Dead

Reactions to death in primitive societies are so astonishingly varied that no archaeologist could hope to reconstruct ritual, much less sentiment, on the basis of what he finds in or near a tomb. Corpses may be immediately buried or burned, given a place of honour, or exposed for months as carrion, or simply abandoned altogether. They may be studiously preserved, or dismembered or even eaten. The rituals preceding burial and accompanying it were, and are, of equal variety, ranging from orgiastic parties to total abstinence, from massive feasts to a shut-down of all social intercourse. If we look for universals in these diverse patterns of behaviour, the most notable fact that emerges is that death focuses the attention of a society upon those cultural values that determine the conduct of life. (This is apparent, too, in the modern world: Mitford 1963 is a classic text for an industrialized urban state.) Thus the structure of a society and the preoccupations of its members are powerfully expressed in funerary ritual and in the monuments which commemorate the dead (Huntington and Metcalf 1979). Although we cannot penetrate to the heart of the mystery in the case of the prehistoric inhabitants of Britain, this oneness of funerary rites with the social order is something of which we must not lose sight. How the dead were treated tells us much about the living. But we cannot deduce what the living *thought* from what they *did* (see the popular but useful discussion in Ragon 1983).

Earthen long barrows of types familiar in the chalklands of southern England appear to be rare in the South West. The concentration of such monuments closest to the peninsula is the group about the Dorset Ridgeway. To the west, a number of long cairns and cairns enclosed in elongated mounds are known but classic long barrows have yet to be clearly demonstrated. The monument which comes closest to the long barrows of Wessex is a long mound at Woolley Barrows, Morwenstow in north Cornwall, near the crest of a ridge above the Tamar. The mound, still 2.4 m high, is a rough oval, tapering towards the west, 62 m in length and 21 m at its widest, with a quarry ditch clearly flanking its northern side. There has been no orderly excavation of the mound itself (Higginbotham 1977 reports an excavation of the ditch), so that nothing is known of chambers or other structures within it. A round barrow lay 50 m away to the south-west, but no other monuments are known in the near vicinity. A small number of other possible long barrows exist, but none has yet been tested by excavation.

Long cairns containing one or more stone chambers are much better represented, notably on the fringes of the granite uplands, and these may fairly be regarded as the south-western version of the earthen long barrow. Although now sadly wrecked, these structures seem commonly to have comprised a pointed oval or pear-shaped mound up to 48 m in length, with a chamber sited close to the broader end. Three monuments on the south side of Dartmoor exemplify this type of tomb, Corringdon Ball, Butterdon Hill and Cuckoo Ball. It is likely that the chambers which still survive on the eastern side of the moor were originally enclosed in similar mounds, of which virtually all trace has vanished. The best known of these is Spinster's Rock, though the chamber now visible is a reconstruction after collapse in the mid-nineteenth century and its adherence to the original plan is uncertain. Other chambers which may once have lain within mounds survive at Meacombe and Gidleigh. Long cairns are also known in Cornwall, on Bodmin Moor and in West Penwith. One of the finest surviving chambers is that at Trethevy around which an oval mound once stood. On Bodmin Moor the remains of a probable long cairn are evident at Catshole near Altarnun. The most familiar of all Cornish chambered tombs fairly certainly belongs to the same type of monument. This is Lanyon Quoit, another chamber re-erected after collapse in the nineteenth century. Here a pear-shaped mound 20 m long surrounds the reconstructed chamber, while a group of slabs at the east end may represent another chamber now largely destroyed. None of these structures has been excavated in recent times and most of them are probably to be regarded as archaeologically sterile. Dates and associations are thus largely a matter of guesswork. A chambered mound at West Lanyon, now almost completely destroyed, produced a disorderly scatter of human bones, recalling the successive burials in megalithic chambers in later Neolithic Wessex. Over these bones lay a cremation urn, presumably a Bronze Age interment. Otherwise the long cairns are eloquent only of the long period of neglect and dilapidation which has brought these monuments almost to extinction. Others may yet be located, especially on Dartmoor and Bodmin Moor. An unknown number must have suffered destruction in lowland areas. (The place-names 'quoit' and 'shilstone' may point to the former existence of several.)

It has long been the custom to regard the small chambered tombs that occur mainly in west Cornwall as a distinct group (the 'Penwith tombs' of Daniel 1950: 93–5). In actuality there is clear overlap, in the matter of megalithic chambers, between these western tombs and at least some of the long cairns. Bearing in mind how little is known of the original superstructure of the 'Penwith' monuments, it will be safest to avoid any emphasis upon morphology as an indicator of date or cultural association. The most familiar of the 'Penwith' tombs are those which lie on the uplands of the Lands End peninsula, the quoits at Chun, Mulfra and Zennor. These chambers are small and tightly enclosed by flat slabs. Occasionally, as at Zennor, the front uprights are made to project, forming a shallow porch, as in the portal-dolmens of Wales and Brittany. This feature is also seen in the chamber of Trethevy Quoit (Daniel 1950: 93).

It is, of course, impossible to judge how many chambered tombs have fallen victim to destruction in later periods. The two pierced slabs set up on edge, the Tolvaen near Gweek and the Men-an-Tol in Madron parish, have often been seen as likely remains of chambered tombs, providing a means of

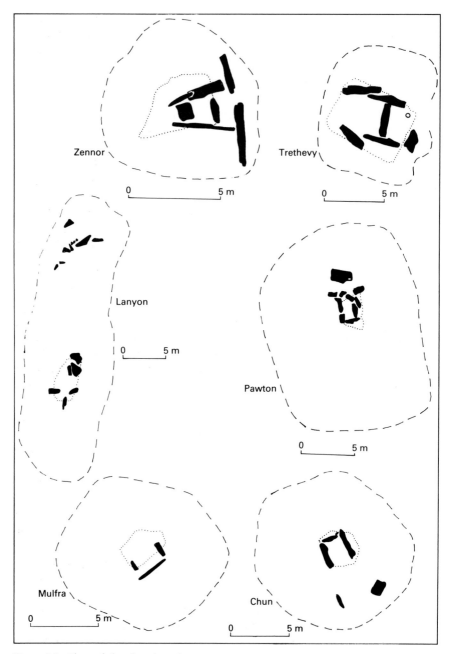

Figure 4.5 Plans of chambered tombs

communication with the chamber to facilitate the deposition of later burials or ingress for ceremonial purposes. There is, however, no proof that either slab ever formed part of a tomb. Even the present lay-out of the Men-an-Tol, with a stone to either side of the pierced slab forming a short alignment, is not original. Borlase's plan shows the three stones in a triangular setting (Borlase 1754: Pl. XIV), as does a sketch in the margin of an estate map dated 1778. Both the Tolvaen and the Men-an-Tol remain enigmatic as regards their original function and also their date, which need not be as early as the late Neolithic.

Monuments less elaborate in design but equally massive stood on the heights above the west Cornish coast. An oval cairn at Tregaseal, near St Just, covered a long cist or chamber 4.5 m long, 1.2 m wide and 1.4 m high (Lukis 1885: Pl. XVII). Immediately outside it near the centre of the cairn lay a small, square cist which contained an inverted, handled cremation urn. The long chamber is a carefully built megalithic structure, its sides lined with trimmed granite blocks up to 2 m long, and floored with flat slabs. Unfortunately, there appears to be no record of what it had contained.

A Penwith tomb which must be distinguished from the entrance graves and chambered tombs is the large oval cairn at Chapel Carn Brea, over-looking Whitesand Bay behind Sennen. This was originally a lofty structure and large enough for its summit to be crowned with a medieval chapel. It was still 5 m high when it was excavated by W. C. Borlase (Lukis 1885: Pl. XIV). Within the body of the cairn, five short lengths of revetment wall had been inserted to stabilize the mass of loose stone. In the centre was a well built chamber 3.5 m long, 1 m wide and 1.3 m high, open at one end and pointed at the other. It has been floored and roofed with slabs throughout. A large cist was found at a higher level in the cairn. Neither chamber nor cist had apparently been disturbed, but neither contained any evident traces of human remains or of artifacts. A deposit of cremated bone was located at one point within the cairn and scattered throughout the structure were found fragments of blackened pottery and charcoal. The absence of human remains from the enclosed spaces is puzzling, as we might have expected at least some trace of bone to survive within the chamber or the cist, sealed from the prevailing acidic soil conditions.

These three remarkable monuments have little or nothing in common with the majority of Penwith chamber tombs and little in common with each other except their megalithic chambers and the fact that they are sited on prominent hills and thus must have been clearly visible over great distances. Links with other megalithic structures in other parts of western Europe, which some have tried to establish, seem still less plausible. Safer is the line of argument that these are the result of local initiatives to provide striking tombs for the distinguished dead. Their individuality may owe as much to the intractable materials which were to hand as to any striving after originality. The evidence for their date is meagre, the middle Bronze Age vessels from Carn

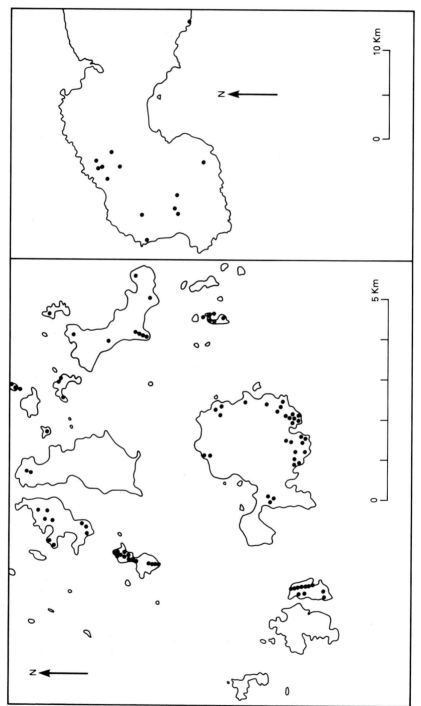

Figure 4.6   Passage and entrance graves in Scilly and west Cornwall

Gluze being accompaniments to later burials. All three monuments are now in a sadly mutilated condition and it seems unlikely that they could now reveal much about their date of construction.

There are numerous other megalithic structures in Cornwall which fall into no well-defined category and which are to be seen as the work of isolated communities in honour of their dead. On Crouza Downs, St Keverne, stand The Three Brothers of Grugith, an odd work combining a natural rock outcrop with two large stones to form a simple chamber, the horizontal capstone of which is covered with cup-marks. This may be regarded either as a burial chamber or a large surface cist, probably the former. At Tregiffean Vean, in St Just parish, a small barrow contains a central chamber 2 m long, 1.3 m wide and 1.4 m high, with a low cist only 50 cm high adjoining it. Although a strange monument at first sight, it is probably no more than the juxtaposition of two cists of different dates, and very different sizes. A number of other sites have been noted in Cornwall of which some may be the remnants of megalithic tombs, others natural groups of exposed granite blocks.

In west Cornwall, about twenty entrance-graves can be distinguished from the other megalithic tombs. Their place in the cultural sequence is not well defined since few have been examined. The most important investigation is that conducted on a kerbed cairn at Bosiliack (Madron), a small structure with a narrow entrance leading into a gradually widening chamber lined with slabs laid horizontally. The primary deposit in the chamber was a partial cremation placed within and around a coarse ware pot in the late Neolithic/early Bronze Age tradition of the region. This deposit had then been closed off by thin granite slabs. This first modern examination of a Cornish entrance-grave (by Professor Charles Thomas) suggests that the monument is to be placed in the late third or early second millennium. What is still not known is how these small tombs were related, if at all, to the larger chambered tombs. Were they broadly contemporary, did they steadily replace the larger monuments, or were they substantially later in origin? A programme of work now in progress, directed by Professor Thomas, may lead to resolution of this and other questions.

Scilly

The entrance-graves of the Isles of Scilly form one of the most remarkable groups of burial monuments in Europe. Although known to archaeological scholarship since the mid-eighteenth century, no full study of them has yet been undertaken and not even a comprehensive inventory has been published. The best accounts of the Scillonian tombs are those of Ashbee, and that scholar's excavation at Bant's Carn is the most important examination of one of the group (Ashbee 1974: 1976). Up to fifty megalithic tombs survive in the islands: many more have fallen victim to agricultural and other destruction over the past two centuries. Of the survivors, more than half lie in three groups or cemeteries: one on the eastern side of St Mary's, one on Samson and one on Gugh. The others are rather more scattered, though small clusters occur on Bryher and on St Martin's.

The graves are very similar in their plan, most of them consisting of a circular cairn with a regular and massively constructed kerb, containing a roughly rectangular chamber which opens from the very edge of the cairn, and usually extends to beyond the centre-point of the monument. The chambers tend to be rectangular, though a few are coffin-shaped or have slightly bowed sides. One or two have partial corbelling in their roofing. The structures have generally been carefully built. Large slabs were commonly used in the kerbs as well as in the walls and roofing of the chambers, though coursed rubble was also employed. The majority of the monuments are between 7 m and 20 m in diameter, though a few smaller examples are known. Their siting appears to have no special significance except perhaps that entrances tend to open on to a downward slope. Orientation of the chambers seems to follow no discernible principle and is likely to have been determined by purely local or personal factors. In a small number of cases, an outer platform appears to have surrounded the cairn, though whether this was originally a normal feature is unknown.

The concentration of monuments in groups or in linear cemeteries is one of the most striking features of the Scillonian chamber tombs. On Gugh, seven tombs lie on the slope of Kittern Hill and three more occupy the crest in a parallel line. A line of twelve lie on the North Hill of Samson and a further four on the spine of South Hill. The tombs on St Mary's, once probably more numerous, give the impression of a more dispersed cemetery, or series of cemeteries, on Salakee Down, Porth Hellick Down and Normandy Down.

There are smaller groups, as on the northern tip of Bryher, the northern end of Tresco, the southern end of St Martin's, and Little Arthur in the eastern Isles. In most cases the tombs are mingled with unchambered barrows and other funerary monuments and generally the groups include monuments of very varied size. Although the tombs sited on ridges and higher slopes now catch the eye, it is clear that a number of monuments lie on low ground, in some cases only a few metres above the modern shore-line. So far as can now be determined, such sitings were not frequent and the number of monuments lost to marine erosion must be small. One further feature, particularly evident on Kittern Hill, Gugh, must be noted. Linking tombs and other burial monuments, the lines of boulder walls are evident in several places, for example on the North Hill of Samson, on St Mary's near Old Town and on Bryher. The purpose of these walls has not been determined archaeologically. Clearly they respect the burial monuments, but they may have been built at a very much later date as part of a scheme of land-allotment similar to those evident on Dartmoor and Bodmin Moor (below, p. 115).

The overall uniformity of the Scillonian entrance-graves makes them unique among such monuments in the British Isles. Their builders were clearly following fairly closely a basic design which was echoed in certain monuments in West Penwith but not elsewhere. This close adherence to a structural pattern is perhaps the most striking single feature of the monuments, no doubt reflecting the closely knit community on the prehistoric island. In one further respect the chamber tombs of Scilly appear to be unique. There is evidence from a small number for the use of mortar in the rubble walling. Borlase remarked on the presence of mortar in one of the chambers on Buzza Hill, St Mary's, and more recent observation in other monuments bears out that early record (Borlase 1756: 30). Hencken noted a coarse mortar between the wall stones of a chamber on North Hill, Samson, and O'Neil's excavation of Knackyboy Cairn on St Martin's revealed not only a bonding of granite-clay paste, but a rendering of the walls in the same substance (O'Neil 1952: 23). The possibilities which the latter raises for internal decoration of the chambers, and indeed for other burial monuments, are intriguing but no further evidence on the point seems to have been noted.

The character of the burials for which the chambers were designed, their disposition and the grave-goods which accompanied them are all matters which require more detailed field-work. Unfortunately, the majority of the chambers now stand empty and exposed and it will require a major stroke of fortune to reveal intact deposits in one of the known monuments or, better still, a new, undisturbed chamber. Very little in the way of careful excavation has yet been carried out on the tombs and only one, a small cairn, has been completely dug. One of the most important and informative excavations to date is O'Neil's work on the largely intact Knackyboy Cairn on St Martin's (O'Neil 1952). The chamber in this cairn, which had been so built as to take advantage of a natural rock outcrop, contained eight urns, six of these standing in two rows of three near to the inner end of the chamber. All eight probably contained cremated remains. Around and partially over these urns lay a thick deposit of ash, charcoal and cremated bone, in which was included several large fragments of pottery, a number of beads and bronze scraps. Over this in turn lay more urns, including three sited along the central axis of the chamber. The urn at the outer end of this row had probably been the final deposition before the chamber was closed off. Two further urns were found, surrounded by stones, a metre away from the chamber in the body of the cairn. The pottery vessels apart, the most distinctive of the grave-goods are the beads found in the deposit of charcoal and cremated bone. Seven of these were of glass, one of faience, a further glass bead being recovered from one of the urns. The bronze fragments from this same deposit are not certainly identifiable, though one may be part of a pendant ornament or an ear-ring.

It is reasonably certain that a considerable number of individual cremations is to be inferred from the material recovered from Knackyboy Cairn. O'Neil estimated that there were twenty-two urns which could be reconstructed and as much as 4 cwt of pottery in all from the chamber. It is impossible to estimate how many individuals might be represented by the mass of cremated bone outside the urns. Ashbee's guess is 'at least sixty', though the figure could be somewhat higher.

Another entrance-grave which has produced relatively large quantities of material, both skeletal and ceramic, is Obadiah's Barrow on Gugh, examined by Bonsor (Hencken 1933b: 21; Ashbee 1974: 92–4). The unburnt remains of a skeleton were found in the middle of the chamber, these being interpreted by Bonsor as the primary interment, much disturbed. Subsequent to this burial, about a dozen cremation urns had been placed in the chamber, of which only one was intact. These had apparently been inverted so that their breakage or removal had allowed the cremated remains to spill out on to the chamber-floor. Further urn-fragments and burnt bones were found close to the entrance. The entire deposit gives the impression of a sequence of burials, beginning with an inhumation and continuing with cremations, earlier deposits being perhaps partially cleared away to make way for other interments as the available space became cramped. A reasonable alternative view is that the remains were brought in from another place, perhaps an earlier burial-place, the better preserved urns being placed in position, and the fragments of other ash-containers being more casually disposed about them. On the whole, the former view seems preferable on the evidence from Knackyboy Cairn, but the matter is not beyond doubt. There were grave-goods other than pottery in Obadiah's Barrow, including part of a bronze awl, a hammer-stone and a battered pebble. Other burial chambers have produced finds of broadly similar character, inurned cremation being the normal rite.

The most recent careful excavation of one of the Scillonian monuments has been that by Ashbee at Bant's Carn on Halangy Down, St Mary's (Ashbee 1976). This was first examined by Bonsor in 1901, a record of which was published by Hencken (Hencken 1933b: 22). Knowledge of the tomb was further enlarged during restoration in 1970 and a considerable quantity of pottery was recovered during that operation. The forms of the vessels are generically similar to those from Knackyboy Cairn, the barrel- and bucket-shaped urns in particular. Rim-forms were either plain or internally bevelled. Decorative schemes included finger-tipping, combing, corded ornament and grooves, again recalling the Knackyboy pottery. Urns of broadly related types were found in the small tomb on Salakee Down, St Mary's, excavated by Grimes (Grimes 1960: 174–6) and on Par Beach, St Mary's. More important is the fact that urns of the same forms and similar decoration were in use on domestic sites, as the material from Halangy Porth demonstrates. Here, the common decorative elements are comb-stamping and impressed cord. Much of pottery, however, has no ornamentation and is surprisingly thin-walled for such large vessels.

The pottery from the better recorded tombs is characterized by a number of distinctive traits. The forms of the principal vessels are biconical, barrel- and bucket-shaped urns, their rims either plain or internally bevelled. The decorative schemes, much in evidence at Knackyboy Cairn and Bant's Carn, include finger-tipping, combing, cord-ornament and grooving. Pierced and solid lugs appear on the larger vessels. Much of the pottery is unornamented and surprisingly thin-walled. A few vessels are generically similar to the plain Neolithic vessels of the mainland, though the latter have not been reported from Scilly. Substantial quantities of the same barrel- and bucket-shaped urns have been found on the domestic site at Halangy Porth, as Hencken long ago pointed out, and again the decorative elements are usually comb-stamping and impressed cord-decoration. Such vessels are obviously related to mainland vessels of the mid- to late second millennium BC; such as the urns of the earlier Trevisker series and the related urns from Gwithian (layers 7 and 8) (below, p. 136). Behind all these lie a wide range of biconical and bucket-shaped urns of the mid- to later Bronze Age.

What these grave-goods demonstrate, then, is the continuance of collective burial on Scilly long after it had been abandoned on the mainland. The conventional divisions of British prehistory cannot be applied to the cultural record of Scilly.

The extraordinary profusion of megalithic tombs on Scilly, long ago noted by Hencken (1932: 17), has not been satisfactorily explained. Yet there is a real problem here. More than forty, probably up to fifty entrance-graves exist in the islands, an exceptional concentration in so small an area. Even allowing for the destruction of monuments in west Cornwall, the contrast with the mainland is sharp. An explanation which takes account of the economic imperatives is obviously required and thus the suggestion put forward by Clark is to be carefully weighed (Clark 1977). The distribution of entrance-graves in Scilly, west Cornwall, western Brittany and southern Ireland could be connected with the pursuit of sea-fishing, especially of hake and mackerel, until recently a major preoccupation of coastal dwellers in these regions. Line-fishing from the shore and from boats is well established for the north European Neolithic (Clark 1948) and a likely cause of the close similarities between grave-forms in these Atlantic coastlands is contact between groups who crossed the seas in the pursuit of fish-shoals. Unfortunately, the contemporary shore-lines in the South West have been drowned by the rising level of the sea making difficult the detailed examination of the hypothesis. There may, however, be a reflection of sea-fishing in the accumulations of shells of limpets and other marine crustaceans on certain south-western sites, including one or two megalithic tombs. About a dozen such shell deposits are known on Scilly (Ashbee 1974: 264), a smaller number on the north Cornish coast, and occasional instances

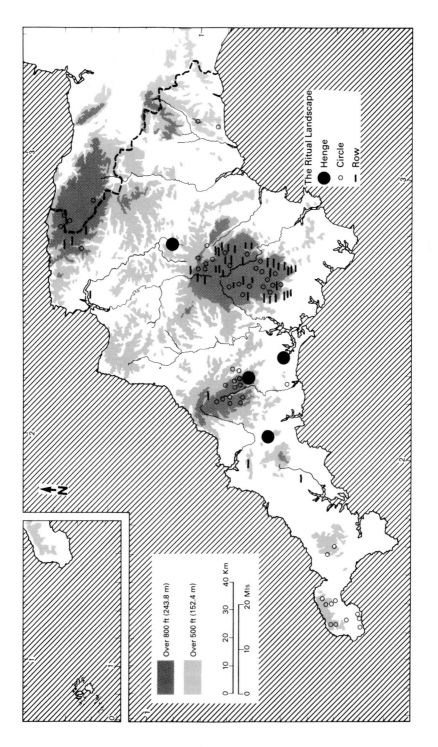

Figure 4.7   The Ritual Landscape

in Devon, including Westward Ho! (Jacobi 1980: 183). Limpets have been eaten in the South West in recent times, but they are neither appetizing nor nutritious. It is easier to believe that they were used as bait in line-fishing.

The harvest of the sea will not, however, provide an adequate explanation for the unusual concentration of megalithic tombs and, to a lesser extent, in west Cornwall. Human activities on land should provide a more convincing answer. One of the most interesting demonstrations of recent years has been that many megalithic tombs, including both chambered monuments and entrance-graves, stand on lynchets and other elements in field-systems. This is true, for example, of Bant's Carn, Innisidgen, Obadiah's Barrow and Carn Valla (Ashbee 1982a: 17; Thomas 1985). This relationship between funerary monuments and the agrarian landscape is a compelling one and it urgently requires elucidation by excavation. As Fowler and Thomas put it,

> the tombs, and the extensive agrarian structure . . . (were) parts of the same evolving cultural landscape. Perhaps it needs to be stressed that it is we, today, who make this functional distinction between farming and the funerary; . . . psychologically both activities may have been part of the same process
>
> (Fowler and Thomas 1979: 187).

This approach is without doubt correct. But what it was that impelled the erection of funerary monuments on the cultivated landscape remains elusive. It may represent a call for aid or protection from the ancestral dead for land which was declining in its fertility. Or it may signify no more than that land which was recognizably inferior in quality was chosen to house the monuments of the dead. Whatever the truth, the placing of these structures in the landscape is a sure reminder that to Neolithic man the living and the dead inhabited one world.

Although the large monuments of the Neolithic and early Bronze Age may be judged to have had specific purposes, burial, ceremonial, assembly, it is reasonable to think of them as functioning in other more general ways in society, not least as symbolic expressions of power, territoriality and possession. In the case of the tombs, the association of ancestors with a particular locality might be seen as an essential proof of possession which none could question, just as the great house and its policies proclaimed the landowner of later European societies. The henge monuments, still so poorly known in the South West, may also have been in essence expressions of power, power to direct the efforts of many to construct a great work, power to attract to a centre the allegiance of a population which was normally dispersed.

Ceremonial observance, as in most primitive societies, will have been an integral part of the mundane cycle, for the most part undifferentiated from everyday tasks and acts. But specialized monuments connected with this aspect of human preoccupations were also found essential, as in other parts of

Neolithic Britain. Surviving instances are mainly on the uplands, though we must extrapolate from these a distribution which originally embraced the entire region. There is probably significant overlap with burial and the rites of the dead, so that these monuments are to be considered next. The most notable categories are henges, stone circles, menhirs and stone rows.

The south-western henges are monuments of relatively modest scale. Three of the sites which may be regarded as certain henges lie in east Cornwall: Castilly, Castlewich and the Stripple Stones on Hawks Tor Down, Bodmin Moor, the last-named being the largest and most impressive, part-destroyed though it is. We might with reason expect a henge to lie undetected somewhere in west Cornwall. The unlikely gap in Devon has recently been filled by the discovery of a henge near Bow in the Culm Measures.

Only the Stripple Stones monument has been examined (St George Gray

Figure 4.8   The Stripple Stones

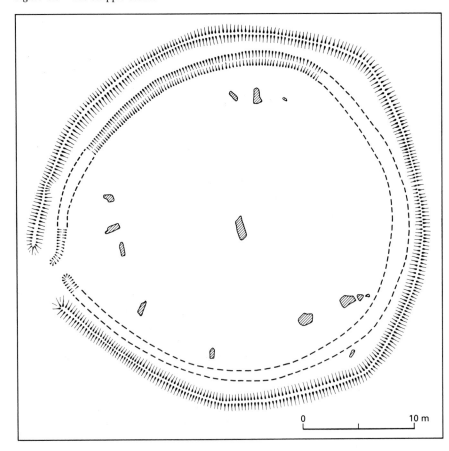

0   10 m

1909). This is a circle of 60 m bounded by a shallow and rather irregular ditch (comparing with the 58 m for the henge at Arbor Low in Derbyshire). Within the earthwork there stood a circle of some twenty-eight stones, only two of which are still upright. A further eleven lie roughly where they have fallen. Near the centre of the circle there once stood a single large stone over 4 m in length. There is only one entrance, on the south-west side. The most unusual feature of the monument is the presence of three apsed recesses in the surrounding bank, on the western side, the largest of these being 11 m wide and 4.5 m deep. The closest analogy seems to be with recesses in the enclosure at Durrington Walls. Those at the Stripple Stones have been linked with observation of the equinoxes. This is not entirely out of the question but they could equally well have served as the sites of ceremonies which were thought to have no place within the central circle itself.

Within a short distance of the Stripple Stones lie four other stone circles, suggesting a major focus of ritual and ceremonial activities on this western side of Bodmin Moor (St George Gray 1909). The largest of these is at Fernacre, slightly larger than the circle of the Stripple Stones, and Stannon, each of these comprising small stones and being somewhat flattened in form. The almost perfect circle of the Trippet ('dancing') Stones, 33 metres across, has much larger uprights. In the centre of the group is the smallest and best preserved circle, at Leaze, 25 m in diameter. The close similarity in size between the circles at Fernacre, the Stripple Stones and Stannon is to be noted, as is the fact that similar numbers of stones were used to form the Leaze circle (28), the Stripple Stones (28) and the Trippet Stones, a feature also evident in the Dartmoor and West Penwith circles. Why these circles stand where they do is impossible as yet to understand. They do not lie close to trackways or obvious routes across the moor. Nor are they close to obvious areas of Neolithic and early Bronze Age settlement, though that is something on which little is known. Perhaps they were deliberately sited at a distance from the mundane activities of man, but where they could still be seen.

The eastern side of Bodmin Moor also had its foci for non-worldly observances, the largest being the three adjacent circles on a rough north–south alignment, the Hurlers. This group does lie on a routeway, between the rivers Lynher and Fowey, and a considerable number of burial monuments stand in the vicinity, including Trethevy Quoit and the Rillaton barrow. Excavation of these circles by Radford revealed that the stones in the central ring had been placed in pits with stones packed round their bases to hold them firm. They had also been hammered smooth, the chippings being then strewn over the interior. Care had been exercised to make the tops of the stones roughly level with each other. Little was found within the circles (Radford 1935b: 134). That in the central position contained an upright stone placed off-centre, and that to the north had been paved with granite blocks. Between the central and the southern circles lay another patch of paving and a small pit. To the south-west and 120 m away are two standing stones, the Pipers, possibly remnants of another circular monument or an alignment running down to the River Fowey, or even a cove like that which lies to the south-west of the Stanton Drew circles in Somerset. None of these monuments is in any sense dated, either in its construction or its period of use. It seems highly likely that circles were being built over a lengthy time-span, and a single site might retain its significance for centuries. The Hurlers, for example, might comprise monuments of different dates with perhaps the central circle at the nucleus. A connection with the world of the dead is often assumed, since a substantial number of circles lie close to burial monuments. But the chronological relationship is impossible to define and it is perhaps notable that no circle has produced unequivocal evidence of a formal human burial within its circumference or its close proximity.

A series of smaller circles is evident in west Cornwall, most of these between 18 m and 25 m in diameter. Boscawen-Un is a slightly ovoid circle with an eccentrically placed tall internal pillar of quartz, sited like that of the Stripple Stones and the central circle of the Hurlers. The other monuments now appear as circles of similar size, with similar numbers of stones (between 20 and 22), and standing at similar heights above sea-level, between 100 m and 300 m. These include the Merry Maidens, the pair of circles at Tregeseal and Boskednan. Apart from their smaller diameters, these circles have much in common with those at Bodmin Moor, for instance in the height of individual stones and in the spacing between them. None now appears to have stone alignments, standing stones or other monuments closely associated with them, though of course we cannot be sure that none ever existed. Precise setting-out is evident at some: the Merry Maidens form almost a perfect circle. Others, including Boscawen-Un, are far from regular in their lay-out and must always have been so. There has been no digging to modern standards of any of these western Cornish monuments so that we have no information about rebuilding or other alteration, about possible earlier monuments of simpler design, or about remains of ceremonies or depositions. Since most have been disturbed to some degree, the prospects here are not bright.

The considerable number of stone circles on Dartmoor contains no large monument, the biggest being the south circle of the Grey Wethers near the headwaters of the Dart, which is 33 m in diameter (Worth 1953: 258–60). Most of the sizeable circles, between 25 m and 30 m across, lie near to the rivers which flow southward from the moor, including Sherberton near the West Dart, Brisworthy near the Plym, and a series, including Scorhill, about the upper Teign (Burl 1976: 106–15). A favoured location is a saddle or a pass between valley-heads where routes might converge. The distribution of the smaller circles is much more general, though most lie on the south and east moor. These modest monuments, often only 10 m or 12 m across, and built of small stones, have not been well studied in recent times. Excavation within them, as at Fernworthy, the Grey Wethers and Merrivale, has produced little to enlighten us as to their purpose and history, apart from deposits of ash and charcoal (which might be of any date) and an occasional flint object. Small circles set around central cairns or cists form a class of monument which must be distinguished from the open circles. Some of these are very small, only 3 m or 4 m across and seem to do no more than provide an edging to a burial place.

Most of the known circles are single rings of stones. There are, however, more complex works consisting of several concentric rings, like Yellowmead Down (Sheepstor) and Shovel Down, both of these with four rings (Worth 1953: 187–9). More elaborate still is a pair of monuments at Glasscombe, near the Coringdon Ball long cairn (Robinson and Greeves 1981), which are made up of multiple rings of small stones. Interestingly, all of these complex circles have stone rows either directly associated with them or very close by.

The design and layout of the circles have usually been carried out with care. Stones of roughly equal size were generally selected and their spacing, so far as can now be judged, was even. Many are true circles, others are oval or show a slight irregularity from the true. It must be remembered that several of the larger monuments were heavily restored in the nineteenth century. Internal features such as central stones now seem to be exceptional, but their appearance at Boscawen-Un and the Stripple Stones suggests they may once have been more frequent. Choice of site was obviously a major preoccupation

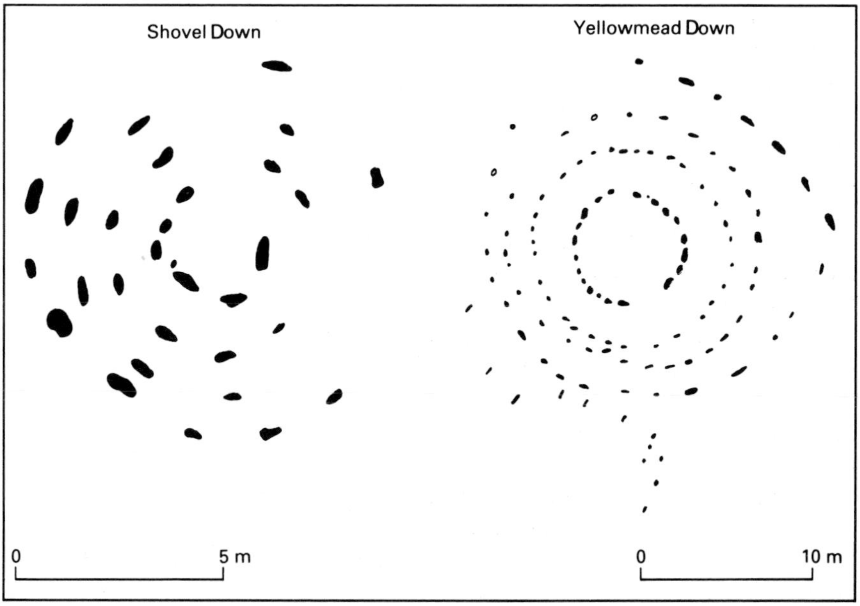

Figure 4.9 Two Dartmoor multiple circles: Shovel Down and Yellowmead Down

of the builders of circles. Apart from placement on saddles or passes, a striking number of circles are so located that dominant local features are in prominent view, normally hill-tops or tors. This seems unlikely to be due merely to chance, but arguments advanced by some for astronomical purposes behind the siting of stone circles have failed to establish any satisfactory basis for this aspect of the subject, even though some connexion remains a possibility (Thom 1967; 1971).

It follows from what has been said above that the dating of circles and their relationship with other monuments present enormous difficulties, insoluble as yet. None has yet produced a radiocarbon estimate or range of artifacts that can reasonably be linked with its period of use, which might in any case be prolonged. Beaker graves and long cists lie close to the circles at Merrivale and Fernworthy, but in no sense can they be regarded as associated with them. The relationship with stone rows – themselves undated – seems to have a firmer base, which would strengthen the argument for a ceremonial function for the rows. But absolute evidence of date is still wanting and should be sought, preferably at the conjunction of a circle with a row.

Frequently a single standing stone or menhir is positioned near a circle, as at Merrivale. Much more commonly a menhir or a pair stands at or near the end of a stone row. But the commonest position adopted by menhirs is in isolation, often on a slope rather than an exposed hill-top. These stones are still widespread on Dartmoor and Bodmin Moor, but commonest of all in West Penwith and the Lizard, where about 90 exist or have been recorded. Their functions were various, ranging from utilitarian markers to simple ceremonial markers or grave-monuments. Some may well have marked out property or other territorial bounds. Excavation at the base of several has produced no finds at all, but in the case of others pottery vessels, as at Tresvennack, and burials, as at Trelew, Pridden and the Blind Fiddler, have been found (Barnatt 1982: 97). A Beaker burial in a cist found at the base of a menhir at Try (Gulval) is the earliest certain burial (Russell and Pool 1964). The pottery from the stone-hole of a menhir at Kerrow suggests erection in the middle Bronze Age, but this may have been only the final act in a long series.

A few other menhirs have small cairns at their bases, but only one has been examined, the Long Stone at Pilton near Barnstaple, a large limestone pillar standing nearly 3 m high. Unfortunately this stone has been moved in modern times so that its relationship with large blocks of stone found buried nearby could not be established and no dating evidence was found (Arkle, Spencer and Lomas 1968).

The stone alignments traditionally called stone rows (at least from the nineteenth century) are the most distinctive monuments of prehistoric Dartmoor in particular. Although considerable variety is evidenced in these monuments, they form a genus with unmistakable characteristics. There are at least seventy known examples, the great majority on Dartmoor, a few on

Exmoor, one on the flats of Bideford Bay and two in Cornwall. They present formidable problems of dating and interpretation (Emmett 1979). They will be treated here as part of the monumental expressions of later Neolithic and early Bronze Age man but this is mainly for the sake of convenience. There is virtually no evidence which bears directly on the date of any one stone row and as a class they may span a lengthy period between the fourth and the second millennia BC. Only one row, at Cholwich Town on Lee Moor, has been recently excavated, without any results for the date of the alignment (Eogan and Simmons 1964). It is fairly certain that they do not represent a single short phase of construction. Some rows are clearly of more than one phase and there are cases of rows which have been renewed or realigned, as on Shovel Down. Monuments which are in some way associated with rows, such as cairns, cists and barrows, have produced datable material mainly of the period 2000–*c*. 1600 BC, but these objects cannot be used as reliable guides to the history of stone rows. It is obvious that a number of burial monuments are earlier than the rows, others may be contemporary or later. All that can be said with reasonable confidence is that where a Bronze Age field-bank or other earthwork such as a reave encounters a stone row, the row appears to be the earlier feature (below, p. 112).

The topographical layout of rows, their length and disposition, the size of stones used, all show variation. The two longest lie in the Erme valley, that on Stall Moor and Green Hill being over 2 km long and that on Butterdon Hill over 1.5 km, both of these single rows. The double and more complex rows are mostly much shorter, between 100 m and 200 m in length. Little emphasis can be placed on the matter of length for in most cases it is unknown how much has been lost, particularly of the rows made up of small stones, which may have been buried by blanket peat or moved by later users of the moor. A few rows are composed of very large stones, up to 2 m high, the best example being that on Stalldon Moor, Cornwood. Most, however, employed relatively small stones, between 50 cm and 1 m long. These were clearly intended to mark out something on the ground rather than to present alignments which could be seen from a distance. Sizes of stones can be mixed and often there seems to have been no attempt at careful setting out, either in detail or in the alignment as a whole: often there is no obvious topographical constraint which might account for this. Compared with the layout of henges and stone circles, the design of stone rows seems much less deliberate. Most are straight or roughly so, but a fair number are slightly curved or even sinuous in their course.

The often observed association with cairns, barrows and stone circles is obviously of significance for any assessment of the role stone rows were intended to perform. As has already been noted, the relationship in time is not always clear, but the incorporation of cairns in rows at Merrivale and Shovel Down, and the use of a stone circle as a terminus, as at Stall Moor, is not casual. The linearity of the rows for the most part, the absence of any attempt

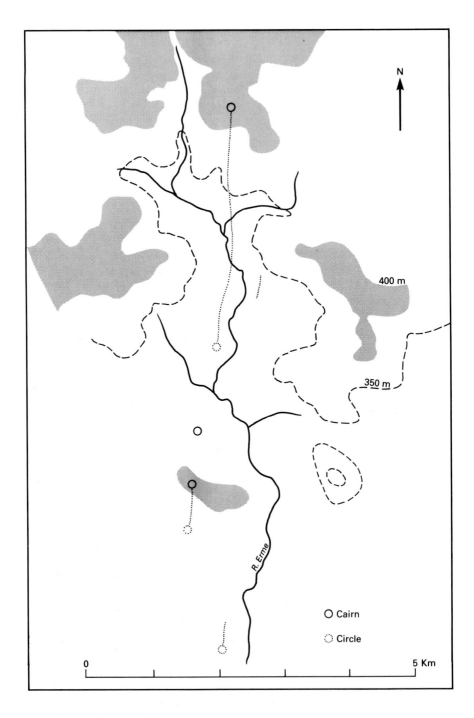

Figure 4.10 The Erme Valley stone rows

to *enclose* ground, is basic to their purpose. So, one might argue, is the fact that few of them would be visible from a distance. Essentially, they mark a line, be it track or boundary or both, which could easily be traced, but not discerned with ease from afar. Boundaries between properties or other blocks of land might explain some of the single rows. Others, particularly the double and multiple rows, are better regarded as ceremonial markers, perhaps for observances at particular monuments, or as monuments in their own right, akin to the long mounds and cursūs of the Neolithic in southern England, none of which is known in the South West. It is probably unwise, however, to make any sharp distinction between ceremonial functions and the marking out of land. The latter might be attended by ceremonies which were repeated at regular intervals (as they still are in several parts of Europe), the power of ancestors in their graves being invoked to protect and fortify the bounds. But there is still much that we do not know about these evocative stone alignments and opportunity should be taken to excavate one or more, preferably with the specific objective of defining the relationship with other structures, especially funerary monuments and circles.

It is sometimes forgotten that stone rows also occur on Exmoor and elsewhere in north Devon. Since three major rows have been noted on Exmoor in the past few years it seems certain that others will emerge. Closest to the Dartmoor rows in character is that on the west side of Wilmersham Common above Chetsford Water (Somerset) (Corney 1967). This was originally a double row running north-east to south-west, ending to the north-east in what now appears as a jumble of stones but may originally have been a triple row or a more elaborate setting. The whole measures about 70 m in length. The most recent discovery, in 1981, is of a row of some twenty small stones in a row 400 m in length at Culbone (Mold 1983). This is aligned east–west, possibly with a barrow at either end. The row on Mattocks Down between Lynton and Ilfracombe, now largely destroyed, was recorded as long ago as 1630 by Thomas Westcote in one of the earliest accounts of any south-western antiquity:

> First there stand two great stones in nature or fashion (though not curiously cut) of Pyramids, distant one from the other 147 foot; the greatest is in height above this ground nine foot and a half, every square bearing four foot. The height of the other stone is five foot and a half, but in square well nigh equals the other, being somewhat above three foot. These two stones, or as may be said Pillars, stand in a right line, one opposite to the other. Sixty six foot on the side of these, are laid a row or bank of 23 unformed stones also, but not equalling the other two by much, and reaching from one of these stones to the other in direct line and making a reciprocal figure as having the sides equally proportioned but double as long, or more than square (which as I am told is called a Parallelogram) (Westcote 1845: 90–1).

The row has now vanished and only one of the standing stones, the larger of the two, can now be seen.

Several shorter rows are known, though none now seems to bear any relation to other structures. The only possible exception is a row of three small stones south-west of Setta Barrow. At Little Tom's Hill a group of six stones arranged in two rows of three each about 18 m long may represent a somewhat different type of monument, for the spacing between the rows is unusually wide, varying from 6.5 m to 8 m (Grinsell 1970: 46). A more closely set pair of parallel rows, three stones in each, occurs at East Pinford, and there are other possible rows at Trout Hill (Exmoor parish), Ilkerton Ridge (Lynton), Hold-stone Down (Combe Martin) and North Regis Common (Challacombe).

That stone rows also existed on low-lying ground (perhaps replaced by rows of timber uprights in terrain where stone was scarce) is demonstrated by the remarkable survival of a row at Yelland in the estuarine flats of the Taw, now some 3 m below the level of the spring tides (Rogers 1932; 1947). This is a double row 35 m long and with a gap of 2 m between the rows so that it has more of the aspect of an avenue than many such monuments. The stones are small and spaced at their closest about 2.3 m apart. There is no sign of any associated barrow or cairn, though it is possible that any such work could have been destroyed. The stones had been inserted into an earlier land-surface which yielded Mesolithic flint objects, but no evidence for a closer dating was obtained in an excavation around some of the stones, although a barbed and tanged arrowhead was found nearby.

At least eight stone rows are now known in Cornwall, seven on Bodmin Moor and another on St Breock Downs, the Nine Maidens. The latter is a striking alignment of nine tall uprights, the former a short row of small stones reminiscent of the Dartmoor examples. The fact that only seven rows have been noted on Bodmin Moor, where the survival of early Bronze Age structures is so extensive, seems to indicate that this feature was never common on these uplands.

Notes

1. Radiocarbon estimates were later obtained from burnt material found in the ditch-filling: 3150 ± 150; 3240 ± 150; 3330 ± 150 (Fox, A. 1963). It is worth noting that the material which yielded these estimates may be associated with the *end* of occupation.

2. On radiocarbon estimates from Carn Brea, see Mercer 1981: 62–3.

Chapter 5

The Stable Communities

Early Metallurgy and Wider Contacts

The origin of metallurgy is generally taken to mark a significant stage in the development of prehistoric society as well as technology, though the first metal objects in Britain were on the whole of limited use and circulation: copper daggers, awls, knives, a few axes, gold ornaments. Few of these have been found in the South West, an awl from Gwithian and a knife from a Beaker burial at Fernworthy on Dartmoor being the most notable. Flat axes of copper shortly afterwards appear in the record and these are commoner in Devon and Cornwall (e.g. Paul, Ipplepen, Burleigh Camp). Broad, flat axes in tin-bronze probably overlap with these (Harlyn Bay, Hemyock and Kentisbeare: an unfinished example at Drewsteignton hints at manufacture here). Slimmer types with narrower blades were soon developed and an open mould for such axes was found at Altarnun on Bodmin Moor. Decorated forms followed, represented by pieces from Axmouth and two with chevron ornament from Trenovissick. Other bronze forms, such as the daggers so well known in Wessex, are very rare in the South West (Pearce 1983: 81). Later, by 1600–1500 BC, daggers, flanged axes and other weapons and tools were more widely distributed in the region and were probably being made here. The major testimony comes from the Plymstock hoard, buried about 1500 BC, which contained sixteen flanged axes, three daggers, a spear and a punch. The ensemble looks like that of a metal-smith who had acquired elements in his repertoire from central European sources, not necessarily directly (below, p. 133). Daggers, mainly of Camerton-Snowshill type, are at this time in a number of graves, at Caerloggas I, Harlyn Bay, Farway, Hameldon, Rillaton, Pelynt and Huntshaw, echoing the deposition of these prestigious objects in contemporary burials in Wessex (Gerloff 1975; Miles 1975a: 32–4). Other dagger-types of the same period are known from Woodbury, Newquay, Upton Pyne and East Putford, all from burials.

Metalwork in gold appeared alongside the early copper and bronzework, most strikingly in the gold *lunulae* from Harlyn Bay, St Juliot and Gwithian,

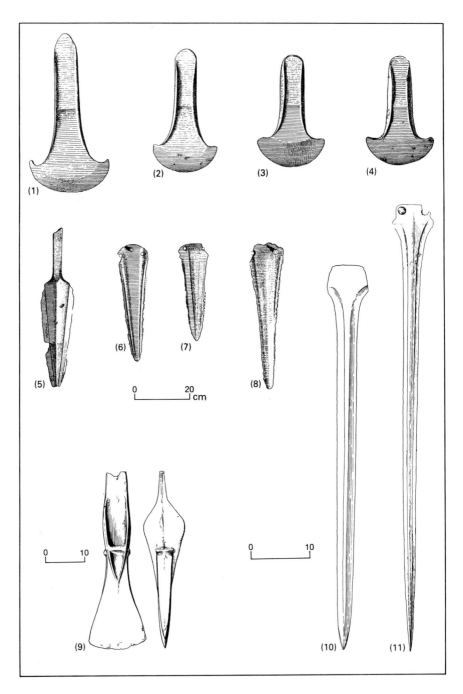

Figure 5.1　Metalwork of the second millennium BC: (1)–(8) Plymstock hoard; (9)–(11) Crediton hoard

and the famous gold cup from the Rillaton barrow. The *lunulae* underline the links in craftsmanship and materials with Ireland which some of the flat axes reveal (Taylor 1970: 53; 1980), but it would be mistaken to see this connexion as the only formative one. Before examining the wider links suggested by this metalwork, we must look more closely at the limited evidence for metal-extraction in the peninsula in this period.

Small quantities of gold and silver could have been acquired in certain localities. Small gold nuggets, up to about 20 g, are occasionally found in west Cornwall to this day and small deposits of natural gold also occur in the St Austell area and at Hope's Nose, Torquay. Gold could also have been found in the same alluvial and eluvial deposits that produce tin around Par, Pentewan, Carnon and Marazion. Silver sources are much more limited, the most significant deposits occurring along with copper near Callington.

Exploitation of tin and copper sources during the second millennium BC is a subject of obvious significance but one which has not yet been elucidated by major discoveries in the field or by detailed analysis of artifacts. The latter is particularly urgently required for it offers the most promising line of enquiry towards the date at which the south-western metal deposits began to be used, as against, for instance, those in Brittany, central Europe and Spain. The transition from tin-bronze to an alloy with higher tin values is firmly attested by 2000 bc (for example at Newgrange), but we do not know where the early metallurgists found their tin and how it was distributed.

Finds of Bronze Age objects, mostly of second millennium date, made in tin-streams in the eighteenth and nineteenth centuries convey the general impression that these alluvial tin-deposits were being worked at that time, but no clear picture emerges from these occasional discoveries. The earliest discoveries are a flat axe found in the tin-rich Carnon valley and a rapier from St Ewe (Borlase, W. C. 1872: 41; Shell 1979: 257). A socketed spear-head and a 'chisel' (? a flat axe) came from a stream-work in the Pentewan valley, and a later Bronze Age hoard from Lanherne, St Mawgan, immediately above the tin-stream (Shell 1979, 256). The flat axes from Trenovissick also came from close to a tin-stream. Most interesting of all are the antler-pick and other antler tools found with a wooden shovel bound with plant-fibre in the Carnon valley (Worth 1874: 56). Although undated, these seem likely to be early prospecting implements, quite possibly of early Bronze Age date. Objects of tin or tin-alloy which may have been produced in the South West are rare indeed. The most important is a bulb-headed pin with a tin/lead head and tin/bronze body, found in one of the parishes of St Columb (Shell 1979: 257–8). This, too, should be an early Bronze Age object, its closest relatives being objects found in central Europe about 2000 BC. The objects earlier identified as tin-slag, found with a dagger of Camerton-Snowshill type in a barrow at Caerloggas (Miles 1975a: 32), may be corroded metal rather than remains of tin-working and thus cannot be used to demonstrate smelting here, though they give us yet another instance of early Bronze Age tin which is of Cornish provenance.

109

Continental connexions (specifically with north-western Germany) can be traced in the south-western material in the form of imported flat axes or British copies of such imports. One, or possibly two, flanged axes in the Plymstock hoard are either imports from north-western Europe or local products based on continental models, and a smaller example from Teignmouth is probably another (Butler 1963: 44; Needham 1979: 275). The Plymstock hoard also contains a distinctive long-butted axe with a waisted body similar to axes found in Aunjetitz culture hoards in central Europe (von Brunn 1959: Pl. 45, 1, 4; Pl. 85, 14). Relations with Ireland have long been recognized in this early metalwork, for instance in the Trenovissick flat axes, and it is reasonable to assume that north-western France also lay within this zone of contact. There were, then, several regions of north-western Europe which could have provided models for imitation as well as implements for use. The distances traversed by some of the imported items may seem surprising but they are no greater than, for instance, those covered by flint axes of Scandinavian type which occur in Britain in the later Neolithic.

Settlement in the Second Millennium BC

The most extensive programmes of work on the settlement and environment of the second millennium have been conducted on Bodmin Moor and Dartmoor. At Colliford in the central part of Bodmin Moor buried soils beneath four barrows constructed between 1650 and 1500 bc reveal marked variation within a small area. Soil deterioration had set in during the period immediately preceding barrow construction, perhaps due to over-use of the land. By the middle of the millennium little woodland remained in the area and what there was lay on the lower slopes of the valleys. It is highly likely that the process of general removal of trees had been proceeding for long before these monuments were built, at a guess from early in the third millennium if not earlier. The variation encountered within so limited an area, however, indicates the degree of caution with which we must proceed from the particular to the general. From the later second millennium onward moorland developed, the soils below the growth of heather and gorse steadily turning into the peat deposits seen today. Broadly similar results have been obtained from below Bronze Age barrows on the granite near St Austell. Only hazel was prominent among the tree pollens, with oak and alder also present, on most of the sites. Below one monument, Caerloggas III, oak and alder made a stronger showing, especially in the period shortly before barrow-building. Interestingly, none of these sites produced any cereal pollen, although Caerloggas I did yield weed spectra suggestive of arable cultivation. There was no indication of the development of moorland at this time, a predominantly grassland landscape being the most likely (Miles 1975a: 60–6).

The best evidence for Dartmoor comes from Shaugh Moor in the south-western corner. Woodland had evidently been cleared during the later Neolithic and this may have led to the degrading and waterlogging of soils. Hazel and alder scrub developed in patches and on the higher moor heather began to colonize small areas. In the valleys and on lower slopes open grassland dominated, an obvious indicator of pastoralism. This grassland reached its fullest extent by about 1000 BC, by which date the population of Dartmoor was probably at its peak (below, p. 151). Cereal pollens and the pollens of weeds associated with arable ground were present but only in quantities that suggest limited cereal-growing. The absence of lynchetted fields supports the idea that arable cultivation was of minor significance and this seems to hold good for most of Dartmoor, except for the eastern and southern fringes. This is the general picture, an open, upland grassland; no doubt there was a considerable degree of local variation.

Bronze Age Settlement on the South-Western Moors*

The moors and heaths of south-west England, particularly the granite areas of Dartmoor, Bodmin Moor, Hensbarrow, Carnmenellis and Penwith, display as field monuments the remains of ceremonial monuments, houses, walled enclosures, field systems and land boundaries; to judge from the few investigated examples, a fair proportion of these are likely to date from the Bronze Age. Although Bronze Age people lived in lowland areas as well, preservation conditions have ensured that the most complete picture comes from the uplands. Indeed Dartmoor and parts of Bodmin Moor contain some of the best preserved 'prehistoric landscapes' in north-west Europe, and provide the opportunity, not yet fully exploited, to compare the visible remains of fields and settlements with the vegetation record indicated by fossil pollen preserved in neighbouring peat-bogs. It is sometimes assumed that because these well-preserved settlement patterns and field systems are located on the moors, they must have been on marginal land, and are thus not representative of Bronze Age settlement in general. However, it is by no means clear what the proponents of this argument are defining as marginality, or whether such a concept existed in the Bronze Age. It should not be assumed without argument that upland settlement patterns represent distorted or incomplete versions of low-land settlement patterns.

* By Andrew Fleming.

111

The uplands of south-west England have deteriorated, from the point of view of human settlement and exploitation, since the Bronze Age; the climate has worsened, soils have become more acid, blanket peat has deepened and spread. In Neolithic times, areas like Bodmin Moor and Dartmoor would have had a positive attraction as hunting zones and grazing grounds. For Bodmin Moor, Brown (1977) suggested that the tree pollen frequencies, not normally exceeding 20–30 per cent, implied the prevalence of open country above about 250 m: 'at most an extensive cover of hazel scrub on the more, but not totally, exposed valley sides, with oak woodland restricted to sheltered hillsides and birch/alderwoods best developed on the wet valley floors around the mires'. Exposure factors, Brown suggested, were responsible for the thinning out of woodland above 250 m; others put forward the view that on Dartmoor the corresponding heights would have been about 400 m (Simmons 1969: 204: Caseldine and Maguire 1981: 6). Neolithic peoples would have been able to graze their livestock on more nutritious grasses than are present in these areas today, growing on higher grade soils with greater earthworm populations (Maltby 1980), land which could be occupied by moles (Fleming (in preparation)). Peat bogs were largely confined to badly drained areas; the blanket bog so familiar today spread out only gradually from the higher ground, at a rate which has still to be accurately determined. It is probable that peat growth intensified during the climatic deterioration of the first millennium bc (Barber 1982: 110) and that many areas favoured for prehistoric habitation were thus affected for the first time during this period. For peoples of the Neolithic and earlier Bronze Age, then, an area like Dartmoor would not have been an extensive, continuous moor, but an area of scrub and open grazing land, interspersed with isolated bogs which were no doubt the haunts of various edible wildfowl.

Chamber tombs and long cairns occur at altitudes of around 370 m on Gidleigh Common, north-east Dartmoor (Turner 1980) and around 300 m on southern Dartmoor (Corringdon Ball, Cuckoo Ball, and Butterdon – Worth 1967: 180; Fletcher 1974). This suggests that Neolithic communities were exploiting these upland areas; chamber tombs in Penwith and recently discovered long cairns (Herring 1983) in the north-western zone of Bodmin Moor suggest a similar interest in the granite uplands. Since individual communities would have used only as much upland grazing land as they required and could defend, areas like Bodmin Moor and Dartmoor would have developed as intercommoning land from Neolithic times.

The early part of the second millennium bc was marked by the construction of over 70 stone rows on Dartmoor (for a concise account see Emmett 1979). The dating evidence for the rows is poor, but consistent as far as it goes; the origins of ceremonial monuments in a small region may be expected to lie within a fairly short time period. The reave builders of the late second millennium bc (see below, p. 115) respected some stone rows and ignored, or perhaps even robbed, others (Fleming 1983: 239) suggesting that the rows were erected at a time neither very remote nor very recent. Their regular spacing around the periphery of Dartmoor, frequently at altitudes of 300–400 m, indicates a sustained interest in the exploitation of the uplands at this time, as does the density of the roughly contemporary small cairns, 3–4 m in diameter and usually but not invariably containing burials in stone cists.

Some of the longer stone rows on Dartmoor must have been built in open country – that is, if they were planned in their entirety from the outset. These include the row in the upper valley of the Erme (nearly 3.5 km in length), the Butterdon row (1.9 km, altitude 350 m) and the Stannon row (300 m, altitude 400–450 m). The stone row at Cholwichtown, on the other hand, was built in an abandoned clearing in oak woodland, in which cereals had been grown (Eogan and Simmons 1964). The clearing was taken over by heather and grass, as hazel and alder expanded at the expense of oak. A good example of the mosaic of vegetation which must have existed on what was probably a rather intermittently used upland common was produced recently on Shaugh Moor (Balaam *et al.* 1982: 212 and fig. 7). Here a major later Bronze Age land boundary, Saddlesborough Reave, provided a convenient transect across the local landscape; the soil pollen sealed beneath it documented the association of alder with the wetter, low-lying ground, the increase in hazel up the slope away from the boggy area, and the greater proportion of heather towards the higher ground.

On Bodmin Moor seven stone rows are now known and one or two are now coming to light farther west (Johnson, *pers. comm.*, Herring, *pers. comm.*). At least three stone rows are known on Exmoor (Eardley-Wilmot 1983 and *pers. comm.*) as well as nearly thirty stone settings. Whether all the stone rows and settings of south-west England will turn out to belong to the earlier part of the second millennium remains to be seen.

Also of second millennium date, but probably mainly later than the stone rows, are the large cairns and barrows which form such conspicuous skyline features, particularly on Dartmoor and Exmoor. Few of these have been excavated with modern techniques. Five recently excavated barrows on the St Austell granite (Hensbarrow Downs) could be placed in chronological order on the basis of tree/non-tree pollen ratios in the pollen preserved in soils beneath them; Bayley (in Miles 1975a) comments that 'even in the earliest phase recorded here . . . the forest was already well on the way to total destruction' and suggests that clearance proceeded outwards and downwards from the hill-tops. As Grinsell (1978: 110) has pointed out, many of the larger cairns on Dartmoor were built on summits and in other impressive locations, and it is possible that traditional or newly acquired rights to grazing areas were being asserted by this means, large hill-top cairns indicating to transhumant groups arriving from lowland Devon that certain areas had already been claimed (see also Fleming 1983: 216). Perhaps the groups entitled to use the commons were now being defined more closely, a process which, according to Hoskins (1958: 150–1) also occurred in the Middle Ages. It is probable that most of the fine

Plate 5.1 The Veryan Barrow, Cornwall. This is the largest surviving barrow in the South West and gives a good impression of how prominent such features will have been in the Early Bronze Age landscape.

stone circles on the south-western moors were constructed in the earlier part of the second millennium bc, although as a class they are very badly dated.

Some of the settlement sites and field systems of the uplands must date from the earlier part of the Bronze Age – the period of the stone rows, large and small cairns, and stone circles. On Dartmoor the field systems demarcated by the broad, low walls known as reaves, which were laid out around 1300 bc, are so extensive that they cannot avoid incorporating settlements and field systems which, in terms of horizontal stratigraphy, are earlier. Some of the sites in question are roughly ovoid walled enclosures; because they are relatively rare in field systems, and in some contrast to the settlement sites more usually encountered there, it may be surmised that they are older than the boundaries marked out by reaves. In another type of early settlement, up to about half a dozen small fields, irregular in plan, form a small field system, with circular or slightly ovoid houses located in nodal positions in relation to the junctions of field walls, or strung out along the walls, string-of-beads fashion. Good parallels for these simple types of field system occur in north Wales and northern England, for example, at Dewbottoms, West Yorkshire (Raistrick and Holmes 1962: fig. 3). These irregular field systems have not been dated, and it is only the presence of circular houses within them that suggests that they are more likely to date from the metal-using period than to the Neolithic. It must be stressed that the stone-built settlements of Dartmoor display considerable variability, and that only four sites with houses have been excavated in modern times – the so-called Round Pound at Kestor (Fox 1954), the enclosures at Dean Moor (Fox 1957) and at site 15, Shaugh Moor (Wainwright and Smith 1980) and two house sites on Holne Moor (Fleming (in preparation)). Several very distinctive types of site have escaped the attentions of the Dartmoor Exploration Committee (reports issued 1894–1936 – see Worth 1967: 132) so that even a rough ascription to the Bronze Age on the basis of early excavation finds is ruled out. The situation is even worse for the enclosures and houses of Bodmin Moor, and for the sporadic settlement sites which can be traced on Exmoor.

Around 1300 bc a remarkably extensive system of land boundaries was laid out around the fringe of Dartmoor (Fleming 1978, 1983, 1984). It is known that some of these boundaries started life as fences or banks, perhaps for hedges, but they are now almost always visible in the field as reaves – walls about 1 m in breadth and originally some 50–80 cm high. Reaves presumably supplanted these early, stone-free boundaries after a short time interval; possibly field clearance problems were one of the factors which encouraged the building of reaves. It is possible, judging from the characteristics of modern reave-like walls in, for example, north Wales (Lynch, *pers. comm.*) that reaves were surmounted by hedgerows, and certainly the occasional presence of gates, normally not more than 1.5 m wide, suggests that reaves were intended to serve as functional barriers. The apparent scarcity of gateways may indicate that they were often blocked with stones; after peat growth such gateways would be impossible to detect from surface inspection. In some areas modern field systems have preserved the orientation of the prehistoric field systems.

The field systems defined by reaves are coaxial – that is to say, the fields are laid out in a grid-like pattern to respect one major axis of orientation. On Dartmoor such systems have been termed parallel reave systems. Coaxial field systems are quite widely distributed in the British Isles; the best-dated examples are those of the late Neolithic at Behy-Glenulra, north Mayo, which are dated to the later half of the second millennium bc (Caulfield 1978) and those from Fengate, just outside Peterborough, which were apparently in use for much of the second millennium bc (Pryor 1980: 177). The chronological position of the coaxial 'Celtic field systems' of Wessex, like the well-known Dorset example, group 45, analysed by Bradley (1978: 270 and fig. 3) is less clear. If such systems do turn out to have Bronze Age origins, it may be possible to see Dartmoor as part of a broad southern (?) English province of coaxial field systems (although this is not to say that all Bronze Age field systems within this area were of this type). The preoccupation with ordered design which is displayed by the coaxial field systems seems to be visible in other aspects of material culture in Wessex and the South West; this is the area of stone 'circles' which are truly circular, of carefully designed funerary monuments in the form of bell and disc barrows, of high standards of design and craftsmanship in the grave-goods of the Wessex culture and the architecture of Stonehenge IIIa and

115

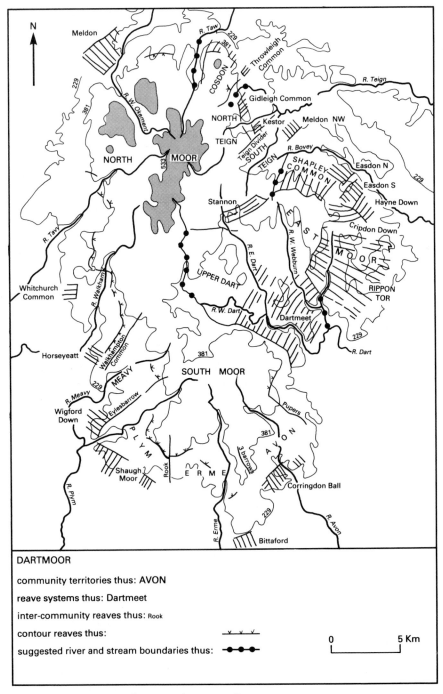

Figure 5.2 Territories and systems of reaves on Dartmoor

IIIb. We are probably seeing here the symbolic expression of a distinctive form of social order.

The coaxial field systems of Dartmoor were large. Their original sizes are often hard to estimate, owing to the fact that large portions of them have been incorporated into more recent field systems still in use today. However, it can be seen from a recently published summary table (Fleming 1983: 220) that areas of 200–300 ha and 500–600 ha were quite common, that two or three systems may have exceeded 1,000 ha, and that the Dartmeet and Rippon Tor systems, which met near Wind Tor on eastern Dartmoor, exceeded 3,000 ha. The Rippon Tor field system, the largest known prehistoric field system in Britain, may have covered about 4,500 ha, since some present day boundaries may be fossilizing prehistoric ones. These two very large systems are essentially imposed upon the landscape; they are not responsive to major features of relief and drainage. Thus the Dartmeet system is stretched across the Dart gorge and the valley of the West Webburn, and its western sector has to cross both the West Dart and the East Dart valleys. It is over 6 km from end to end. The Rippon Tor system runs right across the broad valley of the East Webburn, taking in the modern village of Widecombe-in-the-Moor. Most of the reave systems disposed around the edge of the Moor have a terminal reave on which the parallel reaves end, the equivalent of the 'head dyke' of modern Scotland; beyond the terminal reave presumably lay upland pasture, probably an essential feature of the economy and a major determinant of the parallel systems' locations. This is most noticeable on the eastern side of the Moor, where parallel reaves of both the Shapley Common and Rippon Tor systems climb very steep slopes to reach their terminals on the flanks of the great ridge of Hameldown.

The two very large parallel reave systems on eastern Dartmoor contain extensive tracts of 'prehistoric landscape' – houses, settlement enclosures, lanes, etc. – which reveal the character of the settlement pattern and should permit population estimates as well-founded as any for prehistoric Britain. A further seven or eight systems, less complete, provide essential further detail. The best-preserved area within a system is usually at its upper end, including the terminal reave and a critical zone which tends to contain droveways and moorgates, at the interface between two land-use zones. This zone also tends to contain ceremonial monuments, located on the moor-ward side of the terminal reave.

The settlement pattern within a parallel reave system can be said to consist of 'neighbourhood groups'. A neighbourhood group is an open cluster of houses, numbering perhaps up to twelve or fifteen, the individual houses loosely spaced in ones and twos at distances of about 100–200 m. The neighbourhood group occupies a distinct area within the parallel system as a whole, often a relatively sheltered locality. A house may be associated with one or several small 'enclosures' or 'fields' (the distinction is not always an easy one to make and may turn out to be false); such enclosures and fields

117

Plate 5.2a The Venford reave, Dartmoor, under excavation. This was the terminal reave of the Dartmeet parallel reave system, here viewed from immediately outside.

Plate 5.2b A reave on Holne Moor, Dartmoor, within the Dartmeet parallel reave system, showing a different method of construction from that of the Venford reave. The rough wall approaching from the left is a medieval work. The stones beyond stand on a bank which formed part of an earlier prehistoric boundary system.

may fit into the grid of the system, or they may be more irregular. A few houses are approached by short lanes. Others seem to stand in isolation among fields of normal size. There is no such thing as a typical Bronze Age homestead, although there are certain recurring layout motifs which are found in more than one parallel system. The situation is complicated because, as a result of the excavations on Holne Moor, it is known that some of the houses with stone wall-bases ('hut-circles') had wooden predecessors and companions; there is no reason why an enclosure which is bereft of hut-circles today should not once have contained several buildings of wood or turf. There is evidence from Holne Moor for fenced enclosures and other stake-built structures. At present it is not clear how many reaves were preceded by fences and hedge-banks, and how many hut-circles had wooden predecessors (although this has proved to be the case for three out of three recently excavated on eastern Dartmoor, two on Holne Moor in the Dartmeet system and one at Gold Park in the Shapley Common system – Gibson, *pers. comm.*). Substantial numbers of post- and stake-holes must lie concealed within these field systems, some belonging to structures contemporary with hut-circles and reaves, others documenting an earlier phase, some of whose features may have influenced the character and detail of the stone-built features visible now.

The relationship between individual homestead, neighbourhood group and coaxial field system cannot be expected to reflect directly the relationships between their inhabitants. However, a model suggested by the very poor correlation between house locations, blocks of land defined by reaves and the size of such blocks, postulates that this was not a landscape of single farms with fixed boundaries, even if households did operate as distinct economic entities for some purposes. In this model land is managed and 'owned' at a higher sociopolitical level, probably that of the community responsible for the system as a whole. Between the household and the community, the neighbourhood group, presumably consisting of closely related households co-operating in all manner of agricultural operations and participating in exchange networks of various kinds, must have been of critical importance, a social unit corresponding in some respects to the Irish clachan or the hamlet typical of medieval Dartmoor. In some places, there seems to be a rough line of transverse reaves, at right angles to the system's axis, which could mark the outer boundary of land worked by a neighbourhood group. The slightly awkward junctions between fields associated with a neighbourhood group and fields further away suggest that the fields and enclosures near habitations were marked out first, as one might expect, and that the boundaries running through less intensively used land between neighbourhood groups were added slightly later. The whole layout

---

Plate 5.3a and b (overleaf)   Bronze Age wattle fence under excavation, on Holne Moor, Dartmoor. There is clear evidence here that its builders had access to coppiced woodland.

appears to provide glimpses of the articulation between different levels of sociopolitical organization.

Within the fields, the evidence on Holne Moor is that some cereals and beans were cultivated (Maguire, Ralph and Fleming 1983) although it is unclear what proportion of the land would have been cultivated or what proportion of the diet was cereal-based. Hoof-marks preserved at the base of a Bronze Age ditch running just inside a terminal reave on Shaugh Moor (Smith *et al.* 1981: plate 14) are mainly those of cattle. On the other hand, various factors, including the presence of enhanced phosphate levels in the corners of one of the Holne Moor fields (Ralph, *pers. comm.*) and perhaps the relatively high level of bracken in the Holne Moor pollen diagram, may suggest that sheep were an important component of the economy too; it is unfortunate that animal bones do not survive in the acid soil conditions.

Beyond the enclosed land lay great expanses of upland pasture. On southern Dartmoor, reaves run along the watersheds between the river valleys, and it is possible to suggest a territorial pattern, each community having a parallel reave system and a valley grazing zone some 4–5 km broad (Fleming 1978). On north-east Dartmoor, streams seem to have been used as territorial boundaries, with their valleys treated as buffer zones or access corridors, flanked by reaves running towards the upper pastures. If this is correct, blocks of grazing land were 3 or 4 km broad. Such blocks of grazing land are not visible on eastern Dartmoor, but the relationship between enclosed land and upland grazing seems clear enough. The west and south-west sectors of Dartmoor also include 'contour reaves' which seem to be marking off the upper slopes and hill-tops above about 350–400 m, possibly a zone of intercommoning beyond the valley grazing zones. The most remarkable contour reave, the Great Western Reave, runs along the western edge of the Moor for a minimum length of 10 km, with further apparently unfinished stretches farther to the north; it may indicate that the land division system on Dartmoor transcended the community level, and might have been planned by some kind of regional political authority.

The economic and social context of the occupation of these zones of pasture, and the highly variable and largely undated settlements within them, is unclear. Fox's excavations at an upland enclosure on Dean Moor, in the Avon valley, which contained about a dozen buildings, suggested that grain-processing, spinning, pottery-making and possibly cheese-making were carried out here (Fleming 1979: 125) and some 25 km of iron ore had been brought to the site from its origin at least 5 km away. The doorways of the buildings faced in various directions, suggesting that this may have been a summer occupation site (Fleming 1979: fig. 4). It is uncertain how far the Dean Moor site is typical of the upland 'pastoral' settlements; the same can be said of Shaugh Moor site 15, excavated recently (Wainwright and Smith 1980). Here it was shown that the enclosure wall post-dated four of the five houses. The low phosphate levels within the enclosure and the apparent absence of an entrance gateway (although there must have been a stile of some sort) suggested that the enclosure was intended to exclude animals. Although few cereals were recovered during an extensive water-sieving programme, the settlement was well-supplied with saddle-querns (an average of over six per house, although not all the querns were found in association with the houses). Near site 15 was the Shaugh Moor parallel reave system, which must have been in use during much of the occupation of site 15. Beckett, discussing the pollen record for Wotter Common, within this parallel system, comments that

> the demise of trees and spread of weeds of cultivation indicates a
> grazing pressure which has only been exceeded in very recent times . . .
> arable farming appears to have been on only a minor scale . . . as much
> cultivation may have taken place at this time as at any time since
>
> (Beckett in Smith *et al.* 1981: 262).

The reasons for the development of these elaborate patterns of land division on Dartmoor, and perhaps also on the eastern side of Bodmin Moor (Brisbane and Clews 1979) are unclear. It looks as if these systems represent the seizure and/or colonization of an upland grazing zone perhaps under only intermittent pressure (note in the Shaugh Moor area both alder and hazel had expanded in the period before the major land boundaries – see Beckett in Smith *et al.* 1981: figs. 22 and 26). If so the imposition of these large systems on the landscape may reflect the freedom of action of the land surveyors, as well as the size of communities and the amount of land they felt they required. Because of the similarities in internal detail between the parallel systems, and the interdependence of many of the boundaries, it is felt that many of these boundaries were laid out at around the same time. Whether control of large blocks of land on the edge of an upland grazing zone was taken by several independent communities during a time of pressure on the land, or whether there was a higher level of political authority organizing land division in the region as a whole, is debatable; some of the arguments have been rehearsed elsewhere (Fleming 1984). It is also uncertain how far tin and copper were included among the resources which these communities were seeking to control. Pearce, in a recent review of the evidence, has suggested that the exploitation of local ores began on Bodmin Moor by her Harlyn phase and on Dartmoor by her Wessex II/Plymstock phase (1983: 115, 116) and that a tradition of working local ores continued for the remainder of the Bronze Age. The period when the reave systems were occupied must have coincided with her Chagford and Taunton phases, during which palstaves were probably being manufactured in the Chagford/Moretonhampstead area (Pearce 1979: 1983). If the interpretation of Northover's metal analyses is correct, there is no evidence that the South West was supplying other regions of Britain with metals at this time (Pearce 1983: 123) so any increased control of metal sources which might be implied by these land

Plate 5.4 The parallel reaves at Kestor, Dartmoor, with round houses characteristically scattered among the fields. Two droveways or lanes can be seen passing through the enclosures. The modern road swerves around the enclosure of Round Pound, an Iron Age settlement which has been partially excavated. To the left is the terminal reave.

boundaries would have importance within the South West only – and in any case it is known that metals from other regions were able to reach the area. A further uncertainty is whether 'control' of metal sources in the Bronze Age implies an intention to expand production for exchange purposes, or to restrict it, so that the value of metal is maintained. In other words, we do not know whether it is the *scarcity* of metals or their *abundance* which is the truer index of their significance. Further complications are caused by the melting down and reuse of metals and their withdrawal from circulation. Probably the value of land in agrarian terms was the main consideration for those who were so assiduously subdividing it at this time. Such a division of land may have been an attempt to solve problems of management and distribution of land among communities holding collective title to agrarian resources, at a time of increasing population or growing economic competition. However, how this might have worked in concrete cases has not yet been explored.

The duration of occupation of reave systems is not yet clear; C14 dates and various commonsense arguments suggest that it is unlikely to have been less than two or three hundred years. There is no reason to disbelieve the idea that the climatic deterioration of the early first millennium bc accelerated the spread of blanket peat and diminished the grazing values of the upland commons, leading to the (probably gradual) abandonment of Dartmoor's settlement sites. However, there is enough first millennium material associated with these settlements to suggest that abandonment was not total (Silvester, 1979; Wainwright and Smith 1980: 109, 115).

Second Millennium Settlement Types

Two main settlement-forms are evident on Dartmoor: enclosures of varying size, usually referred to as 'pounds' following nineteenth-century usage, and looser concentrations of round houses without an enclosing wall. Over much of the moor except the high ground in the north single houses or small groups also occur. A sharp distinction between enclosed and open settlements is not possible: enclosing walls were added in some cases at a later stage. Although we are dealing with a phase of settlement which lasted for more than a thousand years, it is apparent that parts of the moor were relatively densely settled, the peak being reached in the period 1300–1000 BC, but continuing for some time thereafter. Our knowledge of the settlements is not yet so extensive that we can discern the way in which the settlement pattern developed; whether for example small groups of houses developed into more nucleated settlements, some of which were in due course enclosed. It is known that some enclosures already existed by 1450 BC at the latest, but some of the larger 'pounds', like Rider's Rings and Grimspound, could represent cumulative growth which only reached its ultimate form much later.

The round houses within enclosures are for the most part small, often only 4 or 5 m in diameter, though larger structures do occur. The walling in some huts is still preserved to a height of about a metre and may originally have been only a little higher. The roofing was probably of turf or thatch resting on timber rafters, in a flattish cone, the better to withstand the strong winds. Most of the excavated houses had an internal ring of roof-supports or at least a group of three or four posts. A centre-post was usually provided. Doorways were

125

invariably narrow and were often protected by curving wing-walls or simple porches. The interior of the house was often at a slightly lower level than the ground surface. Occasionally, rough cobbling had been laid down inside: in a few cases the bedrock had served as flooring. In a few enclosures, for instance Grimspound and Dean Moor, houses comprising two adjacent chambers existed, the additional space offering a degree of privacy or perhaps more storage room. Internal fittings which have survived are simple: a cupboard niche, a bench or bed, a stone hearth. Small objects recovered in excavation are rare and of poor quality. It is important to remember that what we now see on Dartmoor are merely the *surviving* remains. There has been considerable destruction, especially over the past two centuries, though not on the scale that Baring-Gould suggested: he believed that tens of thousands of houses had been removed. Buildings in timber and turf also occurred within enclosures (as at Shaugh Moor) and in some 'pounds' there are evident house-platforms, now with no structures occupying them. In some of the larger enclosures, such as Rider's Rings and Grimspound, there are rectilinear stone structures built against the inner face of the enclosing wall. Not all of these are necessarily prehistoric, but some certainly are. It is tempting to see these as providing accommodation for stock rather than humans.

Settlements of the early second millennium are still elusive, though the burial record is sufficient proof that the moor was settled at this time (above, p. 115). We will begin with an examination of the enclosed settlements on which more work has been carried out. The enclosures take various forms, some as small as 1,000 sq m, the largest more than 2 ha (about 5 acres). Their siting is extremely varied, often on slopes, commonly on valley floors, only occasionally on or near hill-tops. Most contain houses or at least one house. A few have no visible traces of internal structures, but these could have been of timber. One or more entrances may exist, but some have no evident gates – which clearly has a bearing on their function. Agglomerations of enclosures also occur, most strikingly at Legis Tor where there are five or six contiguous enclosures and at Gripper's Hill where there are four. Some were divided internally by lengths of walling, perhaps to form pens or to frame plots for cultivation. Only one enclosed settlement unit has been completely excavated, one of a group at Shaugh Moor, and while the results of this work are of the greatest interest, they cannot be regarded as a paradigm for all such enclosures on Dartmoor (Wainwright, Smith *et al.* 1979, 1980, 1981).

Occupation of the Shaugh Moor site began about 1500, an open settlement at first, continuing for some three centuries until a number of long established houses were surrounded by an enclosure wall. This was continuous, with no gate-openings, and would thus seem to have been intended to ward animals away from the living area and not to impound them. The houses within the enclosure were of familiar Dartmoor types, rather small, often provided with wing-walls covering the entrance. Larger timber buildings lay at the centre of the enclosure. The environmental record

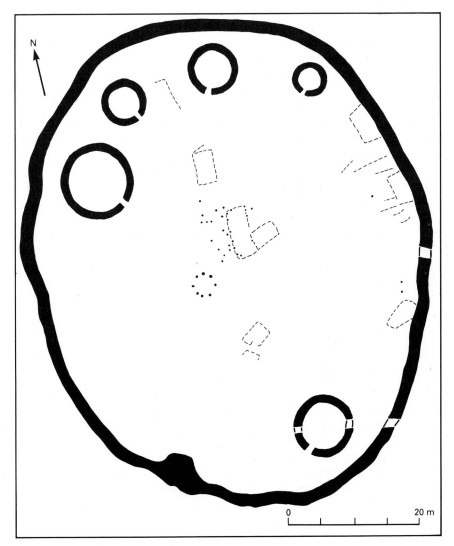

Figure 5.3 The Shaugh Moor enclosure

bespeaks a largely pastoral landscape with a little cereal-growing, probably confined to the sheltered valleys below the settlement. Total excavation of the enclosure failed to reveal any trace of metal-working or extraction, even though alluvial tin deposits lay nearby and outlets by water to the sea were within easy reach. As elsewhere on the uplands, the prevailing impression is of a community heavily dependent on pastoral farming, other activities being secondary in importance, if they were pursued at all.

The Dean Moor enclosure, one of several in the upper Avon valley, is

127

Plate 5.5 The enclosed settlement and associated fields and other enclosures at Bellever Tor, Dartmoor, a group of settlement remains typical of the south-western uplands in the second millennium BC.

---

the next most extensively examined (Fox, A. 1957). Here, about 12 visible huts lay within the wall and 9 of them were examined. They were small, usually about 5 m across, stone-walled and an internal ring of timber uprights. There was one double hut, one with an annexe, and two rectangular buildings butted up to the surrounding wall. Two narrow gates gave entry into the interior. A surprisingly wide range of activities was carried on at Dean Moor. The cassiterite pebble and slag and the enigmatic mass of ironstone attest an interest in local metal deposits. A large number of whetstones, from all over the enclosure, suggest the frequent use of metal tools, while the stones had themselves been brought to the site from some way to the south. Use of puddled clay, presumably for pottery-making, may indicate fairly settled occupation, as does the evidence, in the form of spindle-whorls, for the spinning of wool. Finally, a quern and a rubber represent the grinding of grain, either grown or acquired nearby. In sum, these activities point to a stable community which was in command of all the natural resources of its immediate environment. The point is of significance when considering the economy of these upland settlements.

Exmoor has much less to show of Bronze Age settlements than the other south-western uplands, though the large number of barrows and cairns indicates that it was intensively settled at this time. There are few signs of the enclosures so common on Dartmoor and even groups of huts are relatively scarce. Most of the huts identified by J. F. Chanter seem to be ruined cairns or clearance heaps, though a few may be dwellings. The most convincing sites are those on Shallowford Common, where there are traces of a field-system as well as ruined huts, and at Hoaroak where a few huts lie among clearance heaps. A much better field-worker than Chanter, St George Gray, found virtually no huts in his survey of the Somerset portion of Exmoor (St George Gray 1931; 1932). We might well conclude from this that the Bronze Age inhabitants of Exmoor had used timber rather than stone for their structures and perhaps for their boundaries.

Away from the uplands the number of well excavated settlements is small. Trevisker (St Eval) lies between two indented valleys only 4 km from the sea near St Mawgan (ApSimon and Greenfield 1972). Here two timber houses within a ditched enclosure have been examined, rather larger than the majority of upland structures at 8 m in diameter, and closer to lowland dwellings elsewhere in southern England. One of these was later replaced by a rectangular structure with stone footings about 6 m in length. This could have served as a byre or work-shed, the latter suggested by a large deposit of cassiterite pebbles lying in rubbish over the floor. The yield of pottery from Trevisker was appreciably larger than that from the upland sites: otherwise the range of artifacts is unremarkable, with one exception. In one of the houses there were found two loom-weights and in the same building a pair of post-holes were convincingly interpreted as occupied by the supports for an upright loom. This is the only firm evidence for a Bronze Age loom in the South West and one of very few in Britain as a whole. One radiocarbon estimate may relate to the close of occupation and it points to the later second millennium, perhaps in the fourteenth century BC. In the absence of other published data, Trevisker (and presumably Gwithian) may be taken as typical of the single farmsteads which existed in the lowland areas from at least 2000 to 500 BC and beyond. It was well placed to benefit from the upland pastures to the south-east, from the cultivable coastal plain and from the sea, though there is no sign of the products of the last-named in the excavated record.

The higher ground of West Penwith and the Lizard was extensively

Plate 5.6 The West Penwith landscape, from Zennor Hill. Large areas of the West Penwith uplands contain systems of prehistoric fields and other enclosures which are often still in use, though now suffering destruction at an alarming rate.

colonized in the second millennium, the former still retaining the mark left on its landscape by Bronze Age farmers. In many areas the small irregularly walled prehistoric fields with hut groups scattered among them are still farmed, though increasingly they are threatened by fast-moving mechanical destruction. Structurally the dwellings are similar to those of Dartmoor and Bodmin Moor, stone-walled and with an internal ring of timber uprights. A few have porches or other coverings of the entrance. Groups of huts much less numerous than those on the large granite masses occur, at Sperris Croft (Zennor) and Bodrifty by the later Bronze Age, but truly nucleated sites do not seem to have emerged. Enclosures like those on Dartmoor are rare and seem to have come in after the settlements had existed for some time, as at Bodrifty (Dudley 1956: 20–22), Wicca Round (Zennor) may be such an enclosure, with at least three huts arranged around a yard. The prevailing settlement pattern is dispersed, as is well seen at Trewey Foage (Zennor (Dudley 1941)) and at many places in the parishes of Madron, Gulval and St Just (Russell 1971), where the huts still lie among their fields and terraces. Material remains found in these dwellings are meagre in the extreme, being mainly rough friable pottery, stone rubbers and a few flint tools.

Scilly was extensively settled during the second millennium and later as

130

is revealed by house-sites and extensive field-systems as well as many burial monuments (above, p. 91). The extent and importance of the field-remains has only recently been made apparent and further work will undoubtedly reveal much more (Thomas 1985). The Bronze Age settlements are generally small in comparison with those on the mainland. Isolated houses are common and when they occur in groups these are usually small (Ashbee 1974). Enclosures have not yet been reported on Scilly. Some of the hut-groups form tight clusters, the result of successive additions to an original core. This is well seen at Nornour, Little Bay and, later, at Halangy Down (Butcher 1978; Neal 1983: Ashbee 1974: 186–96). The house-types are unexpectedly varied, more so than on the mainland. As well as substantial round-houses, oval and rectilinear structures are found. Massive walling is often in evidence, a thickness of 2 m being not uncommon. Internal radial walls and other divisions occur in some of the larger houses, as at Nornour (Butcher 1978: 33). Dating these buildings is always difficult for the range of associated finds is narrow and few of them are distinctive. Moreover occupation might be prolonged and some houses were reoccupied at a much later date (e.g. Nornour; Butcher 1978: 65).

It is hardly surprising that settlements on Scilly betray the interest of their inhabitants in the resources of the sea and its coasts. Shells and fish bones are reported from these sites, along with remains of seal and whale. Even sea birds may have had their uses. Certain pottery vessels found at Halangy Porth, St Mary's, bore traces of an oily substance, probably derived from the fat of sea-birds such as shear-waters. Such oil might have been used in lamps, for cooking and for the lubrication of leather in boats and furnishings.

Fishing provided much to the Bronze Age diet on Scilly. Fish bones at Nornour included specimens of conger eel, ling, bass, wrasse, turbot, plaice and pollack. At Little Bay on St Martin's the range of species was somewhat different, cod, saithe, red and black sea bream, and gilthead being caught as well as conger, wrasse and pollack. Most if not all of these could have been caught by lines from the shore or from boats anchored inshore. Even cod move into coastal waters in winter, while the other species are still found around the rocky coasts of western Britain or, in the case of gilthead, over sand and mud floors.

Close examination of fields and the techniques used to work them remains to be fully developed. But at Gwithian fields of the late second millennium and later have been carefully studied, with striking results (Megaw 1976; Fowler 1981: 185–98). In a horizon dating from the fifteenth to the fourteenth century BC, a group of at least eight fields was recorded, each unit about 30 m square. These had been succeeded by a series of fields of the thirteenth to eleventh centuries. For both horizons, excellent evidence was obtained for ploughing with an ard, in the form of V-shaped grooves cut into the plough-soil. These grooves covered sizeable areas with a criss-cross pattern suggestive of cross-ploughing. The areas covered imply the use of an

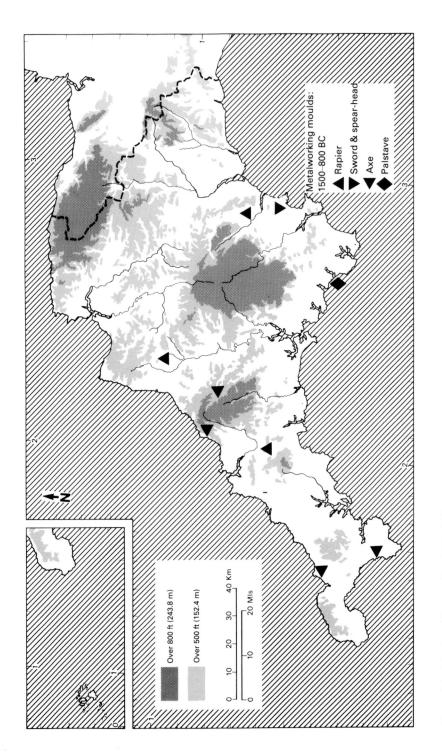

Figure 5.4 Metalworking moulds: 1500–800 BC

animal-drawn ard but there is other evidence for the use of spades on the headlands where the ard could not easily operate.

The Development of Technology

The introduction of bivalve moulds allowed the production of flanged axes of higher quality and a wider range of other metal types, including spear-heads, chisels and riveted daggers. These are usually comprised under the heading of Arreton after the type-hoard on the Isle of Wight (Britton 1963). Palstaves too began to appear at the middle of the second millennium, the earliest occurring in the Plymstock hoard. An important group figured in the Crediton hoard, an odd collection of material, quite possibly scrap for resmelting. This heavy palstave takes its name from the deposit (Hawkes 1955) and is fairly certainly a south-western product. Rapiers and dirks also entered the record after 1500 BC, among the earliest being the dirks from Mullion and Harlyn Bay, and the rapier from North Crofty and the lost example from Benallack. A stone rapier mould from Bodwen (Lanlivery) probably produced blades of this type and is the earliest of an interesting series of such finds in the peninsula. The moulds found at Chudleigh (now lost) were for similar weapons, while a mould from Holsworthy would have produced related dirks. The rapiers in the Talaton hoard belong to the same general class of weapon, the currency of which seems to have been prolonged, perhaps for three or four centuries.

These rapiers are often elegant, narrow-bladed weapons, up to 80 cm long, the classic side-arm of the warrior who selected his opponent for the duel. The contrast with the heavy, slashing swords of the later Bronze Age is sharp and should imply a substantial change in fighting methods before the end of the millennium. The rapier and the dirk were of course for close-order combat, but we need not assume that rapiers and spears were not carried by the same warriors (*contra* Pearce 1983: 191). The association between the throwing weapon and a short sword is a perfectly natural one and occurs frequently in proto-historic and early historic Europe. Shields or shield-parts are not represented in the south-western finds and may in any case have been frequently, even normally, of leather. Personal ornaments are also absent so that it is difficult to summon up the image of the Bronze Age warrior dressed up for war.

Unfortunately, little of this metalwork can be satisfactorily related to the rest of the archaeological record. The Crediton and Talaton hoards could be the stock-in-trade of metalworkers or deliberate depositions of a votive kind. The Bodwen mould was an unstratified find near a later round. The Tredarvah bronzes (Pearce and Padley 1977) were associated with domestic debris and slag but the details of the find are poorly recorded. The famous gold hoard of

Towednack (Hawkes 1932) had been buried in or under a field-bank close to a small hut and there are other records of metal goods being concealed in field-walls, including the later hoard found near Kenidjack Castle and the axes from Week (North Bovey). But it remains the case that, Gwithian bronzes apart, not a single metal object of the second millennium has been found in conjunction with other material under conditions which would allow the find to be properly recorded.

A number of implement types can be distinguished as south-western products on the grounds of distribution or through the finding of appropriate moulds. These include the heavy palstaves named after the Crediton hoard and the related palstaves with side-loops, a mould for which has come from Bigbury in south Devon (Pearce 1983: 433). Rapiers were also produced here: indeed all of the four known rapier-moulds in Britain have been found in the South West (Chudleigh (2), Holsworthy and Bodwen). The range of bronze goods greatly enlarged towards the close of the second millennium, perhaps partly under the stimulus of implements imported from other parts of Britain and from western Europe. The Moor Sand wreck find and the Horridge palstave are more than hints of imported *goods* as well as metal for recycling, as are other objects from farther afield.

We need not be surprised that bronze weapons and other fine metalwork of Mediterranean and western European origin should have found their way into the South West from time to time. Nor should we be tempted to see any regular pattern of trade behind these exotic pieces that filtered through to the periphery of Europe. The sword fragment from a barrow at Pelynt (Macnamara 1972) is the most widely known instance of an import from the Aegean and the most variously dated. The most convincing attribution is to Mycenaean Greece IIIB and the date, on the basis of Aegean tomb-groups, should fall between 1300 and 1200 BC (Branigan 1972: 281–2). Cypriot hook-tang blades of earlier date are known from Torrington and from Sidmouth (Branigan 1983; Pearce 1983: Fig. 2b), the latter find a hoard of at least five objects. A double axe from Topsham is ultimately of Aegean type, but such objects are well known in western France and in central Europe generally (Hawkes 1936–7: 156–7). The occasional piece from central Europe, like the palstave from Horridge Common, is only to be expected, given the existence of trade-routes from the eastern Mediterranean across the Alps and westward across France (Fox and Britton 1969).

One of the most striking demonstrations of these overseas contacts is the discovery of a group of bronzes on the sea-bed in about 6 m of water at Moor Sand, 3 km east of the Salcombe estuary (Muckelroy 1980; 1981: 287). This is virtually certainly the site of a Bronze Age wreck, though no traces of a vessel have been recovered. Among the seven bronze objects so far retrieved, at least three pieces have come from France or farther afield. The finest item is a hook-tanged sword which belongs to the Rixheim/Monza series of weapons, found most commonly in eastern France, northern Italy and southern Germany shortly after 1000 BC. Four other damaged blades may also be exotics, but no diagnostic features are now visible. Two palstaves were also present, probably northern French or Armorican in origin. The Moor Sand wreck (if we accept it as such) invites comparison with the much larger cargo of bronzes found in Langdon Bay near Dover. The latter, however, was plainly a cargo of scrap metal destined for recycling in Britain. The Moor Sand objects look more like imports of fine pieces, especially the Rixheim sword. The date of this lost cargo is to be set about 950 BC.

A striking proportion of the larger metalwork of middle and later Bronze Age date occurs in hoards on dry land and in deposits in water, rivers, pools and peat-bogs. The latter category of deposit is less to the fore in the South West than elsewhere, but it does occur (in general, Torbrugge 1971–2; Bradley 1979; 1984: 96–127). Allowing for chance losses and erosion from the sides of streams, there is still a considerable body of material which can only be explained as the result of deliberate deposition in water in pursuance of some ritual or votive act of a kind so well demonstrated in later prehistoric Europe (Fox, C. 1946; Todd 1975: 187). Of the south-western instances, the most likely to fall into the class of votive finds are the spears of about 800 BC found in Bloody Pool near South Brent, and the looped palstave and two torcs (probably of about 1000 BC) found in a pool at Cothelstone House on the Quantocks in the late eighteenth century (for similar practices in the Iron Age, see below, p. 183). Certain of the hoards concealed on dry land (e.g. Crediton and Talaton) may also have been buried with no intention that they should ever be retrieved. The disposal of some prestigious items to enhance the value of the remainder is a widely attested practice in ranked societies. The 'potlach' or deliberate abandonment or destruction of fine goods as a mark of status or wealth provides yet another possible explanation for Bronze Age hoards, especially those containing weapons. A few hoards, though not in the South West, are distinguished by careful disposition of the contents, as though ceremonial had accompanied concealment (Coombs 1975: 68).

The scale of the industry which produced the metal goods, reflected as it is in the wholly inadequate sample which we happen to possess, is most impressive. When we have made allowance for what has been lost or never recorded, for what has never been found and, above all, for what was resmelted in antiquity, we have a brief glimpse into a world of craftsmanship which was barely surpassed in north-western Europe for a thousand years. There is little doubt that seen as a whole the metalwork of the second millennium is the product of a society in which differences of rank and/or wealth were marked. In this respect the metalwork is likely to be a surer guide to the framework of social organization than the settlements, which convey an impression of uniformity which cannot have been maintained in actuality. The hoards of weapons and other metalwork reveal the active presence of a social group which was raised above the rest by its warlike avocations, either itself dominant or in the service of a leading warrior or chieftain. We may see the origins here of the warrior-following, the *comitatus*, of later Celtic and Germanic Europe. If so, it is a small step further to see the smiths of the second millennium working for individual members of the warrior-elite and not itinerant in search of occasional patrons. The relationship of patron and client, however, remains resolutely obscure and archaeology alone may never illuminate it.

By 1000 BC, new weapon forms had emerged, socketed leaf-shaped spearheads and the characteristic later Bronze Age slashing sword, a weapon better designed for fighting in a *mêlée* than the narrow rapier. Both weapon types occurred in the deposit of bronzes found in an enclosure at Worth in the middle Exe valley. Palstaves were replaced by a wide variety of socketed axes and a new range of tools appeared, chisels, knives, gouges, called into being by innovations in a number of crafts. The most important single discovery relating to this phase is the debris, mainly moulds and crucible, of bronze-casting found at Dainton in south Devon. A variety of weapons was produced, probably in two episodes, including spear-heads with basal loops, and others with lunate openings, the ferrules of spear-shafts and leaf-shaped swords of the Wilburton and Wallington tradition (Silvester 1980: Needham 1980). A date in the tenth century is proposed. The context of the Dainton find is of interest, for the site appears to be an open agricultural settlement and the casting seems to have taken place out in the fields. Though we cannot know how he distributed his goods or to whom, it is certain that the Dainton craftsman was a skilled specialist and that he found, or had in mind, a local market in fine weaponry.

The ceramics of the second millennium are familiar from the contents of graves and increasingly from settlement sites. By the mid-second millennium if not before, it is apparent that the pottery of the South West had departed from the line of development followed by much of the rest of southern Britain so that the region formed a separate ceramic province. Later, after about 1000 BC contacts with Wessex are evident in the pottery, though they did not extinguish entirely local traditions.

Food vessels are rare in the South West, but the contexts in which they occur are broadly similar to those of the northern examples, that is, as cremation containers, adjuncts to cremations, as at Broad Down and Tregulland Burrow (Ashbee 1958). Another instance, from Cataclews, Harlyn Bay, was associated with a fine stone battle-axe. The remainder are of simple forms, weak reflections of a burial rite whose epicentre lay far away (Patchett 1944: 38; Simpson 1968).

After *c.*1750 BC a new ceramic series had emerged, in which the predominant forms were tall jars, some of them very capacious, usually with heavy, clubbed rims and frequently with a broad decorated zone on the upper part of the vessel. Broad handles or suspension-lugs were often attached to the upper body, usually at the angle on carinated vessels. These distinctive and often imposing vessel-forms were long-lived, certainly from before the middle of the millennium to about 1000 BC and the degree of change evinced within the series as a whole is relatively slight. The area over which they were distributed and made includes all of Cornwall, where they are commonest, Devon (a much thinner scatter), west Dorset and south Somerset. The main bulk of this pottery is designated the Trevisker series after the site where it has been most coherently studied, and four major 'styles' have been distinguished on the basis of fabric and decoration (ApSimon and Greenfield 1972: 326–33). It is not yet clear whether or not these internal divisions which are typologically based, have any chronological significance as they stand. Style 1 seems to have been the first to emerge, but it may have continued alongside the others later, while it could be that styles 2, 3 and 4 were either broadly contemporary or overlapped in time to a considerable extent.

The Trevisker series is remarkably independent of the other major pottery traditions of the second millennium. The forms and decoration of Beakers left little impress on these wares, not surprisingly in view of the relative scarcity of Beakers in the South West. The biconical urns of Wessex, although related in a general sense, do not share in the bold and detailed decoration of the Trevisker series which is its most distinctive characteristic. Even the handles on Trevisker vessels have no obvious antecedents or congenors. Taken all together, these handsome vessels belong to a distinct south-western tradition, locally founded and owing little to external influence during its currency.

Decorative schemes were handled with great skill by the Trevisker potters. Plaited cord ornament and incised chevrons are the common zonal treatments but others occur, including finger-tipping and other impressed ornament, and occasionally fine grooving. The large handled urns in particular are well made, stylish vessels, almost certainly the work of specialist craftsmen producing wares for more than single communities. Firing vessels of this size must have posed considerable problems. They were employed as grave furniture and as domestic containers without distinction. In the latter context they would seem to have served as storage jars in the main. That they were valued possessions is suggested by a careful riveted repair made to one used as a cinerary urn in a cairn at Stannon. Areas of production have not yet been clearly defined, though several of the Dartmoor vessels contain granitic inclusions and are thus to be seen as local products. Certain of the Cornish urns have been attributed to the Lizard on the basis of igneous inclusions among which gabbro figures, but the evidence has not yet been set out in full (ApSimon and Greenfield 1972: 333). A few of the Devon vessels were probably produced from Cretaceous clays, others possibly from material derived from the Culm Measures and the volcanic rocks of east Devon (Wainwright and Smith 1980: 95–6).

Not all the pottery of the second millennium can be accommodated within the Trevisker series. The Shaugh Moor vessels include biconical forms, occasionally with lugs, and with simple everted rims. An associated radiocarbon estimate points to 1330 ± 90 bc. These utilitarian pots are closer to Wessex *biconi* than to Trevisker and may represent a considerable substratum of domestic wares which have not yet been fully revealed. Some of the cist-burials on the uplands have yielded even simpler vessels (Patchett 1944: 42 fig. 10, F6; 45 fig. 12, G8).

Burial Ritual and Craftsmanship

Early Bronze Age single graves originated in the burial ritual of the late Neolithic. Both inhumation and cremation were current, the remains of the dead being laid in a simple pit or a stone cist or a wooden coffin. Flat graves with no surface marker are known, though more commonly there was a covering cairn or mound. Such is the variation in grave form even within a single region that only a selection can be presented here. A constant theme throughout the south-western Bronze Age is the inurned cremation, though this could take many forms.

About or shortly after 2000 BC the cultural record begins to reveal the beginnings of major change. The first metal objects appear, most of them imports from adjacent areas. Richly furnished burials in large funerary monuments, with grave-goods which are clearly related to those of Wessex graves, hint at social differentiation, perhaps even at the emergence of local dynastic polities. The record of settlement soon becomes very full, fuller than for any comparable region of Britain. Over the following thousand years, the cultural landscape seems thronged with human inhabitants, probably not without good reason. The population of the South West may have grown enormously during this period, to reach a level not surpassed until the early modern period. Behind all this we seem to witness the growth to maturity of that social order established in the Neolithic, which was to endure down to historic times. These centuries were the most formative in the history of the South West and we are fortunate that they have left so many traces still visible in the modern landscape.

The appearance of inhumation burials containing Beakers and their associated metal and flint goods made little impact on the South West. The region lay beyond the main distribution of Beaker graves and none of the typologically early Beakers has been recorded here. Classic Beaker graves containing daggers, metal ornaments and archers' gear are also very rare, the burials at Fernworthy, Archerton and Langcombe – all on Dartmoor – coming closest to the familiar assemblage. There is, then, even less reason here than elsewhere in southern Britain to link the Beaker phenomenon with a movement of population, rather than with the spread of a particular burial rite, associated though it may be with a certain social group. The Langcombe Beaker is perhaps the earliest of the south-western examples, probably dating from shortly after 2000 BC. Most of the others fall late in the typological series, for what that is worth. These include the vessels with chevron ornament from Trevedra (St Just), Tregiffian (St Buryan), the handled Beaker found at the base of a menhir at Try (Gulval) and the devolved vessels from Farway and Burnt Common in east Devon. Burials containing Beakers are often in small cists which cannot have held an extended body (Tregiffian, Try, Trevedra) and the corpse must thus have been crouched or even trussed up. But other burial-forms were employed, as at Burnt Common, where a ring of stone had surrounded a shallow inhumation pit lined with chert (Pollard 1967).

Domestic sites with Beaker or Beaker-related pottery in association are few indeed, the most interesting being the timber round houses at Gwithian (Megaw 1976) and unspecified settlements at Praa Sands, Harlyn Bay and possibly Topsham (Jarvis and Maxfield 1975). A puzzling site at Poldowrian (St Keverne) has produced the largest concentration of Beaker pottery, about a hundred sherds (Harris 1979). This material came from a stony, oval mound, some 9 m by 6 m, otherwise devoid of domestic debris or structures. Burnt clay and stone suggest that this may have been a cooking-place, perhaps for communal meals or extended feasts, like those known in other parts of western Britain. Radiocarbon estimates place the mound about the middle of the second millennium (Harris 1979: 19).

The collared urn tradition is also sparsely represented in the South West, a small scatter of urns in west Cornwall providing the most significant body of material, most of it assignable to Longworth's Primary Series. Most of the urns are plain or have a minimum of decoration (e.g. Longworth 1984: Pls 43–5), though two handsome vessels with handles from Gwinear and St Mawgan in Pyder have zones of bold ornament near the rim. Small urns, some with lugs, are otherwise the common type, these also occurring sporadically in Devon (Longworth 1984: Pl. 77, 355).

The richly furnished burials of the early Bronze Age are obviously generically related to those of Wessex about 1500 BC and the evidence has been discussed in full elsewhere (Fox, A. 1948). Connections at an elevated level between south-western communities and their eastern neighbours need cause no surprise and certainly need not be explained in terms of colonization from the east. What the rich grave-goods of the mid-second millennium do demonstrate is that south-western chieftains were able to recruit the services of craftsmen who were as competent as those who worked in Wessex or could otherwise obtain their products, perhaps through gift-exchange. The rich graves also indicate something else, which is attested widely in southern Britain in these centuries, the internal colonization of land which hitherto had not been intensively settled or worked. This is markedly true of the burials on the Hameldon ridge on eastern Dartmoor and of the large barrows on the eastern side of Bodmin Moor. It probably also applies to those on Exmoor and to the Farway cemetery. These monumental burials can reasonably be seen as the work of the leading families in a major episode of land-taking which began in the early second millennium and which was in full swing by 1500 BC.

The rich graves of the early Bronze Age include at least two in the Broad Down barrow cemetery, one of the large monuments on the Hameldon Ridge in east Dartmoor, a cist-grave at North Molton, the famous Rillaton (Linkinhorne) barrow on Bodmin Moor and a few less splendidly furnished burials (Fox 1948). Close contacts with the Wessex communities which were inhuming their honoured dead from about 1600 and cremating them from 1500 need not be inferred, though of course there could have been dynastic links through marriage or other forms of alliance.

There can be no doubt about the high standards of craftsmanship attained in the finest of the objects in these graves. The shale or lignite cups from Broad Down are products of an exceptionally confident skill, involving use of a simple lathe. Equally ambitious was the amber dagger-pommel from Hameldon, drilled with hundreds of tiny holes into which pins of gold were fitted, and later repaired by pinning on a detached piece (Kendrick 1937). Faience beads, whatever their ultimate origin, also appear in a few graves, as at North Molton, Shaugh Moor and at Knackyboy on St Martin's, Scilly. We must also allow for fine perishable goods such as furs, leather and perhaps textiles.

The gold objects are the most outstanding products of the fine craftsmanship of the time and they further illuminate the ambitions of the patrons for whom the craftsmen worked. The finest of these, the so-called lunulae, probably ornaments for the neck and breast, are Irish in inspiration if not in manufacture. Three such finds have been made in Cornwall, a pair at Harlyn Bay (possibly found with a flat axe), one at St Juliot near Boscastle and another at Gwithian (Taylor 1970: 54). One of the Harlyn Bay lunulae is so close in technical detail and in ornament to one in a hoard found at Kerivoa in Brittany that it can be ascribed to the same craftsman, though we can form no idea about where he worked. The other gold find which is to be related to a wider circle of craftsmanship in metal is the Rillaton cup.

The Rillaton cup is often compared with the gold-handled cup at Fritzdorf near Bonn (von Uslar 1955). The similarity is not markedly close. The Fritzdorf vessel is sharply carinated, with a rounded base, unlike the smoother profile and flat base of the Rillaton cup. It is also plain, in contrast to the corrugation of Rillaton. Direct links with objects in the gold-rich shaft-graves of Mycenae have seemed attractive to some, but examination of the gold cups in those tombs reveals few items which are at all similar to the western European pieces (Karo 1930: Pls. CIII–CXI for gold vessels; CIV 392 and 393 are corrugated mugs, far removed from Rillaton in form). The possibility of technical influence of eastern Mediterranean goldsmiths on the work of western craftsmen is plausible enough, but the connection has yet to be demonstrated beyond doubt. Much closer to Rillaton is the elegant little beaker found at Eschenz (Kanton Thurgau, Switzerland). This has no handle but is otherwise very similar in form, also having corrugations on the side and base. In technical detail, too, the Swiss find is related to the Rillaton vessel, and perhaps to the beaker from Gölenkamp near Hannover (Hardmeyer and Bürgi 1975; Schuchhardt 1914, Abb. 12).

There are other objects which must be considered as members of the same class of prestigious objects. Two come from graves in Brittany. At Ploumilliau (Côtes-du-Nord) there was found in 1840 the upper part of a gold cup with a gold ladle, the latter bearing punched ornaments similar to that on the Eschenz vessel. More recently a silver-handled cup with a rounded base came to light in a large barrow at St Adrien (Côtes-du-Nord), not far from Ploumilliau, while an earlier find at St Fiacre (Morbihan) may have been another silver vessel. The well-known amber cups from Clandon and Hove and those in shale from Amesbury and Broad Down (below, p. 144) belong to the same *milieu* and to the same period of time.

Connections at an elevated social level between the South West and Wessex in the mid-second millennium have been frequently discussed in the past, usually in the context of Wessex 'influence' on rich burials in the peninsula. It is possible to overstate the case. Certainly, there are objects, of metal, shale, amber and other materials, in south-western burials which have been imported from a variety of sources including Wessex as well as the Continent and perhaps Ireland. But their presence indicates no special or close relationship with the rich burials of the Wessex chalklands. What they do reveal is the fact that about 1500 BC the wealthiest members of south-western society were able to share in the expanding north-west European *koine* of patronage and fine craftsmanship. It is difficult to see in these richly furnished graves the emergence of a well-defined class or caste, but there seems little doubt that they do bear witness to the elevation of individuals above the mass of the population, presumably on the basis of their wealth or status or both.

The burial monuments of west Cornwall were already being summarily revealed by the excavations of W. C. Borlase and the surveys of W. C. Lukis in the later nineteenth century (Lukis 1885). The inadequacies of Borlase's investigations were in some measure redeemed by the clarity and general accuracy of Lukis's drawings. Several of the structures examined by Borlase were very complex and the durable materials in which they were built preserve detail rarely in evidence in other parts of the peninsula, and indeed allowed more ambitious and more permanent constructions than are likely to have been attempted elsewhere. One of the most striking of these western Cornish monuments is Carn Gluze, on the cliffs at St Just. At the heart of this elaborate tomb lay a T-shaped pit, either an inhumation burial or a ritual *puteus*. About this were sited four small cists containing small pottery vessels

141

dating from the middle Bronze Age and probably originally holding offerings rather than cremated human remains. Over this sacred place a remarkable cairn was built, perhaps after a relatively brief interval. This was an oval, corbelled dome, 8 m across at the base and originally about 5 m high, consisting of two walls 1.5 m apart, the intervening space being loosely filled with stone. The domed chamber was sealed off completely and subsequent depositions were made outside it. At a later stage, the dome was engulfed by a massive circular cairn, 5 m across, revetted by an external stone wall. Later still an entrance grave was inserted into the cairn on approximately the same axis as the approach to the primary pit.

The most famous of early Bronze Age graves in Cornwall is that which produced the Rillaton gold cup. This is one of four barrows on the eastern side of Bodmin Moor in Linkinhorne parish, 30 m in diameter and still

Figure 5.5   A Dartmoor cist: Crock of Gold, Royal Newtake

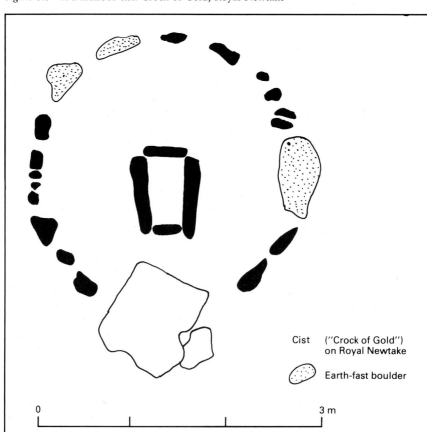

Cist   ("Crock of Gold")
       on Royal Newtake

       Earth-fast boulder

0   3 m

standing 3 m high. Built into the edge of the mound above ground level, that is in a secondary position, is a large rectangular cist, 2.4 m by 1 m and 1 m high. The nineteenth-century workmen who opened the cist found there human bones, the gold cup, a bronze dagger, a pot, beads (possibly of faience) and 'pieces of ivory', presumably bone. All the finds except the gold cup have now vanished, but even the outline description reveals the characteristic components of a richly furnished early Bronze Age burial comparable with many others in Wessex, south-east England and Brittany. The fact that the cist was a later insertion into the barrow is not always appreciated. The primary burial has still to be located, though it is unlikely to survive intact.

Other inhumations in cists are known, but none has been examined by modern techniques. One of the Trevelgue barrows covered a burial furnished with a fine stone battle-axe, recalling types current in Wessex. A number of large cists, probably for inhumations, are still visible on Dartmoor. A rectangular example over 2 m long lies close to the Merrivale stone rows, its broken capstone still in place but its contents unrecorded. Another, comparable in length but of squarer plan, is evident at Roundy Park near Postbridge.

The largest agglomeration of burial monuments of the second millennium BC is that on the Greensand plateau of Broad Down and Farway (Fox, A. 1948; Fleming 1971). Several of the numerous barrows here were examined by Kirwan, Hutchinson and Worth, the considerable variety and wealth of the burials being apparent despite the poor quality of the excavation. The grave goods were restudied by Lady Fox and their relationship with the wealthy burials of Wessex fully elucidated. Numerous as the barrows and other monuments on this plateau are, it is certain that others remain to be found. Several have been revealed by chance in recent years; others have been destroyed without record. The total is commonly said to be about sixty. More probably there are at least eighty and perhaps rather more. The variety of structure evident in the small number of barrows excavated is remarkable, even when due allowance has been made for the inadequacies of the nineteenth-century observers. Several monuments are conical mounds covering pavements of flat stones on which the burials were placed. One contained a substantial cairn ring of boulders, not unlike that at Tregulland Burrow. The most striking was a mound covering a central stone cist and surrounded by a circle of small standing stones. Another had a stone cairn at its centre, surrounded by a stone circle buried in the mound. The surviving mounds reveal major variations in size and form. The largest are 45 m in diameter and up to 4 m high. The smallest are no more than 6 m across and exist now as low flat mounds or ring-cairns. Burning off of the dense vegetation which covers much of the area occasionally reveals small rings of stone which appear never to have been covered by a mound. Many of the medium-sized barrows, between 12 m and 16 m across, are markedly

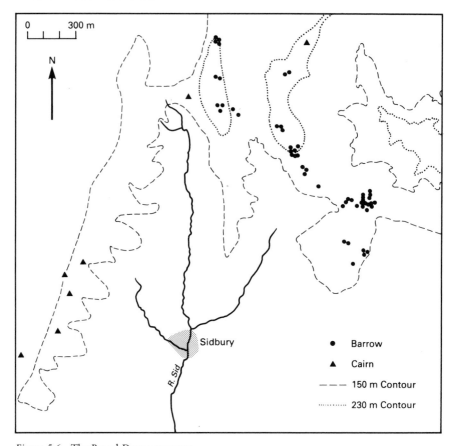

Figure 5.6 The Broad Down cemetery

flat-topped and steep-sided. One has a distinct ledge or terrace about half-way up its side.

This variety extends to the contents of the recorded graves. It has long been recognized that several of the Broad Down barrows contained burials akin to those of the early Bronze Age in Wessex. Three large monuments, each over 30 m in diameter, have revealed particularly close links with the Wessex graves. Barrow 36 in Fox's list contained a small cup cut from a single piece of shale, and Barrow 47 produced a second shale cup and a small bronze grooved dagger of a type well known in Wessex. Another monument, no. 51, produced another link with Wessex, probably from a secondary interment, a decorated pygmy cup containing the cremated remains of an infant. The pottery vessels are mixed in character though the small sample of burials which has produced them is a warning against their use as representations of local funerary tradition. Barrow 52 contained an urn derived from the food vessel series and, from a secondary burial, a Beaker with upright neck and decoration of horizontal grooves. Other fragmentary vessels are suggestive of early Middle Bronze Age ceramics but are now lost, making certainty unattainable.

The barrows of Exmoor, although not well known to the modern excavator, are the most familiar and characteristic monuments of that upland region, visible from afar on the broad ridges. On the higher ground a considerable number of barrows are strung out on the crests above the 500 m contour, evidently related to ridgeways which later served as territorial boundaries of various kinds. A striking series of monuments forms a linear cemetery along the ridge still followed by the boundary between Devon and Somerset, from Wood Barrow to Two Barrows, 7 km to the south-east, some of the individual barrows being among the most impressive of any in the South West. Another linear series on a ridge ran southward from Rowley Down above Parracombe to Stoodleigh Down 10 km away. Other series stand on shorter ridges and small groups of barrows and cairns stud the rounded humps of moor, and still succeed in catching the eye. The best known of all the Exmoor barrows form a linear group on Challacombe Common, the Chapman Barrows, nine in number and including four very large monuments.

It is unfortunate that the early excavations of Exmoor barrows, notably by J. F. Chanter, were not of high quality. It is equally unfortunate that not one has been examined by modern techniques, so that our knowledge of structure, burial rites and contents is very scanty. These fine monuments have deserved a better fate. As in the Broad Down barrows, structure is very varied. One of the Chapman barrows was composed of a solid stack of turves covering a central mound of stones and clay. Alternate layers of clay and 'charcoal' or other carbonized deposits were noted in one of the barrows at Huntshaw near Torrington, recalling similar instances at Broad Down and Upton Pyne. Internal stone rings enclosing the primary deposit are also known, for instance at Heydon Hill and Sparborough Field. Outer retaining walls or kerbs are still visible on some of the larger monuments. The most striking of these surrounds the base of the Setta Barrow, even in its despoiled state one of the finest of Exmoor monuments. Some of the individual stones in the retaining wall are large and solid rectilinear blocks set four-square on the old ground surface: others are thin slabs pitched on end and held in position by smaller stones. Many of the upright slabs have been forced out of their original positions by later settlement of the mound. Two adjacent large barrows appear to have had similar kerbs and this must have been a most imposing group of structures. Surrounding ditches are still evident in a number of cases, for instance, among the Five Barrows group, around the Longstone Barrow at Challacombe and the Thorncombe Barrow in the Quantocks. Many of the smaller monuments on Exmoor and on the Quantocks appear to be stone cairns, many of them enlarged from their original form by the addition of stones collected in agricultural activities, a process which continues in parts of Exmoor. It is likely that careful excavation of more of the Exmoor and Quantock mounds would reveal central cairns covered by deposits of turf, earth and clay, in some cases in a later structural episode. Ring-cairns like those on Broad Down and Haldon are known in small numbers on Exmoor, for example on Thorn Hill behind Lynton, and more intensive field-work would reveal many more.

The size of the Exmoor and Quantocks monuments is a point to be emphasized for, although they do not attain the dimensions of the largest barrows on Broad Down, a substantial proportion rank among the largest burial mounds in the peninsula. Setta Barrow is 23 m in diameter and must originally have stood some 5 m high. The adjacent barrow to the north of it is 26 m across, a measurement exceeded by several of the Chapman Barrows, one in the group at Narracott near Bittadon, and another in Five Barrows (actually nine in number) which is over 30 m in diameter. Those on the Quantocks tend to be smaller, though one nearly 30 m across stands on West Hill and another of 28 m on Hurley Beacon. Thus, although these monuments are much less frequented than those on Dartmoor or in many parts of Cornwall and are, in general, less well known in the archaeological literature, they are considerable works in all senses of the term. Above all, perhaps, it is their majestic setting which makes them so memorable.

Although the excavation record is poor, it is clear that a considerable number of the Exmoor barrows were erected over primary cremation burials. A small number are known to have been richly furnished and to reflect, in less spectacular fashion, the splendidly adorned burials of Wessex nobles in the early to middle Bronze Age. A round barrow on Darracott Moor near Great Torrington produced a fine three-riveted grooved dagger, while another on Bampfylde Hill, North Molton, contained an urn and a necklace made up of beads of faience, lignite and amber. There are general similarities between Exmoor burials and contemporary graves in South Wales, clearly visible across the Bristol Channel only 30 km away. But links with burial traditions in other parts of the south-western peninsula were also at work. A barrow on Berry Down, Berrynarbor, contained a cremation covered by a fine urn of Trevisker Style I, a vessel that would hardly be out of place in west Cornwall.

An area of upland where groups of cairns and other monuments exist in abundance is the Greensand ridge of Haldon, west of the Exe estuary. For long neglected by field-workers, mainly because the visible remains are not impressive, Haldon has recently revealed many monuments for the first time, including many isolated small barrows, cairns and ring-cairns as well as two sizeable cairn-groups. Large barrow mounds like those at Upton Pyne and Broad Down are as yet not in evidence, though large areas of the ridge have never been intensively surveyed and are now covered in dense forest, furze and bracken, making field-work difficult. Some of the small groups of cairns may well prove to be more extensive than they seem at present. The two major concentrations of cairns lie about the 200 m contour on the western side of the ridge. In one group, west of the A380 road, at least forty cairns have been noted and others have probably been destroyed. The majority of the survivors are small mounds between 2 m and 5 m in diameter and now less than 50 cm high. The destruction of one of these in 1982 revealed that it had been built of chert blocks, larger stones being set at the edge, smaller lumps in the body of the mound. There was no ditch and surface indications suggest that ditches were rarely dug around the smaller mounds. The other cairn-group includes a linear series of seven ring-cairns, with a cluster of small mounds 200 m away on the top of the ridge and an isolated ring-cairn, much larger than most, 300 m to the east. This has a circular bank, probably accompanied by a ditch, 32 m in diameter, and with an entrance on the northern side. A slight hump in the centre of the ring may mark the remains of a small cairn. Other monuments on Haldon take this form but this is probably the largest surviving example.

The larger Haldon mounds were a particular target for early barrow-diggers and for road-builders who found in them convenient heaps of stone. It is quite possible that the scarcity of larger barrows on this ridge is due to the fact that they were such obviously attractive quarries. The urns and other grave-goods located by eighteenth- and nineteenth-century excavators seem all to have been lost, though some of the early descriptions suggest similar burials to those attested on Dartmoor and North Devon. The investigations of Mr Tripe (or John Swete) of Ashburton in 1780, as related by Polwhele in his *History of Devonshire*, produced a series of inurned cremations from a number of cairns, one of them inverted over the cremated remains, and another in a stone cist. Lysons refers to these and other discoveries (including Roman coins in some of the cairns). He mentions also Swete's opening of a huge mound on the eastern side of Haldon, 70 m in circumference and 3 m high, which also covered a cist containing an inverted urn. This barrow now appears to have been completely destroyed.

The small Haldon cairns have much in common with certain cairn-types on Dartmoor. A number of cairnfields on Dartmoor contain 20–30 monuments, ranging in diameter from 2 m to 5 m, some of them over stone cists. Like those on Haldon, the record of what they once contained is very poor, but the general indications are that they belong to the first half of the second millennium BC. Three recently examined small cairns on Shaugh Moor produced radiocarbon estimates about the middle of that millennium. The few Dartmoor cists that have produced grave-goods contained Beakers or objects commonly associated with them. Thus, the Langcombe cist contained a Beaker and three barbed and tanged arrowheads, that at Fernworthy, a Beaker, a lignite dress-ornament and a fragment of bronze, those at Watern Down and Wigford Down each a Beaker, and that at Archerton Newtake a stone wrist-guard. This is a modest sample from several hundred burials, but coherent enough. Individual monuments might pass through many vicissitudes before losing all significance for Bronze Age man. Some were completely or largely rebuilt in successive phases of use.

Tregulland Burrow, Treneglos, in north-east Cornwall had comprised in its first phase two or three concentric rings of timber stakes, the innermost circle measuring 4.5 m in diameter. A central rectilinear pit, badly disturbed or robbed, may have been the primary grave. From its filling came a number of cup-marked stones suggesting a stone-lined or covered chamber. A satellite cremation burial containing two arrowheads, one barbed and tanged, the other hollow-based, lay between the second and incomplete third ring of stakes, as did a shallow pit the floor of which had been scorched by fire. The monument was subsequently completely remodelled. A stout ring-cairn of stone now formed the focus, this being girt by a bank thrown up from an encircling ditch. Within the cairn-ring stood a large slab of slate, cup-marked and bearing other deliberate incisions. Turf capping was then added to the cairn and bank, producing a small, neat arena, within which a cremation was placed and, a short distance away, an undecorated food vessel. This was, then, a complex ritual structure which had passed through three distinct phases and apparently served changing ceremonial needs over a long period in the early to middle Bronze Age. The cup-marked stones found in two phases of the monument are uncommon in the south-western peninsula. Another instance has been reported in the Nancekuke barrow at Portreath near Redruth and a third may adorn the large cist known as the Three Brothers of Grugith in the Lizard. Further examples are known in barrows and cists in South Wales.

The record of Bronze Age burials tends to be dominated by barrows and other more or less prominent, above-ground monuments. Other less striking burials undoubtedly existed in the second millennium, though they do not yet figure. The occasional burial in a pit, with no surface marker, has been noted. Such a pit burial, covered by a single capstone, has been excavated at Rose Ash in north Devon, one of the few to be carefully recorded (Wainwright 1980). It contained an undecorated, ovoid urn with a simple, slightly everted rim, which had held the cremated remains of an adult. A radiocarbon estimate of 1030 ± 70 bc was obtained from charcoal in the pit, suggesting broad contemporaneity with the Shaugh Moor settlement and with Trevisker. The vessel shape is very simple and not notably distinctive, but it may be related to the Middle Bronze Age upright jars in evidence on the Dartmoor settlements and in west Cornwall.

Not all barrow groups were sited on high ground. North of Exeter in the parishes of Upton Pyne, Brampford Speke, Thorverton and Nether Exe, a loose concentration of over thirty barrows occupies low ground to either side of the River Exe. A small number survive as prominent mounds, the most impressive, north of Bramble Lane in Upton Pyne, still measuring 2.5 m in height and 40 m in diameter. The majority, however, have been reduced or extinguished by ploughing and are now barely visible as flattened mounds on the ground, or as crop-marks from the air. Four members of the group were partially excavated in the later nineteenth century, with limited results but with slight indications of similarity with the barrows on Broad Down and Farway. No burials were encountered, but observation of the structure of the mounds suggested that the mounds were constructed of successive layers of clay interleaved with bands of charcoal, while a thick deposit of charcoal was noted in the upper part of the mound in two barrows. The description of this stratigraphic sequence is not as precise as one could wish, and it is possible that the 'charcoal' layers are actually the result of chemical weathering or even the remains of turf used in the building of the mound. No traces of surrounding ditches were noted in these early excavations and the only barrow in the group to be examined more recently certainly had no such encircling work. Aerial survey, too, has produced no sign of barrow-ditches so that the mounds appear to have been raised from material scraped up from the adjacent ground. Interestingly, ring-ditched earthworks which may include funerary monuments are known in the Exe valley, and indeed two are recorded amid the Upton Pyne barrows. Unfortunately, none of these ring-ditches have been excavated and their chronological and functional relationship, if any, with the barrows is thus unknown. Several of the barrows were constructed, not by scraping up earth from the vicinity, but by cutting a terrace into a natural slope and heaping up the spoil into a mound. This distinctive practice was not only economical of labour but also provided a level space around the barrow which might have been used for ceremonial.

The only carefully excavated monument in this group is one of the cluster in Upton Pyne. Some 20 m in diameter and originally perhaps about 4 m high, it had been constructed on a level platform terraced into a natural slope. The core of the barrow structure was a mound of sand, covered by a mass of laid turf, presumably stripped from the site in the levelling process. Over this in turn lay a thick deposit of clay and sand. The principal funerary deposits had been laid in the sand at the centre of the mound. They comprised an inverted urn containing the calcined remains of an infant (probably the primary burial), two further inverted urns containing cremations, and a small stone cist containing a collared urn, inverted like the others. Two further cremations, not in urns and with no other grave-goods, lay in the same deposit. The possibility of secondary burials in the outer body of the barrow, not destroyed, must clearly be allowed for.

The four urns are of the greatest interest, being virtually the only middle Bronze Age vessels recovered by careful excavation from any of the numerous barrows in Devon. The collared urn in the cist is a fine example of the Primary series in Longworth's classification, the only one so far known in Devon or Cornwall and so divergent from the other collared urns of the South West as to be fairly regarded as an import from farther east. The other three vessels share much in common, in their forms, decoration and fabric, with the Trevisker series, best known in Cornwall and west Devon and on

149

Dartmoor, but with relatives in Dorset. These Upton Pyne vessels, however, are the first clear indication that pottery in the Trevisker styles was distributed over east Devon and the date of its occurrence is thus a matter of some interest. The sole radiocarbon estimate obtained from this barrow is of *c.* 1386 bc, about the beginning of middle Bronze Age and thus according well with the other C14 determinations for the Trevisker series. This slender support for the chronology of middle Bronze Age pottery receives a measure of confirmation from other evidence.

Assuming that the majority of the barrows in this group are now recorded, as seems reasonably certain, their local distribution presents a further feature of interest. The linear pattern of distribution of several barrows along a line from the river Creedy to the Exe and on towards the Culm suggests a routeway as determining the siting of the monuments. A green lane still exists along part of this line. Another alignment of barrows may link the Upton Pyne cluster with the higher ground to the north and here too an old track, still followed by the parish boundary, appears to act as a link between the barrows.

Relatively few burials of the latest Bronze Age are recorded in Devon and Cornwall. The urnfields so well known to the east are absent here and the building of barrows and cairns ceased in the centuries after 1000 BC. The commemoration of the dead underwent profound change, presumably reflecting the steady transformation of the social order that is evident in settlement-types and material equipment in the same period.

Chapter 6

Towards a Wider World

The remarkably stable prehistoric communities established in the second millennium were increasingly subject to change after 1000 BC. The upland settlements were progressively abandoned and the material record in general alters markedly, becoming in several respects poorer than that of the preceding thousand years. Since the Neolithic, the economic progress of south-western communities had been steady. Now came interruption, probably recession, certainly change. Why this should have occurred is matter for debate. Climatic deterioration after 1000, reaching a peak about 600–500, could have had serious effects on the upland settlements in particular. Variation of a few degrees in temperature or a modest increase in rainfall, or both, is likely to have reduced drastically the quality and extent of grassland on the higher ground. The increase of peat-growth in some areas well before 1000 has already been noted (above, p. 125). The relatively high population density may further have led to over-grazing on the hills, leading in turn to gradual depopulation or displacement. In consequence, more intensive exploitation of the lowland areas may have ensued, one eventual result being perhaps the emergence of a new range of enclosed settlements in most parts of the region (below, p. 157). What does seem clear is that the late Bronze Age in the peninsula did not see the same degree of material advance registered elsewhere in southern England. The artifact record is rather limited and it reveals little that is truly innovatory.

The pottery of the later Bronze Age, that is, from about 1000 BC when the Trevisker series ended, to 600, exists in simple forms with a minimum of decorative treatment. Straight-sided, bucket-shaped vessels akin to the Deverel-Rimbury urns of southern England (and especially Dorset) are found in both Cornwall and Devon, even though the characteristic urnfields evidently did not extend so far to the west (Petersen 1981; White 1982). Most of the south-western urns come from graves, especially in West Penwith, but this reflects no more than the incidence of archaeological enquiry. Seen as a whole, the pottery of this period is a very mixed bag, apparently reflecting the co-existence of several local ceramic traditions which are still imperfectly known (Patchett 1944: 41–8). This will help to explain the marked

151

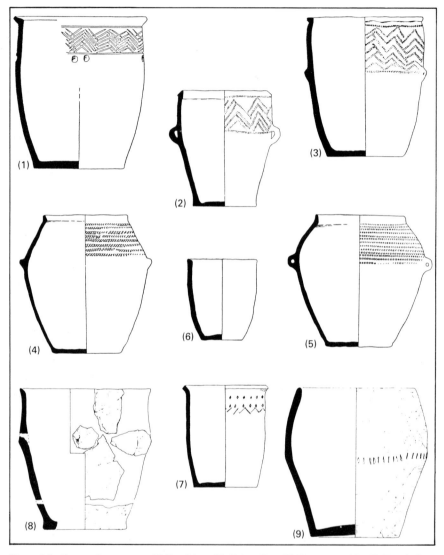

Figure 6.1 Bronze Age pottery: (1) Trevisker; (2) Gunwalloe; (3) Tresawsen; (4)–(5) Knackyboy Cairn, St Martin's; (6) Place, Fowey; (7) Cape Cornwall; (8)–(9) Shaugh Moor

differences seen between contemporary sites not far from each other, for example between Gwithian and Kynance in the Lizard. At the latter site comb-stamped decoration appears, an otherwise unknown treatment in west Cornwall (Helston Museum, unpublished).

The metalwork of this period is similarly unremarkable. Socketed axes which might have many functions are the most prominent component of late Bronze Age metalwork. Stone-valve moulds for socketed axes have been found at Helsbury near Camelford, Gwithian (Needham 1981: 37) and on a site in the Quantocks (Grinsell 1970: 34). The exceptional number of axes in the hoard at Stogursey in north Somerset yields further proof of local production of these tools. That huge hoard contained copper ingots as well as scrap metal and new tools, and is thus safely identified as a metalworker's stock-in-trade. The same is true of the Kenidjack Castle (St Just) hoard, a collection of thirty pieces of tin and copper, along with two unused socketed axes of south-western pattern, found close to the defences of a coastal fort and the hoard of forty axes buried at Higher Roseworthy, Gwinear. These sizeable collections of a particular tool-type raise the possibility that these axes had served a limited function as a means of exchange, as Breton axes may also have done and as iron in the form of bars was later to do (below, p. 155). Copper ingots appear elsewhere in the South West at this time and are a useful reminder of the natural occurrence of the metal near Callington. The principal finds are those at Mount Batten, Kent's Cavern, and Churston in Devon, and St Hilary and Lelant in Cornwall.

There are a few finds of gold. The hoard of six gold bracelets found at Morvah in west Cornwall (Hencken 1932: 90–3) contained three instances with decorated loops and trumpet terminals. These have close analogies with Irish material and are most probably Irish imports. But there is also a bracelet with a flat, thin bow and simple, coiled terminals which is not an Irish type. For this piece the analogies are with eastern England if with anywhere in particular. Somewhat earlier, of the ninth century BC, is the group of gold objects from Towednack in West Penwith. This included two magnificent twisted torcs or neck-rings, four bracelets, two of them unfinished, and three coiled gold bars or ingots (Hawkes 1932). The unworked and unfinished items suggest that this was the stock of a smith, either a migrant from Ireland or someone fully conversant with Irish goldworking techniques.

The settlement-context of this late Bronze Age metalwork is as uncertain as that of the preceding period. A small number of bronzes have been found at or close to the sites of hill-forts or other enclosures, which we would imagine were coming into existence in or before the middle of the first millennium. These sites include Woodbury Castle, Hembury (near Buckfastleigh) and the Trendle in Devon, and Carn Brea and Kenidjack Castle in Cornwall. But in no case is there any clear connection with any kind of settlement, whether enclosed or otherwise. No light is thus thrown from this quarter on the origin of south-western hill-forts, though the lack of extensive excavation in hill-forts in the region prevents us from drawing any conclusions on the point (below, p. 157).

The most striking concentration of late Bronze Age metalwork occurs at Mount Batten, a rocky promontory projecting into the eastern side of Plymouth Sound, and it points to a major port of entry here about the middle of the first millennium and later (below, p. 184). There are bronzes from northern France, a Breton socketed axe, a tanged sickle which may have come from much farther afield, and four cakes of copper as well as scraps of other implements. There is no indication that these objects stemmed from a hoard. Most, if not all, were probably single finds from a midden on the eastern side of the promontory (Clarke 1971). In view of the exotic pieces in the earlier Plymstock hoard, buried not far away, it is at least possible that foreign goods were being introduced into the South West *via* the Sound over a lengthy period.

Increasing evidence for trade and exchange-networks involving metals and metal goods spanning the English Channel at this time may be leading us towards a clearer perception of where the main nodal points in those networks lay. The Isle of Portland has long seemed to be an outstanding example of a major point of entry with many fine goods from this great promontory (earlier an island?) and its hinterland, material which includes several important Iron Age pieces. The Mount's Bay area of west Cornwall and Tor Bay in Devon may be others, along with possibly Stogursey and Helsbury (Pearce 1983: 250). Most of these places could offer safe anchorages and easy access to the interior; they would thus have been attractive to traders crossing the Channel. The trading-places later visited by Mediterranean sailors may have had a long history before the Classical world became aware of them (below on Ictis, p. 187).

The conventional division of British prehistory about 600 BC at the introduction of iron technology is even less significant in the South West than in the rest of southern Britain. In essentials the record of settlement and material culture underwent no sudden or drastic alteration in the mid-first millennium, the disappearance of a dominant bronze technology being gradual after about 750 BC and the emergence of new settlement forms, including hill-forts, evidently making little impact until after 500. The material record remains poor in mid-millennium, making both dating and cultural assessment very difficult. Not until the last two centuries of the pre-Roman Iron Age do the archaeological sources expand, but even then they do not match those for the rest of southern England. Pottery is scarce, metalwork even scarcer. Settlement sites are abundant for the second half of the millennium, but very few have been well studied. Within the slowly evolving settlement pattern, in which a major feature was the appearance of a wide range of enclosed settlements, the familial group seems to have remained the main determinant in how the land was occupied and used. In other words, the framework of the social order established over a thousand years earlier still survived.

The metal resource which has given its name to this division of prehistoric time is present in various localities on the eastern and southern sides of Dartmoor, varying in composition from brown haematite to the specular material generally known as micaceous haematite. The richest deposits lay in the Ilsington area while at Haytor the ore could have been reached near the surface. Also at or near the surface were the deposits below

Holne Chase, where, interestingly, the only Iron Age currency bars known in the peninsula have been found. Other near-surface deposits lay on the south-western flank of Dartmoor around Hemerdon and Plympton. There are no very early iron objects in the region, the nearest being certain weapons and implements in the Llyn Fawr (Glamorgan) deposit of about 600 BC. An interest in the local iron deposits was alive about that date as the Kestor evidence shows (Fox 1954: 59) and earlier iron ore might have attracted some attention even if only as a curiosity, as at Dean Moor (Fox 1957: 73). Isolated deposits of surface iron occur in various places and one or two may have been worked. The most interesting case is at the promontory fort of Trevelgue near Newquay, where bands of iron occur in the cliffs.

Settlement-types and Settlement-pattern

Settlements of the mid-first millennium and immediately afterwards are few when compared with the preceding and following periods. What is known about them suggests that no major change in settlement type had occurred. Bodrifty (Mulfra, W. Penwith) illustrates the continuity from the later Bronze Age tradition admirably. Here a scatter of round houses, five of them rather larger than the Bronze Age dwellings on the uplands, lay amid an extensive field-system. At a later stage a wall was built around eight of the houses, thus creating an enclosure which resembled the 'pounds' on Dartmoor. The earliest pottery vessels adhere to the plain styles of late Deverel-Rimbury urns, but they were shortly superseded by forms distinctive of the fifth and fourth centuries in regions farther east. These include carinated jars and bowls, jars with upright rims and large storage vessels with finger-tip or impressed decoration on the shoulder (Dudley 1956: 23–4). Other west Cornish sites, like Gwithian (Thomas 1958: fig. 21, OLS 203 and PT 81) and Maen Castle (Crofts 1955: fig. 23), have produced similar wares though perhaps somewhat later in date. The cliff-castle of Gurnards Head also had a small number of plain vessels, one of them close to a late Bronze Age flat-rimmed jar (Gordon 1940: fig. 7, 10). A small group of sherds of upright jars at Carn Euny is associated with two stamp-ornamented vessels which may be Armorican imports or copies of late Hallstatt Armorican stamped wares of the fifth century (Christie 1978: 402): for the whole group there is a radiocarbon estimate of 420 ± 120 bc. The Bodmin Moor upland has little to offer as yet, though earlier Iron Age houses have been excavated at Garrow Tor (unpublished).

Sites of this period in Devon have been scarcely more productive. One of the most interesting is that at Dainton, on the limestone behind Torbay, a field-system with clearance-cairns but with no visible houses. The pottery is all coarse ware, with plain rim-forms (Silvester 1980: fig. 9). Most, and probably all, the vessels were produced locally, as petrological examination suggests. The hoard of metalwork moulds attests late Bronze Age activity at Dainton, but some of the pottery should be considerably later, probably of the fifth or fourth centuries (notably Willis and Rogers 1951: fig. 6).

The mid-first millennium on Dartmoor has for some time been regarded as a period of agricultural recession and thus of depopulation of the upland. While this may be true as a general statement, it would be wrong to visualize Dartmoor as a deserted wilderness from 500 BC. Not only is there a considerable number of hill-forts around the fringes of the moor (below, p. 161), but a small number of settlements on the drier eastern flank were certainly occupied in the early Iron Age. What we may be seeing, as yet very indistinctly, is a large-scale realignment of settlement after the sixth century, in which the more exposed uplands were abandoned in favour of more sheltered positions, the open moor still being used for grazing. It must also be borne in mind that only a tiny proportion of the hut-groups on the moor has yet been investigated by modern techniques and that so small a sample can be no reliable guide to fluctuations in settlement history.

The Round Pound at Kestor and its associated field-system and subsidiary huts is the best known of the Dartmoor settlements of this period (Fox 1954). The focal point of the settlement was a single round-house, 11.3 m in diameter and thus unusually roomy by Dartmoor standards, occupying its own small enclosure to which it was attached by radial walls. Within the hut lay a small bowl-furnace and a forging-pit, used in the production of iron, probably from ironstone found at Lustleigh 16 km away. This is so far the only indication of iron-smelting on Dartmoor at this period, raising the suspicion (without, however, independent support) that the metalworking installations are intrusive and medieval in date. The sparse pottery finds from Kestor suggest a date in the sixth to fifth century or a little later (Fox 1954: fig. 12). Of broadly the same date are two vessels from the settlement at Foales Arrishes, where other large round-houses lie within a rectilinear field-system like those at Kestor and Shovel Down.

Some of the early Iron Age vessel forms seen at Bodrifty are also in evidence at Mount Batten, for example the carinated bowl and straight-sided jar (Clarke 1971: fig. 6). Hill-forts in the region, however, have so far yielded remarkably little pottery which can confidently be assigned to the earlier Iron Age. Blackbury Castle in east Devon is the most helpful in this respect, but most of the pottery seems to fall after the middle of the millennium, perhaps in the fourth or third century. The few sherds from Woodbury Castle are perhaps of similar date, while the most extensively excavated hill-fort, Hembury, has produced only one or two vessels which might be dated to the early Iron Age. This sparseness cannot be due to chance. Pottery does appear to have been a far from common utensil in the earliest phase of the Iron Age and in consequence elucidation of the chronology of this period will never be easy. This problem is one that bedevils the study of the hill-forts of the region in particular.

Hill-Forts and Hill-Slope Enclosures

It is to be expected that the occupation and enclosure of hill-tops was proceeding in the earlier first millennium, but as yet little clear evidence has been obtained. The occupation of hill-tops might be unenclosed, as at South Cadbury, or within an earthwork, as at Norton Fitzwarren. A number of sites later occupied by hill-forts have produced chance finds of later Bronze Age metalwork, but the original context of this material is not known. The Armorican and other socketed axes from Carn Brea (Borlase 1754: Pl. XXIV) are the best known of such finds but there are others from Cornwall (Kenidjack Castle) and from Devon (Woodbury Castle, the Trendle and Membury). That use of these hill-top locations began in the early first millennium need not be thought unlikely, but no excavated settlement has produced satisfactory evidence for a late Bronze Age origin. Radiocarbon estimates in the tenth and ninth centuries obtained for the site at Killibury in north Cornwall are not certainly referable to the earliest phase of fortification (Miles 1977b: 100–1). In view of what has emerged from hill-forts in other parts of western Britain, however, it is probably only a matter of time before clear evidence for late Bronze Age occupation and probably enclosure of hill-top sites in the region is obtained.

The South West is not a region of large and powerfully defended hill-forts like those of Wessex and the Welsh Borders. Many fortified enclosures do exist, but the great majority are not hill-forts in the sense in which that term is generally used. They do not occupy positions well defended by nature and their earthworks are not well designed to withstand attack. They commonly lie on hill-slopes or low ground and are thus overlooked from nearby hills or ridges. Among hill-forts proper, most are small, less than 2 ha (5 acres) in area, and equipped with simple univallate defences. The smaller works are virtually undistinguishable from the larger rounds. Against this background the larger fortifications (Hembury in Devon, Castle Carnyke and Castle an Dinas in Cornwall) stand out sharply, but even these are not huge in scale.

The most extensive examination of the defences of a hill-fort is that carried out at Hembury in the period 1930–35 and 1980–85 (Liddell 1930, 1931, 1932, 1935; Todd 1984). Miss Liddell's work had suggested the existence of a palisaded enclosure (or enclosures) in the early phases of defensive building, stone-filled slots for large upright timbers having been identified at the gates of the later fort. The recent excavations have clarified this considerably. The first phase of hill-fort defences took the form of a box-rampart, faced and rear-revetted by timber walls which were founded in continuous trenches (the 'palisades' seen by Miss Liddell). The total width of this rampart was 6.1 m, rather wider than the similar constructions at Maiden Castle (3.8 m) and South Cadbury (3 m). The body of the structure was composed of sand, earth and stone derived from an accompanying ditch, or ditches. No date can be attached to this powerful defensive work, no

157

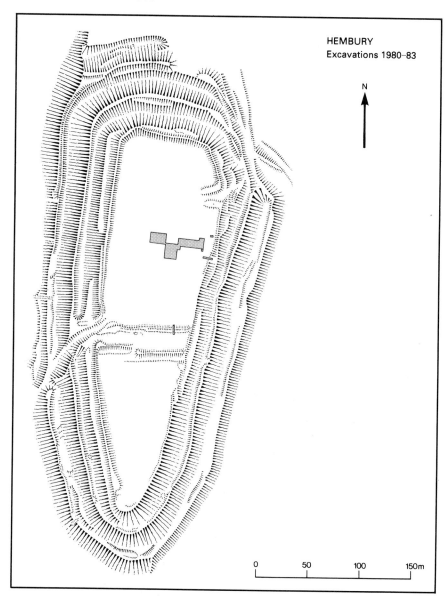

HEMBURY
Excavations 1980–83

N

0   50   100   150m

Figure 6.2   Defences of the fort at Hembury

pottery or other finds being associated with it. On analogy with other such works in western Britain, it is reasonable to place it in the middle of the first millennium, probably between 600 and 450 BC.

Another east Devon hill-fort has produced evidence for a timber-fronted rampart, though of a somewhat different kind from the Hembury

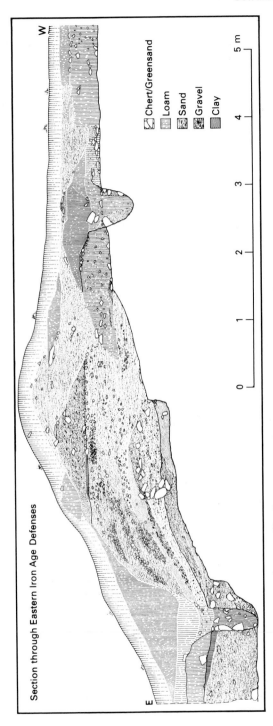

Figure 6.3 Section of the defences at Hembury

159

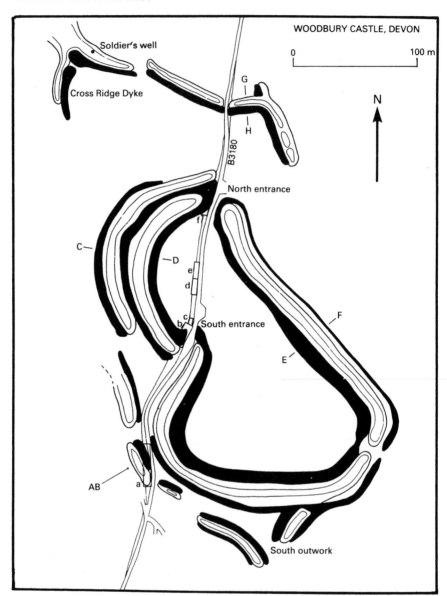

Figure 6.4 Woodbury Castle

box-rampart. This is Woodbury Castle, where a palisaded enclosure seems to have preceded the massive visible earthworks, it too undated (and probably of only brief duration), but possibly of the same period as the Hembury rampart (Miles 1975b). A short length of earthwork immediately north of the fort was crowned by a timber structure. The foundation for this had been embedded in the bank, so that this was a very different kind of construction, though it may have been contemporary with the palisaded enclosure.

The later defences of Hembury are akin to the massive works so familiar in the great hill-forts of Wessex. The box-rampart was replaced by a dump rampart 8.9 m wide and standing originally some 5 m high, revetted by a low stone wall at the front. Material for this rampart had been derived from two large ditches which ran around the entire circuit. A third ditch covered the vulnerable northern side. Since the rampart was sited on the very edge of the scarp, the vertical height of its top above the bottom of the ditch was 18 m. Even in their present weathered state, these works are not easy to scale. Two large gates set between inturns of the rampart gave access to the fort in the west side and near the north-east angle. The date of this phase of defensive building can be placed in the late Iron Age, after 300 BC and perhaps as late as the early first century BC (Todd 1984: 260–1).

The Greensand uplands of east Devon and the area about the Exe valley contain a relatively large number of rather small hill-forts, the exceptions being Hembury and Dumpdon, many of them univallate with a single gate-opening and measuring less than 2 ha (5 acres) in area. Of the few that have been excavated, Blackbury Castle near Beer has produced the best evidence for its chronology (Young and Richardson 1955). Here a simple dump rampart and a single ditch were constructed at a date which should probably be placed in the fifth or fourth century BC. A single, narrow gate gave access into the oval enclosure of 2.7 ha (6.5 acres). Little is known of the interior, though part of a possibly rectangular timber building was found close to the gate. The most remarkable feature of the site is the earthwork which protected the gate in the manner of a barbican. So elaborate an external work is without parallel in the South West and the closest analogy elsewhere is in an early phase at Maiden Castle (Wheeler 1943: 33–4). In a small fort like Blackbury Castle this might seem to be a case of *folie de grandeur*, though the earthwork may have had some practical use, perhaps in the droving of cattle.

An interesting series of small hill-forts lies on the fringe of Dartmoor, suggesting continued use of the upland for grazing in the later first millennium. Once again it is the eastern and southern edges of the moor that were the favoured areas. Cranbrook Castle, near Chagford, is one of the largest, a work of two major phases, the later of which was not completed (Collis 1979). Not the least interesting feature of this fort is the apparent association with reave-like boundaries, suggesting continuation of long-established practices of land-allotment down to the construction of the hill-fort, whenever that was. Hunter's Tor near Manaton may be another unfinished fort, the defences of which resemble those of the earlier 'pounds'. On the southern edge of Dartmoor lie Hembury near Buckfastleigh, Holne Castle near important iron deposits at Ausewell (above, p. 155) and Boringdon Camp near Plympton. The northern and western sides show only

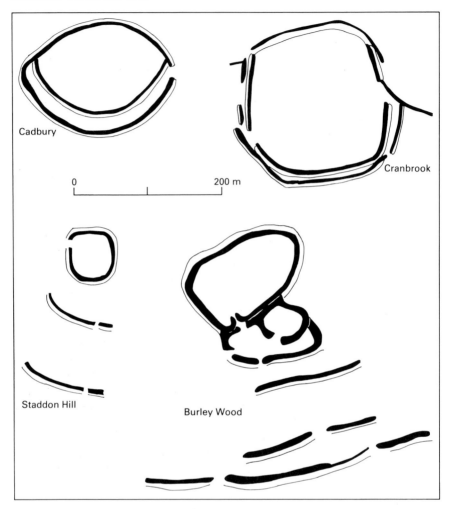

Cadbury

Cranbrook

0   200 m

Staddon Hill

Burley Wood

Figure 6.5   Hill-forts and hill-slope enclosures

the occasional defended site, the small promontory work near Okehampton being the best known. There is obvious scope in these forts for further study of a crucial period of south-western prehistory. It would not be unreasonable to expect some of them to be relatively early cases of fortified settlements, products of a formative period of social change.

True hill-forts are few in Cornwall, the conspicuous exceptions being Castle-an-Dinas and perhaps Carn Brea and Trencrom (but see above, p. 76). Several of the small forts, however, are outstandingly strongly defended, chief among these being Chun Castle on the West Penwith moors (Leeds 1926–7). This little fort, only 100 sq m in area, was surrounded by two massive granite walls 6 m apart and by two ditches. In the nineteenth century the inner wall still stood almost 4 m high. The single gate with its narrow, funnelled entrance was shielded by the outer wall so that access lay along a dog-leg track overlooked by the inner curtain-wall. The known structures were set against the rear of the inner curtain. These include sub-rectangular as well as circular and less regular plans, but not all need be of Iron Age date. It is not surprising that a strong place like Chun was occupied in the Roman and post-Roman periods. Among the Roman wares here are amphora sherds which may be imports of the late Iron Age (Leeds 1926–7: 220). A similar stone-walled fort may have stood at Caer Brane, Sancreed, also in West Penwith. This has now been largely destroyed, but it seems to have been a double fortification like Chun, though the outer wall was of earth.

The fretted coast of the peninsula provided many promontory sites, some of considerable scale, which could be economically fortified by laying defences across the neck. Some of these promontory forts, or 'cliff-castles' as they are commonly called, are among the most striking and distinctive prehistoric works in the South West. For some earlier writers they represented a clear link with Brittany where similar forts are numerous, especially on the coasts of Finistere and the Morbihan (Wheeler and Richardson 1957: 103–12). Commercial activities promoted by the Veneti in the later Iron Age (Caesar: III, 8) seemed to provide a plausible historic context for the introduction of this type of fortification (Cotton 1958–9: 116; Fox, A. 1973: 141) and certain elements in the associated pottery (e.g. stamped wares at Gurnard's Head, Gordon 1940: 110) seemed to hint at import from western Gaul or even Spain. There seems little substance in a direct link between the south-western promontory forts and those of Brittany. Headlands girt by precipitous cliffs were obvious sites for strongholds and no one would need instruction in how they should be fortified. Nor is the evidence for a connection with Venetic traders very impressive. The very nature of promontory forts renders them unsuitable as trading-posts. The long, sheltered estuaries could better serve that function. Such evidence as is available to us indicates that these forts do not represent a distinct type of defended site. They can reasonably be seen to be of the same genus as other hill-forts, differing only in their topographical setting.

Promontory forts are found in numbers along the northern coast, less frequently on the English Channel coast as far east as Bolt Tail in south Devon, and in Scilly. Most are relatively small, but a few (Dodman Point, Trevelgue near Newquay and Wind Hill, Countisbury) are among the largest of south-western hill-forts. Morphologically, the forts are varied, univallate, bivallate and multivallate forms all being represented. Maen Castle, Sennen, is an excellent univallate example, the stone rampart here being faced with large orthostats and accompanied by a U-shaped rock-cut ditch with a small counterscarp on its outer lip. The builders of these cliff-top forts often faced

Plate 6.1 The promontory fort of Gurnard's Head, west Cornwall. The Iron Age defences crossed the narrow neck of land in the middle ground.

the problem of cutting through hard rock, though the quarried material could then be used to construct a solid rampart. Multivallate forts are common, several of them obviously works of more than one period. This is true of The Rumps, St Minver, where three phases of building are evident in the three ramparts (Brooks 1974). The works cutting off the inhospitable promontory of Gurnard's Head (Gordon 1940) are similarly complex. The innermost rampart here had a vertical front and a stepped back providing a platform or protected walkway, the whole presenting a more carefully designed defensive arrangement than was normal. At Trevelgue, four closely set ramparts closed off the narrow neck of the large promontory, certainly indicating several stages of defensive building. An outer annexe is plainly a further late addition to the fort. Exceptionally, there are also defences which are designed to ward off an approach from the sea, though these are not certainly Iron Age in date.

Some of the coastal forts are very large by south-western standards. Among these are Dodman Point, near Gorran Haven, Hillsborough near Ilfracombe and Wind Hill above Lynmouth. The last-named is probably the largest, a massive bank and ditch cutting off a wedge-shaped bloc of land 52 ha (150 acres) in area between the sea-cliffs and the steep gorge of the East

Lyn river. Its Iron Age date has been doubted, but for no good reason. It seems likely to have been the stronghold of a ruler with some pretensions to authority and may thus have been one of the few centres of political power which can be discerned in the south-western Iron Age. The strongly defended bivallate fort at Hillsborough may be another and it may be significant that both of these lie immediately adjacent to good harbours, as does Trevelgue.

Promontory forts also exist on Scilly, the best known being the Giant's Castle on the eastern side of St Mary's, a small work defined by two granite walls and ditches (Borlase 1756: 11). The northern tip of Bryher, Shipman Head, is also cut off by a substantial wall of granite blocks in which a gate with guard-chamber is still visible. Another imposing work lies on Burnt Hill, St Martin's. This is a roughly rectangular fort bounded by steep cliffs and with a stout stone wall on the landward side. Within are indications of stone houses. The date of these Scillonian enclosures is unknown and we may not assume that their occupation was limited to the conventional Iron Age. They could well have served as the centres of communities at any date from the first millennium BC to the Middle Ages.

There has been so little excavation in the interior of hill-forts that information on overall planning and even on the types of structures is scarce and fragmentary. As is to be expected, round houses are widespread, the excavated instances being rather small by the standards of Wessex. Square buildings of the kind often referred to as granaries appear at Castle Dore (Radford 1951: 65–6) and no doubt elsewhere. Rectangular structures of larger size have not yet been identified, unless we include a sub-rectangular building at Blackbury Castle (Young and Richardson 1955: 52–3). All this amounts to a very modest sum of evidence. Some fort-interiors seem not to have been densely built up. At Hembury a large area near the northern end of the enclosure was free of huts and other features throughout the life of the fort (Todd 1984: 261). On one point the evidence is unequivocal. The large storage-pits familiar from Iron Age settlements in Wessex do not appear in the south-western hill-forts, even in the east of the region. No large pits existed at Hembury, nor apparently at Blackbury, Killibury or Castle Dore. Large-scale storage of grain was evidently not practised by these communities, unless it was in above-ground structures. The predominantly pastoral economy was still the basis of subsistence in the later Iron Age, as a further range of Iron Age sites strongly suggests.

Much commoner and more widespread than hill-forts proper are enclosures of various kinds which are sited on hill-slopes or occasionally on flat ground. These were first brought to attention by Lady Fox's studies of them and similar works in South Wales (Fox, A. 1952a). The characteristic form of these earthworks is a small enclosure, usually roughly circular or sub-rectangular, and less than 3 ha in area, with widely spaced outer works, sometimes completely surrounding the inner enclosure, in others only in part. Additional short lengths of earthwork might mark off other spaces farther

165

out. These sites are clearly not in the usual sense defensive, as hill-top positions are almost invariably eschewed, and they must be regarded as serving purposes which were essentially different from those of hill-forts. Apart from their situation on slopes, these enclosures almost invariably lie close to an abundant water supply. In not a few cases the earthworks run down to a stream or a river.

Hill-slope enclosures are found in most parts of the peninsula but are commonest in west and north Devon, and in east and central Cornwall. Only in the far west of Cornwall do they appear not to have been recorded. Although most are in essence a single enclosure with subsidiary spaces defined by annexing banks, outworks or cross-banks, a number consist of a series of fully concentric earthworks, covering in all up to 8 ha or more (about 20 acres). The most elaborate of these multiple enclosures are Clovelly Dykes above Bideford Bay and Milber Down behind Torbay. Only Milber Down of this important group of sites has been excavated. Here a sub-rectangular central enclosure (1.25 ha: 3 acres) is surrounded by two further dump ramparts, the intervening spaces being 25–30 m across. A smaller earthwork defined a broader tract of ground to the south, and possibly also to the north, of the enclosures, swinging round towards the main entrance to form the bounds to a sunken entrance-way. Limited excavation in the interior of the central enclosure revealed the existence of buildings but none was completely revealed. Occupation began in the later Iron Age and continued at least into the early Roman period, a useful indication that such works might continue in use beyond the Roman conquest (Fox, Radford and Shorter 1949–50).

The most imposing of the multiple enclosure works is Clovelly Dykes, lying on level ground above the cliffs of the Hartland peninsula, a complex work which has undergone two or three major enlargements. The original core was a sub-rectangular enclosure with two widely spaced surrounding banks. Another enclosure was subsequently added to the eastern and southern sides, perhaps in two stages, and finally two narrow rectilinear blocs were attached to the western side. In its ultimate form the whole site covered 8 ha (19.2 acres).

Large or small, the design of these works has been influenced by economic not defensive requirements. The widely spaced ramparts were intended to provide safe accommodation, not to repel attackers. As Lady Fox argued thirty years ago, the siting and layout of these sites accord wholly with the needs of pastoral farmers, the outer enclosures being intended to house cattle and other livestock, particularly perhaps in the winter season (Fox, A. 1952a: 18–20). The central enclosure, often no bigger than a round, presumably housed the main dwellings and other structures for human use. As in the second millennium BC, Dumnonian farmers were above all else pastoralists and they were to remain so for centuries to come.

Several hill-slope enclosures have linear earthworks in their vicinity, often crossing a spur or watershed or otherwise linking valleys or areas of low ground. These works have attracted surprisingly little attention, despite the fact that they are clearly related to similar earthworks on the Downland of southern England (Bradley 1971). The best examples are those close to the hill-forts of Largin Castle, Braddock, and Hall Rings, Pelynt, in Cornwall, but they are recorded also in the east of the region, for example near Blackbury Castle and below Belbury, near Ottery St Mary. The earthwork south of Largin Castle illustrates the type admirably, crossing a high knoll and linking the headwaters of two small streams flowing into the Fowey. A roughly rectangular block of land was thus defined, about 65 ha (156 acres) in area, within which lay the hill-slope enclosure, another linear earthwork and a part-enclosure on the upper slope. A similar disposition of linear earthwork and hill-slope enclosure is evident at Hall Rings, Pelynt, again resulting in the enclosure of a sizeable area of land (about 50 ha, 120 acres). Some of these outer works may have been complete enclosures or nearly so, as at Pencarrow, Egloshayle.

So few hill-forts have been extensively examined that conclusions on the history of their occupation, in the Iron Age and later, must be limited. As in Wessex, there may have been a move away from hill-top settlement in the later Iron Age. Hembury seems to have been abandoned by the first century BC and the same may be true of Blackbury Castle and Castle Dore. But at least some enclosed sites continued in use down to the Roman conquest and perhaps beyond, for instance The Rumps, Milber Down and Caerloggas. No uniform picture emerges nor should one be expected.

In the fragmented south-western landscape it is not surprising that there was so little conducement to political centralization or even association. The overall picture of later prehistoric settlement is one of a multitude of small fiefdoms, of which the hill-forts were the centres of power and the hill-slope enclosures the main repositories of wealth. No large central place is known to have developed, along the lines of the great oppida of other parts of Britain. No coinage was issued by any ruler or dynasty to proclaim authority or reward allegiance. Any unity that existed must have been expressed in intangibles. Like most, if not all, the tribes of southern Britain, the people who came to be called the Dumnonii were in all probability an amalgam of several groupings of varying size and significance. Some of these may be faintly distinguishable in the archaeological record (for example in west Cornwall), but none can be reconstructed with real confidence. We may fairly believe that before the Roman conquest unity did not become even a formal reality.

The heterogeneous enclosed settlements commonly called 'rounds' multiplied in the later first millennium, especially in Cornwall and west Devon, and must represent a major phase of internal colonization of the region in that period. It is possible that this type of enclosed familial homestead or small nucleated settlement had its origins in the later Bronze Age, though this is not demonstrable on the available evidence. The most

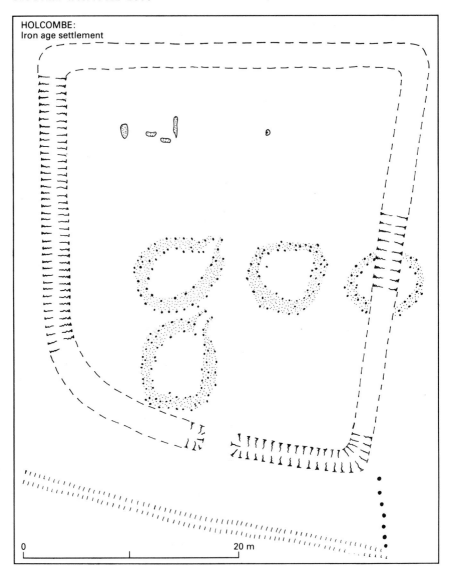

Figure 6.6   Rectilinear enclosure at Holcombe

fully examined rounds date from after 200 BC in origin and extend well into the Roman period. They are thus dealt with more fully in a succeeding chapter (below, p. 223). In central and east Devon, rectilinear or sub-rectangular enclosures seem to have been common features of the later Iron Age landscape and are to be regarded as a phenomenon broadly comparable with rounds: these too appear to continue until well after the Roman conquest.

About open settlements we are less well informed, but they certainly

0   50 m

Figure 6.7   Courtyard houses and fields at Bosullow Trehyllys

existed, for instance in west Cornwall, and no doubt in other parts of the region. The most striking representative of these is the courtyard-house, now known only in the Land's End peninsula, though a small number of related structures are recorded in Scilly. Within the Land's End, the majority of surviving examples lie on the high ground and on the slopes which fall to the cliffs between Zennor and Morvah. Further south, in St Just and Sancreed they are much sparser and hardly any are known around Sennen. And they appear to be absent from the slopes behind St Ives. The building type is best known from the excavated settlements at Carn Euny and Chysauster but

Plate 6.2 A courtyard house at Chysauster, west Cornwall. The central courtyard, crossed by drainage channels, is surrounded by living quarters, stalling and other chambers.

more typical is the isolated courtyard-house or small group, often with other structures associated with it, set within a system of fields.

The courtyard-house is usually roughly oval in plan, its surrounding wall being a massive structure, commonly 2 m or 3 m thick, with well-built faces of granite retaining a mass of rubble and earth. The whole may measure up to 35 m on its long axis. More commonly it is between 15 m and 25 m in length. A single entrance passageway, flanked by upright jambs and closed by a timber gate, gave access into a central courtyard, almost certainly unroofed and in some cases partly paved. Around this central space a varying number of rooms was arranged, often three or four, though up to seven are known in a few examples. Opposite the entrance there was most commonly a large, round room, often containing a hearth and clearly serving as the main dwelling area. In some instances the floor of this chamber is raised above the level of the courtyard, presumably to provide some protection against damp and dirt. A small number also have a doorway allowing passage through the outer wall without entering the courtyard. On one side of the court, usually to the right at the main entrance, lay a narrow rectilinear chamber and opposite this a long recess on the outer wall. The former would be well suited to a work-place and store, the latter perhaps as a small animal-pen. Other small rooms, usually circular or oval, were set in the thickness of the

170

surrounding wall. These elements in the plan do not occur in all courtyard-houses, but they are present in a sufficient number of examples to prove that they served a set of functions that were common to the majority of such settlements. The better preserved houses reveal a high standard of building. The masonry in the walls is often well finished, given the nature of the building material, angles are neatly turned, paving is carefully laid and drainage often provided. The door or gate at the main entrance was often hinged to a pivot which rested in a stone socket like those found in Roman buildings. The overall impression gained is of a stoutly built house designed for occupation by a nuclear family numbering up to about six.

Although best known in groups like those at Chysauster, Carn Euny and Bosullow, most of the courtyard houses either stand alone in the landscape or form small groups of not more than three. Most of the sixty or so known examples lie in the open, a few within a round or other enclosure, for example, Goldherring and Porthmeor. They are normally set within their own field-systems and several have small terraces immediately outside them, perhaps gardens or paddocks. The origins of courtyard-houses have not yet been adequately explored. None has yet produced any clear sign of occupation in the mid-first millennium. Like so much else in the south-western Iron Age, they appear to belong to that period after 200 BC when so many changes were wrought in settlement on the land and in material culture.

Plate 6.3 A courtyard house within a round at Goldherring, west Cornwall, late Iron Age and Roman in date.

The origin of the building-type is likewise obscure, but it is unlikely to have sprung into being fully developed. An example on Scilly, at Halangy Down (St Mary's) grew out of a number of structures loosely disposed around a central space (Ashbee 1974: 187–93) and gradually unified by progressive building. This may also have been true of some of the Cornish houses, though few have been recently examined. Those at Carn Euny were certainly occupied over a lengthy period in which many modifications were made (Christie 1978: 349). The building of these distinctive dwellings continued well into the Roman period, to which indeed the larger groups belong. As late as the second and third centuries AD new structures on this plan were still being erected, at Chysauster and Porthmeor (Hencken 1933a: 266; Hirst 1936: 74–6).

Fogous

The underground structures of west Cornwall known as *fogous* comprise a type of monument unknown in other parts of southern Britain. Since the days of William Borlase there has been speculation, not always informed or reasonable, about their date and purpose, but even now it cannot be claimed that their place in prehistoric settlement is fully understood. About their approximate chronology there is now a measure of certainty. They were built in the later first millennium BC and probably continued in use until well into the Roman period, perhaps in some cases until later. Their physical relationship with various forms of settlement can also be defined within broad limits. With the results of several recent excavations before us, we can be somewhat clearer about their original function. But there is still much that we do not know, for example about the structural history of the more complex monuments, or about the full economic significance of these structures as a class.

Fogou, or its now superseded variants *googoo*, *vouga*, *hugo* and *oogo*, means 'cave', 'a place of concealment'. Borlase called *fogous*, 'hiding-places, dens or caves'. They were, then, normally wholly or mainly subterranean structures, though at least one surviving example was built on the surface. Most take the form of a passage of varying length lined with drystone walling and roofed by large slabs. The simplest of all are short lengths of underground passage, little more than a recess, as at Chysauster. But the range of plans is wide and it is clear that the builders were not constrained to follow any particular design. More than one passage may be provided, a separate chamber may be included, the number of entrances might vary. There is also considerable variation in the relation of *fogous* to settlements, but all those which can still be examined or for which adequate documentation exists lie in or close to

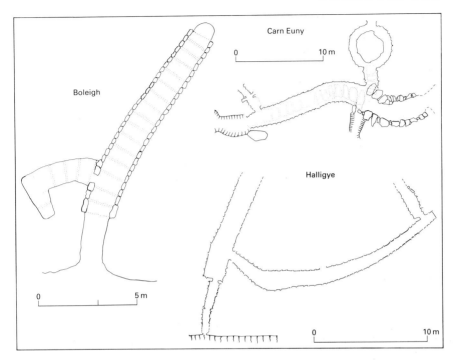

Figure 6.8   Plans of *fogous*

sizeable settlements. There is little doubt that these structures are to be re-garded as a phenomenon peculiar to west Cornwall, most of the known instances lying in the Land's End peninsula. The granite upland of central and east Cornwall contain no certain *fogous*, the reported structure at Altarnun on Bodmin Moor being very dubious (Clark 1961: 118) and none is recorded in Scilly.

For long the most striking of underground structures has been the circu-lar corbelled chamber and associated passages in the settlement at Carn Euny. Excavation has shown that the circular chamber and its entrance passage were the first to be constructed, followed by the long, curving passage which was subsequently given an imposing entrance lobby at the east end. The corbelled chamber is a reminder of how much skilful building in large blocks has been lost to us. It had been built in a pit and in its ultimate form was 4.5 m in diameter at the base and 2.4 m high. The main passage, over 20 m long, 2 m high and 1.8 m wide, is another imposing structure, built with considerable confidence in a mixture of large blocks and smaller rubble. The dating of these various elements is not straightforward. A radiocarbon estimate centred on the fifth century BC was obtained from a sample taken from the area of the *fogou*, but there is no particular reason to link this with the construction of the circular chamber as has been done in the excavation report (Christie 1978:

173

331). Nor is a single estimate admissible evidence for anything. We are on somewhat safer ground with the long passage. Here, sealed deposits contained pottery of the second and first century BC, and further yielded a radiocarbon estimate centred on the same period.

Another complex and imposing structure is the *fogou* at Halligye, Trelo-warren. This lies within an enclosure, one of its exits giving on to the surrounding ditch. Originally it consisted of a broad, straight passage, about 2 m wide, with a narrower curving gallery leading off from it at about the halfway point. Later, the access to the ditch was considerably narrowed, the curving gallery lengthened and a short blind passage or 'creep' added to it. The entrance within the settlement must have been at the south end of the straight passage. Little was found within the *fogou*, probably because of earlier clearance. Alterations were still being made to the structure in the late Iron Age and possibly later still. In the Roman period it may have been deliberately blocked up and the enclosure ditch filled in (Startin 1982).

Alongside these elaborate structures there existed much simpler *fogous*, often consisting of a single passage lined and covered with stone, entered from one end and provided with a small exit at or near the other. Among these are the *fogous* at Trewardreva in Constantine parish, Chysauster and Boleigh in St Buryan. There is no need to suppose that these structures of simple plan are necessarily earlier than their complex relatives. Numbers of the smaller *fogous* have probably been destroyed by later stone-robbing, the large cap-stones being a particular attraction. *Fogous* which stood on the surface or projected well above it, as in the case at Porthmeor, will have been particularly vulnerable in this respect. Other above-ground buildings may once have existed which were functionally related to *fogous*. The famous 'beehive-hut' at Bosporthennis may be an aberrant member of the same class of buildings (Lukis 1885: Pl. XXXIX).

Before considering the purpose of *fogous*, it must be recalled that wholly or partly subterranean structures are found in other parts of western Britain and France. Souterrains, as the genus is commonly termed, are well represented in various forms in northern and western Ireland, in northern and eastern Scotland and in western Brittany, but not in Wales or north-western England (Thomas 1972). Although variant functions may be expected over this broad geographical spread, most of these structures are essentially cellars associated with individual houses and settlements. So intimate is that connection that a function related to daily life seems the most likely explanation. Few would now agree with Hencken (1932: 139) that they were temporary refuges or bolt-holes: for that they could scarcely have been worse designed. Nor do the associated finds suggest that they served as places for the disposal of the dead in the longer or shorter term, or as sites of ritual observance. The carved figure holding a spear and a snake (if that is what it is) on an entrance jamb of the Boleigh *fogou* is not convincing evidence for use as a sacred place, nor is the figure likely to be of Iron Age. More plausibly, these underground chambers and passages served a variety of purposes as store-places, the larger instances being communally built and maintained. Preserving an even temperature throughout the year, they could have housed large quantities of dried and salted meat, containers of grain, fruits and vegetables, cheese, milk and other forms of drink. At least one *fogou* (Trewardreva) contained ash-pits in which gulls' eggs might have been preserved (Polwhele 1793–1806: II, 129). Subterranean storage for food-stuffs ('hulls') are found in Cornwall much later, even down to the present century, and before refrigeration they provided the only efficient means of bulk-storage of food over months or even years.

If interpreted in this way, *fogous* are not to be seen as any kind of cultural indicator and links with other regions in which souterrains occur need not be postulated. More important for our purpose, they point to the maintenance of a sizeable surplus of food and other commodities, at least by some communities, which in its way is comparable with the bulk storage practised by Iron Age communities in other parts of southern Britain. Although they are a striking response to peculiar local needs, *fogous* are thus firmly to be accommodated within the framework of the wider Celtic Iron Age economy.

Burial

Unlike most areas of southern Britain, burials of later Iron Age date are well recorded in the South West. The datable graves, however, begin in the second century BC, thus leaving a gap of some five hundred years between the later Bronze Age burials and the Iron Age graves, almost invariably inhumations in cists. Once established, the rite of extended inhumation in a stone-lined grave persisted for many centuries in the peninsula and in Scilly. In the late- and post-Roman period this was still the most prevalent burial form (Whimster 1981: 60–74).

Cemeteries of Iron Age burials placed in stone cists are well attested in Cornwall, at Harlyn Bay, near Padstow, and Trelan Bahow, St Keverne, and in west Devon at Stamford Hill, Plymouth, though not yet in any other part of Devonshire. The Harlyn Bay cemetery is the best known of these and is often taken to be typical of later first millennium BC cemeteries (Bullen 1912; Whimster 1977). The excavations of 1900–5 on this site, on a broad, sandy bay backed by a low cliff, revealed over 130 inhumation burials, originally ascribed to the Neolithic. The great majority of the graves had been lined and covered with slabs of stone. Deviation from the norm of a single inhumation in a cist was very rare, the most notable exception being a circular grave divided

175

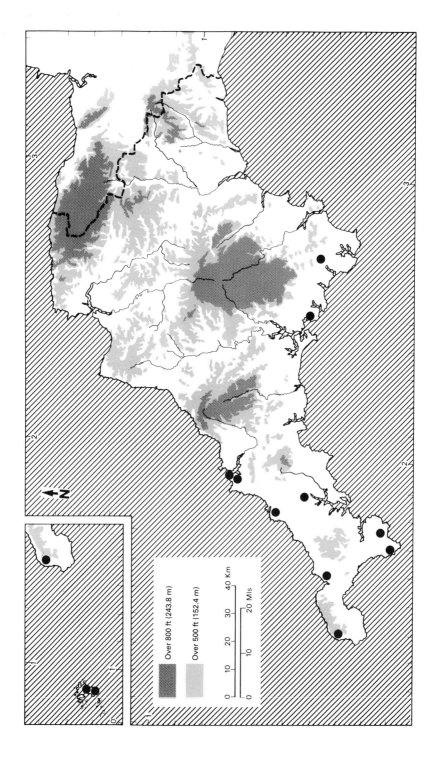

Figure 6.9 Iron Age cist cemeteries

by a central partition, which contained two crouched adult skeletons and an infant in one compartment, and a further adult in the other. Four other burials contained two skeletons, a phenomenon also recorded in La Tène cemeteries in France and in east Yorkshire. Interments had evidently been made over a considerable period, for some of the earlier burials had been disturbed or even destroyed by later depositions, notwithstanding the fact that a degree of order is evident in the alignment of more than half of the recorded graves in rows running from north to south. It is possible that the remains of disturbed burials had been collected together in antiquity and placed in a charnel-pit specially dug for the purpose. Another interesting feature of the cemetery is the presence of two pits containing skulls but no other bones. These could represent careful reburial of skulls disturbed by later grave-digging, or the detachment of skulls before burial in some apotropaic rite, or even the ritual burial of battle-trophies.

Most of the Harlyn Bay burials were unaccompanied by goods. Regrettably, the record of furnished graves is imperfect and an unknown number of objects are now dispersed or have no secure provenance. This is all the more unfortunate as certain of the surviving items are of great interest. The most famous are two very similar, though not identical, disc-footed bronze brooches with a high, arched bow. A third object, of iron and now badly corroded, may be a third specimen (Whimster 1977, 77). In Britain these distinctive objects are matched only by a pair from Mount Batten, Plymouth, and we must turn to the Atlantic coastlands of Europe, to Spain and to south-western France, to find their place of origin. The type was current in later Hallstatt cemeteries in Aquitaine in the sixth and fifth centuries BC. In Spain, these brooches are found later, in the fourth and third centuries and it is probable that the examples in south-western England were derived from this source at that later date. The other metal objects include a bronze ring-headed pin and another specimen in iron, both of these well known in the middle and later Iron Age in southern Britain, bracelets of Kimmeridge shale and a glass bead. After the imported brooches, the most interesting objects are a series of polished slate artifacts, clearly of local manufacture and revealing ingenious use of a somewhat un-promising raw material. These included two broad needles, an awl and a broad knife with a curved edge. All could have been used in the working of leather or skins. No pottery vessels were certainly found in the graves, the sherds reported on by the early excavators apparently coming from a rubbish dump of late Iron Age or early Roman date to the south of the cemetery.

It cannot be claimed that the Harlyn Bay cemetery can be closely dated on the evidence at present available. Beginning in the fourth or third century BC, it may have continued in use until the late Iron Age or even into the Roman period, though no Roman object was certainly found in a grave. Sadly, no search has yet been made for the contemporary settlement which cannot be far away. More recent excavation has revealed part of a substantial circular building with an outer wall in stone, but there are reasons for seeing this as a non-domestic, possibly mortuary structure, and in any case it antedates the cemetery, perhaps by an appreciable margin.

Other cemeteries of long cists have been recorded in west Cornwall and, although the evidence of date is very poor, the cumulative impression is that they belong to the second half of the first millennium BC and to the earlier Roman Iron Age. Closely related burials are well known on Scilly during the same period. Only 3 km north-east of Harlyn Bay a group of cist-graves was found at Trevone in 1848 (Dudley and Jope 1965). These may have fallen into two distinct chronological groups separated by an interval in which blown sand had covered the earlier graves. Records of the cemetery are very poor, but one grave contained, as well as shale and iron bracelets, two La Tene II brooches of the third or second century BC, imported from southern Britain. Similar grave-forms are in evidence from the cemetery at Trelan Bahow in the Lizard peninsula, and here the grave-goods clearly prove that interments of this type continued into the early Roman period. One richly furnished grave contained a decorated bronze mirror of the first century AD, a La Tène III Nauheim-derived brooch, several bronze rings and glass beads. A number of other cist-burials of the later Iron Age confirm that this form of interment was widespread in Cornwall and extended into west Devon. It has not yet been recorded in north and east Devon, nor, with a solitary exception at Woodleigh near Kingsbridge, in the South Hams.

The most striking of Iron Age burials in Devon are those recorded on Stamford Hill, Plymouth, overlooking Plymouth Sound to one side and the Cattewater to the other, at the base of the Mount Batten promontory. These discoveries were made during the construction of Stamford Fort in 1865 and the circumstances were not ideal for careful record of what was found (Spence Bate 1866). The graves had been dug deep into the limestone rock, up to $1\frac{1}{2}$ m in some cases. The number of burials encountered cannot be estimated but it seems certain that the cemetery was large and parts of it may remain intact. Several grave-pits had intruded upon others, as though the cemetery had long continued in use. The grave-goods date from the very end of the Iron Age and the early years of the Roman period, and they include several notable items, among them a decorated bronze mirror and the handles of two others, a La Tène bracelet, several late La Tène brooches and a range of imported Roman pottery otherwise rare in the South West. The mirror is not the finest product of the western school of metalworkers which was responsible for the magnificent mirrors from Birdlip and Holcombe, but it is a luxury item only likely to come the way of a member of a wealthy community. It is worthy of note that the only other late Iron Age decorated mirror in the South West came from the similar inhumation cemetery at Trelan Bahow.

It is unfortunate that the funerary evidence from Devon is so limited. Among other matters, it would be interesting to know whether or not the small cemeteries of crouched inhumations so well known in south Dorset extended westwards, or whether some local burial tradition prevailed west of the Axe.

Given the highly acidic character of much of Devonshire soils, the chances for early solution of the problem seem remote.

Cist-grave cemeteries of a similar kind occur at several locations in the Isles of Scilly. The most completely examined are three on St Mary's at Porth Cressa and Poynter's Garden (Ashbee 1974: 120–47). Although the Scillonian cists are not the carefully constructed rectangular graves found at Harlyn Bay, the burial site is in other respects comparable. The graves on Scilly were usually much more roughly built boulder-lined cists, often sub-rectangular or even rounded in plan, and covered with a number of rough blocks or natural boulders. Occasionally a more massive chamber was constructed, as in the case of two graves at Porth Cressa. Contracted inhumation seems to have been the common, perhaps the normal, rite on Scilly, though skeletal remains are usually poorly preserved. In three of the Porth Cressa graves, two brooches accompanied the corpse, in another grave a single brooch. Two further graves each contained a brooch and a pot, one of these also having a glass bead. The appearance of brooches in all six of the furnished burials suggests that they had played a special role in the funerary ritual, perhaps holding together a shroud. The date suggested by these brooches, and with less precision by the two pottery vessels, is the first century AD, though of course the depositions could have been made later. The burials at nearby Poynter's Garden were similar in type and the few items of grave-furniture suggest that they were contemporary with Porth Cressa and both are to be related to settlements close by.

Other Scillonian cists indicate that this form of inhumation was widespread on the Isles and was probably normal for the Scillonian Iron Age from at least the first century BC until well into the Roman period. Certainly, no contemporary cremations seem to have been recorded.

Material Culture

Reference has already been made to the scarcity of early Iron Age pottery. For the middle and later Iron Age, the available material is relatively abundant and of great variety. Well excavated assemblages, however, are still few and in consequence dating presents many problems for all the known wares. What has already emerged is the existence of a number of regional groupings, partly evident in the forms and decoration, partly in the material composition of certain wares, especially the decorated vessels best known from Glastonbury and Meare and often designated inadequately 'Glastonbury ware'. More such groupings remain to be defined by further study.

The pottery of the period *c.* 400 to 200 is characterized by very simple forms, usually with no decoration or with ornament simply impressed by the thumb or a stick. The forms are so elementary that any attempt to see them as representing a distinct unit in cultural terms is gratuitous. They are found all over the region, for example at Blackbury Castle (Young and Richardson 1955: fig. 8), Hembury (unpublished), The Rumps (Brooks 1974: fig. 32), Carn Euny (Christie 1978: figs 53 and 54), Carvossa (unpublished) and Chysauster (Hencken 1933a, fig. 9). These look like locally produced wares and certainly those from Hembury and Blackbury Castle were made from the Greensand clays of east Devon. Alongside these plain vessels, and probably overlapping in date, there are more refined forms with spare, incised ornament. These have often been confused with the elaborately ornamented 'Glastonbury ware' types, and indeed their forms are similar. But a distinction is worth preserving between the two, particularly as the former group may begin at an earlier date.

The introduction of vessels with distinctive curvilinear decoration, possibly from Somerset, has been variously dated, to 400 BC, 150 or as late as 100. Scarcely any real evidence of absolute date exists. The radiocarbon and dendrochronological estimates obtained at Meare in Somerset suggest that the decorated wares were current by about 200 or 150 at the latest, but they do not tell us when they first appeared (Orme, Coles and Sturdy 1979). A date in the third or even in the fourth century cannot be excluded, though an origin before about 350 seems unlikely on present evidence. Localized production of these handsome vessels is certain, it having been demonstrated by Peacock (1969b) that at least six (and probably more) distinct groups can be identified on the basis of their constituent clays. One of these (Peacock's Group 1) is represented widely in Cornwall and south Devon, and two other groups (5 and 6) seem to have their origin in the Permian clays of the Exe valley and east Devon (Peacock 1969b: 43, fig. 2). There seems little doubt that a substantial proportion of these wares was produced by specialized, centralized workshops, relying on a limited but interchangeable series of curvilinear motifs. The vessels are often very well made and carefully finished, frequently with burnishing. The use of a turntable or a slow wheel seems likely, though not wholly certain. A general similarity with the decorated La Tène wares of Armorica has often been remarked, but apart from a general kinship in artistic design there is nothing to indicate a close connection. Armorican pottery occurs in the South West in very small quantities and it appears to have had little or no influence on the decoration of locally produced wares. The imported vessels bear stamped ornament, probably produced by a wooden or bone die, giving them a curiously Anglo-Saxon air. The Cornish instances include two sherds from Carn Euny (Christie 1978), and single occurrences at Porthmeor (Hirst 1936: Fig. 6, VII, 1), Trevelgue and Halligye (both unpublished). The closest analogies are found in Finistere and the Côtes-du-Nord, notably at Le Miniou and Pembrat-Vihan.

The decorated vessels continued to be produced into the first century BC but may have come to an end before AD 1. Certainly there is not yet any indication that they were still current at the time of the Roman conquest. At

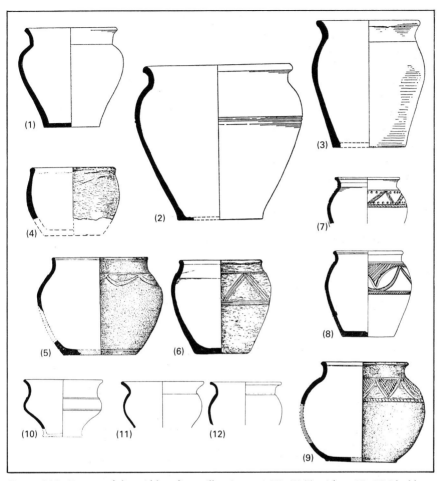

Figure 6.10 Pottery of the mid-late first millennium BC: (1)–(3) Trevisker; (4)–(6) Blackbury Castle; (7)–(8) Caerloggas, St Mawgan; (9) Blackbury Castle; (10)–(12) Caerloggas, St Mawgan

some date between 50 BC and AD 40, probably in the later first century BC, a distinctive series of cordoned vessels appeared in the South West, generically related to material found in northern France but representing a regional offshoot. The principal forms are tall jars with cordons on the shoulder and upper body, often of a size suitable for storage. They are usually very well made, probably on a wheel, and are often highly burnished or smoothed on the outside. More rarely there occur cordoned bowls with elegant S-shaped profiles, along with small carinated jars, these certainly wheel-turned. Such vessels are not found at Glastonbury and Meare, or at Maiden Castle and Hod Hill, though there are related forms at Hengistbury Head which might suggest that the ultimate models were Gaulish (Bushe-Fox 1915, Pl. XVII, 2; Cunliffe 1978: 46, fig. 21).

181

Surprisingly little pottery reached Devon and Cornwall from the late Iron Age production centres in Dorset. The 'Durotrigian' vessels at Mount Batten, Hembury and Carvossa are reasonably certainly imports of the early Roman period. A little may have been introduced before the Conquest, but the wares never appear as a major component of the pottery on any site before AD 50.

Fine metalwork of the later Iron Age is more common in the South West than is often appreciated. One of the finest of all the decorated mirrors was found at Holcombe in east Devon, in an otherwise undistinguished settlement

Figure 6.11 Iron Age mirror from Holcombe

(Pollard 1974: 70), while two others came from cemeteries at Stamford Hill and Trelan Bahow in the Lizard (above, p. 175). The Holcombe mirror is related technically to the most accomplished pieces in the mirror series, those from Birdlip and Desborough in particular (Fox 1973: 27–8), which may be dated to the years AD 10–30. There is other metalwork which shows similar motifs and styles of engraving from Somerset (notably the Polden hoard and the Meare scabbard-mount), and in Dorset (the Verne mirror and the Portland collar), all of these plainly indicating the activity of a group of craftsmen in the West Country in the decades immediately before the Roman conquest. The motifs on the Stamford Hill mirror bring it into the same series of objects, though its workmanship is not of the highest quality. The Trelan Bahow piece is decidedly inferior and may be of later date, perhaps of the period 30–50.

A striking group of heavy 'collars' or rings occurs over broadly the same area, one representative being found in Cornwall, at Trenoweth (St Stephen in Brannel). This is an extraordinarily complex object, with a core of lead-tin alloy, a decorated front-plate of brass (copper, tin, lead and zinc) and a back-plate of bronze (Megaw 1967). The use of brass may suggest that this piece is of Roman date but this is not beyond doubt. The metallic composition of the Trenoweth collar raises once more the question: to what extent do these fine objects reflect external interest in the metal resources of the region, rather than exploitation by skilled local craftsmen. There is little sign of any tradition of expertise in the working of bronze and the precious metals over the previous five centuries and there is a strong probability that the smiths responsible for these objects had been imported or that the pieces themselves had been acquired from farther east.

The three other late Iron Age bronzes complete the survey. One is a shallow bowl with rounded base from Rose Ash in north Devon (Fox 1961c). A single ring for suspension had been held on a loop formed by a stylized ox-head in cast bronze. This is so similar to another bowl found near Warbstow in north Cornwall that the two may be assigned to the same workshop (Smith, R. A. 1926). Both were found in peat bogs and may well represent votive deposits (above, p. 135). Finally, the shield-mount, if that is what it is, from Caerloggas (St Mawgan in Pyder) offers a rather developed design related to the mirror-backs. But this is still an elegantly fashioned piece and may be the work of one of the craftsmen who produced the mirrors (Fox, C. in Threipland 1956: 80–1: Fox, C. 1958: 115–16). The attractive and amusing small bronzes of a stag, a duck and other bird found in one of the ditches of the hill-slope enclosure at Milber Down may be from the *atelier* of a native smith, but are almost certainly of Roman date (Fox, Radford and Shorter 1948: 40–4).

Horse equipment and war gear are almost entirely unrecorded. The only major exception is the fine bronze horse-bit found somewhere in Devon and later acquired by General Pitt-Rivers for his collection at Farnham, now dispersed. This is an Irish type, two curved side-links being joined by an 8-shaped centrepiece. The rein-rings hang from small loops. This may fall late in the series of bridle-bits (Ward-Perkins 1939: 181), in the later first century BC or even early in the following century (Fox, A. 1959: 170–1).

Coins were not struck by the Iron Age leaders of the Dumnonii and Iron Age coinage is otherwise so rare in the South West that when it occurs in quantity on one site we are bound to question why. The only concentration of coinage is at Mount Batten, where we have already seen a wide range of imported goods. Either one or two hoards of coins was found here in the early nineteenth century, one containing Dobunnic gold and Armorican silver, the other silver pieces of the Dobunni, Coriosolites and Redones. Later finds of Armorican and other Gaulish coins from the site, along with issues of the Dobunni and Durotriges, confirm the influx of coinage from north-western Gaul, analogous to that into Hengistbury Head in Dorset but on a smaller scale. Both hoards, assuming there were two, date from about 30 BC, the revised date of the Le Catillon, Jersey, hoard (Sellwood 1983) and the other pieces recorded at Mount Batten could fall within a restricted date-range of about 30–1 BC. There are several ways of explaining the arrival of an exceptional number of such coins in a brief space of time. They may have been brought in by refugees. But there seems no reason for such a movement in the last third of the first century BC. They may represent a short burst of trading activity, or a short-lived search by Gaulish and/or Roman traders for particular supplies such as minerals or animal products. This seems much more likely and may be matched by the somewhat earlier appearance of Gallo-Belgic gold coins at Carn Brea (Borlase 1754: Pl. XXIII) and perhaps in another gold hoard buried near Penzance, to which we should add the hoard of north Italian silver drachms imitating Massiliote issues buried before or about 100 BC at Paul, also near Penzance, and a few other Gaulish pieces in the same neighbourhood (Allen 1961). A scatter of Dobunnic gold and silver staters, at Camborne, Plymouth and Bellever Tor on Dartmoor may reflect sporadic trading contacts, along with a few Durotrigian issues. The only hoard of such coins is known at Cotleigh Farm, near Axminster, close to Durotrigian territory itself.

Currency bars of iron, which occur generally in the south Midlands and in Wessex, put in one appearance in the South West, in a hoard of twelve such objects found on the slope below the small hill-fort on Holne Chase near Ashburton. These were possibly shorter and broader than the majority of bars, but all have now perished or been reduced to fragments (Amory 1906). It can hardly be a coincidence that this isolated hoard was buried close to the largest deposit of near-surface iron-stone in the Dartmoor area, while from close by came two Greek silver coins which also suggest that prospection for metals may have been taking place here (Fox 1950).

Wider Contacts

The trade in tin between the South West and the Mediterranean world is probably the most generally famous aspect of the protohistory of the peninsula, not least because the attractive tale of Greek and Phoenician prospectors opening up the sea-routes of Atlantic Europe was at once enhanced and given authority by Camden and others. The literary sources for the tin-trade have been exhaustively discussed and there is no need to go beyond the examination of certain crucial points here, though a complete understanding of this important subject is still some way off (Hencken 1932: 167–76; Rice Holmes 1907: 483–514; Hawkes 1977: 22–32; Mitchell 1983; Hawkes 1984). The literary sources are precious testimony to contact with the civilized world, but we must not forget that they were compiled several centuries after the trade in tin was first established and are usually repeating details drawn from a variety of sources of different dates and about which we know little or nothing. Thus, when one writer mentions the Cassiterides, the Tin Islands, we cannot be sure that he is referring to the same Tin Islands which occur in other sources, or even that reference is being made to a precisely located group of islands. As we will see, the Cassiterides are better studied under Myth than under Geography. By and large, Classical sources repeating snatches about trade with barbarians on the fringes of the known world, or beyond it, are about as reliable as second-hand references to American Indians in the sixteenth century by historians who had never sailed the Atlantic.

The severe limitations of the written evidence are most apparent when we try to penetrate the mystery of when the connection between the Mediterranean and south-western Britain was first established. The tradition of Phoenician or Carthaginian trade with Britain is deeply rooted in secondary writing on the subject, but the merest glance at the ancient sources is enough to reveal that this is myth, arising perhaps out of the smokescreen in which Phoenician captains enshrouded lucrative operations in any part of their world. At the root of the myth lie the Cassiterides, islands set in Ocean at the edge of the world. Herodotus, the first to mention them (III, 15), knew nothing of their location and was not even sure they existed. Five centuries later Strabo reported that the Phoenicians based at Gades (Cadiz) in southern Spain traded with the inhabitants of the Cassiterides, receiving from them tin, lead and animal skins in exchange for pottery, salt and bronze objects. But he offered no specific information about the location of the islands, noting only that the Phoenicians were anxious to conceal their whereabouts from rivals. Diodorus Siculus writing in the late first century BC and drawing on similar or related sources, mentions tin found in islands called the Cassiterides which lie in the Ocean opposite Spain. Interestingly, he does not say that they lay close to Britain. Indeed he makes a clear distinction between the tin they produced and the tin from Britain which he discussed elsewhere in significantly greater detail. Long after southern Britain had passed under Roman domination and when her coasts were well known to Roman fleet-commanders and traders, writers like Pliny and Ptolemy could still refer to the Cassiterides without saying anything about their position or their products. This is curious if the islands did lie close to Britain. Still more curious, and damning, Tacitus makes no mention of them at all. In other words, as Roman knowledge of the coastlands of north-western Europe increased, the Cassiterides melted away in the Atlantic mists whence they had been conjured. The islands were mythical, though the commodity that gave them a name was real enough. When, then, did merchants from the Mediterranean world begin their search for minerals in the South West? Might the brooches imported from western Gaul or Spain (above, p. 177) find their true context here?

There is nothing to support the romantic notion that Phoenician or Carthaginian entrepreneurs concerned themselves with any form of commerce in British waters. Their world embraced the secure harbours of the western Mediterranean. Forays beyond the Pillars of Hercules would be attempted by few captains, for the hazards of the Atlantic coasts were infinitely greater than the chances of finding profitable cargoes. These were not gambling men. Nor is there anything to indicate Greek exploration in western waters before the voyage of Pytheas in the later fourth century BC. The Greek pottery vessels from Halamanning in West Penwith are certainly modern imports, those from Teignmouth probably so, though they retain some shreds of credibility. Greek coins do, of course, occur in Devon and Cornwall, though none is to be dated as early as the fourth century (below, p. 214). There is little doubt that Pytheas was interested in deposits of tin and other minerals, but what he learnt of such deposits in the South West has not come down to us, unless he was the source of what Diodorus records (V, 38, 5; V, 22, 2). More probably this information derives from a later writer, perhaps Poseidonius. If that is so, then there is no secure testimony to Greek involvement in the tin trade before the second century BC. By then, Massaliote traders were certainly operating in western Gaulish waters, but reaching them not through the Straits of Gibraltar but overland *via* the Carcassonne Gap and the valley of the Garonne. A major target was the emporium at *Corbilo*, probably on the lower Loire or its estuary. In or about 150 BC, Scipio Aemilianus tried to find out what sea-crossings to Britain were in use by interrogating men of Massalia and Narbonne, entirely without success. 'None had an answer, none worth recording: so monstrous had been Pytheas's lies' (Strabo IV, 190). Some modern commentators have read much into this, seeing it as part of a jealous web of evasion which concealed the profitable route to Britain. Another explanation is possible: that there really was nothing to record because Pytheas had not been followed by others and no regular trade contact had resulted.

The absence of reliable information persisted until the middle of the first century BC (Caesar: IV, 20, 4), though at least one successful attempt was made to learn more about the tin route, by one Publius Crassus, probably the P.

Licinius Crassus who governed Further Spain in 96–3 BC. (A less likely candidate is the son of Crassus the triumvir, one of Caesar's officers in Gaul (Caesar: III, 7–11; Frere 1978: 43; Mitchell 1983: 82–3)). Crassus visited the 'Cassiterides', found that tin was easily accessible and the natives accommodating, and thus laid open the route to anyone who was prepared to follow him. It is probable that after Crassus's expedition, knowledge of the tin-deposits and the export of the metal did increase. The best known passage referring to British tin, that of Diodorus, clearly reflects a well informed source, possibly Publius Crassus himself (Mitchell 1983: 86–7), certainly someone who had been to Britain. Significantly the passage makes no mention of the Cassiterides. A new era had begun.

The inhabitants of the peninsula of Belerion, we read in Diodorus (V, 22), were remarkably civilized due to their frequent contacts with merchants from other lands. They extracted the tin, ground down the ore and smelted it into ingots shaped like *astragaloi* (knuckle-bones?). The ingots were then taken to an island called Ictis, which lay just off the coast of Britain and accessible to wagons at low tide. At this market the merchants bought the metal from the natives and transported it thence to Gaul and then overland on horseback for thirty days to the mouth of the Rhone. This circumstantial account clearly originated in the observation of an eye-witness and it must be accepted as an accurate statement of how the trade in tin was organized before the Roman conquest of Britain. It leaves one major question unanswered: where was Ictis?

Attempts to identify the site on the report of Diodorus, clear as it is, are bound to fail. This has not prevented several bold ventures, some better equipped than others, but all in vain. St Michael's Mount long held the field, understandably so being an island linked to the mainland and situated in a bay which offered safe anchorage (Hencken 1932: 176–8 for the earlier literature). But there is nothing to support the case, not even the relationship of the rock with the mainland, since this may have been very different two millennia ago. More recently Mount Batten has been proposed, but again this was probably not an island at the appropriate date. It does lie close to important tin deposits, but that is not enough (Cunliffe 1984; Hawkes 1984). There are other candidates, not least the largest island off the Cornish coast, St George's Island off the Looe estuary. This is now 1.5 km offshore but it was possible to reach it on foot until the seventeenth century at low water and the channel is still shallow. A bronze ingot has recently been found on a reef close to the island, but there is no other evidence for a trade in metals based here. None of these sites fits the bill at present and further search is fruitless until we know much more about changes in sea-level and the coasts in later prehistory. Much more important than the location of Ictis is the fact that it now appears clear that the traders whom ancient literary sources report as coming to the South West were following routes established long before, probably before 1000 BC, and they may have made for a number of trading places with a long history of overseas contact already behind them (above, p. 154).

These trade contacts with western Europe and ultimately with the Mediterranean world foreshadowed the advance of Roman power into Gaul in the first century BC and, a century later, into southern Britain. The co-operative inhabitants of the peninsula of Belerion were to be absorbed in the world-empire of Rome.

Chapter 7

The Conquering Power

Literary sources for the Roman conquest of southern Britain are sparse. For the conquest of the South West, they are non-existent. Much has been hung upon the famous abbreviated account by Suetonius of Vespasian's command of a legion in Britain in the invasion of AD 43 and immediately afterwards (Suetonius: 4, 1). But the thirty engagements with the Britons, and the subjection of two powerful tribes and more than twenty strongholds can hardly have involved the legate with the South West. At most, his operations, and perhaps those of his successor in the command of the Second Legion, were directed towards the reduction of the Durotriges of Dorset and south Somerset, and perhaps the Belgae of Hampshire and Wiltshire. Other literary sources report nothing of the Roman advance towards the South West or of the eventual conquest of the peninsula.

Despite, or perhaps because of, this lacuna in history, there has been a tendency for modern commentators on these early years of Roman Britain to assume too readily that the advance of the Roman army was a steady, uninterrupted progress towards the subjection of south and midland Britain, following the early successes of Aulus Plautius against the heirs of Cunobelin. Rapid campaigns through eastern England, across the midland plain and towards the South West carried Roman arms to the valleys of the Trent and Severn by AD 47, and did so without encountering serious opposition. The thrust towards the South West seemed to have been crowned with a conspicuous, early success, and one moreover which was documented in the archaeological record. Wheeler's discovery of a British war-cemetery at Maiden Castle (Wheeler 1943: 64–8) and Richmond's elucidation of a Roman siege at the hill-fort at Hod Hill, followed by the siting of a Roman fort within the prehistoric stronghold (Richmond 1968), gave welcome substance to the spare sentence of Suetonius. But, though Roman forces did penetrate lowland Britain with speed, there is no warrant at all for assuming that they were as quickly able to assume total control of the territory they have overrun. The siting of a fort housing a detachment of legionaries within the Iron Age hill-fort on Hod Hill has long suggested that the early Roman hold on this part of the

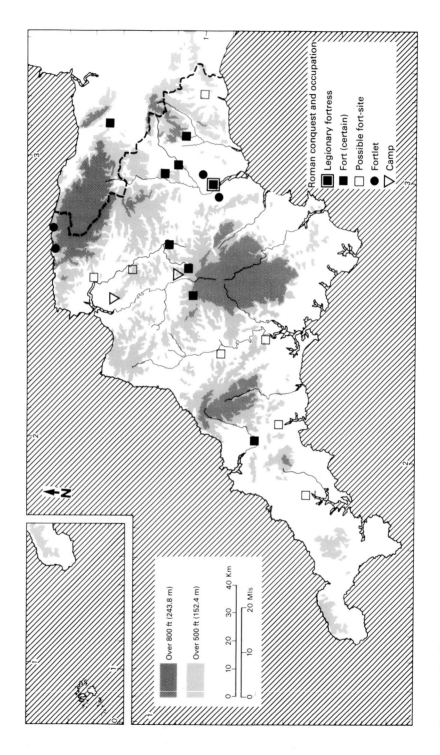

Legend (within figure):

Roman conquest and occupation
■ Legionary fortress (box outline)
■ Fort (certain)
□ Possible fort-site
● Fortlet
▽ Camp

Over 800 ft (243.8 m)
Over 500 ft (152.4 m)

0   10   20   30   40 Km
0   10   20 Mls

Figure 7.1 The Roman conquest and occupation

Durotrigian lands was tentative. Evidence from other hill-top sites in the same region supports the idea. The large hill-fort on Ham Hill in Somerset has produced a striking array of Roman military equipment, as well as quantities of mid- and late-first-century pottery (Webster 1958: 80–3). Within the hill-fort at South Cadbury in the same county, a group of military buildings was erected, perhaps in the late 50s, and there are clear indications here of a battle or a massacre at a somewhat later date (Alcock 1969: 35). Another hill-top site, at Waddon Hill near Beaminster in Dorset, was occupied by a fort about 50, this time within no prehistoric circuit of defences (Webster 1979). Finally, the powerful Iron Age fort at Hembury, near Honiton in Devon, had a sizeable Roman establishment set within its northern end (Todd 1984). The implications for our understanding of the course of the Roman conquest are considerable.

The excavations of 1930–35 on the Iron Age hill-fort at Hembury yielded significant clues to the site of another early military establishment (Liddell 1935: 153). Quantities of Roman pottery of pre-Flavian and early Flavian date, including *terra sigillata* and other imported wares, along with two coins of Claudius and a number of metalwork items were found in several parts of the site. But the most interesting discovery was made in a narrow cutting immediately inside the eastern rampart of the Iron Age fort, some 30 m south of the north-east gate. The corner of a rectangular timber building aligned east–west and a length of foundation-trench belonging to a second timber structure were located in this trench and identified by Miss Liddell as parts of late Iron Age buildings. The construction details, however, pointed clearly to an early Roman date (as did the associated finds) and hinted strongly at a military origin. Unfortunately, no large-scale examination of the interior of the hill-fort was undertaken so that no further information about these, and other, structures was obtained.

A new programme of excavation at Hembury, begun in 1980, quickly demonstrated that the hill-fort had indeed been taken over by the Roman army (Todd 1984). The northern end of the prehistoric stronghold had been adapted for military use and substantial timber buildings erected. As these are known at present, they include a courtyard building, probably a *fabrica*, and a narrow block which may have been a barrack. The total extent of these early Roman structures has not yet been defined, but it is worth note that a rectangular area of about 2.4 ha (6 acres) was available to the builders in the northern half of the hill-fort. It may be that such an area was indeed cut off by defences running across the ridge. The date of this occupation of the hill-top is at present fixed as *c.* 50–70, though these dates may prove to be too wide a bracket [1]. No evidence of Roman attack of the hill-fort has been recovered and the very small quantity of late Iron Age pottery from the site suggests that the site may have been vacant when the Roman army arrived. Both of the Iron Age gates appear to have been either rebuilt or substantially remodelled in the early Roman period. The evidence is particularly clear at the west gate, where a series of small, square posts appear to have been inserted into the remains of the earlier gate-foundations in order to revet the ends of the rampart on either side of an entrance some 4 m wide.

This clearly attested use of earlier fortifications on hill-tops implies that the first penetration into the region was made by an army which was not yet sure of its ground. Hill-tops like Hembury, Hod Hill and Ham Hill impose several difficulties on those who occupy them, not least that of maintaining an adequate supply of water. It seems unlikely that a fort would be established at Hembury by a commander who felt entirely in control of the military situation. Its occupation may have been brief, but the fact that it was thought necessary at all must warn us against an assumption that the Roman forces swept through this area without opposition. We do not yet know how the initial conquest was achieved, but the evidence from Hembury, along with that from the hill-forts further east, suggests that the task facing the army was not light.

West of Hembury and within clear view lies the valley of the Exe, an obvious strategic target for the early Roman thrust.

The Fortress of the Legion at Exeter

The existence of a legionary fortress at Exeter was finally demonstrated in 1971, when the remains of a fine Neronian bath-house – plainly of military origin – were located outside the west front of the Cathedral. Before this discovery, the remains of pre-Flavian timber structures appeared to point to the presence of a military establishment on the site, without providing any clear indication of its character and size (Fox 1952c: 1968). Another clue was afforded by Ptolemy's description of Britain. Relying principally upon first century source-material, but up-dating certain sections including the stations of legions, his list (II, 3, 3) placed the sixth legion at York and the twentieth at Chester, where indeed they were in the second century. The Second legion he located at *Isca Dumnoniorum*, which may be seen as a simple confusion with *Isca* (Caerleon), where the legion was based from the 70s. But the reason for the confusion was that the unit had earlier been stationed at the Dumnonian *Isca* and Ptolemy (or his source) had failed to carry out the up-dating correctly. Since the discovery of the legionary baths, excavation in several parts of the city has revealed other parts of the fortress and the outline of the plan is steadily emerging (Bidwell 1979: 3–66; 1980: 16–45; Henderson 1984).

The fortress lay on a spur between two narrow valleys. To the north-east the ground rose fairly steeply to the knoll of Rougemont, now crowned by the medieval castle. To the west and south, the land fell away in cliffs towards the Exe. The south-western part of the site sloped sharply down towards the river, but provided no formidable difficulties for the soldier-builders. The ground

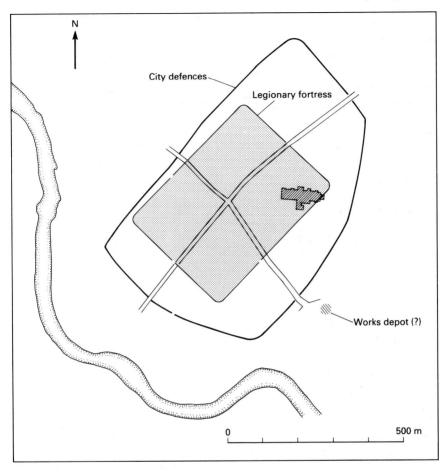

Figure 7.2 The Legionary fortress at Exeter

close to the river below the spur is likely to have been marshy in antiquity, though it is worth note that the medieval bridge and a ford lay here. It is not yet clear whether the site had been occupied in the later prehistoric period, but at least the possibility of settlement in the later Iron Age must be entertained. The remains of two circular huts, unfortunately undated, were found below one of the fortress buildings and a small quantity of pottery in a pre-Roman Iron Age tradition has been recovered from several parts of the site. Such pottery, however, continued to be made and used until well after the Roman conquest and it cannot be used to demonstrate pre-Roman occupation. The same may be said of the two Iron Age coins which have been found at Exeter. It must be remembered that very little of the earliest levels of the site has yet been examined on a satisfactory scale and until this has been achieved the question must remain open.

The dimensions of the fortress within the rampart are about 440 m by 350 m, an internal area of 15.4 ha (38 acres). This appears to be considerably smaller than the mean size of early Imperial fortresses, which is about 20 ha (50 acres). In actuality, several pre-Flavian fortresses are similar in area to Exeter, for example, Nijmegen (16.5 ha), Haltern (16.7 ha) and Lincoln (16.8 ha). The significance of the size of the fortress for the garrison is examined below (p. 195).

The main axis of the street plan is still echoed in the thoroughfares of central Exeter. The line of the *via principalis* is approximately represented by North Street and South Street, the *via praetoria* by High Street and the *via decumana* by Fore Street. The site of the *principia* can thus be located at the modern, busy junction of these streets. There seems very little chance of its plan ever being recovered. Since the course of the defences is known, the only major uncertainty relating to the north-east side, the positions of the four gates can be fixed fairly closely, though opportunity for the excavation of any of them has not yet arisen. As has already been mentioned, it was the fortunate discovery of the baths in 1971 that first demonstrated the true character of the military site. They are a rather small example of a well-known type of bath-house which was symmetrically planned about the central axis. Both military and civilian representatives of the type are known, the former at Vindonissa and Caerleon, the latter at Leicester and Avenches. At Exeter, only the *caldarium*, and its furnaces, and part of the *tepidarium* have been excavated: the whole of the *frigidarium* and most of the *palaestra* are yet to be examined. A considerable number of purely decorative elements had been included in the building. Some of the floors were paved with grey and white flags, while at least one figured mosaic, one of the earliest known in Roman Britain, had been laid in either the *caldarium* or *tepidarium*. Some of the mouldings and veneers were of Purbeck marble from Dorset and antefixes had been applied to the eaves (Bidwell 1979: 136–9).

The sites of other principal buildings remain unclear. The *praetorium* presumably lay on one or other side of the *principia*, perhaps to the east below South Street. Provision of a hospital is reasonably certain and this is likely to have lain in the *retentura*. A granary, or granaries, lay in the *praetentura* and between it and the defences was situated a *fabrica*. Accommodation for the troops is best known on the north and west sides of the fortress. Between the *fabrica* and the north defences there is space for eight barracks, of which two have been completely excavated and a further two in part. Another group of four barrack-blocks has been defined in the south-west corner and one of these has been almost completely revealed. The barracks are rather shorter than was usual in first century legionary fortresses, at about 62 m. The centurions' quarters, however, were maintained at the normal size, the scaling down being achieved in the *contubernia*. These were only 3 or 3.5 sq m, comparable with the *contubernia* at Hod Hill, but markedly smaller than those in contemporary fortresses.

It is reasonably certain that the unit in garrison at Exeter was the Second Legion Augusta. The evidence of Ptolemy already referred to is usefully supported by the fact that antefixes from the Exeter baths were produced in the same mould as others found at Caerleon, certainly the station of the Second Legion from about 75 (Bidwell 1980: 23). But was the *entire* legion housed in the Exeter fortress? The relatively small size of the work might seem to suggest that the full complement of ten cohorts was never based here at one time. The earlier history of the legion provides some support for this view. There are good reasons for thinking that detachments were outstationed in several small forts during the early years of occupation, at Hod Hill, Waddon Hill and perhaps Lake Farm near Wimborne. Perhaps this deployment of small legionary detachments, with auxiliaries in support roles, continued for much of the period during which Exeter was held or even to the close of occupation. This would help to solve another problem of the legionary garrison of western Britain, the apparent fact that Exeter and Gloucester were simultaneously garrisoned in the late 60s and early 70s. The Second Legion, with appropriate auxiliary support, could have occupied both fortresses during those years.

This is by no means the only possible explanation of the evidence. The internal planning of pre-Flavian fortresses is not yet so well documented that we can be sure that a full legion, or a legion which was slightly under strength, could not be accommodated within Exeter's 15.4 ha. It is probable that the barracks for sixty centurions could be fitted into this space, if the buildings were set closely together. The small *contubernia* in the barracks already excavated could adequately be explained as a response to the need to fit sixty blocks into a space which was determined by other factors, not least by the constraints of topography.

On the evidence at present available to us, there are at least three hypotheses, any one of which may account for the size of the Exeter fortress.

1. An entire legion was housed here, perhaps in somewhat cramped conditions. If the unit was under strength, as units on campaign not infrequently were, this would have provided some easement [2].

2. Small detachments were permanently outstationed in forts elsewhere in the South West. The use of legionaries for such duty is now well attested in provinces other than Britain at this date.

3. From the later 60s at least, the Second Legion garrisoned both Exeter and Gloucester. This arrangement could have succeeded the phase in which small detachments were outstationed. That phase is in any case unlikely to have lasted more than ten or fifteen years.

Since the complete plan of the fortress can never be recovered, we will always be compelled to consider the widest range of reasonable possibilities.

The date of foundation and occupation can be established only on the evidence of the pottery, still meagre on quantity, associated with the structures and deposits so far excavated. The sum of the decorated *terra sigillata* sherds indicates that there is no ground for supposing that the fortress was built before about AD 50 (Bidwell 1979: 16–17). Only one vessel has so far been recovered which might date from about 45 at the earliest. Sherds from vessels with a date of first emergence in the decade 50–60 number 23, there being 30 from the period 60–70. Those with opening dates between 50 and 60 divide into two fairly even groups, one of 11 starting about 50, the other of 12 beginning about 55. The same is true for the decade 60–70, with 14 vessels in the earlier group and 16 in the later. So small a sample of vessels can provide no secure statistical base, but, so far as this evidence goes, it suggests a fairly steady supply of *terra sigillata* during these twenty years. When did the supply begin? Bidwell argued in the report on the excavations of 1971–7 that the fortress is more likely to have been founded about 55–60 than earlier. This is a far from secure conclusion. Since the same number of vessels with a starting date of 50 is represented as those of 55, the possibility of foundation about 50 is at least as likely. Further, use and loss of pottery will normally be appreciably less around the date of construction than during occupation of a site. The start of occupation at Exeter may thus be dated to about 50, in the governorship of Ostorius Scapula or very shortly afterwards.

The siting of the Exeter fortress at the head of the estuary underlines the importance attached to water-borne transport by the army. Similar positions were chosen for several other fortresses in the conquest period and later, for example, Colchester, Gloucester, Caerleon and Chester. The remains of works associated with the supply of the fortress, and other forts in the region, might thus be expected. Two possible sites have so far been noted. One is at Topsham, on the east bank of the estuary some seven miles from the open sea. This has been claimed as the site of a port or naval supply base operating in conjunction with the fortress. The grounds for this suggestion are very weak (Maxfield 1980: 305–7). First, there is nothing military about the site as it is known at present. The most recent excavations indicate that it was a first-century farmstead with no other contact with the Roman army than that its inhabitants were acquiring their pottery from the same market as the legionaries. Secondly, the position of Topsham is a strange one for a port designed for military use. The Exe was almost certainly navigable as far as the site of the fortress itself, so that it would have been logistically simpler to carry supplies directly to Exeter than to unship them at Topsham and transfer them to other means of transport for the remaining 5 km.

The other possible site has more to recommend it. A flat area of ground between the Coombe and Shutebrook valleys, to the south-west of the fortress, has produced evidence for pre-Flavian buildings of military type and of considerable complexity in planning and chronology (Bidwell 1980: 41). A substantial ditch containing pre-Flavian pottery and on the same alignment as the buildings appears to have bounded a sizeable enclosure on this platform. This is best interpreted as a supply depot, served perhaps from the Exe bank by way of the Coombe valley. If this was indeed so, wharfs and other installations must have existed on the river and would repay careful search and discovery.

The Occupation of the Canton

If, as has been argued above, a legionary fortress was established at Exeter about AD 50, progress must already have been made before that date in the conquest of the peninsula. Sites such as marching-camps are not well attested in the South West so that the earliest operations of the invading army are ill known. But the number of recorded fort-sites, especially in Devon, has substantially increased in recent years, and as a result the pattern of the early garrisons is steadily emerging. The key to the conquest was provided by communications and Roman emphasis upon the control of major routes will undoubtedly lead to the identification of further military sites.

North of Exeter the valleys of the Exe and the Yeo and Taw offer the most direct routes to north Devon and both are likely to have been employed in the conquest phase. The area of Tiverton has long seemed likely to contain a fort which commanded the crossing of the Exe and within the town there is a platform of about 2.5 ha (6 acres) which seems well suited to military use. No finds, however, have been reported from the site and there has been no excavation in the town. At Bolham Farm, 2 km north of the town, on a low bluff overlooking the Exe valley, lies a work of 1.35 ha (3.3 acres) surrounded by a single ditch. As it is at present known, this resembles a temporary camp, but so much pottery has been recovered from trenching of the defences that a more permanent occupation seems likely.

The most significant fort-site yet recorded in central Devon is the imposing group of earthworks at Bury Barton, 1 km south of Lapford (Todd 1985). This occupies a tactically strong position on a flat spur above the west bank of the River Yeo, immediately opposite the confluence with the Dalch. The visible earthworks form two rectangular enclosures, one superimposed on the other, both with neatly rounded angles. The larger, and plainly earlier work, appears to enclose somewhat over 9 ha (21 acres), covering most of the spur and extending down the slope to the south. The smaller work (1.8 ha, 4.4 acres) survives as an impressive earthwork, especially on its north, east and south sides, being obscured to the west by the fine medieval and later farm buildings. Air photographs indicate three ditches on the east side and at the north-east

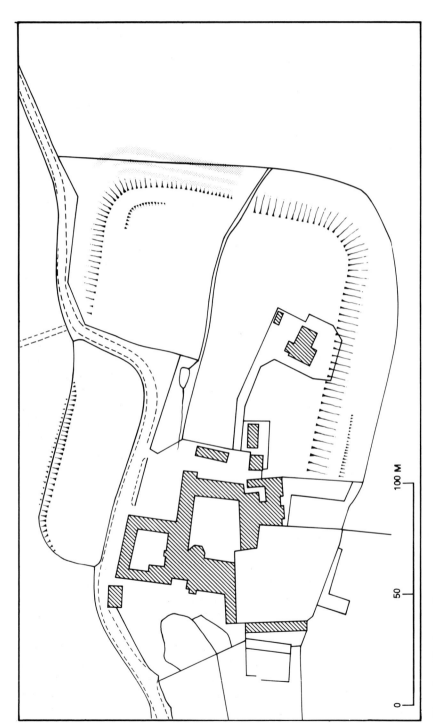

Figure 7.3　The Roman fort at Bury Barton

angle. There is no interruption for a gate in the south side, which suggests that there was no *porta decumana* and thus that the work dates to the middle decades of the first century AD. The north side seems to be pierced by a gate-opening at its centre point, while the sites of the east and west gates may be linked by the lane which crosses the spur. Excavation has demonstrated the first-century date of this fine earthwork. Its rampart was composed of clay dug from the surrounding ditches, revetted by turf-work.

The larger enclosure at Bury Barton is fairly certainly to be related to the late Roman period and it may have served as an official *statio*. The site lies in the centre of the series of place-names including the element *nymet* and it overlooks the Yeo, the earlier name of which was *Nymet* (Stevens 1976; Rivet and Smith 1979: 424–5). There seems, therefore, to be a *prima facie* case for identifying Bury Barton as the *Nemetostatio* of the Ravenna Cosmography (below, p. 203).

The fort at Bury Barton confirms the existence of a route which linked the Exe estuary with that of the Taw by way of the Creedy, Yeo and the Taw itself. This in turn implies the existence of a fort near the head of the Taw estuary, possibly at Barnstaple or a little to the south at Bishops Tawton.

The route along the Culm valley, now followed by the railway and the M5 motorway, provides the most obvious approach from the north-east. A fort near Cullompton and possibly another at Killerton indicate military use of this line, which probably extended north-eastwards to Wellington and Taunton where other forts are to be looked for.

Beyond the Exe, the route which passes around the northern flank of Dartmoor offers the most direct approach to the west and two forts on this line are well established. The larger is at North Tawton at a crossing of the River Taw (St Joseph 1958: 98). This is 2.8 ha (6.4 acres) in area and has an annexe on its western side. A temporary camp nearby may represent the earliest advance on this route [3]. There has been no excavation here and only a few first-century objects are recorded from the site. Farther west, a small fort (1.0 ha, 2.6 acres) lies on the eastern outskirts of Okehampton on the west bank of the river Okement (Bidwell, Bridgwater and Silvester 1979). Nothing is known of its internal planning and little pottery has been recovered from small-scale excavation. A Neronian to early Flavian date has been suggested on very slender grounds. Opportunities exist for identifying other sites along the route. A possible fort has been pointed out at Colebrooke, 10 km east of North Tawton close to the little river Troney, but this awaits confirmation (Stevens 1976).

The conquest and garrisoning of north Devon is still largely unknown. The presence of two fortlets or look-out posts on the coast at Martinhoe and Old Burrow, however, does at least demonstrate military interest in the security of the Bristol Channel and suggests that forts are still to be found around Exmoor and perhaps on the coast itself. Porlock Bay and the vicinity of

Lynton present themselves as possible sites. The two fortlets, long known as visible earthworks, were carefully studied by Fox and Ravenhill in the 1960s, Old Burrow having been trenched by St George Gray in 1911 (Fox and Ravenhill 1966). Both sites stand high above the cliffs and command excellent views across the Channel to South Wales roughly 30 km away. They are not, however, inter-visible, a fact which raises the possibility that other fortlets in the series have yet to be found. There are no obvious candidates.

The two fortlets are similar in size and in the planning of their defences. A bank and a pair of ditches surrounded the fortlet proper, while a further bank and ditch described a rough circle about the whole. No coherent plan of buildings was recovered at Old Burrow, though less than half of the interior was examined. At Martinhoe, however, barrack-like structures were identified, the whole perhaps representing the accommodation for a century and its centurion. Evidence of date was not extensive but both works were probably manned in the Neronian and early Flavian period, perhaps from *c.* 55 to 75. It seems highly likely that similar fortlets existed to east and west of these. Bull Point west of Ilfracombe and the great promontory of Hartland both call out for examination with this in mind.

The Roman advance farther west into Cornwall is still remarkably ill-known. Only one certain fort-site has been identified west of the Tamar and few other known sites, on present evidence, seem likely to contribute to our knowledge of how the conquest was achieved. The positions of the forts at North Tawton and Okehampton indicate that at least one major route through the peninsula was that which passed to the north of Dartmoor. This is still followed by the most direct road into Cornwall from the Exe valley and is likely to have been employed in the earliest Roman thrust to the Tamar and beyond. The Tamar crossing at or near Launceston clearly calls for a fort, though as yet no hint of its site has been given. Beyond the Tamar the route down the central spine of the peninsula will fairly certainly have caught the attention of Roman commanders. This ran across the south-eastern side of Bodmin Moor to the broad valley of the Camel in the vicinity of Bodmin. Here, 4 km west of the modern town, lies the only Roman fort yet known in Cornwall, at Nanstallon.

This earthwork, set on a flat spur on the south side of the river Camel, had long been suggested as a fort, on the grounds of its position and of chance finds of first-century Roman pottery, before the fort was demonstrated by the extensive excavations of Lady Fox and Professor Ravenhill (Haverfield 1924: 4–5; Fox and Ravenhill 1972). It is a small work, only 0.88 ha (2.2 acres) in internal area. About half of the fort has been selectively excavated. A very small *principia*, only 20 m by 15 m overall, lay in the customary position at the junction of the *viae principalis* and *praetoria*. Next to it was the *praetorium*, on a relatively generous scale and having a small compound attached to it. Three barracks, or possibly four, were identified in the eastern half of the fort, along with a small workshop and storesheds. No granaries were located: presumably

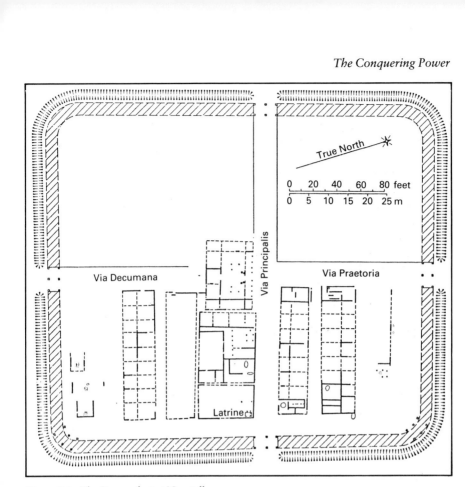

Figure 7.4 The Roman fort at Nanstallon

these lay in the unexcavated half. If the planning of the fort was approximately symmetrical, there would have been ample space for the barracks of the six centuries appropriate to a *cohors quingenaria*. Stabling and additional troop accommodation for a complement of cavalry might have been provided, though there is no direct evidence of the presence of mounted men.

The dating of Nanstallon depends on a rather small amount of pottery. As elsewhere, this is likely to be related to the phases of occupation and abandonment rather than the episode of construction. The earliest datable objects are of the later 50s or early 60s. No certainly Claudian material was found, so that the date of construction may be set in the period 55–60. No substantial rebuilding occurred during the occupation of the fort and its abandonment probably came only 15 to 20 years later.

It is important to stress that Nanstallon is, as yet, the only certain fort-site known in Cornwall and the temptation to assume that its history mirrors precisely the course of the Roman conquest of the far west must be resisted. The possibility of penetration into the region before the mid-50s is very real.

There were minerals to be exploited, or at least assessed, and these included gold and silver as well as tin. From one site comes a hint of Roman activity, probably military, well to the west of the Tamar and rather earlier than the occupation of Nanstallon. An earthwork at Carvossa, near Probus, four miles east of Truro, has produced surprisingly large quantities of high-quality imported Roman pottery of the mid- and later first century (Douch and Beard 1970). Much of it is closely paralleled in the pottery from the Exeter fortress. The earliest vessels may well date from the later Claudian period, *c.* 50/55, and all in all the Carvossa assemblage appears to point clearly to the Roman army as the agent of introduction. The character of the earthwork itself, however, betrays no Roman influence in its planning or its internal buildings. Apart from its exceptional pottery finds, the site is an unremarkable enclosed settlement of a familiar Cornish type. We might look elsewhere in the vicinity for a military work and across the valley of the Fal at Garlenick (or Garlinnick) there is a possible candidate. Here, a rectangular earthwork existed until the earlier nineteenth century on a low eminence above the river. The position and the name of this now-vanished site, Burghgear, accord well with the site of a fort and relocation of the work is desirable [4].

The Evidence of Place-Names

Another source of information bearing on the early occupation of the region is available to us, though its content and significance cannot yet be interpreted in full. This source is a number of names recorded in documents, the *Geography* of Ptolemy, the Antonine Itinerary, the Peutinger Table and the Ravenna Cosmography. The earliest of these is Ptolemy, a mid-second-century compilation of mainly earlier sources, and of particular interest as it is apparent that much of his evidence for southern Britain as a whole derives from Claudio-Neronian and early Flavian sources. A strong case can also be made out that Ptolemy included 'Roman' places, that is, fortresses, forts and cities, and not purely 'native' sites. In the South West, therefore, his place-names should refer to Roman military sites, since no notable centres of civilian population existed. Apart from *Isca*, Ptolemy gives us *Voliba*, *Uxella* and *Tamara* as Dumnonian *poleis*. About the last-named there can be little doubt. This should be a fort on the river which Ptolemy calls the *Tamaros*, the Tamar, probably the fort which has been posited above at or near Launceston. *Uxella* may be connected with the river of the same name also listed by Ptolemy, a stream not certainly identified but possibly the Axe. If that is so, the fort *Uxella* might lie near Axmouth or Axminster. *Voliba* defies any identification. It has been linked with the hill-fort of Golden, near Probus, but that is sheer guesswork. A fort such as Nanstallon, or an as yet unrecorded work in Cornwall or Devon, is a more plausible candidate.

The south-western names supplied by the seventh- or eighth-century Ravenna *Cosmography* are more numerous but even more difficult to interpret. The first sixteen names listed in the document lay in the South West, apparently west of Exeter since *Scadeum Namorum* (= *Isca Dumnoniorum*) occurs at the end of this group. Unfortunately it is not clear whether or not this list is in any kind of order. Such tentative identifications as can be offered suggest that it is not and that we are here dealing with a number of routes which found their terminus at Exeter. Two names also occur in Ptolemy: *Tamaris* and *Uxelis*. Another, *Nemeto(s)tatio* has commonly been identified with the fort at North Tawton (e.g. Fox 1973: 171), principally on the ground that the *nemeto*-element appears to be preserved in a number of place-names in the upper Taw valley (e.g. Kings Nympton, Nymet Tracey, Nymet Rowland). Another name containing the element *statio* is listed here: *Devionisso Statio*, probably a corruption of *Derventio Statio* and derived from a river-name *Derventio* (the River Dart?). This is followed by the obviously garbled name *Deventiasteno*, which is probably a doublet of the same name. *Statio* must here denote an official establishment, perhaps a centre for the collection of tax and tribute, and possibly originating in a fort (Rivet and Smith 1979: 335–6).

The prominence of river-names in the Ravenna list is notable and two further clear examples may be pointed out. The names *Eltabo* and *Elconio* are most unlikely as they stand. The initial letter may be convincingly emended to F, giving *Fl(umen) Tabo* and *Fl(umen) Conio*. The latter name, further, is presumably the *Cenio* of Ptolemy, perhaps the Fal or one of the streams flowing into the Fal estuary. *Tabo* gives us *Tavus*, which should be the Taw. A further name may also refer to a river, either directly or by way of a settlement-name. *Giano* may be safely emended to *Glanum*, and the element *glano*- appears in several Celtic river-names, meaning either 'pure' or 'shining', or 'bank'. No plausible identification can be suggested.

Most of the other names are baffling, in several cases because they are plainly corrupt. These include *Pilais*, *Vernilis* or *Vernalis*, *Vertevia* and *Arduaravenatone*. *Melamoni* may be a garbled form of *Moridunum*, which occurs in the Antonine Itinerary and on the Peutinger Table. *Duriarno* has been linked with Durnovaria, Dorchester, but could be an unidentified site in Devon or Cornwall. The most interesting of the corrupt names is *Purocoronavis*. Its original form was probably *Durocornovium*, 'fort of the Cornovii'. This is the earliest certain mention of a people who presumably formed a sept of the Dumnonii and who in a later period gave their name to Cornwall (Kernow). The name contains the element *corn-*, 'horn' which has led to the suggestion that the Cornovii were seen as promontory dwellers, or dwellers in promontory-dwellers, or dwellers in promontory-forts. Equally plausibly, the 'horn' may have been the peninsula itself, especially its western reaches, the true home of the Cornovii (below, p. 217).

The Antonine Itinerary, the Ravenna Cosmography and the Peutinger Table refer to a site called *Moridunum* ('sea-fort') fifteen Roman miles, according to the Itinerary, east of Exeter. No other south-western place-name has provoked so much controversy as this. Hembury was the site favoured by many nineteenth-century writers, being later replaced by Seaton when Roman material began to appear there. The most recent suggestion, Sidford, has nothing to recommend it apart from its distance from Exeter, about 15 Roman miles. The claims of Hembury, which is also of the appropriate distance from Exeter, have been considerably strengthened by the discovery of an early Roman fort inside the Iron Age stronghold (Todd 1984, and above, pp. 191–2). Against it, it may be argued that the sea is at some distance, although it can be seen from the hill-fort in clear weather. But this objection applies to Sidford, too, and for the present Hembury, or a site near Honiton on the Roman road, seems to be the most likely solution to the *Moridunum* problem.

The place-name *Nemetostatio* recorded in the Ravenna Cosmography attests a *nemeton* in the region north-west of Exeter, possibly at Bury Barton, near Lapford. *Nemeton* is Celtic for 'sacred place', possibly a wood or grove as the word is cognate with the Latin *nemus* which carries that meaning. Later sources make it clear that *nemeton* could mean simply wood or forest and this is of particular interest for central Devon, since there are several names in a more or less closely defined area which are clearly related to *nemeton*, a large proportion of them still in use. Most of these names occur in the valleys of the Yeo and the Mole, several being borne by villages (Kings Nympton, Nymet Tracy, Nymet Rowland), others by farms and hamlets (Nymetwood, Nicol's Nymet, Broadnymet). These are beyond doubt ancient names for thirteen Domesday manors in this same area bear *nemeton* names, eight of them still extant on the map. The broad distribution is in a band to either side of the rivers Taw and Yeo from the northern foothills of Dartmoor to just south of Exmoor. Clearly they are to be related to a tract of land, not merely a single site, although a sacred place of some significance obviously must have lain hereabouts.

Notes

1. More probably occupation was confined to the period 50–60 AD.
2. We are ill-informed about the *actual* strength of a legion. It may often have fallen well below 5,000.
3. A large military work identified from the air here in 1984 by Miss F. Griffith underlines the importance of this route.
4. Several strategic positions in Cornwall are likely to have received garrisons. The head of the Tamar estuary opposite Bere Alston is one obvious site. Others include the Fowey crossing near Lostwithiel, perhaps at Restormel, and the estuary head in the area of Truro (see Fig 7.1).

Chapter 8

The Dumnonii

The Dumnonii

The long-term effects of Roman military occupation on the South West were remarkably limited. None of the auxiliary forts in the region appear to have attracted to its vicinity that motley crew which is so commonly attested at the forts of the pre-Flavian period in much of southern Britain, and subsequently no *vici* or road-stations developed over their sites as happened frequently elsewhere. North Tawton, Okehampton, Nanstallon and the rest faded into the landscape and were no more. Only at Bury Barton is there any hint of later occupation and its nature is still uncertain (Todd 1985). The most substantial legacy of the Roman army to the *civitas Dumnoniorum* was the site of Exeter, which was to remain the focus of Imperial administration until the end of Roman Britain and a centre of authority for long after that.

Isca Dumnoniorum

The site earlier chosen by the legionary surveyor for the fortress sloped gently southwards below the knoll of Rougemont, then more steeply towards the river (Fox 1952c; Bidwell 1980). Most of the ground later occupied by the city was covered by gravels, the main exceptions being the volcanic boss of Rougemont itself and the red sandstone breccia at the southern end. The place had been well chosen. To the north the River Exe has cut a narrow channel through the Culm Measures, leaving to either side steep-sided bluffs which offer no convenient site for a large settlement. Exeter lies precisely at the point where the valley begins to widen into a broad flood-plain up to 2 km wide. Today the river flows on the eastern side of this plain, against a wall of steep cliffs. In the Roman period it is virtually certain that it tended to flood the low-lying marshy area below the city, as it does on occasion now. The course of the main stream-bed, or beds, at this date is not known, but it may have lain close to its medieval and modern successor. Down to the sixteenth century the tide reached Exeter so that Roman ships could easily have reached the city directly from the open sea. The possibility of an inland harbour immediately below the Roman city is thus a real one, though unfortunately no opportunity has yet arisen to examine the appropriate area.

The long debated problem of whether or not a native settlement of any size existed on this site before the Roman arrival still remains unsettled. It is true that very little of the pottery and other objects, such as Iron Age coins, so far recovered from the earliest levels must of necessity be dated to before AD 43. But it must be borne in mind that a bare 5 per cent of the total area covered by the Roman city has been excavated to undisturbed subsoil and several parts of it have never been examined archaeologically at all. The latter include the northern corner which embraces the summit and southern slopes of Rougemont, which a pre-Roman community (if it existed) is unlikely completely to have ignored. It must be noted, too, that one excavated area (near the Guildhall) has produced evidence of pre-Roman occupation in the form of two probable hut-circles (Bidwell 1980: 34). These, however, are not dated with any accuracy and could be much earlier than the first century AD. No decisive evidence on the question has yet been obtained. It is remarkable that only a single sherd of decorated La Tène pottery or of cordoned ware seems to have been reported from Exeter or its immediate environs. A negative can in these circumstances never be conclusive, but for the present no convincing case can be made out for the existence of a sizeable pre-Roman nucleus on the site of *Isca*. The possibility remains that the inhabitants of Iron Age settlements nearby, including perhaps that on Stoke Hill (Radford 1937), were quickly drawn towards the new focus provided by the legionary base. But the evidence has yet to be assembled and the native contribution to the earliest civilian settlement at Exeter is still shadowy.

The name of the site *Isca*, as reported by Ptolemy, is plainly related to the British word for water, as are the names Esk and Usk. Like them, the name was clearly a river-name which was subsequently transferred to the site. Philological problems surround the descent of the name (Rivet and Smith 1979: 376–8) to Asser's *Cair Uuisc* and Lhuyd's *Kar Esk*, which seem to demand an original *Esca*, but this does not invalidate an ultimate derivation from the Celtic name of the River Exe.

The Forum

The building which, above all, marked the emergence of the urban community is the forum and basilica, as normally in Romano-British cities unified in a

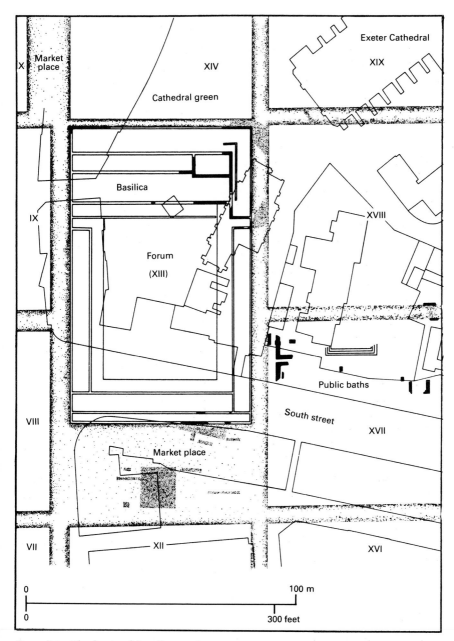

Market place

X

Cathedral green

XIV

Exeter Cathedral

XIX

Basilica

IX

Forum
(XIII)

XVIII

Public baths

VIII

South street

Market place

XVII

VII

XII

XVI

0

100 m

0

300 feet

Figure 8.1 The forum of *Isca Dumnoniorum*

single structure, part of the plan of which was revealed by excavation in 1971–7 (Bidwell 1979; 67–82). The demolition of most of the legionary baths was followed by the erection of a large timber structure, fragmentary traces of which have so far been recovered. This may have housed the workshops which must have been established for the masons and other craftsmen charged with the building of the forum. Another possibility is that this was part of a timber forum and basilica, like that recently identified at Silchester. Parts of the legionary baths were left standing to form the end and side walls of the basilica, the hypocausts being filled up with rubble to form level surfaces (the succession of legionary *thermae* by a civilian forum also occurred at Wroxeter: Atkinson 1942: 55–6). The plan of the forum is in general outline unexceptional and is clearly related to other first-century fora in Britain, though with minor variations in detail. Forum and basilica formed a unitary whole in which the basilica was the dominant architectural feature. As in almost all the other British fora, there is no indication of the existence of a religious focus such as a Capitolium or a temple of the Imperial cult. The entire complex measured 106.5 m by 67 m, the nave of the basilica being 10.4 m wide, reduced to 9 m at the south-east and where a large chamber, 13 m by 7.6 m, lay across the aisle and projected into the nave. This may have been the *curia* or some other official chamber such as the record-office. The other end of the basilica, where a tribunal might be expected, has not yet been available for excavation.

Around the forum-piazza there will have stood the customary shops, booths and offices fronted by porticoes. Little of these ranges has yet been examined, though it is clear that small commercial premises were certainly present there by the second century at the latest. Outside the south range lay a large metalled space around which more shops and stalls may have been sited. In such a setting a temple or small shrine might also have stood (Fox, A. 1952c: 17).

Pottery and coins associated with the building phase of the forum point to a date of construction not earlier than about 75. Of four coins of Vespasian, two are of the year 72–3 and one of these had circulated for some years before loss. It is clearly possible that the building of this public complex was stimulated by the kind of official encouragement commonly associated in Britain with the name of the provincial legate Julius Agricola (Tacitus, *Agricola*: 21). But a date about 80 seems to be the earliest possible date for the construction of the Exeter forum on present evidence and a later date, perhaps as late as 90, is by no means excluded. Other Romano-British cities which were developing about this time have produced evidence for the building of public structures in the last decade of the century and in the opening years of the next (e.g. Silchester (Boon 1974: 49–56); Leicester (Hebditch and Mellor 1973)). Allowance must also be made in the case of a canton like the Dumnonii, dispersed as it was over a wide area and probably lacking cohesion among its leading members, for a protracted phase of construction. The initial impetus provided by provincial administrators may not have been maintained with notable fervour by the tribal magnates as they contemplated their future as members of the local curial order.

Although little is known of their plan, the public baths are known to have been situated immediately east of the forum in Insula XVII, beneath the Deanery and the present South Street. Structural remains of a very large building were reported from this site from time to time throughout the nineteenth century, firm identification as the baths being achieved in 1932 when excavation in the Deanery grounds revealed part of a large open-air swimming pool or *natatio*, 16.75 m long and over a metre deep, surrounded by a sandstone pavement with a gutter down its centre (Montgomerie-Neilson and Montague 1933–6: 72–8). A column-base 50 cm in diameter was found in the filling of the bath and it was believed that the positions of other columns could be discerned along the inner edge of the pavement. The nineteenth-century reports stress the massive size of some of the foundations located in this insula and some of these at least are to be explained as the underpinning of a large building erected on a fairly steep southward slope. The plan of the whole cannot, however, yet be reconstructed in detail. Nor is the date of the baths certain. Bidwell (1980: 53) suggests it may have been contemporary with the forum, that is, Flavian, but the grounds for this are inadequate. It could equally well be of the earlier or middle second century.

Other urban amenities were modest in character. A supply of water was carried into the centre of the city in a timber-lined leat which may have tapped the water-flow in the old legionary aqueduct diverting it around the northern flank of Rougemont to enter the city near the north corner. Why the builders of this strange structure should have decided on this tortuous course is difficult to grasp. The line of the first century aqueduct is the obvious one to follow (Henderson 1984: 2–4). At all events the life of this installation was brief, from about 100 for no more than twenty years or so.

The Urban Defences

The defences of the legionary fortress were not systematically levelled after the end of military occupation and thus continued to provide some kind of boundary for the emergent town. But they were little more than a boundary and there is no sign that they were deliberately maintained in good order (Bidwell 1980: 46–7). The rampart remained standing, but its interval towers were probably demolished. The large ditch on the south side of the fortress was left open and later filled up with stagnant water. Other stretches may have been levelled over at a later date in the second century. On the south side, the old intervallum road was taken over into the street system of the new city, though its width was considerably reduced. By the mid- or later second century the old circuit can only have been in a ruinous condition and several sectors are likely to have been levelled or otherwise removed to make way for new streets and buildings. The building of a new circuit was undertaken shortly afterwards.

As early as 1934, the possibility of an early earthen bank was suggested after excavation by the Exeter Excavation Committee.

> An earth bank and ditch with timber defences was first erected and was then strengthened by a stone wall. . . . We may tentatively assign the bank to the period of the foundation of the city and the wall to the late first or second century, when many Romano-British towns appear to have received their defences.
>
> (Radford and Morris 1933–6: 184)

The bank, as revealed in a section at St John's School, was at least 6.5 m wide, composed of reddish clay derived from the digging of an external ditch. It survived to a height of about 1.3 m and may originally have been some 3 m high. The bank is best preserved in the grounds of the Bishop's Palace and the adjacent Cathedral School. In the Palace gardens it stands 5 m high, though excavation in 1939 revealed the upper deposits to be of medieval date. In Bedford Circus the bank measured 7 m in width and stood 1.6 m high. On this site Lady Fox observed that the bank had been in existence long enough for a 10 cm layer of vegetation to develop on its slope before the city wall was built (Fox, A. 1952c: 59). As normally, dating evidence from the body of the bank was very sparse. The few sherds dated to the first half of the second century, suggesting that it had been thrown up not before about 150 and probably rather later, perhaps in the final quarter of the second century. There is continuing uncertainty about the dating and purpose of these earthwork defences in Romano-British cities (Hartley 1983; Frere 1984). Exeter adds nothing to the debate except a fairly clear example dated before AD 200 and in a region where any external threat can have been of minimal proportions. The needs, and the prestige, of the local community must have carried more weight.

In their developed form the defences provided the city with a strong and well-planned circuit of walls, 2.35 km in length and enclosing in all 37 ha (89 acres). These continued to frame the city until the nineteenth century, one result being the survival of nearly three-quarters of the circuit, though all sectors have been subject to some degree of rebuilding and certain lengths of walling have been wholly replaced in the medieval centuries. Topography played a major role in determining the course of the wall. On the north-western side the steep-sided valley of the Longbrook offered a clear demarcation. Farther north, the prominent knoll of Rougemont called for inclusion within the circuit while to the south the steep fall of ground towards the Exe marked a clear line for the wall-builders. On the eastern side the demands of topography were less severe, the fairly gentle fall from Rougemont towards the Shutebrook valley being broken only by the relatively shallow Coombe. The main expansions of the enclosed area were thus to the north-east and east of the old circuit.

The city wall was constructed of volcanic trap, most probably quarried from Rougemont. It measured at the base 3.2 m to 3.4 m in width and rose to a height which was probably at least 6 m and perhaps a metre higher at the rampart walk. The best preserved section seems to be that close to the south gate, where it is still 3.5 m high, its width reduced by three offsets from 3.4 m at the base to 1.9 m. It is difficult to be certain about whether or not any of the original facing still survives. It has long been held that several lengths of neatly coursed square blocks of trap preserve the original facing but this has never been demonstrated beyond doubt. Recent work in the Cricklepit Street area suggests that this masonry may be late medieval or even sixteenth century (Bidwell 1980: 64). A stretch of wall in Northernhay Gardens, north of Queen Street, includes much of the Roman fabric, its footing and plinth being still visible. The eastern side of the town wall has been the most heavily rebuilt in post-Roman times.

At least four gates, and possibly five, gave access through the wall. The east and west gates occupied sites on or close to those of their medieval successors, on High Street and Stepcote Hill respectively, though nothing is known of their structure. The site of the north gate is less certain, though it is most likely to have lain close to the medieval gate on North Street. The south gate alone has been examined archaeologically (Fox 1968). Excavation of its western tower showed it to be roughly square in plan, measuring 5.2 m by 5 m. A single entrance-portal seems likely, perhaps flanked by a footway to either side. The arch at the rear of the gate survived down to the nineteenth century and drawings of that date show it to have been semicircular in form. William Stukeley (1724, 15) and some later writers have argued that this rear arch was a Roman survival, partly because of its form, partly because it was built flush with the rear face of the wall. Neither point is conclusive and the probability is that all the Roman gates had vanished by the late medieval period at latest. This is borne out by the best source for the medieval gates, the drawings brought together by Sprake (Sprake 1832). The most Roman in appearance (for what that is worth) was the north gate, but that is scarcely reliable evidence.

One internal tower or turret is known, on the northern defences at Paul Street, and others may be expected to appear elsewhere on the circuit (Henderson 1984: 8–9). The known instance was an addition to the town wall, perhaps in the middle or later third century, a time when defences were being remodelled in a number of Romano-British cities. There are as yet no indications that external towers were added to the defences in the late Roman period.

Away from the central *insulae* the plan of the city is patchily known. Urban housing is a particularly ill-recorded subject, hardly a single substantial house being yet excavated in full. Early chance discoveries revealed few of the familiar features of wealthy town-houses, tessellated or mosaic floors, painted walls and hypocausts, while more recent work suggests that sizeable areas close to the defences were not built over at any time in the Roman period. Such buildings as have been excavated reasonably fully were of simple plan and lacked elaborate ornament. It must be remembered, however, that many of the *insulae*, including several close to the centre of the city, have never been examined archaeologically, and the same is true of most of the major street frontages. Secondly, Exeter was a thriving place in the medieval centuries and much of the Roman city has been destroyed by building activity from the eleventh century onward. At present the sample of our recorded information is woefully small, too small to be regarded as representative in any way. It will be many years before it is significantly greater and it will never be more than a fraction of what existed in the four centuries of Roman rule.

Present indications are that for the first century of the city's existence, private buildings were timber structures of modest type. The earliest stone buildings are of the late second century, the clearest case being an L-shaped dwelling of five rooms in Insula XVIII (Bidwell 1979: 121). Even well after AD 200 many timber structures remained in use and it is reasonably certain, as in other Romano-British towns, that many buildings which had stone footings were largely timber-framed above their dwarf walls.

There is no sign as yet that the early years of *Isca* saw a rapid expansion in private houses, shops and workshops. The second half of the second century appears at present to have been the first phase of appreciable growth, so far as this can be measured in the construction dates of buildings. From several parts of the city comes evidence to suggest a period of lively building activity in the third century, especially in the middle and later decades, extending into the first half of the fourth century, a state of affairs now evident at several cities in Upper Britain. No doubt this is to be related to the increase in agricultural prosperity mirrored in the rise of estates in the adjacent lands of the Durotriges which may have had repercussive effect farther west.

The sequence of buildings revealed in *Insulae* IV and V is one of the fullest obtained so far and may give a fair impression of what Roman Exeter's dwellings were like (Bidwell 1980: 69–72). Simple timber buildings on both sides of the intervening street were the first to be erected, in the second half of the second century. At the end of the century, by which time the street had gone out of use, both buildings were completely rebuilt, though still to simple plans, and one of the structures had been given an apse in masonry and a small chamber with a hypocaust. After perhaps half a century these buildings fell into disuse and the site lay empty for a time. In the late third century a long, narrow masonry building of three rooms went up, to which were later added (at the rear) two small chambers, one with a hypocaust and a verandah. These small rooms were subsequently demolished, leaving the original narrow block with verandah as the final form of the building in the late fourth century.

Another substantial fragment of a town-house has been examined in Insula XVIII, immediately opposite the forum-basilica (Bidwell 1979: 121). This may have had modest origins as a single range of rooms in the second century, but was later given an L-shaped plan by the addition of a second range running along the street frontage, thus bringing it close to the layout of some of the houses at Verulamium and Silchester. Again the development seems to be one of the third century. One of Exeter's rare mosaics floored a room in the later range.

Remains of shops and workshops are not yet as well recorded as one would expect in so large an urban community. Aside from commercial quarters in the ranges around the forum, few of the familiar shops-cum-workshops have yet appeared, though this is principally due to the fact that relatively little of the main street-frontages has been excavated. A small workshop containing four small ovens lay close to a dwelling in Insula XXXIII close to the southern defences, where more of such installations are to be expected (Bidwell 1980: 74–6). This dated from the first half of the fourth century and had replaced a third-century timber workshop, also equipped with small ovens or furnaces. From several other sites in the city there are indications of small-scale craft-working, relics of the trades which any sizeable provincial community called into existence: metalworking, smithing, the manufacture of objects in bone, antler and shale, and presumably also in wood and leather. Of industrial working on any larger scale there is no trace and probably none is to be expected. Even the production of pottery seems to have been for the local market, though small quantities may have found their way westwards in the first century (below, p. 234). No kilns have yet been identified, but there are wasters of jars in a sandy grey fabric from a site in Topsham. From the second century onward, the vast bulk of Exeter's pottery was supplied by the black-burnished ware kilns of south Dorset, with support from the customary sources in central Gaul and the Rhineland/Moselle centres, as well as from Oxfordshire, the New Forest and the Nene valley. It may seem strange that no substantial production centre of pottery developed in or near Exeter in the heyday of the city, as the raw materials are to hand and the position of the place is ideal for the distribution of goods by water. The same state of affairs is evident in other parts of Roman Britain and can only be explained by reference to the tenacity of established patterns of trade and manufacture. In Exeter's case, it seems at least likely that there was a substantial surplus of commodities for trade from the hinterland, so that there will have been ample capacity for the import of finished goods such as pottery. This may not have been true farther to the west.

There are few signs that Isca enjoyed more than a modest prosperity in the later Empire. Large urban houses like those of Cirencester, Wroxeter or Dorchester in this period are virtually unrecorded and there are no other indications of burgeoning wealth. The position of the city close to the eastern end of the tribal territory may not have been conducive to the concentration of native wealth upon the *chef-lieu*. Once the first impulse towards urbanization was past, the Dumnonian landowners seem to have gone their own way, and that was the way of their forefathers. The absence of villas in the lower Exe valley close to Exeter, where they might have been expected, reinforces the point. In this respect *Isca* was unlike the other *civitates* of southern Britain. No doubt its links with the immediate hinterland were as close as those of any other Romano-British city, but the hinterland itself was more purely Celtic than Romano-Celtic. And what the tribal landowners did not do in the countryside they probably also did not do in the city. This does not mean that Roman Exeter was not exposed to any external stimuli to change. But present information suggests that resistance to such influence was generally effective.

Like most or all Romano-British cities, Exeter depended upon its agricultural hinterland for its prosperity. Of the animals bred in the vicinity of the city, cattle predominated, followed by sheep and pigs in roughly equal numbers (Maltby 1979: 82–4). Horses were also present but in small numbers. The domestic fowl was also kept. The cattle seem to have reached maturity in great numbers, suggesting that they were reared for dairy products rather than meat, and for use as draught animals. Sheep were killed when still relatively young, up to two years old, so that they could have provided their first fleece as well as meat. Hunting was evidently a source of food as well as a pastime, roe deer, red deer and hare being well represented among the finds of bone, along with wild geese, ducks and other game birds.

It has long been known that surprisingly large numbers of Greek coins occur in the lists of coin-finds from the city of Exeter. This first came to attention in the mid-nineteenth century with the publication of W. T. P. Shortt's *Sylva Antiqua Iscana* (1841a). Shortt was particularly interested in coins and published some of the most detailed coin-lists of his day (Goodchild 1947). One section of his book was devoted to 'Greek coins found in Exeter and its neighbourhood'. He had already contributed a short account of these finds to the *Gentleman's Magazine* in 1837, but his notice was not kindly received. Shortt himself was at some pains to record his early scepticism about these finds, but his doubts were removed, he tells us, by the repeated discovery of coins in circumstances which appeared to exclude the possibility of fraud or relatively recent import and loss. The 'salting' of a site with modern imports from the eastern Mediterranean by workmen who knew of Shortt's preparedness to purchase coins would certainly have been relatively easy. But Shortt was no fool and he appears to have satisfied himself that a considerable proportion of the finds he recorded were genuinely ancient losses, either by inspecting the find-spots or by interrogation of the finders. His own copy of *Sylva Antiqua Iscana*, now held in the West Country Studies Library in Exeter, contains a number of notes in his own hand expressing doubt about certain items. About most of the finds, he was certain.

The first reference to Greek finds in Exeter was made not by Shortt but by Alexander Jenkins in *The History and Description of the City of Exeter* in 1806. Excavations prior to the installation of a main sewer on Fore Street in the south-western part of the city in 1810 produced a large number of coins, including 'a great number of Greek coins of Egypt, among which 8 of the

Ptolemies already alluded to, and a number of the Imperial ones'. Most of these pieces were acquired by the Jenkins family and were subsequently dispersed. In 1823, another group of Greek issues was found on a site near Broadgate, among a total of 120 coins. Again, in 1834 the construction of vaults in the cemetery in the Bartholomew Yard area on the north-western side of the city brought more Greek coins to light, while in 1838 what Shortt describes as a hoard of Greek and Egyptian pieces was found near Poltimore, two miles north of Exeter. Shortt left Exeter in 1855 and settled in Germany where he spent the rest of his life. The recording of coin-finds in the city was continued by W. D'Urban and Edward Parfitt and the latter reported further Greek issues in 1878, Greek 'Imperials' of the second and third century AD (Parfitt 1878: 343–7). There the matter rested, though some later numismatists roundly rejected the ancient origin of the Exeter Greek coins, arguing that Shortt had been the victim of a hoax.

In more recent times the coins have lain in a dubious twilight, rejected as modern imports by some, including the most recent commentator on Roman Exeter (Bidwell 1980: 87), accepted by others, but usually as freak finds with no real significance. Their principal champions have been J. G. Milne and R.G. Goodchild, who published a well argued reply to Haverfield and Macdonald in 1937 (Milne and Goodchild 1937). Milne later studied as many Greek coins found in Britain as he could trace and demonstrated a clear concentration of Hellenistic silver and bronze pieces of the third to first centuries BC in Dorset and Devon (Milne 1948). He was careful to exclude all finds about which there could be doubt and still recorded a respectable total. Goodchild subjected the Exeter coins to detailed study in an unpublished dissertation, outlining the problem with admirable clarity and good sense. His conclusion was unequivocal. To reject all of the nineteenth-century finds as modern imports was to ignore a number of discoveries which had been made in conditions which excluded recent loss and deception. Furthermore, a large proportion of the coins were common bronze issues, unattractive in themselves and unlikely to have been carried to Britain by collectors in the eighteenth and nineteenth centuries. Goodchild could also point to the recent discovery of a further group of Greek coins during excavation in Exeter by the Devon Archaeological Society (1939: 10). Having drawn attention to other finds of Greek issues in the South West, he suggested that the Exeter finds indicated visits by east Mediterranean seamen to the Exe estuary over a lengthy period from the third century BC to the later Roman period, and perhaps later in the fifth and sixth centuries (below, p. 255).

First of all, the notion that all the Exeter finds are the result of a hoax can be swiftly disposed of. Discoveries repeated at intervals from the early years of the nineteenth century until the 1930s must be regarded either as genuine or the work of several generations of hoaxers operating with a single-mindedness and persistence rare in Devon. As Shortt recognized, certain individual pieces must be regarded as questionably ancient imports. The majority are genuine.

Secondly, the Exeter coin-finds are not to be seen as an isolated and freakish phenomenon. Greek coins of a wide range of dates have been reported from a number of sites in the south-western peninsula and extending eastwards into Dorset (Milne 1948; Fox 1950). As Milne argued in his study of the coins contained in the Rackett collection (derived mainly from sites in Dorset), this concentration in a particular area cannot be explained away as the dispersal of pieces brought to Britain in modern times. The distribution is too wide for such a thing to be plausible and there is nothing in the circumstances surrounding many of the finds to suggest that they are anything other than ancient losses. The Exeter finds must thus be accepted as one aspect of a wider phenomenon, for which as yet we have no well-defined archaeological context. The presence of so many Greek and Greek Imperial issues is best viewed in the light of the fact that Exeter may well have been the first port of call for many vessels arriving from the Mediterranean. That small change of ultimately Mediterranean origin was dispersed in the town is understandable enough. Once there, the small value bronze coins in particular are unlikely to have been distributed very widely.

Settlement on the Land

Seen as a whole the *civitas Dumnoniorum* was one of the least Romanized regions of Roman Britain. *Isca* was a recognizably Roman provincial community. Most of the rest of the canton in its outward form was no more Roman than tribal communities on the northern frontiers or even beyond them. So slight was the penetration of Roman provincial culture in most of the peninsula that some fieldworkers of the early twentieth century doubted that the Romans had ever conquered Cornwall. Even Hencken (1932: 190–1) believed that the far South West had been left unadministered by Rome. There are still many who believe that the Roman advance ended at Exeter. As we have seen in the preceding chapter, the conquest of the Dumnonii was completed in the reign of Nero and less than a decade after his death the Roman garrisons could be withdrawn from the peninsula, never again to be imposed. The tribal name as it is reported to us by Ptolemy and the Antonine Itinerary was Dumnonii, a name philologically linked with the *Fir Domnann* of Irish legend, a people said to be of British origin. There are other related names recorded in Ireland, for instance *Erris Domnann* and *Inber Domnann*, in which the element *Domn-* is probably to be derived from a divine name Domnu. If this is so, then the Dumnonii will have been the worshippers of the god or goddess *Dumnū* or *Dumnonū*. Other derivations have been suggested, but none is satisfactory (Rivet and Smith 1979: 343). A tribal grouping which covered so large and varied a tract of country will certainly have embraced a number of smaller septs or populations. There is one positive indication of this in the far South West. The Ravenna Cosmography records the name *Durocornavis*, in which the first element is the familiar Celtic prefix *Duro-*, meaning fort, stronghold. The second element, Cornovii, refers to a population group or sub-tribe, presumably resident in the far South West since the name is perpetuated in that of Cornwall itself. The meaning of the name is disputed. The element *Corn-* should mean 'horn' or 'promontory', which some have seen as referring to the cliff-castles of the Cornish coast. More probable is an origin in a divine name (which might have found expression in cult-images or totemic devices) of a horned deity of fertility, cognate with the Gaulish Cernunnos or the unnamed horned god of the Brigantes. The possibility that other septs were subsumed under *Dumnonii* must clearly be allowed for. The population of the Exmoor fringes may well have comprised one such grouping, that of the South Hams another [1].

The ancient name of Scilly, at least in the form in which it is presented by Roman writers, is known to us. In the earliest of these references, in the *Natural History* of the Elder Pliny, an island lying between Britain and Ireland is called *Silumnus* or *Silimnus* (*Nat. Hist.*: IV, 103). *Silimna* or *Sillina* would be a reasonable emendation to agree with the noun *insula*. Solinus, writing in the third century AD, gives *Silura* as the name of an island off the coast occupied by the Dumnonii (*Polyhistoria*: 24). There is perhaps confusion here with the tribal name *Silures* and it is noteworthy that other versions of Solinus' text give *Sillina* as this island name. Two centuries later, an island situated 'beyond' Britain and called *Sylina* appears in the *Chronicles* of Sulpicius Severus, when the exile of two heretics to this remote spot is recorded (Severus: 11, 51). The nearest we can get to the Roman name is probably *Sillina* or *Sulina*. Not the least interesting feature of the record is the fact that these widely different and independent sources agree in presenting the name in the singular form (above, p. 11).

Roads and Ports

On present evidence it might seem as though a network of roads did not develop in the canton of the Dumnonii. Scarcely any lengths of road have been proved to exist by archaeological means and the alignment of only a few major routes can be proposed, and then on meagre evidence. It must be borne in mind, however, that roads in the Roman provinces were not always well metalled or paved and in remote areas, like the South West, were not always well maintained. Cleared tracks might suffice the needs of Imperial officials, traders and any other travellers who penetrated to these districts, and archaeological traces of them might never appear. There is, at least, no doubt about the course of the Fosse Way, which terminated not at Seaton, as is sometimes claimed, but at Exeter itself. This major highway, in its origin a route surveyed and laid out by legionary surveyors in the first century, entered the region over the Greensand hills on the Devon–Somerset border and then took a fairly direct line to *Isca*. From Honiton to Exeter the present A30 follows the Roman line closely. A major road left the Fosse Way, probably in the Otter valley, and ran eastward towards Dorchester, crossing the River Axe near Axminster.

The alignment of the main route west of Exeter, since one may be safely assumed, is only partially known. Like the medieval route which was its successor, it ran down the spine of the peninsula on a course largely dictated by topographical features, especially the massive bulk of northern Dartmoor. Immediately west of Exeter the road must have swung into the Creedy valley and thence due west to avoid the broken hill-country north of the Teign. The northern flank of Dartmoor was best skirted along the Okement near Okehampton, as today, and from there a more or less direct line could be followed, along the line followed by the modern A30, to the Tamar crossing at or near Launceston. The continuation westward is not clear and several routes might have crossed east Cornwall. A direct east–west route across Bodmin Moor is possible and was preferable to a long detour to north or south of the upland. Beyond, the most direct route through central Cornwall is that pursued by the present A30, but there is nothing that suggests that this was the line of the Roman highway. Nevertheless this spinal route seems the most likely course of the main east–west road even though direct testimony is yet to be found. The milestone of Gordian III found, apparently *in situ*, at Gwennap Pit near Redruth (*RIB*: 2234) is the only indication that the modern highway may be following a Roman line in this part of west Cornwall.

Records of road-maintenance (commonly called 'milestones') found at Breage and St Hilary (*RIB*: 2232; 2233) reveal the existence of a length of road which ran from the Lizard along the south coast towards the Land's End peninsula. Much more surprising are two records of road building or repair on the north coast of Cornwall. One, of the reign of Gallus and Volusian (251–3) lay in the churchyard at Tintagel, the other, of Licinius (308–24), at Trethevy, 2 km to the east (*RIB*:2230; 2231). It is difficult to see what compelled the erection of these records in this district. There is no obvious route approaching Tintagel from the east, though there is a plausible line now followed by the A395. More puzzling is the absence of any reason for such a route. Why should imperial officials be concerned with the maintenance of a road which terminated at Tintagel, or any other site on this rocky, inhospitable stretch of coast? No rich mineral deposits lay in this area and there was certainly no harbour which might have sheltered sea-borne traffic. This problem remains unresolved, along with much else connected with late Roman Tintagel (below, p. 262).

Other lengths of road have been proposed as Roman, but none is certain.

A road running through Stratton in north Cornwall, a place which may retain a memory of an early road in its name (Old English: *straet*), appears to be aligned on the harbour at Bude. In south Devon, an embanked road running over the Haldon ridge and making for the lower Teign could be of medieval or later date, and the remains of a bridge over that river are likewise not closely datable. Certain routes seem almost certain to have caught the eye of the Roman surveyor, as for example that which led from the Creedy valley into that of the Yeo and Taw and thence to Bideford Bay. But no structural remains of a road have come to light and it is likely that, as over most of the canton, no well built *agger* was ever constructed.

Ports and small harbours suitable for Roman merchantmen could have existed at numerous points along the indented south coast. Exeter, of course, will have attracted much of whatever traffic crossed from north-western Gaul and vessels would have been able to reach the city's quays from the Exe, without transferring cargoes to barges on the estuary. It seems at least possible that a second port lay somewhere on Plymouth Sound, this in addition to the site at Mount Batten which still saw some use in the Roman period. A scatter of late Roman coins and a little building material from the site of Plymouth itself hints at a port-site at the mouth of the Tamar but gives no clearer indication of where it might have lain. A port on the Sound could have served as a major collection-point and exit for supplies of metal, especially from Dartmoor. In the east of the region the likeliest site for a port is Axmouth. A harbour still existed here in the sixteenth century, as Leland reports, but at that date what he calls the 'mighty rigge and barre of pible stones' was threatening to close the estuary (Leland: I, 242). Down to the nineteenth century a few boats managed to use the haven before it became completely choked with shingle. A harbour so close to the open sea has obvious attractions and the possibility of a Roman installation here is a real one (above, p. 202). The Atlantic coast offered little in the way of shelter to craft making for the Severn estuary. The estuary of the Taw and Torridge in the Barnstaple area is the most obvious haven for major craft. From Hartland Point (*Promontorium Herculis?*) to the Camel estuary the harbours are small (e.g. Boscastle) and unlikely to have been in regular use. The Camel estuary itself is a likely point of entry and exit. A site near St Enodock's Church which has produced a wide range of later Roman metal-work and pottery may point to a harbour here, at one end of a major route across Cornwall (Haverfield 1924: 6).

Villas

The sole fully excavated villa at Holcombe, originated in, or at least on the site of a farmstead of the first century AD, though the Iron Age settlement need not have existed for more than a decade or two before the Roman conquest, if indeed as long as that (Pollard 1974). The first buildings of the Roman period at Holcombe were going up about AD 70, perhaps after a break in the occupation of the site which may have lasted for twenty-five years. These were rectangular buildings in timber, the plan of which could not be recovered in full, the several phases of which extended down to the later second century. At the end of that century, an aisled hall with outer walls in stone was constructed over the site of the earlier timber buildings and this was accompanied or shortly followed by the erection of a large and unusual timber structure immediately to the east. This may originally have been a rather wide-aisled hall, subsequently modified by the insertion of a through-passage about the centre of the building, the addition of a verandah or service-corridor along its northern side, and subdivision of the east end into a number of small chambers. These alterations are unlikely to have been made all at the same time. No close analogy for this remarkable structure has been recorded among the earlier villas of Roman Britain.

The main development of the villa came in the peaceful and prosperous third century (Pollard 1974: 84–6). Further rooms and a verandah were added to the stone-walled aisled hall in the early decades of the century and there were further extensions of the main dwelling before 300. The appointments of the third-century villa were simple but the diet of its inhabitants was varied enough: ox, pig, sheep, chicken, mallard, woodcock and thrush, salmon and sea-bream. Further development of the plan in the earlier fourth century turned the villa into a long narrow range more than 50 m long with a verandah running along the entire length. After the mid-fourth century came the most ambitious 'improvement' of all, the provision of a bath-house entered from the southern end of the long verandah (Swann 1880; Pollard 1974: 94–101). This was in the form of an irregular octagon, arranged about a central sunken bath or pool. Around this focal point lay a series of irregularly planned rooms, three of these having internal apses. The structure had been badly damaged, first by excavation in the nineteenth century, later by ploughing, so that many of the internal details cannot be reconstructed. This particularly applies to the system of heating, the supply of water and the drainage. The remains of one furnace were identified in one chamber on the east side, but precisely how the flow of heated water was regulated in the baths as a whole remains unknown.

The Holcombe bath-house is a highly ornamental building, unexpectedly so for so modest a villa. Architecturally, it has much in common with the octagonal baths at the Lufton villa in Somerset (Hayward 1952), also of the fourth century and quite possibly the work of the same designer/builder.

Though it is an exceptional building in the east Devon landscape, it serves as a reminder of the considerable prosperity with which Britain was visited in the later Empire and a proof that that affluence was enjoyed in the borderlands of the Dumnonii and the Durotriges. The site of the villa was abandoned as a dwelling-place at the end of the fourth century or shortly thereafter.

Scavenging among the ruins went on for as long as usable objects and materials could be obtained. Then the site became overgrown and was forgotten.

The other villas in this landscape are very imperfectly known. A substantial stone house is reported to have been excavated by the Rev. F. E. W. Langdon in 1914 at Membury Court seven miles north of Seaton, and another lies at Whitestaunton just across the Somerset border. Other small villas may well emerge in this area to reinforce the distinction between a rural scene in which villas were relatively common features and a landscape farther west from which they were wholly absent. Although it cannot be insisted upon, it is possible that this distinction is a reflection of the tribal boundary between the Durotriges and Dumnonii.

The history of a complex of buildings at Seaton, published as a villa but possessing very unusual features for such a site, was briefer than that of Holcombe (Miles 1977a; Silvester 1981b). A native farmstead of the first century AD is represented by a pair of enclosures, possibly pounds for stock. The Roman-period buildings so far revealed are rectangular blocks without embellishment or refinements, dating from the second to early-fourth centuries. A detached bath-house of simple scale but some pretension was built in the third century 75 m east of the domestic quarters. The most interesting buildings are two large timber structures which stood on the slope to the north of the baths. These were long narrow ranges only 4 m wide but up to 45 m in length, each with a verandah. The western building had at least two internal partitions, the eastern none, though they may have been destroyed by later ploughing. No closely similar buildings seem to have been recorded in Romano-British villas. They seem ill-suited to such agricultural purposes as the stalling of animals and the storage of crops. They look more like simple living quarters and their barrack-like plan suggests some official connection. Indeed the entire complex at Seaton is with difficulty identified as a villa. We might well wonder whether we are dealing with an official installation connected with a nearby harbour, at Axmouth perhaps (above, p. 202). This would account for the absence of a villa-dwelling as well as helping to explain the paramilitary character of the buildings. The presence of a tile-stamp of Legio II Augusta must also be remembered. The later history of the buildings seems to point in this same direction. The baths and the long timber buildings were deliberately demolished and their foundations carefully back-filled and levelled, this probably in the third or early-fourth century. This would, of course, be standard military practice. The main house continued in use into the fourth century but without elaboration of its plan or furnishings. Before the end of the century it too had come to an end.

As is well known, the villa at Holcombe lies on the western borders of Romano-British villas. Even in the broad vale of the lower Exe and in the South Hams, few sites resembling even simple villas have yet been recorded [2]. It is, therefore, astonishing to be confronted by a site in west Cornwall, more than 150 km from Holcombe, which bears all the outward marks of a villa. This is the building at Magor Farm, Illogan, near Camborne (O'Neil 1933). This was a small portico villa with projecting wings, in its first phase dating from the mid or late-second century. The east range was later extended by the addition of four small chambers, and there was further extension of the western end at an unspecified date. At no stage was the house lavishly appointed. The portico had a tessellated floor and some walls were painted. But there were no heated rooms or other refinements. The excavator believed that the building was abandoned about or shortly after 230–40, the date of a small hoard of *denarii* found in a wall-recess, but the evidence is hardly convincing. Coins of the later third century were found in upper levels within the house, these being linked in the excavation report with 'squatter occupation'. More probably they denote occupation down to the late-third century, the relevant archaeological deposits having been disturbed by ploughing. There was no organized search for other buildings in the vicinity, though a small trial trench did reveal a sequence of walls immediately west of the house, of which at least one was apparently Roman, the others being undated.

The Magor villa is not easily explained. It is difficult to see it as a villa in the proper sense of the word. Thomas (1966, 92) has suggested it may be the 'sunset home of a Dumnonian official once on official service' and this may be near the truth. Might it not be the residence of an official *still* on imperial service, for example a member of the procurator's staff or even a *beneficiarius consularis*? There need be nothing 'official' about such a residence in an apparently peaceful area like second-century Cornwall. We might reasonably expect other buildings in the vicinity and there is ample room for these. The site is so unusual as to call for further examination.

Settlement Pattern and History

Among the larger enclosed sites are a number which have produced evidence for their being settlements of wealth and status. The site at Carvossa, Probus, 1.5 km from the west bank of the Fal, is a case in point (Douch and Beard 1970). This was a sub-rectangular enclosure of about 2.3 ha (5.5 acres), girt by a massive rampart 4 m wide and still standing 2 m high in places, with occupation extending beyond the defences to east and north. This was not a hill-fort. The settlement occupies gently sloping ground of no great height and therefore does not dominate its immediate environs. Indeed, before excavation took place the site would have seemed unremarkable but for its unusual size. Nor does the late Iron Age occupation appear to be in any way exceptional. But early in the Roman period, about AD 50–55, considerable quantities of high-quality Roman pottery began to arrive at Carvossa, along with glass and bronze brooches. So unusual is this phenomenon in first-century Cornwall that it invites explanation. The position of the site is worth note, close to the Fal which was probably navigable to at least this point in the early Roman period. The place could thus have been accessible to Roman merchants beginning to explore the possibilities of new markets beyond the fringes of the emergent province of Britannia. Or the Roman army may have established itself at a site on the Fal and the imported items could thus have passed into native hands in exchange for various goods and services. Less than 2 km to the south of Carvossa lies the even larger enclosed site of Golden, on a hill-slope but in a tactically stronger position than its neighbour. There has been no excavation here, however, and no objects have been reported from the site. Its position close to the Fal could have caught the eye of a Roman commander. Equally, it may have been the principal nucleus of Iron Age power in the area and the imported goods at Carvossa may be simply a reflection of the prominence of Golden.

Another enclosure which has produced early Roman material of high quality is the smaller work at Caerloggas, St Mawgan in Pyder, sited on a sloping ridge above the River Menalhyl (Threipland 1956). This was a univallate enclosure of only about 1 ha (2.4 acres) with a surprisingly powerful gate-structure, more appropriate to a large hill-fort. The metalwork finds are of particularly high quality for a Cornish Iron Age settlement, including the well-known shield-mount (above, p. 183). Roman imports included amphorae, flagons and fine wares of pre-Flavian and Flavian date, and presumably the wine that normally accompanied such wares. Here too was the residence of someone who could offer something to Roman traders. It must be appreciated that before excavation took place at these two sites they betrayed no hint that they were in any way unusual. So many earthwork enclosures in Devon and Cornwall have never been examined at all that it would be unwise to assume that we are anywhere near a true picture of the extent of early Roman contacts as revealed by imports, still less of social differentiation between settlements. But the first indications of such differentiation are evident and more will appear as work proceeds.

By far the commonest type of settlement in west and central Cornwall was the enclosed homestead or 'round' (Thomas 1966; Wells 1978). These appear in the local place-names as car-, caer-, ker- and -gear, reflecting the survival of their surrounding earthworks, in many cases down to the present day. Definition of a round is difficult and, as a precise term for a settlement-form, unsatisfactory. Though commonly circular or oval, subrectangular and even triangular plans also occur. Most are univallate with a single entrance. The great majority are less than 1 ha in area, many are only half that figure. They are usually now taken to be essentially agricultural in their functions and not designed with defence in mind. But some of the larger rounds do possess strong defences akin to those of hill-forts and a number are sited in strong positions. The few excavated instances have been shown to contain buildings of various kinds, but it would be rash to assume that all were enclosed settlements. Stock-pounds and other agricultural enclosures might well figure among the known sites (e.g. Stoke Gabriel in Devon, below, p. 228 (Thomas 1966: 87–9; Wells 1978)). Rounds cannot be considered as an exclusively south-western phenomenon. Enclosed homesteads and hamlets are found all over upland Britain and in the great river valleys of the Midlands and the South. *Mutatis mutandis* there are clear resemblances with rounds in scale and disposition.

The total known to exist or to have existed is in excess of 1,500, the great majority lying in west Cornwall where in some areas their density may be as high as one per 3 sq km. Farther east the density of rounds is more difficult to determine, as agencies of destruction have removed a greater proportion of ancient earthworks, but they occur up to the Tamar valley and in smaller numbers in north and west Devon. The most common siting is on hill-slopes or valley-sides between 75 m and 120 m OD, much less often on hill-tops. They are densest in the coastal plain of East Penwith, around the Helford river and on the slopes of the West Penwith uplands. The higher bleak moors of West Penwith and the Lizard show very few instances. There seems to be no marked relationship between rounds and other settlement-forms such as hill-forts and hill-slope enclosures (Wells 1978: 52–3). Groups of huts occur fairly frequently close to rounds, but this may not signify anything other than successive use of land by different types of settlement. In some cases it is certain that a round replaced an earlier open settlement of huts (e.g. Trevisker, Porthmeor). Nonetheless, there is a possibility that some hut-groups were socially dependent on rounds. In west Cornwall there is a distinct grouping of rounds, with over 80 per cent lying within 1.5 km of another (Wells 1978: 55–6). Even when allowance is made for sites of different date, this is impressive and may be related to the 'budding-off' of settlements as the population grew. By and large, the later *tref* settlements formed a quite distinct horizon of land-colonization, although a few rounds were reoccupied (Thomas 1966: 97).

Extensively excavated rounds are still so few that generalization about their internal arrangements and history is hazardous. Goldherring, Castle Gotha and Trethurgy present the largest body of information yet available for sites occupied in the Roman period and the variety evident in these three alone underlines the need for caution in treating these works as a distinct phenomenon. Goldherring began as a strongly walled and ditched enclosure in the late Iron Age. The main occupation, however, was from the second to the fifth centuries AD and took the form of courtyard houses and sizeable huts, set for the most part against the inner face of the rampart. The settlement was a small one, measuring only 0.8 ha (1.6 acres) and seems to represent a single family holding (Guthrie 1969). Castle Gotha was of similar size but rather more elaborately planned. At least two large, oval houses and a number of smaller huts lay within the enclosed space of 0.8 ha, while a possible rectangular building resting on timber sills was also postulated by the excavator. Metalworking of a modest kind was practised by some of the inhabitants but only as an adjunct to their normal agricultural pursuits (Saunders and Harris 1982).

The most completely examined enclosed settlement is Trethurgy, 4 km inland from St Austell Bay (Miles and Miles 1973). This site has all the outward characteristics of a round and it is thus of interest that occupation did not begin before the later Roman period. The roughly oval enclosure, measuring 55 m by 48 m internally (0.2 ha) was bounded by an earthwork up to 6 m wide at the base. A single narrow entrance lay on the downhill side. As so often, the ditch was a far from formidable obstacle some 3–4 m wide but only 1.5 m deep. The structures within lay mostly close to the enclosure bank, leaving a large open space in the centre. The buildings included four or five substantial oval structures with rather roughly built outer walls of stone. In two cases timber uprights had been embedded in the inner faces of the stonework. It is unlikely that all these structures existed at one and the same time, since occupation may have extended over a century or rather more. Essentially, the site may be yet another example of the *Einzelhof*, owned or at least inhabited by a single family and its immediate adherents, and thus is analogous with many peasant sites found all over Roman Britain. One further structure heightens the impression of a native agricultural milieu. This is a rectangular timber construction consisting of four stout posts such as could have supported an above-ground store for grain and other perishables.

Prehistoric and early Roman material is absent from Trethurgy. Occupation may have begun in the third century, reaching its peak in the fourth and early fifth. But the place remained inhabited until much later for relatively large quantities of imported pottery were arriving here in the first half of the sixth century, from the Mediterranean lands and from western Gaul (below, p. 253).

In addition to the common detritus of settlements of this kind, there is one object which suggests an interest in the nearby mineral deposits on the part of the late Roman inhabitants. This is an oval ingot of tin, broadly similar to those from Chun Castle, Madron and Par Beach on St Martin's (below, p. 232). But there is no other sign of any preoccupation with metal extraction at Trethurgy and there is certainly no reason to see the place as a major centre of tin- or pewter-working in late Roman times.

Another enclosed settlement occupied principally in the late Roman period is that at Grambla, Wendron, near the Helford river. The surrounding earthworks here are rectilinear in form, forming almost a square with sides of 60 m internally. Limited excavation in the interior revealed parts of two stone-walled structures of unusual interest. One was oval, 18 m long and 9 m wide in the centre. The other was longer, about 20 m, and with straight sides on the long axis, giving it almost a boat-shaped plan. There are general similarities with the oval building at Castle Gotha 6 km to the south and a remoter resemblance exists to the long-houses of early medieval Britain, exemplified in the South West by those at Mawgan Porth (below, p. 305), though the

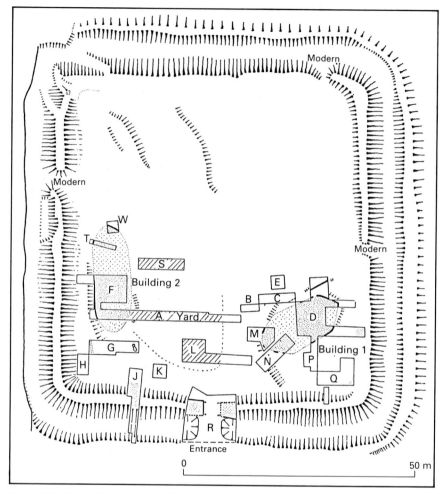

Figure 8.2   The enclosure at Grambla

Grambla buildings do not seem to have possessed internal partitions. As at Trethurgy, occupation continued after 400, perhaps throughout the fifth and into the sixth century (Saunders 1972: 52).

The great number and variety of visible rounds in Cornwall are liable to make us forget the existence of open settlements. But these did exist, not only in the form of isolated courtyard houses and huts, but also as considerable nuclei of both with associated fields still clearly in evidence, notably in the West Penwith uplands. Such open settlements are less well attested in the lowland areas, but enough are known to suggest a substantial hidden factor (e.g. Topsham (Jarvis and Maxfield 1975)). All this tends to the conclusion that the Roman period rural population of the peninsula, especially at its western end,

Plate 8.1 Aerial view of the excavated round at Trethurgy, Cornwall. Several round houses stand immediately inside the perimeter wall around a central space.

was greater than it is today and perhaps than it has been at any time since AD 400.

Few rural sites of the period have been excavated around Exeter and in east Devon generally. A striking feature of the ancient landscape, as revealed mainly in cropmarks to the aerial observer, is the large number of rectangular and rectilinear enclosures in the lower valleys of the Exe and Creedy, and to the west of the Exe estuary (Bidwell 1980: 18; Griffith 1983). Some of these appear to stand alone: others are surrounded by small closes or fields. None has been examined on a large scale, but finds from a few indicate that they at least belong to the Romano-British period and perhaps the preceding Iron Age. The overall resemblance to enclosures of Roman date on the gravels of Trent, Thames and Severn is close. It is, however, possible that some of these sites originated much earlier, possibly in the late Bronze Age. Their distribution pattern is also probably incomplete; the upper Exe valley and the Culm Measures may well some day show that they extended north and west. Some of these enclosures will have contained dwellings and farm-buildings, though finds of building-material from them are so scarce as to suggest that these structures were normally in timber. Others presumably served as stock-pounds and home closes. A group of enclosures at Pond Farm, Exminster probably falls into this category (Jarvis 1976: 67–72). There is evidence for use of one enclosure in the second century, but no buildings were encountered in limited excavation. The most completely excavated site is the enclosure at Lower Well Farm, Stoke Gabriel (Masson Philips 1966). This was in use in the first and second centuries, but not apparently as a dwelling-site. Around it lies an extensive field-system defined by low stone walls and a small hut within these produced pottery of the later Roman period. Another rectangular enclosure close to the Iron Age settlement on Milber Down, Newton Abbot, has a group of small fields or closes associated with it, this too dating to the later Roman centuries (Vachell 1964). Many such settlements must have existed at this time on the good land of the South Hams.

The only farmstead site in the vicinity of Exeter to be excavated on any scale has revealed a mixture of native and Roman in its structural components. This is a site at Topsham, immediately adjacent to the estuary flats of the Exe (Jarvis and Maxfield 1975). Beginning in the first century AD, a series of substantial timber structures, rectangular in plan, formed the nucleus of a farming unit, to which also belonged a number of four-post structures (grain-stores?) as well as the customary pits and working-hollows. The recognizably Roman or Romano-British element is a three-roomed rectangular dwelling, apparently with a verandah on its eastern side. The plan is reasonably close to that of several early villas, in timber and in stone, in southern Britain, and in view of the nearness of the site to Exeter interpretation of it as an attempt to introduce a new building-type in the first century AD (its undoubted date) seems colourable. But if that was the case, it is notable that development into a fully fledged villa (or indeed into anything) did not ensue. Occupation seems not to have continued beyond the first century and was associated only with timber buildings of simple plan and no pretension. It may be that a more imposing residence was constructed on another site nearby, but of this there is no trace. The picture is one of subsistence farming at a fairly humble level, remarkably little affected by the existence of the legionary fortress only 6 km distant, except for the supply of high-quality pottery and probably other goods.

It is unfortunate that so little work has been devoted to south-western hill-forts, for it is to be expected that here, as in Somerset and in Wales, well fortified sites will again have been sought after as secure places of settlement. There are a few indications that this was so. Inside Cadbury Castle in central Devon, a shaft or well 18 m deep had received numerous trinkets, bracelets and beads in the fourth century (Fox, A. 1952b). This looks like a votive deposit, but those responsible for it are likely to have been living close by and presumably in the hill-fort itself. A late Roman community occupied part of the cliff castle at Trevelgue Head on the north Cornish coast, perhaps from the fourth century into the fifth or sixth, and there are hints that this may also have been so at Membury and Berry Head in Devon. The later occupation of sites like

Chun Castle, Killibury and Castle Dore merely underlines the probability that secure places were ever more attractive from the late Roman period onward.

The most interesting settlement site of the period on Scilly is that at Halangy Down near the northern side of St Mary's, partly for the information it affords on contemporary conditions, but chiefly for a connection in settlement type which it betrays with the mainland and specifically with West Penwith (Ashbee 1974: 189–95). A group of structures set on a slope were conjoined to form a complex building which has much in common with the courtyard houses of west Cornwall. A long, narrow entrance passage led into a rectilinear courtyard off which led two sizeable circular chambers, one of which had appended to it a small pentagonal annexe recessed in the stout surrounding wall. The final form was achieved only after several progressive stages of building, beginning in the later Iron Age and continuing into at least the second century AD. Other less well preserved structures lying nearby were rectilinear in plan and these too may have been of Roman date.

The local economy had a varied basis. Terraced plots on the adjacent hillside and finds of querns in the settlement attest at least some grain-growing. A small oven may have been used to dry corn for storage or to produce malt for beer. The domestic animals were principally cattle and pigs, with some sheep and goats. Fishing may be assumed though fish-remains were sparsely represented. A shell midden was almost entirely composed of the shells of limpets, a limited source of protein for man but a useful supply of fish-bait.

The small uninhabited islet of Nornour off St Martin's has produced the most abundant and at first sight surprising finds of Roman date on Scilly (Dudley 1967; Butcher 1978). From the upper levels of a group of Bronze Age and later round houses, Miss Dudley recovered an astonishing quantity of Roman objects, brooches in particular, but also including coins, rings, beads, glass, pottery and ceramic figurines. On any Romano-British site in the South West this would hardly be a normal assemblage. On an exposed rock off Scilly it is even more remarkable. How is it to be explained? Certainly not as a workshop for the manufacture of brooches, as was argued in the first excavation report (Dudley 1967: 9–10 and 16–18). The deposition of these objects here is plainly specialized in character, votive not utilitarian. There are, for example, more than fifty types of brooch represented here and many are unique or very rare in Britain. The suggestion of a votive deposit is strongly reinforced by the presence of thirteen fragments of Gallic figurines, six of the so-called pseudo-Venus, seven of the nursing mother or *Dea nutrix*. This is the vital clue to the nature of the site. This was a shrine, its position on this small but prominent islet indicating a shrine visited by sailors, and some of the objects deposited here suggesting sailors passing from Gaul to Britain and back again. Nornour may thus have been both a landmark and a staging-post on the crossing from south-west Britain to western Gaul and to Spain, a natural spot for observance of the gods of travel and the sea, from which Venus herself was born.

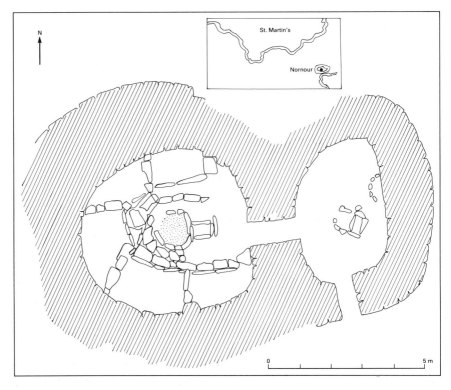

Figure 8.3   The shrine at Nornour

Curiously enough, the most notable Roman object from the whole of Scilly is also connected with religious observance. This is the well-known uninscribed granite altar probably found at Hughtown on St Mary's and now housed on Tresco (Ashbee 1982b). It may have come from a well, shaft or other underground repository like that at Bosence in west Cornwall (Haverfield 1924: 8). Ashbee has suggested the possibility of a cult building in the vicinity of Hugh Town, perhaps within the ramparts of the promontory fort of the Giant's Castle (Ashbee 1974: 218). However that may be, the altar is fairly certainly an ancient import from the mainland and the mere fact of its importation reveals something of the strength and frequency of the connection between Scilly and the main island. Borlase (1756: 12) records a structure in this part of St Mary's which may have been much earlier than the Tudor period and which just possibly may have been the remains of a circular shrine like Arthur's O'on in Stirlingshire.

Just below the lines (of the Garrison) are the remains of an old fort. It is a round hillock and seems to have had a *Keep* on top of it, in the same manere as *Trematon* and *Launceston* Castles, in Cornwall, but smaller:

the walls of it have been stripp'd to build the *Lines*; tis call'd *Mount Holles*.

All trace of this odd structure, which does not fit easily into any category of medieval or later building, has vanished since Borlase's day, but some fortunate chance may bring its foundations to light once more.

Industries

There is scarcely a sign that the tin deposits of Devon and Cornwall attracted any attention in the early Roman period. This is understandable enough. The deposits in the Iberian peninsula were rich and the lodes close enough to the surface to be mined by simple methods. Posidonius reports that Spanish tin was reaching the Roman market by the first century BC at the latest (Strabo: 147) and throughout the first two centuries AD this was the principal source for the Empire. In the third century, the best tin still came from Spain (Davies 1935: 104). Tin from the streams of the South West could be no serious competitor to the riches of Iberia. Only by immense labour could any appreciable quantity of tin be won by tin-streaming and even then the yield could never approach that from Galicia and Lusitania, as the small British ingots reveal so clearly. That streaming continued in the early Roman period is not doubted, but there is no evidence that it was anything other than limited in scale, and probably localized in significance. The recorded ingots and finds of cassiterite pebbles are small and no site of this period can be shown to have been a smelting-site. The mould from Castle Gotha may have been used to produce sheet metal, not tin ingots (Saunders and Harris 1982: 147–8).

It has long been evident that this pattern of localized, small-scale extraction was altered in the later Empire. Production in Spain was drastically reduced by various factors about the middle of the third century and other western deposits were, perforce, more systematically exploited. From a variety of streamworks in western and central Cornwall have come Roman objects which attest this increased interest in tin, while from most parts of southern Britain there is evidence of a notable reflection of increased production of the metal in the pewter tableware, jugs, bowls and platters for the most part, which served as respectable substitutes for the silver vessels of the very rich. One find, which made its way into the possession of William Borlase, reveals that pewter was manufactured in at least one location in the South West, at St Just in west Cornwall. This is the two pieces of a greissen mould which was designed to turn out dishes (Brown 1970). A number of pewter and tin vessels found in the region are likely to have been made here. These include a cup from Halviggan,

St Stephen-in-Brannel, a dish from Carnon found along with a hoard of late-third-century coins, a tin bowl from Parson's Park, St Neot, a tin flagon from Carhayes also with late-third-century coins, a largely tin flagon from Goodrington on Torbay, and, most remarkable of all, an almost pure tin bowl with fitting lid from Treloy, St Columb Minor, in its form resembling the stone vessels of this period in west Cornwall. All of these objects are to be dated to the later third and fourth centuries.

Finds of tin ingots have been few and almost all pose problems of dating. The following includes those ingots which are certainly or most probably of Roman date. In some cases we may be dealing with late prehistoric or early medieval instances.

Tin ingots

Carnanton	Rectangular. 17.8 kg. Stamped impressions of? helmeted heads and inscription IEEN? Truro Mus.
Chun Castle	Oval. Not certainly an ingot. 5 kg. Late Iron Age or Roman deposit in fort. (Leeds 1926–7: 238–9.)
Lanlivery	Oval. 21 kg. Geological Mus., London.
Par Beach, St Martin's	Plano-convex. Late Roman deposit in hut. Unpublished.
Pentewan Valley, nr. St Austell	Two, now lost. *c.* 10 kg.
Penwithick, nr. St Austell	Elongated oval, plano-convex. 7.9 kg.
Praa Sands	Four. Oval, plano-convex. Two of 1.8 kg, one of 3.6 kg. Found on beach with timbers which produced a radiocarbon estimate of AD 660 ± 150, but this may not be a safe guide to the date of the ingots. Unpublished.
Tremathack Moor, Madron	Oval, plano-convex.
Trethurgy	Oval, plano-convex. 12 kg. In late Roman deposit within a round (Miles and Miles 1973: 28).
Vellin Antron, Mabe	Oval, plano-convex. One of 'half a dozen found together'.

The St Mawes ingot, often assumed to be Iron Age or Roman, has been deliberately excluded from the reckoning as there are strong arguments in favour of its being medieval (Beagrie 1983). What seems to bind this group of ingots together is the recurring oval shape and plano-convex section and the weights, between 5 and 17 kg. Such dating evidence as exists points to the later Roman period, for instance at Par Beach and Trethurgy, while the Carnanton ingot (though of rectangular form) bears stamped impressions of what appear to be fourth-century helmeted Imperial heads (Haverfield 1924: 10). Unfortunately these are badly corroded and cannot be identified with a particular emperor. The inscription which Haverfield recorded has also almost vanished. The four ingots from Praa Sands are of great interest, particularly in view of their possible dating in the post-Roman period. But the conditions in which this find was made were not ideal and there may be no true connection between the ingots and the timber which gave a radiocarbon estimate in the seventh century. That tin was still being extracted in some quantity at that date is certain, as the famous tale of the open-handed John, Patriarch of Alexandria, reveals (below, p. 255).

The generally late date of the ingots found in Cornwall is given support by a few objects found elsewhere, notably by eight ingots of pewter found in the Thames near Battersea Bridge, six of them bearing the name-stamp SYAG-RIVS, others the legend SPES IN DEO and the Chi-Rho monogram. Their weights ranged from 3 to 7.5 kg. There can be no doubt about the fourth-century date of these and we can fairly safely refine this to the second half of that century or even the final quarter. This is important evidence that some of the extracted tin at least was destined for official purposes, though it would seem unlikely that all such supplies were passing into the hands of Imperial officers (*Eph. Ep.* ix: 1263; RCHM iii: 43, 175 no. 35).

As has been noted, the most obvious reflection of increased tin-production in the late Empire is the widespread appearance of pewter table-ware in north-western Europe. Probably of greater significance at the time was the use of tin (along with lead) in the alloys used in the Imperial coinage from the time of Gallienus to the coinage reforms of Diocletian and Constantine and beyond. Use of tin as a surface-enrichment in imitation of silver has not been satisfactorily demonstrated, but employment of the metal as a whitening agent is well attested.

Some have seen a link between the heightened interest in tin and the appearance in Cornwall of a number of late Roman coin-hoards, especially in the late third and early fourth centuries (Thomas 1966: 91–2; Pearce 1970). There may be some connection between these two phenomena but it need not be intimate or exclusive. The Cornish hoards fall well within the prevailing pattern of such deposits at this date and they may simply reveal that traders were still interested in anything that the region could offer, and that included metals.

It is possible that the iron deposits of eastern Exmoor and the Brendons were mined in the Roman period. Such exploitation is notoriously difficult to date with any precision but the number of Roman objects, mainly coins, recorded from the ironstone deposits is striking and in at least one instance, at a find-spot near Dulverton, late Roman coins were found embedded in iron-slag and waste. Other possible sites of extraction and smelting lay at Luxborough, where an iron *dolabra* was found, Treborough and Syndercombe.

It is strange that so little evidence of pottery-making should have been recovered from a region which possesses so much estuarine and riverine clay. Yet it is the case that virtually no pottery kilns are known in this vast expanse of territory, though it is possible to identify wares which were certainly made here. Several local fabrics have been distinguished at Exeter in the later first century, among them mortaria, deep bowls and upright jars (Bidwell 1979: 192–3). A kiln on the eastern side of the fortress may have produced some of these vessels. A second kiln-site, at Topsham, is represented by wasters of grey ware jars and beakers dating from the Flavian period. In the second century a range of forms copying the black-burnished wares of Dorset may have been made at or near Exeter. The great mass of the common pottery, however, both in the fortress and in the later city, came from elsewhere, much of it from Dorset and other parts of southern Britain, including the Nene valley, Severn basin, and later Oxfordshire and the New Forest. Gaulish imports are also present, most strikingly in the form of *ceramique à l'éponge* from the West, a ware of the later Roman period (Galliou, Fulford and Clément 1980). There are likely to be several major south-western wares still awaiting recognition. A grey fabric containing plates of black mica, for example, is known on sites in south Devon from the late first to the late fourth century, its granitic inclusions suggesting use of the clays of the Teign or the Dart. Farther west, most of the common pottery used in Cornwall was produced there. This material is generally characterized by simple forms and heavy fabrics, some Iron Age in origin. Vessel-types introduced in the first century of Roman rule also heavily influenced later development. No kiln-sites are known for certain, though a number of local wares can be distinguished in west Cornwall. On Scilly, as is to be expected, most of the Roman-period pottery was locally produced, though some vessels were imported from west Cornwall and farther east.

The production of salt from sea-water may have been important in certain locations. The only salt-working site to be examined, however, is that at Trebarveth on the Lizard coast. Here two rectangular ovens were identified, along with the crude ceramic vessels which were used in the evaporation of sea water. The date of the installation lay in the second century AD (Peacock 1969c).

Search for change during the late Roman period is not very productive. It may be that the beginnings of a major reordering of the pattern of settlement lay in the fourth century. But if that is so, the evidence is still to be sought. More far-reaching change, however, was to ensue in the centuries following the collapse of Roman administration in the early fifth century.

Notes

1. Only two Dumnonians are known to us by name. An inscription found at Cologne names Aemilius, son of Saenius, *civis Dumnonius* (Galsterer and Galsterer 1975: 68). Appropriately, Aemilius was a sailor in the Roman fleet on the Rhine.
2. A building at Thorverton in the lower Exe valley is probably a small villa. Information from Mr J. Uglow.

Chapter 9

Dumnonia: The Church and the Kingdom

The Church and the Kingdom

The ending of Roman administration in the early fifth century can have had little impact on the lives and work of most of the inhabitants of south-western Britain. The only significant alteration to the superstructure of government will have been the removal of the impositions in kind which Rome placed upon her provincial subjects and of the other dues required by the Empire of the *civitas Dumnoniorum* as a whole. The break with the Roman world would thus have been felt mainly at the seat of tribal government, in Exeter, and specifically would have affected the members of the curial order (above, p. 213). Upon them, or at least upon those who were prepared to undertake it, would have fallen the burden of ruling the land of the Dumnonii.

We have, of course, no information about how the territory was ruled after 409 or about how the *civitas Dumnoniorum* was transformed into the petty kingdom of Dumnonia. But a power vacuum will not have remained in being for long and the man or men who filled it would naturally have come from the landowning elite of late Roman Britain. The centre of authority, at least for a time, could well have been Exeter, the largest stronghold in the region, though how long that state of affairs continued is quite uncertain. The main, probably the only, function of a provincial city like *Isca* was administrative. Its magistrates controlled the territory assigned to the city and collected the required taxes. When that function was no more, the remaining attraction of the place lay in the security offered by its walls.

There is at present no sign in the archaeology of post-Roman Exeter that a truly urban community continued to occupy the place. That parts of the walled area were still occupied seems likely (though not yet clearly demonstrated), but no ordered settlement seems to have been maintained in the fifth and sixth centuries. Even occasional objects dating from the period are extremely scarce. Pottery, whether imported or local, has not been recorded.

Attempts to reconstruct a king-list for the Dumnonian realm are vain, for they must rest on material which, however generously it is viewed, is not 'historical'. It may contain the names of kings who did exist, but we are in no position to distinguish the real from the legendary. Like other heroic figures of Celtic Britain, we must leave the early princes of Dumnonia in the poetry and romances where they belong.

'In Longborth was Geraint slain:
Heroes of the land of Dumnonia,
Before they were slaughtered, they slew,
Under the thigh of Geraint swift chargers,
Long their legs, wheat their fodder,
Red, swooping like the milk-white eagles'

(Llywarch Hen: *Death of Geraint*)

The first king in whom we can have total confidence as an historical personage is Constantine, a contemporary of Gildas in the mid-sixth century and denounced by him along with four other western rulers (*de Excidio* 28: 'tyrant whelp of the filthy lioness of Dumnonia'). His offences were heinous enough, adultery and murder among them, but among Frankish rulers of the time Constantine would not have seemed more than ordinarily brutal. When Gildas mentions him he had ceased to be king and had apparently entered a monastery. This had scarcely tempered his violent behaviour for in the guise of an abbot he had slain two young men and their guardians, we may guess rivals in some power play. Another ruler, Marcus, also known as Conomorus or Cumomorus, is to be taken seriously on the authority of the ninth century *Life* of St Paul Aurelian (chap. viii), and he too may be a sixth-century figure. Another glimpse of this man and his son may be given us by the sixth-century memorial stone which still stands at Menabilly near Fowey, inscribed DRVSTAVS HIC IACIT/CVNOMORI FILIVS. The names of these two rulers are faint echoes of the Imperial past: appropriately enough they were also borne by two of the 'tyrants' who seized power in Britain in 407.

A more or less unified kingdom may have developed relatively late, perhaps not before 500, and the geography of the peninsula will have tended to encourage bids for local power. In these circumstances the position of the high king may have depended upon the swaying allegiance of a number of petty rulers. It would not then be surprising if the later rulers of Dumnonia had to invent a bogus list of kings like that which confronts us in the manuscript in Jesus College, Oxford Ms 20 (Bartrum 1966). Even the successors of Constantine in the seventh and eighth centuries are shadowy and none can claim to have left any mark on the history of Britain. Bledericus, *dux Cornubiae*, is at least reported as taking part, and being killed, in a known historical event, the British interception of Ethelfrith of Northumbria early in the seventh century (Monmouth: xii, 13). A century later Gerontius (Geraint) could be addressed by Aldhelm in terms that indicate that he was recognized in Wessex as sole ruler of a unified kingdom (below, p. 272). Others are little more than names, like the ill-fated Dumgarth in the late eighth century (below, p. 273).

Migration from South-western Britain

The most puzzling feature of the immediately post-Roman period is the migration of a considerable body of the population from south-western Britain, and from other areas, to north-western Gaul and Spain. This migration is attested by some of the most reliable authorities of the time on both sides of the Channel and cannot be lightly disregarded. But it raises all manner of questions to which there are at present no answers, especially about the date at which it began and what set it in motion. The earliest mention of the British migration is by Gildas, who implies that it started in the years shortly before the battle of Mount Badon, that is in the later fifth century. He does not specifically link the movement into Brittany with the advance of Anglo-Saxon power in southern Britain, though that is the impression conveyed by the placing of the relevant passage adjacent to his account of the evils brought by the English nation. Nor does he identify the precise destination of the migrants as Armorica. Writing a decade or two after Gildas, the Byzantine historian Procopios seems to rely on a different tradition. He tells us that the inhabitants of Britain (Angles, Frisians and Britons) were so numerous that they migrated with women and children to Gaul where they were settled by the Franks as colonists in the more sparsely inhabited regions (Procopios: viii, 20, 8). Not all the details in this passage can or need be insisted on, but its core cannot be mere invention. There is an echo of this story, perhaps, in Geoffrey of Monmouth, who may have been familiar with both Breton and British traditions. He relates that Magnus Maximus transferred large numbers of soldiers and civilians from Britain to Armorica, thus founding a second Britain (Monmouth: v, 12–16). After Maximus's defeat the remnant of his army joined the Britons already settled in Armorica. The tradition recorded in Nennius also referred to the Britons in Armorica as soldiers taken there by Maximus and destined never to return to Britain (Nennius: 27).

What lies behind these memories of a migration, variously reported in later times? First, it seems most unlikely that there was a major movement from Britain to Armorica in the late *fourth* century, as Geoffrey and Nennius relate (*contra* Chadwick 1965: 258). They have simply hit on the expedient of attaching the story of the movement to the activities of Maximus, whose operations in Gaul were well known. Gildas and Procopios, closer in time and to the realities of the period, are more reliable guides to the chronology. The later fifth century and its disturbances is the more plausible context and we hear from another source of a British king, Riothamus, and a British force on the lower Loire (Jordanes: 237): the size of his army, 12,000, is an obvious exaggeration. The evidence of Procopios is particularly valuable. For him, Armorica was now *Britannia*, from which we must deduce a sizeable settlement of Britons in north-western Gaul in the first half of the sixth century, and he adds the further interesting detail that the migrants were being used by the Franks much as barbarian *laeti* had been employed in the late Roman Empire (Thompson 1980: 498–502).

None of our authorities deals with the cause or causes of the movement, beyond linking it with the doings of Magnus Maximus. It is hard to believe that the English advance westward was capable of dislodging large numbers of people in the later fifth century. Nor can Irish raids and settlements be invoked as a threat of major proportions to the security of the western Britons (Chadwick 1965: 262–9). It is probably mistaken to assume that there was only one stimulus or that the impulse to migrate did not change over the decades in which the movement occurred. In the early stages, in the later fifth century, as the old social institutions began to fall apart, it is plausible that adventurous spirits in south-western Britain began to look outward in the hope of gain and advancement. Employment by those who controlled northern Gaul may have offered the most tempting rewards (certainly better than anything which Britain offered) and this may account for the presence of Riothamus and his Britons in Gaul and for the tradition of settlement on vacant lands in the manner of *laeti*. This was a policy followed by Roman commanders, often with success. Later, in the sixth century the character of the movement may have taken on a different form as larger groups sought land and a future in Gaul. Saxons were doing so as well as Britons at that time and the land of Gaul was still vast and attractive.

In this sixth-century phase some Britons, including some perhaps from the South West, settled in north-western Spain, in Galicia (Thompson 1968). The *Acta* of the Councils of Braga record among the bishoprics of that region an *ecclesia Britonensis* and a Bishop Mailoc, a sound Celtic name. This settlement appears to have been in an extensive tract of country from the west coast inland to Asturia, suggesting a large number of migrants, presumably arriving by sea. We do not know when they arrived, except that the bishopric of the Britons was in existence by 570. Probably they moved in the time of freer migration in the first half of the sixth century.

By the middle of the sixth century, Procopios could refer to north-western Gaul as *Britannia* and no longer as *Armorica*. The movement of Britons left other traces on the nomenclature of Brittany which strengthen the link with the South West. About the mid-sixth century three major political organisms are evident in Brittany. In the north and north-west lay *Dumnonia*, in the south-west *Cornouaille*, the Breton Cornwall and still often referred to as such, while in the south lay *Bro Erech*, the land of Weroch, a sixth-century ruler of the region about whom we hear in Gregory of Tours (Tours: V, 19).

Little is known about these early divisions or petty kingdoms, but what is significant for us is the evident link with the South West of Britain contained in the names of two of them. What lay behind the link can only be guesswork, but that an active part was played in the formation of these divisions by settlers or adventurers from British Dumnonia and Cornovia is difficult to deny. More fundamental still is the linguistic link between the two Atlantic peninsulas, for the Cornish and Breton languages are very closely related to each other in morphology and phonology, while differing from the other Celtic tongues. Until the eighth century at least, Breton and Cornish were truly a single language and there is no reasonable doubt that this link was forged in the early post-Roman period by emigration from Britain to Brittany. These connections provide a colourable background for the movements of saints, monks and missionaries in the period after 500 (Bowen 1969: 51–80).

The Church and Monasteries

There is no evidence (and no real likelihood) that the Christian faith had made significant advance in the Dumnonian peninsula before 400. The Chi-Rho monogram scratched on a pottery sherd from Exeter is the only passing witness to the adherence of the Dumnonii to the religion of the Roman state (Fox, A. 1952c: Pl. X, A). It will be safe to assume that the vast majority of the inhabitants remained pagan down to the end of Roman rule and thus that Christianity had to be introduced afterwards. When this was done, by whom and from where are questions which receive no answers at present. It would seem unlikely to have occurred before about 500, at which time we find the earliest epigraphic testimony to the faith in the South West (below, p. 249). And it may be surmised that western Gaul was the origin of the first bearers. Beyond that, we cannot yet go.

Despite the fact that it has attracted much attention and a fair share of trenchant comment, little is known about the pre-Conquest Church in Dumnonia. Most of those who have written on the period have held firm views on the 'Celtic' Church in the South West, Wales, Ireland and Brittany, but when we come to examine the basis of those views, much of the evidence melts away. Most have assumed that the pre-Conquest Church was a monastic Church. Was this really the case and if it was did monasteries control the major institutions of ecclesiastical government? Was there any space left for the functions of the territorial bishops of whom we hear from the eighth century onward? What do we know of the south-western monasteries, their life and work? As in Wales, study of the ecclesiastical life of Dumnonia from the sixth century onward has been dominated by the image of the 'Age of the Saints', an image projected back upon the canvas of the sixth and seventh centuries from the no less real 'Age of Hagiography', that period of the high Middle Ages in which the cult of saints called into being an extraordinary series of saintly *Lives*. These stories present a powerful and appealing picture of many ascetic monks travelling across the lands of Atlantic Britain and Gaul, promoting the Faith and founding religious communities. A few of the *Lives* do contain veritable historical material. But whether the historical perspective they present as a whole is truly of the sixth and seventh centuries is, at best, a very dubious proposition (Dumville 1977; *contra* Morris 1972). Even when genuinely early material is included, how may this have been altered some five hundred years later?

Drawing on evidence from several parts of western Britain, some outline of what the early monasteries were like can be attempted. Many, probably most, were small and have left no trace behind. In south-east Wales for example as many as fifty may have existed (Davies 1982, 143). They appear to have been settlements, not merely isolated churches, and once established the more successful attracted non-monastic settlers to them. Again on analogy with south Wales, they will have lain on or close to the main lines of communication and thus close to the coast and valley routes. Isolated clerics or monks are little heard of: community life seems to have been the ideal. We will never be able to write a history of early monasticism in the South West on the materials available to us. Even a mere list of monastic sites cannot be compiled with any pretension to completeness since so many monasteries made so little impact on the outer world. A small number of the more prominent sites must be our main concern here.

All over Cornwall and sporadically in Devon there occur place-names containing the prefix *lan-*. Like the Welsh *llan*, this element derives from British **lanon* meaning 'cleared or open space', 'enclosure'. In the majority of the Cornish instances the second element is a personal name (as in the Scottish and Irish names in *cil* and *kil*) and in at least a proportion of these the name was, or was believed to be, that of the holy man who first ministered there. Some of the original names, of rather obscure persons, were subsequently abandoned in the medieval period in favour of more illustrious saints or martyrs. Other names prefixed by *lan-* were those of local landowners or of those who gave sites for churches. Although many *lan* names are not ancient and some refer to secular enclosures such as *corlan* (sheepfold) and *bowlan* (cattlepen), there is no doubting that the early stratum of such names was closely associated with the foundation-period of Christianity in the South West. Among many reflections of this truth is the fact that many of the early monastic sites have *lan* as the first element of their names.

From an early date, certainly from the earlier sixth century, enclosed *lans* contained cemeteries, some associated with a saint or other leading figure and distinguished by an inscribed monumental pillar, others simply inhumation graves in long cists. Many such burial-grounds are known in most parts of Cornwall (though few have been well excavated and published, below, p. 251)

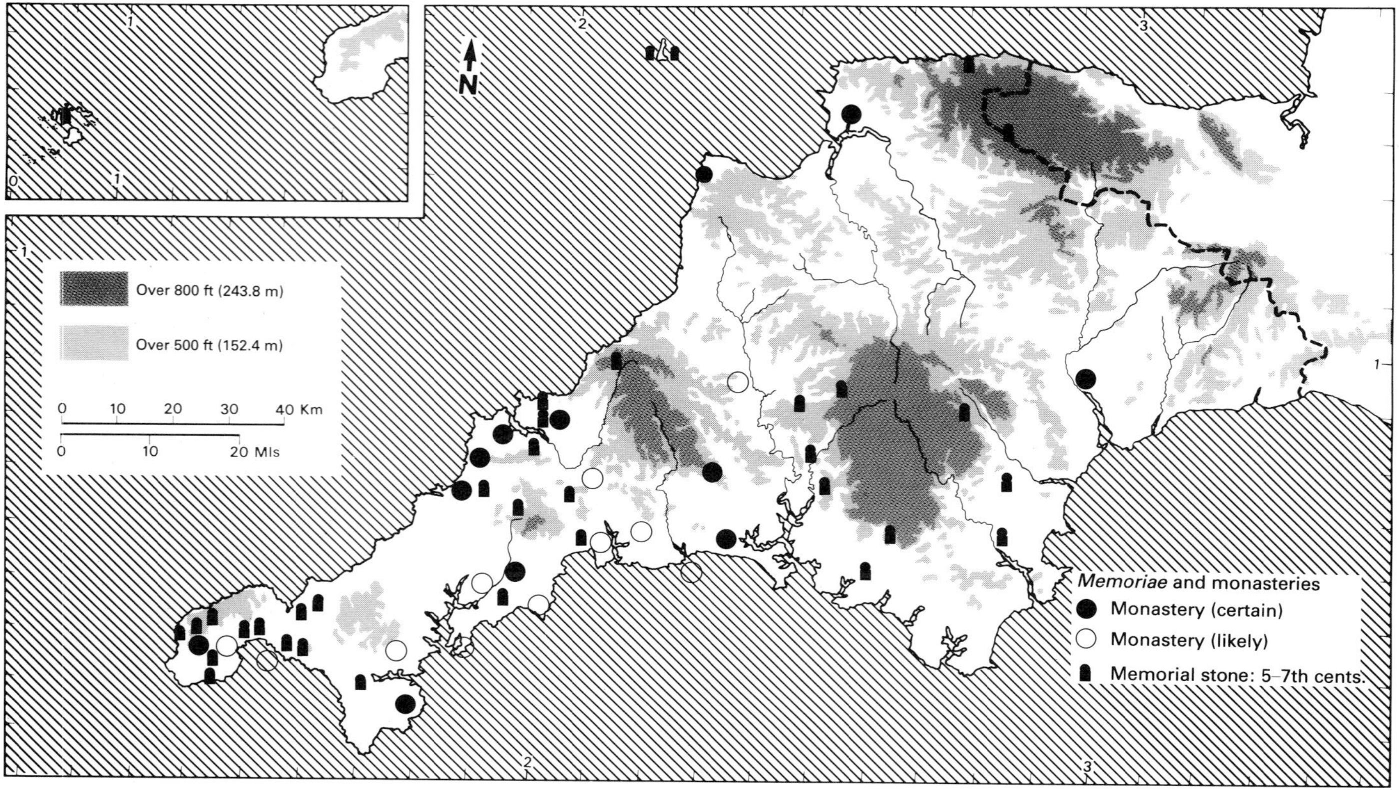

Figure 9.1   Memoriae and monasteries

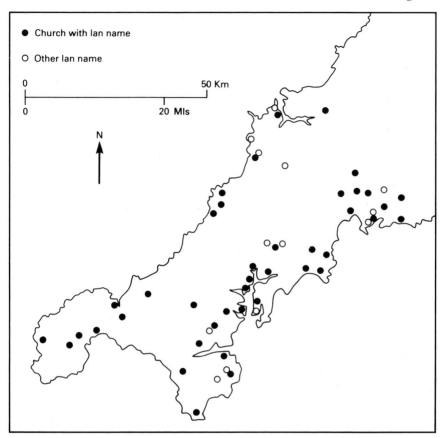

Figure 9.2 Lans in west Cornwall

and a considerable number were continued in use when sites were selected as those of parish churches in the Middle Ages. Thus it is that many churchyards in Cornwall and a few in Devon still bear the evidence of their antiquity in the form of a surrounding bank and a pronounced elevation of the interior above the surrounding ground, as at Lewannick, South Petherwin and Sancreed in Cornwall and at Lustleigh in Devon. This continuity of religious and funerary usage clearly had a formative impact upon the settlement pattern of the region in the post-Roman centuries, one which is still evident in the Cornish countryside today. Unfortunately, not a single *lan* site has yet been examined on an adequate scale nor will this ever be an easy matter. For the present, after a start in the period about 500 AD, it will be sensible to allow for the foundation of *lans* over a considerable length of time, quite possibly down to the beginning of English domination.

Monasteries, some of them to achieve a wide fame in western Europe,

243

were founded in the late fourth and early fifth centuries. Not surprisingly, these foundations were in areas with a long established tradition of learning, both secular and religious, in southern and western Gaul, the most influential being the community founded by Honoratus on the island of Lérins, John Cassian's monastery near Marseilles, and, earliest and most famous of all, the monastic houses inspired by St Martin in the region between Seine and Loire, including Ligugé and Marmoutier (Rousseau 1978). When Martin died, we hear that 2,000 monks gathered together on the day of his burial. We do not know (nor are we ever likely to know) precisely when the first monastic communities were settled in Britain, nor whence the impetus came. Western Gaul seems the most plausible region of origin, and there are some pointers in that direction. But proof is not yet attainable. It is not impossible that individual Christians found a solitary and contemplative life attractive in the latest days of Roman Britain, but such a life could leave no detectable trace behind it. It is unlikely that communities of monks and nuns came into being in Britain or Ireland before the middle of the fifth century. Probably not until the very end of that century or the beginning of the sixth are the beginnings of any form of organized monasticism to be sought and even then the nature of the early monasteries means that secure identification of them on the ground will be a virtual impossibility. We are not dealing with large and highly organized communities which constructed specialized and distinctive buildings. Even their places of worship may not differ in plan from domestic structures.

We must not look for similarities between the earliest monasteries and those which followed the Rule of St Benedict three centuries later. The monastic houses of the sixth century in Ireland, Wales and the South West, so far as we know anything about them at all, were the creation of small, isolated communities, often ascetic and inward-looking, having no regard for the life of other Christians in their neighbourhood. They were not centres of learning and education, nor did they concern themselves with the active propagation of the Christian Faith. The lives of many of their inmates lay in the shade, but not shining. The communities may well have attracted to them some whose need for a life of inward contemplation was not as strong as their desire for a sheltered, relatively carefree existence in which major decisions were made for them. These were not centres of culture in any sense – most were too small for that. The larger monasteries, like that of St Germans, probably did have a somewhat limited cultural and educational role, but these were the exceptions.

Some monks and clerics preferred to isolate themselves from the world still further, choosing to live in some lonely place, an island perhaps or a cave. This was given particular impetus by the ascetic movement of the sixth century. Samson and his three companions living in their fort and cave after withdrawing from the community on Caldy are the best-known representatives of this rigorous form of asceticism, in which hard manual work, abstinence from all bodily pleasures, long vigils and fasting, the avoidance of all possessions were accepted as essential. Asceticism was not confined to hermits. Like St Cuthbert,

Samson and presumably others practised extreme self-denial while acting as head of a community (Davies 1982: 152). There are numerous later legends relating to hermits in Cornwall and there need be no doubt that they did exist and in some cases formed a nucleus for larger communities later (Taylor 1916). But too much influence has been attributed to the eremitical movement in the past, not least on Scilly where a number of early chapels were associated with saintly hermits. As Thomas has demonstrated, there is little or no support for these being hermitages: rather they represent small communities served by a priest (Thomas 1978).

The South West was receptive rather than innovatory in the matter of monastic foundations. When they are viewed as a whole there is nothing in our sources to indicate that any lead in the development of monasticism was provided by personalities or communities in the region. Our most informative source for early monasteries is the *Vita Sancti Samsonis*, a work of the seventh century, possibly compiled in its original form about 650. This is an impressive document by the standards of Saints' Lives, sober, well organized and internally consistent. It mentions two monastic establishments: one called Docco, the other unnamed, established by Samson himself. The author tells us that his source for the early history of the unnamed monastery was an old man whom he met there. We learn that the monastery had been founded some eighty years earlier, that is, about 570/75, and after its creation Samson had departed for Brittany, leaving his own father Amon in charge. It was in touch with other regions, notably Wales and Brittany. It possessed one written work (and perhaps others), an account of Samson's work by one Henoc. Samson had established the monastery near to a cave, having first evicted a fearsome serpent, and he himself dwelt in the cave for a time. (This story, or something like it, is also told of Samson's foundation of a monastery in Armorica and it is difficult to be certain whether it is Cornish or Breton in origin.) We cannot locate the site of Samson's monastery with any confidence. Dedications to the saint are not recorded before 1000 and of the three later instances only two seem even plausible. These are South Hill in east Cornwall, where there is a pillar bearing a Chi-Rho monogram likely to be of sixth or seventh date, and Golant near the Fowey estuary, an attractive site for an early monastery on topographical grounds but with no further support in its favour. We are on safer ground with the other monastery mentioned in the *Vita*, that called Docco. This should lie near the north Cornish coast to suit the topography of the *Vita*, and probably close to an estuary or other harbour. These conditions are fulfilled by a site now called *Lanow* in St Kew parish, but termed *Landochou* in a tenth-century charter and referred to there as a monastic site.

Samson's visit to this monastery gives us a fascinating glimpse of monastic affairs, virtually the only one we are allowed. Before he could reach the place, the monks sent out one of their number, Juviavus, to meet him, their purpose being to fend him off. Although showing due deference to a distinguished visitor, Juviavus urged Samson not to stay, saying it would not be proper, and discord might be aroused between the brothers and their guest. The monks had fallen away from their earlier rules of life and become slack in their observances. Samson made no attempt at remonstrance but set off across Cornwall towards the 'southern sea'. This brief view of a Cornish monastery apart, the *Vita* is instructive in conveying some impression of the regime which Samson himself adhered to, or which the author saw as an ideal. Samson had been trained in a coenobitic monastery in Wales, evidently a large one. He later tended, at least on occasion, towards the eremitic life, but was prepared to serve as the head of a community when called on. He imposed a strict code of conduct on himself but did not insist on this for all monks. To what extent Samson and his followers were concerned with missionary activity is far from clear, but there is a reference in the *Vita* to pagan practice which was promptly stamped out when encountered. While passing through the region called *Tricurius* (plausibly identified as the hundred of Trigg in north Cornwall), Samson came across a group of people who had abjured the Faith and were performing some rite before an idol. They were persuaded to stop, with the aid of a miracle, destroyed the idol and were brought to baptism by their leader. Although this kind of episode is associated with other pilgrim-monks in western Britain, there is little other sign that they were intent on missionary work as distinct from pastoral care. They did their duty as Christian brothers but little more. Samson's response to those saved for the Faith when they asked him to stay and be their bishop is significant. He refused and soon afterwards founded his monastery near the cave. Routine administration was not for Samson and his like.

What of the other monasteries founded in the sixth and seventh centuries? What can be discovered about them? Most were so small and obscure that their history, and even their sites, will never be revealed. But a number can be identified from sources of later date and varying character (Olsen, forthcoming, for a full study of this important subject). Several of the Cornish religious houses in Domesday Book are ancient foundations. All but one are dedicated to Celtic saints and early forms of their names are strongly suggestive of monastic origin, for example *Lanbrabois, Lanpiran, Langorroc* and *Lannachebran*, with their significant combination of *lan* and a saint's name. The full list is: St Germans, St Petroc, St Probus, St Carantoch, St Piran, St Achebran (Keverne), St Buryan, St Neot. Others may be suspected on more localized evidence. These include St Michael's Mount, Goran, Constantine, Lammana (St George's Island) and St Antony in Roseland, to name only the most likely. These were the larger communities, mostly endowed with landed property and capable of keeping some record of their holdings. Small communes of monks left no trace behind.

Of the score or so monasteries we can tentatively identify in this way, most lay near the estuaries of the coasts, notably on the northern coast, a distribution similar to that encountered in south Wales (Davies 1982: 149–55). This number is not large and it is unlikely to grow to any great extent.

Archaeologically, nothing is known of a single monastic site: here is a major objective for future field-work. For so long Tintagel seemed to offer the monastic *locus classicus* in the South West. For reasons examined below, this identification is not accepted here (below, p. 263; Thomas 1982).

An odd document of the ninth or tenth century may cast an oblique light on the location of the major Cornish monasteries. In the Vatican manuscript *Reginensis Latinus 191*, there occurs a list of personal names, unquestionably the names of saints (Vendryes 1938; Godu and Le Roux 1938), and a number of these have strong Cornish connexions. These include Just, Achobran (Keverne), Nioth (Neot), Probus, Berrian (Buryan), Geuedenoc (Gwinniau), Gereut (Geraint), Guron (Goran), Entennin (Antony) and Maucan (Mawgan). The purpose of the list is unknown but it is unlikely to be merely an *aide-memoire* to saints or their churches. More probably it was related to properties, perhaps ecclesiastical or monastic, or to parishes, perhaps those designated for some particular role in ecclesiastical organization. At all events the correspondence between the list and other forms of evidence in the naming of what were clearly major religious foci is remarkable and could be an important guide to the eventual identification of certain early monasteries and their *paruchiae*.

There is little possible doubt that the pre-eminent monastery by the ninth century was that of St Germans in south-east Cornwall. The site cannot easily be examined archaeologically, though excavation in 1928 beneath the Norman church produced some evidence for earlier stone buildings. But the written record offers clear proof of the status of St Germans by the tenth century at the very latest. Mention of a place in Cornwall called *Lannaled* occurs in an incomplete mass, the *Missa Propria Germani Episcopi* (*Codex Oxon. Posterior* fol. 1), a tenth-century text almost certainly written in Cornwall (Jenner 1932). *Lannaled* is described as the 'famed and universally known place, where the relics of Bishop Germanus are preserved'. Another document, the so-called *Lanalet Pontifical* of the tenth or early eleventh century, also refers to this centre, describing it as the *monasterium* of *Lannalet* (by this date indicating a collegiate church or a monastery) and the seat of a bishop. This can only be St Germans, the centre of the Cornish see (below, p. 288). The *lan* element in the name, combined with a place-name, suggests an early ecclesiastical site, and the siting above the great estuary of the Tamar is entirely consonant with an early foundation. The dedication to St Germanus of Auxerre (for it should be to him and not to some local saint) may also be a survival of an early cult, not an imposition of tenth-century date. The relics of a Gaulish saint might well have reached Cornwall along with other treasured items. The unseemly scramble for relics could begin even before the corpse was laid to rest, and *disiecta membra*, clothing and other possessions could be scattered to every corner of Europe.

A larger problem is presented by the location of the establishment associated with the cult of St Petroc. By the tenth century this was sited at Bodmin and by that time the community was both prosperous and prestigious. But this marks the close of a long history of which we catch only glimpses. The *Vita* of St Petroc dates from not before the eleventh century and was probably compiled in Cornwall, which appears in the work as the frame for the saint's entire life. Petroc and a band of monks came originally from Wales to Ireland and then to the 'River Hail', an old name for the Camel estuary where a small cell of monks already existed and where a hermit lived by the shore. Petroc settled here for a time at a place named after the leader of the original cell, one Wethinoc, *Landwethinoch*, an early name applied to Padstow. Later he founded another cell at Little Petherick near Padstow, before departing once more on the final stage of his travels which ended at Bodmin and the foundation of another monastery. There is a sound tradition for the existence of an early monastery at Padstow, the fame of which is reported by William of Malmesbury (II, 95). The reference in the *Anglo-Saxon Chronicle* C-text to the *Sancte Petroces stowe* ravaged by the Danes in 981 is reasonably certain to be to Padstow (below, p. 276). That raid might indeed have instigated the move of the cult to Bodmin, though this is mere hypothesis. The prestige of Padstow survived into a later age in the form of a privileged sanctuary in which asylum could be found (Leland: II, 179, ed. Toulmin Smith).

The religious origins of Bodmin are shadowy. Though the tradition of an early foundation conveyed by the *Vita* of Petroc probably had a firm basis in fact, there is no final proof of an early foundation here and it is possible that the first major establishment only came after 800, its development thereafter being unusually rapid. There is a good case for identifying the house at Bodmin with the *monasterium* of *Dinuurin*, from which Kenstec sent his submission to Ceolnoth after 833 (below, p. 287), so that by then it certainly was an important centre of administration among the west Britons (Olsen forthcoming). But details of the site and its topography are unknown: it need not have occupied the same position as the later medieval church.

A monastic house was in existence at Exeter by the late seventh century and may have been founded a century earlier in this secure place. This was under an English abbot by about 670 but its origins are likely to have been Celtic. The site is not precisely located but it was probably near, or even in, the Roman forum, close to the later cathedral (below, p. 288). A cemetery in this place dating from the fifth and sixth centuries attests very un-Roman usage which is best referable to the presence of an ecclesiastical building in the old public building and this could have formed the nucleus of a monastery in the sixth century, in the way that Frankish monasteries took over public buildings, basilicas, baths, even a granary (Bidwell 1979: 112–13). Other monasteries existed in Devon, at Braunton (*Branocminstre*) and at Stoke St Nectan, but their dates of foundation are not known and need not be early.

It was to the monastery at Exeter that about 685/90 there was sent a boy who was to be one of the most remarkable figures of a remarkable age. The man who was to be known as Boniface, the apostle of Germany, was born and baptized Wynfrith somewhere in the Crediton area. His original name is purely English and he is most probably to be regarded, as later tradition certainly regarded him, as nobly born, a member of an English family owning land in a region which had not yet emerged from see-sawing warfare between English and Britons. Nothing more is known about his origins, except that the Christian virtues were highly regarded by his father and that Boniface himself had felt drawn to the monastic life from a very early age. By the age of seven he had been offered to the service of God at the abbey at Exeter, then ruled by Abbot Wulfhard, apparently as a sacrifice during a serious illness suffered by his father. Boniface thus grew to manhood in a learned community in an age of burgeoning Christian scholarship and missionary enterprise, the age of Bede, Aldhelm and Wilfrid.

Inscribed Memorials and the Dead

It is a paradox almost peculiar to the South West that a part of what had been a Roman province in which written records on stone are scarce and virtually confined to 'milestones' (actually records of road-building and maintenance), should after the end of Roman administration produce a series of stone memorials, inscribed in Latin, commemorating prominent individuals in this part of the Christian Celtic world. About forty of these striking inscriptions are known in Devon and Cornwall, some of them, like the 'Tristan' stone near Castle Dore and the Men Scryfes on the West Penwith upland, among the most familiar of south-western monuments. Farther east they are scarce, there being only one in Somerset and an intriguing group of five at Wareham in Dorset (Macalister 1949: 188–9). The nearest major concentration of comparable stone inscriptions occurs in south Wales where about thirty are recorded in Pembroke and Dyfed.

In the earlier inscriptions, the lettering runs in straight lines across the face of the stone and is usually cut in more or less regular Roman capitals, remotely related to the monumental epigraphy of late Roman Britain. The formulae employed in the earlier instances are well known in Christian funerary monuments of the fifth century in Gaul and the Rhineland. On one of the earliest, possibly the earliest of all the known examples, from Carnsew near Hayle, we read that the woman commemorated, Cunaide, *hic in tumulo requiescit . . . vixit XXXIII annos*. Formulae and arrangement are so close to those of tombstones of the late Roman world that this inscription can safely be dated no later than the late fifth century. The majority, however, are laid out not in horizontal lines but running vertically down the stone. In these instances there are evident signs of later epigraphic usage, for example the letters I and O

Figure 9.3   Memorial inscriptions: Carnsew; Men Scryfes; Lewannick; Menabilly

tend to be of smaller size than the others. A few letters related to those of uncial and half-uncial book-hands also put in an appearance, notably A and T. These forms are unlikely to have entered the stonecutter's repertoire before the beginning of the sixth century and might be somewhat later. Other letter-forms derived from the script generally known as Insular Majuscule are unlikely to be earlier than 600 and could occur as late as the late seventh century, thus giving a total date-range for the entire series of inscribed monuments of about 475–700 (Radford 1975).

Eight of the inscriptions, six in Cornwall, two in Devon, occur in the Ogham script as well as in the Latin alphabet. This group includes one of the earliest inscriptions, at Lewannick. Although Ogham is ultimately Irish in origin, the south-western instances could be more closely related to the considerable number of Ogham inscriptions in south Wales and may have been introduced from that quarter rather than directly from southern Ireland.

The great majority of the inscriptions record no more than the name of the person commemorated, sometimes with a patronymic and frequently with the formula *hic iacet*: here he lies, a formula found on Christian tombstones of the late Roman period. This evidence apart, the position of many of the memorial stones, in or near medieval cemeteries and monastic sites, is a clear pointer to an early Christian *milieu*. A fairly restricted social class may be assumed and we may be sure that the individuals for whom these stones were erected were leading members of contemporary society, kings, nobles, members of the landowning class. Clearly they could only be erected at a time when the Faith had thoroughly permeated society and their testimony indicates that this had been achieved by the late fifth and early sixth centuries.

The siting of the stones is compelling evidence for the continued significance of certain sites for centuries, even down to the present day. Many of them, including several of the earliest, still stand in churchyards on or close to their original positions, for example Lewannick, Lanivet and Stowford. Others lie far from churches or other Christian sites. The Drustanus stone still stands at Menabilly beside the ancient route from Fowey to Padstow, the Enabarrus memorial at Buckland Monachorum on the track from the Tavy valley on to Dartmoor, and the Caratacus stone on Winsford Hill on the fringe of Exmoor. These would be seen by all who used these routes. But a few stones were erected in apparent isolation, possibly on the estate of the person honoured. The Men Scryfes on the West Penwith upland must always have been a lonely witness to the Faith. The inscribed stones in Devon are fewer but of equal interest. The surviving examples lie around the skirts of Dartmoor, with outliers on Exmoor, but these may be no more than the remnants of a once wider distribution. East and central Devon has little stone that would be a useful medium for these pillars and the possibility that wooden monuments may have taken the place of stone must be considered. Some sixteen stones are known in Devon, four of them recording Irish names, for instance at Ivybridge (Macalister 1945: 468).

The erection of memorials of this type continued throughout the seventh century and into the early eighth. One at least must be later still. At Lanteglos near Camelford an English inscription in Roman capitals records the dedication by two people with English names for the soul of a third and for themselves (AELSELTH GENERETH WOHTE THISNE SYBSTEL FOR AELWINES SOUL FOR HEYSEL). This can only have been set up in the ninth century at the earliest and it marks the end of a long tradition of memorial monuments. One of the consequences of the English conquest was to replace the memorial stone with a very different kind of *memoria* (below, p. 294).

The only inscribed memorial stone recorded in Scilly indicates a Christian focus on Tresco close to the Priory of St Nicholas. Burials were found close by in the nineteenth century during the laying out of the renowned Abbey gardens. On St Agnes a cemetery site is known close to the shore at Porteagles, while Leland reports the existence of a chapel here, later turned into a dwelling. At least one cemetery on St Mary's, at the western end of Hugh Town, seems to date from before AD 1000, and there are good reasons for thinking an early chapel stood in the same area.

Burial forms on Lundy are similar to those in Scilly at this time. On Beacon Hill near the southern end of the island, a cemetery of cist burials, none accompanied by grave-goods, accumulated and became the focus of a wider religious observance. A central monument of large stones was constructed over an occupation layer dating from the third and fourth centuries, and shortly afterwards burials in long cists covered by stone slabs began to cluster around this nucleus, to be surrounded in due course by an enclosure of oval plan. From this fairly small cemetery no less than four inscribed memorial stones have come, all of them probably of the later fifth and sixth centuries (Thomas, Fowler and Gardner 1969).

Burials of the period 400 to 800 are in general ill recorded, the inhumation cemetery at Exeter being the only instance which satisfies modern standards (Bidwell 1979: 112–13). From several sites there are reports of long cists containing oriented inhumations without grave goods for which a post-Roman date is the most probable (e.g. Carnanton (Preston-Jones 1984)). This burial form was prevalent in western Britain at this time and later (see Mawgan Porth, below, p. 306). What is lacking in the South West is any clear association between such cemeteries and their contemporary settlements and churches.

The memorial stones raise the much-discussed question of Irish settlers in the peninsula, for some of the personal names are Irish and the use of ogham implies the passage of at least some literate individuals from Ireland to Britain. Whether it implies more than that is a matter for debate, but as yet a debate with no conclusion (Jenner 1917; Thomas 1972). The case for settlers from Ireland in the South West rests almost exclusively upon linguistic and epigraphic evidence, and in its sum that evidence does not indicate an extensive or numerous Irish colony. The inscriptions relate only to the uppermost social echelon and must be treated with care. So far as it goes, their evidence suggests a degree of intercourse between leading families in Ireland, south Wales and the South West, in which intermarriage, dynastic in-fighting, religious activity and mere adventuring could all have played a part. Archaeological evidence for movement from Ireland, or even contact with Ireland, is at best slim and may not exist at all. Certainly little can be made of the appearance of grass-marked pottery in Cornwall in the post-Roman period (Thomas 1972: 260–5: below, p. 286). Nor are place-names convincingly attributed to Irish colonists, rather than to the natural spread of name-forms among communities which used mutually comprehensible languages. The problem still remains, concealed behind linguistic thickets which we cannot yet penetrate. But it is not a problem peculiar to the South West. Its resolution may depend as much on work in Ireland, south Wales and perhaps Brittany. We may be on safer ground in considering indirect contacts *via* south Wales rather than directly with Ireland.

Material Culture and Imports

Since there has been so little excavation of settlements, our knowledge of material culture after 400 is not extensive. Native production of pottery seems to have ceased for some time and metalwork is a very rare commodity in the period. Fortunately, a striking range of imported pottery enables sites to be identified, and acts as a useful, if limited, chronological indicator.

About 500, quantities of fine tableware, coarser wares and wine and oil amphorae began to appear on a wide range of sites in Ireland, eastern Scotland, Wales and the South West. These were first recognized in the South West in the excavations of the 1930s at Tintagel, but not until twenty or more years later did the broader distribution and significance of these wares begin to emerge clearly (Thomas 1981a). Increased attention to late Roman pottery over the same period in the Mediterranean provinces means that it is now possible to set these imports in their proper place in time and to approach with greater confidence the question of their significance (Hayes 1972; 1980: Hautumm 1981).

Among the earliest vessels to arrive in Britain were examples of the red-slipped wares now generally referred to as African Red Slip Ware, material which began to be produced in the mid-fifth century and which was reaching these shores about half a century later. This occurs at Tintagel in some quantity, at Gwithian and at Lydford (Thomas 1981 a: 8–9). It is now thought that the main production centres lay in Tunisia and they seem to have continued in operation until the late seventh century. The other major fine ware which found its way to Britain is Phocaean Red Slip Ware, named after a major centre in western Turkey (Hayes 1980: 1, ix). This too is well represented at Tintagel, and by occasional finds at Gwithian, Phillack, Perran Sands and Trethurgy. Amphorae, which might contain wine, oil or even grain, and other handled jars reached the South West in greater quantity. These originated in several regions of the Aegean, Asia Minor and possible Egypt. The 'Agora' type of amphora (earlier called BI) is widely distributed in Cornwall, again with a concentration at Tintagel, and is recorded also at Mothecombe and High Peak in Devon. The contemporary BII amphorae from Syria, or Cyprus, has a similarly wide distribution, as do other types from Syria, Asia Minor and North Africa.

There were other imports, from other regions. The distinctive western Gaulish grey ware (*terre sigillée paléochretienne grise* to French archaeologists, D ware to British) is sparsely represented in south-western Britain, with only a few fragments at Tintagel. Much commoner is the coarse ware from western Gaul, perhaps from the Bordeaux region, known as E ware. This is workaday pottery, cooking-pots, small storage-jars, bowls and platters and it is surprising that it should have been exported at all. It occurs on Scilly as well as in Cornwall and Devon. Its presence may indicate continued or renewed trading contact with western Gaul in the late fifth and sixth centuries, but it must also be noted that this ware, or something very similar, occurs in fourth century contexts in Gaul and *could* therefore have reached Britain at an earlier date, along with such imports as *ceramique à l'éponge* (above, p. 234). The absence of well-stratified finds in the South West is in this respect a particular handicap.

Imports of fine pottery and of ceramic containers and their contents can no longer be regarded as freakish and occasional. Nor, in view of the wide range of sites from which they have now been recorded, can they be linked with specific elements in south-western society, say with the Church or with the nobility. Secular sites of quite humble standing (e.g. High Peak, Trethurgy) also received these objects, which were after produced in vast bulk. They are remarkable only for the distance they have travelled. At present the main period of importation seems to be the first half of the sixth century, with a smaller quantity arriving in the late fifth and late sixth but none certainly later than about 700. That occasional overseas contacts were effected in this period is well known, but this pottery seems to show us something much more regular

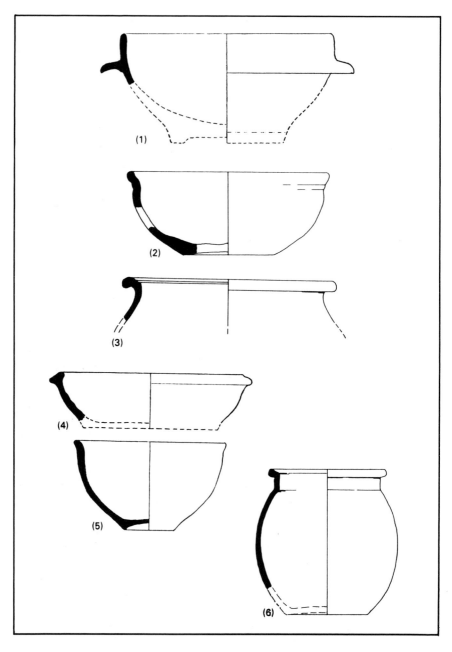

Figure 9.4 Imported pottery: AD 500–700: (1) Porthmeor; (2) Tean; (3) May's Hill, St Martin's; (4) Gwithian; (5) Hellesvean; (6) May's Hill, St Martin's

and most probably commercially based. Most useful of all, it provides firm material evidence for the passage of ships and men and thus ideas from Gaul and the Mediterranean to the South West and thus helps to establish a general context for relations between Dumnonia and the Christian world of the West.

Surprisingly large quantities of these wares have been reported on Scilly. E ware is naturally the commonest and most widespread, occurring on St Mary's, St Martin's, Tean and Samson. Bii amphorae are recorded on Tean, Samson and possibly St Martin's, and a Biv jar on Tean (Thomas 1981a). When compared with the meagre amount of Romano-British pottery found on the islands, this body of material is impressive and it must be recalled that it has been produced by limited excavation. The Gaulish wares D and E hint, if no more, at a connection with western Gaul which was more than sporadic and which might be reflected in other objects. From Tean, for example, comes a small bronze mount which has closer affinities with Frankish metalwork than with anything else. Scilly thus shared in the converse between south-western Britain and Gaul in the period from about 500 onward. What form that converse took, and what inspired it, can only be guessed at. Its basis may have been in part commercial. Minerals and the products of the sea could well have retained some of their earlier attraction. But there were less tangible things that may have been conveyed, especially from Gaul to Britain at this date, ideas and institutions of which archaeology can report nothing.

Among other imported objects of the period may be numbered a few Byzantine coins. Six such pieces are recorded from Exeter, most of them by Shortt in the nineteenth century (Shortt 1841 a: 100–1), two from Poltimore nearby, and single finds from Exmouth and Princetown on Dartmoor. A further example, from near Plymouth, has a less secure background and may be a modern intrusion. Most of these issues date from the end of the fifth century to the beginning of the seventh and could thus have accompanied the fine pottery and other goods. Doubt has often been cast on the Exeter and Poltimore finds, chiefly it seems because they are reported by Shortt. But the presence of coins from two other findspots, both of them untainted by any hint of modern agency, does compel us to take these finds more seriously. Byzantine coins and other objects appear elsewhere in southern Britain and since pottery and glass could reach these shores from the eastern Mediterranean and North Africa, there need be no surprise at this. Contact was evidently not as occasional as our sole literary reference might seem to suggest. John the Almoner, the wealthy and charitable pontiff of early-seventh-century Alexandria, had at his disposal a sizeable fleet of ships which might be used for trade. One such vessel, carrying 20,000 bushels of grain, was driven by storms to Britain (from western Gaul perhaps?) where a famine was raging at the time. The grain was exchanged for tin (which fixes the episode in the South West) and the metal was later sold in Egypt (*Vita Johannis* IX). There is interesting evidence from closer to home for the continued extraction and use of tin in certain Anglo-Saxon coins of the eighth century. Some *sceattas* contain a surprisingly high proportion of tin, up to 8.5 per cent (Metcalf and Walker 1976: 228–9). We do not know how this metal found its way into the moneyers' hands, but it more probably came from deposits in Devon than from Cornwall.

When set beside the relative bounty of imported pottery, the record of locally produced wares is sparse. A number of sites in west and north Cornwall and on Scilly (but not yet in Devon) have produced pieces of generally coarse pottery with impressions of grass and other vegetation on their bases (Thomas 1968b). The earliest in the series are flat platters and deep, straight-sided pots with flat bases, best known from Gwithian and probably of the period from the late fifth to the seventh century. There are remote resemblances between these vessel-forms and certain late Roman types, but any direct connection or continuity seems implausible. Nor is there any need to derive these vessels from a source in northern Ireland. Such simple forms could be produced anywhere, once the usefulness of this basic amenity had been accepted.

Metalwork of the immediately post-Roman period is extremely scarce in the South West, but there are suggestions that the meagre total will significantly increase when settlement sites and cemeteries are identified and examined. Among older finds are two specimens of the penannular brooch usually designated Fowler's Type G, one from a stream-work on Goss Moor, Roche and the other, similarly unstratified, from a probable settlement site near Padstow. These simple brooches are very difficult to date with any precision, though it is probably significant that few have been reported from undoubted late Roman contexts (Dickinson 1982: 53–4). The sum of the slight evidence for date indicates the fifth and sixth centuries as the first main period of currency, with other types continuing into the ninth and tenth. The most interesting of the early penannular brooches is a recent find, also unstratified, from a site at Capton near Dartmouth (Todd 1983b). This is an elegant example in silver, with plain, rectangular terminals and with the hoop covered with interrupted ribbed strokes instead of the more usual regular ribbing. Another unusual feature, reminiscent of Anglo-Saxon brooches, is the twisting of one end of the pin around the shank to produce the loop-fastening. The Capton brooch is probably the finest of the penannulars of this type so far known. It is one of the only two in silver, the other coming from Worlebury in Somerset. It may well not be chance that the only silver specimens have been reported from the South West, where silver was evidently still being mined towards the end of Roman Britain. The discovery of this piece is a salutary warning against judging the material culture of Dumnonia in its sub-Roman phase from the sparse objects presently to hand.

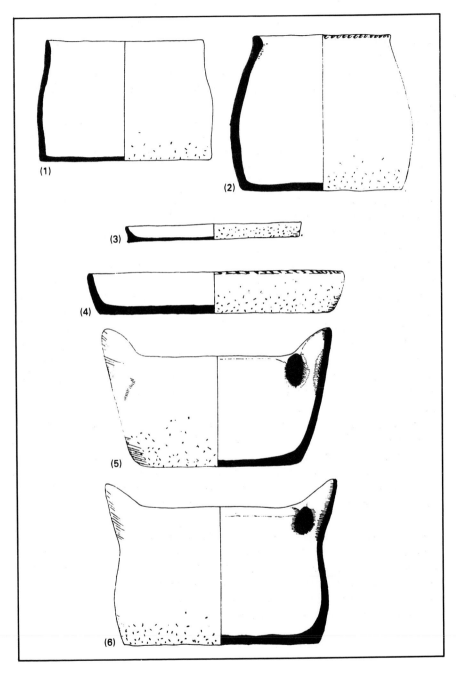

Figure 9.5 Grass-marked pottery: (1) Chun Castle; (2) Gwithian; (3) Tean; (4)–(6) Gwithian

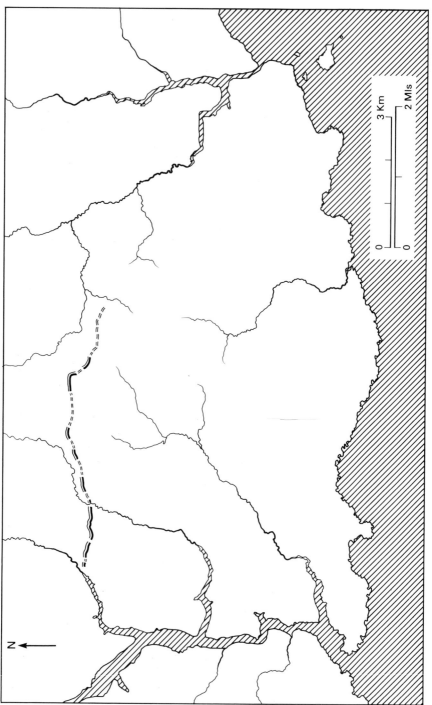

Figure 9.6 The Giant's Hedge

Land and the Social Order

Unquestionably one of the most exciting discoveries about western Britain in this period has been the demonstration that a number of documents in the Book of Llandaff, a twelfth-century collection, are of sixth-century origin. They preserve information about landowners and estates in south-east Wales, revealing that land was still being measured in Roman units and that these processes were being described in Latin terminology (Davies 1978; 1979). Could this have been the case in Dumnonia? There seems no inherent reason why it should not, especially in the eastern part of the region where at least a few late Roman estates had existed. But attempts to demonstrate a continuity from late Roman systems of land-tenure to English estates on the evidence of charters have so far failed in the South West. There is a gap of two to three centuries which cannot yet be bridged and no amount of wishful thinking will forge the vital link for us.

The demarcation of territory by means of large linear dykes is a familiar feature of this period, the most famous examples of such works being Wansdyke (probably a frontier of the west Britons against the Anglo-Saxons), the many dykes of Cambridgeshire and East Anglia, and the western frontier of Mercia built by Offa against the Welsh. Two major earthworks in the South West have much in common with these and may be provisionally assigned to this period, though they are not in any sense dated. The larger is the Giant's Hedge which cuts off a sizeable area on the south coast of Cornwall between the River Lerryn, flowing into the Fowey estuary, and the West Looe river. (Croft Andrew 1936). In all, some 65 sq km are enclosed. In its western sector, the Giant's Hedge is still an impressive earthwork, with a ditch 8 m wide and a rampart which must once have stood 5 m high. It runs in as direct a line as the broken landscape will allow from the Lerryn to Lanreath and is then compelled by steep slopes to turn southward towards the West Looe river near Milcombe. This eastern end of the dyke is now lost. No obvious nucleus of ancient settlement is known within the area enclosed, though there are three substantial enclosed sites, including Hall Wood, Pelynt. Castle Dore is sometimes linked with the territory bounded by the Giant's Hedge, but the site lies several kilometres to the north and there seems no pressing reason to make the connection.

A smaller bloc of land about St Agnes Head on the north Cornish coast is also marked off by a linear earthwork, the Bolster Bank (Johnson 1980). This is 3.3 km long and defines a rough oval 50 ha (1,200 acres) in area. This is a slighter work than the Giant's Hedge and the topography allowed it to adopt a more direct course. It is just possible that a late prehistoric date might be entertained for the Bolster Bank, whereas the Giant's Hedge is so close in character to earthworks known to be post-Roman that its date in that period seems assured. Other small linear earthworks might well emerge. In both

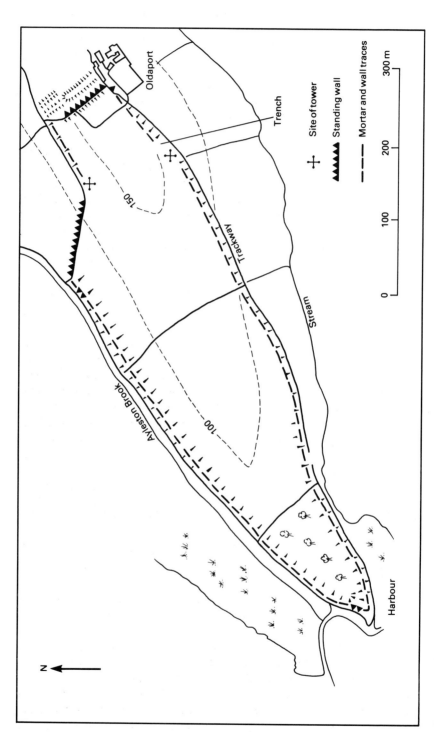

N

Oldaport

Trench

Stream

Trackway

Aylveston Brook

150

100

Harbour

Site of tower
Standing wall
Mortar and wall traces

0   100   200   300 m

Figure 9.7 Oldaport

Devon and Cornwall several lengths of 'hedge' or field-bank are plainly earlier than the medieval fields in which they are embedded and some of these could go back to the early post-Roman period. But it will take preternatural luck as well as intensive field-work to provide a date for them.

High status settlements, the *lys* of local rulers, for the most part remain to be identified. No doubt enclosed settlements and hill-forts were favoured situations, as they were farther east at South Cadbury and Congresbury. Castle Dore near Fowey offers the most familiar example of the reoccupation of an Iron Age stronghold. Timber rectangular buildings have been interpreted as two large halls, one with an attached kitchen with one or more raised granaries sited nearby (Radford 1951: 60–7; Rahtz 1968). These structures are difficult to reconstruct (or rather they permit of reconstruction in many forms) and just as difficult to date. Only small quantities of early medieval pottery were found at Castle Dore, in sharp contrast to Tintagel and South Cadbury. Yet identification as a *lys* hinges on the character and date of these buildings. There is uncertainty about both.

One of the most problematic of sites in Devon may be referable to this period, though little is yet known of it. This is the enclosed site at Oldaport near the mouth of the River Erme (Farley and Little 1968). Here two small creeks join with an arm of the river to form a small, sheltered harbour now completely silted up. As early as the early fourteenth century the place bore the name *Yoldeport* so that at the very least the memory of earlier navigation was preferred. Above the harbour the two creeks define a narrow, steep-sided spur some 700 m long and 150 m wide, tapering to a point towards the south-west. On this spur stands a remarkable group of defensive works in which at least two major building phases seem to be represented. The earlier takes the form of a rectangular enclosure of 1.1 ha (2.6 acres) occupying a flat platform at the head of the spur. This is surrounded by a substantial earth rampart fronted by a mortared stone wall over 1 m thick and still standing to a height of 3 m on the north-east side. A substantial ditch accompanies this wall across the neck of the spur and there are further traces of an outer ditch on this side. The later walled enclosure takes in the rest of the spur, covering 12.5 ha (30 acres). This, too, was surrounded by a solidly built wall of mortared masonry at least 3 m high originally, with an earth bank to the rear. A nineteenth-century visitor to the site (Sir John Dryden in 1863) reported the presence of two towers on the circuit (unpublished manuscript in Northampton Museum), but if these structures ever existed, they have now vanished and there are no surviving traces elsewhere of towers or of gate-openings.

There has been only limited excavation at Oldaport and this has produced very little to assist in the crucial matter of dating these enigmatic works. One section has been cut at the south angle of the earlier enclosure (Farley and Little 1968: 35), but with far from conclusive results. An unstratified Roman sherd was found overlying the bank and an unidentifiable sherd lay below the robbed wall. We are thus thrown back upon such general criteria as the character and position of the site. The latter gives no support to the notion that the earlier enclosure was a Roman military work (Farley and Little 1968: 35–6). No useful military purpose could be served by a site which lay so far from any kind of route. The character of the defences is also firmly against an identification as a Roman fort, there being no gate in the north-east side and no sign of another on the south-east. The position of Oldaport only makes sense in relation to the ajacent estuary and sheltered anchorage. Equally secure sites are available further inland, but the builders made deliberate choice of this spur adjacent to a waterway which gave easy access to the sea. Why that was done is unknown, but the fact is undeniable.

Although a Roman fort is not here in question, a Roman date, and more specifically a late Roman date, remains a strong possibility. The solid mortared masonry of the two enclosing walls is more reminiscent of late Roman work than of anything else before the high Middle Ages and the presence of external towers (if they did indeed exist) would tend to support the hypothesis. If these are late Roman works, all problems are not thereby solved. A military function has already been excluded and a coastal installation serving some official need seems very unlikely here. Could we be dealing with a civilian, private fortification? This may at first sight seem an unpromising line of enquiry, but at least one other site in western Britain, in some respects analogous to Oldaport, does seem to fall into this category. This is Gatcombe, on the Failand ridge west of Bristol (Branigan 1977), a late Roman fortified enclosure situated far from the Roman road-network, though close to the Severn and Avon estuaries, and classifiable neither as a fort nor as a township.

Also to be considered as a settlement of high status is the extraordinary site on the headland at Tintagel. The excavations of C. A. R. Radford here in 1933–4 immediately established the site as one of prime interest and importance in early medieval Cornwall (Radford 1935a). On the eastern side of the almost encircled headland lay an agglomeration of small rectangular chambers, none longer than 6 m or wider than 4 m. These were dated by the excavator to the fifth century and later, and identified as the cells of a Celtic monastery, comparable with (though larger than) the monastic sites on headlands and islands in western Ireland and Scotland. The dating to the fifth to seventh centuries was later supported by the recognition of relatively large quantities of fine pottery and amphorae which had been imported from the Mediterranean world. These vessels were held to be contemporary with the group of rectangular structures. The excavations which brought this site to light were never published in full, but the identification of an early Celtic monastery here was widely accepted until the 1970s (Thomas 1981b, 348).

The thesis involves difficulty. The group of buildings is very much larger than we should expect of an early monastic site. It is true that the structures could have spanned two centuries, but, even so, their scale is surprisingly large. More recent study of the pottery finds from Tintagel enables the character of the site to be more clearly defined. The quantity of material dating from the

Plate 9.1 The later Roman and medieval site at Tintagel, Cornwall, looking north along the coast. The rectangular buildings in the foreground probably date from the Middle Ages. They overlie remains of the late Roman and early medieval aristocratic or royal settlement.

later fourth century is now seen to be considerable (above, p. 218), suggesting an occupation already well established before the end of the Roman period. The exceptionally large quantity of imported pottery dating from the late fifth and sixth centuries can now be more fully comprehended (Thomas 1981b). Much more of these imported wares has been recorded from Tintagel than from any other site in Britain or Ireland, something in the order of three hundred vessels in all. This fact alone suggests that the site was of unusual, much more than local, importance. The natural advantages of the peninsula are likely to have appealed to a lord or chieftain of the period, perhaps even to a king. To explore that possibility further would require further field-work on the headland. For the present, we must be content to note that in the early twelfth century, when Geoffrey of Monmouth was writing his *History of the Kings of Britain*, Tintagel was linked with the residence of the king of Corn-wall. How old that tradition may be is beyond even guesswork, but it is a reasonable assumption that the tradition which Geoffrey of Monmouth re-flects was already long established in Cornish folklore when he was writing. This does not carry us back to the sixth century and to the recipients of the imported wares. But it does underline the extraordinary position which Tin-tagel enjoyed in popular memory over a lengthy period. Whether or not the tradition which survived down to the twelfth century faithfully reflected the

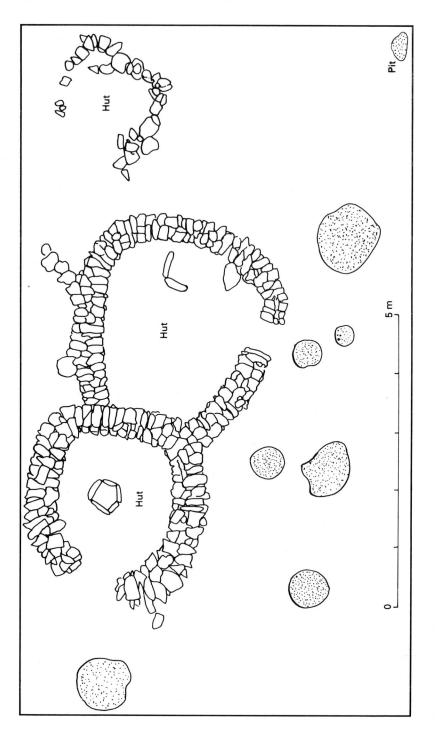

Figure 9.8 Dark Age houses at Gwithian

standing of Tintagel five hundred years earlier, the archaeological evidence indicates that the site enjoyed an elevated status from the later fifth century [1]. Fortunately, further excavation may well be able to elucidate what that status was and whether it had its origins in the fourth century. And it may confidently be expected to demonstrate the essentially secular character of the settlement.

Settlements of more modest degree have been identified in small numbers and a few excavated, notably in the areas of blown sand. Several sites in the Gwithian area have produced evidence of occupation in the late- and immediately post-Roman period, and at least one of these was occupied over a lengthy span of time (Thomas 1958). This lay on a long spit of blown sand projecting into a tidal creek. It originated probably in the fifth century AD, its inhabitants using pottery which revealed its derivation from wares current at the end of the Romano-British period. Part of a small hut associated with this phase of settlement was excavated. The occupation may have extended into the sixth century, as quantities of sherds of imported Mediterranean amphorae and red-slip ware were recovered from these deposits. Later, three huts went up in sequence on the same site. These had stone footings with turf walls above. All were small, the largest being no more than 4 m in diameter, so that a minimum of internal support was needed to hold up the roof. The earlier pottery in use during this phase was broadly similar to that of the preceding occupation, a mixture of fine imported wares and derivations from the late Romano-British tradition. But the common ware underwent a profound change with the introduction of a completely new vessel type, at a date which can be estimated as a few decades before 600. This was a flat-based, straight-sided bowl, hand-made and usually poorly fired, the rim of which was occasionally decorated with impressions of a fingertip or fingernail. On the underside of the base, impressions of chopped grass or straw are usually evident.

The material culture of the Gwithian settlers in this sixth- and seventh-century phase was by no means impoverished. The locally available iron ores were exploited and both lead and bronze were in use. Cattle, sheep, pigs and horses were all kept, fish and wild birds were caught, and shellfish gathered in great quantity. The basics of this subsistence economy thus seem to have altered little, if at all, from those of the Roman period and they were to continue unchanged in the communities of the far South West for centuries to come.

Two sites in south Devon, each at the mouth of a major estuary, have yielded quantities of imported pottery and other objects which demonstrate occupation in the fifth century and later. One of these is at Mothecombe near the mouth of the Erme, where the evidence amounts to sherds of imported amphorae which have not yet been attributed to any stratified context (Fox 1961a). The other is a site on Bantham Ham, overlooking the mouth of the Avon, where small-scale excavation has revealed a little more of the character of the occupation (Fox 1955; Silvester 1981a). Bantham Ham is a rocky protrusion into the Avon estuary. From the dunes to the south of the promontory late Roman pottery sherds were recovered early in the twentieth century. Their true character and date were first recognized in 1953 by Lady Fox, who suggested that they indicated the existence of a trading place in the period 450–650. A small excavation conducted by R. J. Silvester in 1978 added a little more imported material, as well as enlarging the range of metal and other artifacts, but provided no structural evidence. Bi and Bii are to the fore, as at Mothecombe, though at least one sherd of E ware, probably from western France, is also represented.

A third site in south Devon has also produced imported pottery of fifth- and sixth-century date. This is High Peak, a cliff-top eminence 5 km west of Sidmouth (Pollard 1966). Much of the site has been lost in erosion but it is clear that the settlement was surrounded by a ditch and may originally have been on an oval plan. Excavation by P. O. Hutchinson in 1871 produced the first finds of what were much later recognized as late Roman sherds, and these were added to in 1929. Excavation in 1961–4 for the first time demonstrated the true date and context of this material, though again without producing evidence of structures. All the sherds from High Peak are from amphorae, exclusively of Bi, Bii and miscellaneous B types. Despite the quantity of material recovered, not a single sherd of other wares, imported or local, was noted. In other respects the assemblage resembles that from Bantham. Animal bones, chiefly from ox, sheep, pig and fowl, were plentiful, as was charcoal. The spindle-whorls so common at Bantham were here represented by one specimen, in Kimmeridge shale.

It cannot be claimed that we yet have a representative series of early medieval sites in Dumnonia. Present indications are that the period 400–700 was a formative one for the settlement pattern of the peninsula. One result of this is the fact that many sites established at this time are still occupied by farms and villages and are thus not accessible to the field-worker. Much will one day be revealed by the study of sites abandoned in the medieval centuries, but this work has hardly yet begun over most of the region.

After AD 600 the independence of the kingdom of Dumnonia came under increasing threat. Over the following three centuries this enclave of the British steadily fell under the domination of English kings.

Notes

1. Arguably, *royal* status, as Charles Thomas suggests to me.

Chapter 10

Into England: Wessex and Dumnonia

'. . . few questions in early English history are more obscure' (Stenton 1947: 72). Stenton's judgement on the English conquest of Devon and Cornwall is sufficient warning that any satisfactory account of the subject is not to be expected. The process by which Dumnonia fell under English domination has frequently been referred to as the 'expansion of Wessex', an unfortunate phrase as it suggests that the English advance was a steady progress towards an obvious goal. In fact, the assimilation of Devon and Cornwall with the English territories to the east took over three centuries and was achieved sporadically, the main episodes of advance being separated by long periods of inaction or consolidation, not necessarily entirely uneventful, but productive of nothing which seemed remarkable to the compilers of the *Anglo-Saxon Chronicle*. There was no grand design, no great conqueror. The advance of English power was slow and it left large areas of the South West in British hands for long after they had been detached from Dumnonia. This was so in Dorset, for example in and around Wareham, where a remarkable group of memorial inscriptions record the survival of literate and presumably noble Britons in the seventh century and probably until shortly after 700. We may be sure that it was so in many parts of Devon until the eighth century or later, long after the last mention of Geraint of Dumnonia, the last-known ruler of the old kingdom.

At the beginning of the seventh century the Saxons of Wessex were in control of Wiltshire and the northern part of Somerset. Their annexation of Dorset took place in the course of the next fifty years or less but the stages by which it was carried out are hardly to be discerned, either from the written sources or from the archaeological record. It is remarkable how little of Anglo-Saxon material culture of the seventh century has been reported from Dorset, south Somerset and east Devon. No large cemeteries have been found and the few, poorly furnished grave-finds are difficult to date. So far as they indicate anything, they suggest that by the mid-later seventh century the English conquest of the best land of Dorset was complete. There is certainly nothing to support the view that a substantial and permanent English settlement had been achieved in central and western Dorset much before this date. A

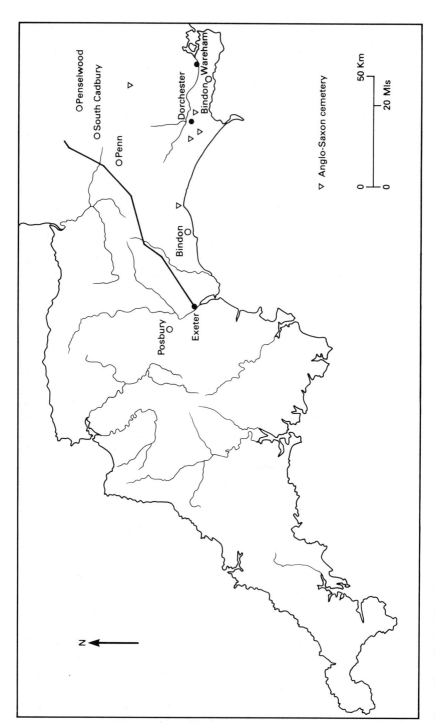

Figure 10.1 The English advance

small group of cemeteries, none of them containing more than a few graves, has been recorded in north-east Dorset, their date centring on the later seventh and early eighth centuries. Farther south, another group lies around Dorchester. This includes Maiden Castle, Mount Pleasant and a particularly interesting cemetery at Bradford Peverell, 5 km north-west of the town. This small cemetery contains one of the few relatively richly furnished graves known in Dorset, that of a girl buried with a necklace containing a gold wire bead, a gold ornament with a stone set *en cabochon* and a silver pendant. This group of objects should date to about 700 or shortly before.

Other burials at Bradford Peverell, though less closely datable, probably fall between about 675 and 720. To that same period belongs another small inhumation cemetery at Hambledon Hill near Blandford Forum. Although burials like these are commonly labelled 'Anglo-Saxon', we have, of course, no means of knowing whether the occupants of such graves were Germanic, British or something of both. The poverty of British material culture at the time encouraged the westward drift of Germanic trinkets and weapons in small quantities and the ethnic origins of their users, and the exact circumstances of their use, can never be revealed by purely archaeological means. Thus occasional finds of Germanic objects from south Somerset need not be considered remarkable and certainly have nothing to tell us about Germanic settlement in that area. The most notable single objects are two disc-brooches from Ilchester of about 500, a shield-boss from Ham Hill, probably of the early sixth century, a sword of the same date in a burial at Queen's Camel, and a button brooch, also of the sixth century, at South Cadbury, a site which has produced unequivocal evidence for the building of a fortification of Britons about 500 and for its occupation into the late sixth century, if not later (Alcock 1972: 174–93). West Dorset has produced very little Germanic material of the fifth and sixth centuries, the only significant finds coming from a series of burials at Hardown Hill, near Charmouth, which require further discussion (Hoskins 1960: 6–8; Evison 1968). One of the most compelling facts about this scant record is the almost total absence of Anglo-Saxon pottery of any kind. Had settlement been achieved and maintained at any level, we might with reason have expected at least a few chance finds in the known burials and from settlement sites. There is nothing of the kind and it must be presumed that a stable settlement on the land had not been achieved.

Much has been made of one group of Germanic objects found in west Dorset at Hardown Hill near Charmouth, in connection with the chronology of English settlement in Dorset and east Devon. These came from what were fairly certainly secondary burials in a barrow and include ten spearheads, a shield-boss, an axe and a small-long brooch. Some of the spear-heads are of types which first appeared in the fifth century and the group as a whole probably dates between 450 and 550. The Hardown graves have been cited as demonstrating an Anglo-Saxon presence in west Dorset well before the mid-sixth century and thus as indicators of the sites of certain major battles noted in the *Chronicle*. It will be clear from what has been set out above that they cannot be so used. They may indicate Germanic intrusion about 500, in the decades of warfare by the battle at Mount Badon, an episode quickly concluded by the rallying of British resistance about this time. They tell us nothing about permanent English land-taking so far west in the sixth century, still less can they be used to assist in the identification of the battle-sites of *Beandune* and *Peonnum*. And the archaeological record as a whole gives no support to the notion that there had been a major influx of English settlers into Dorset during the seventh and early eighth centuries. Rather, so far as negative evidence can indicate anything, it suggests that a colonizing movement from Wessex did not take place before the eighth century at least.

The tale of battles in the *Anglo-Saxon Chronicle* seems to point to an inexorable westward drive of the west Saxons in the seventh century, with Devon deeply penetrated by the 680s, and an English abbot presiding over the monastery at Exeter. Behind the bare outline given in the Chronicle we can detect a much more complicated history (Finberg 1953). In the earlier seventh century Wessex was a relatively minor kingdom of the English, little known to Bede and, apparently, to the compilers of the *Chronicle*. Not until the middle decades of the century can we discern kings who were overlords of all Wessex, Cynegils and later his son Cenwealh. Even then the name of king was borne by several other members of the house, though to what extent this may be taken to indicate divisions within the overlordship is not clear. Even in the later seventh century there is doubt about how Wessex was governed. Bede relates that the kingdom was divided on the death of Cenwealh in 672 and for ten years was ruled by a number of lesser kings (Bede: IV, 12). The *Chronicle* has Cenwealh briefly succeeded by his widow and then by his kinsmen Aescwine and Centwine. Though Centwine appears in Aldhelm's work as well as the *Chronicle* as a strong and successful ruler, the rise of Mercian power to the north made it plain that the bounds of Wessex could not be extended in that direction. And it was not long before Centwine's power was challenged from within, by a young scion of the ruling house, Caedwalla. The name of the challenger presents a further complication. It is the English form of Cadwallon, a British name, and thus hints at intermarriage with a British landed family or at some similar association. The sum of this evidence seems to be that rulers of Wessex were not in a position to pursue major campaigns aimed at permanent occupation of the areas they overran before the later seventh century at the earliest. And even then they could not devote all their energies against Dumnonia.

Two battles fought in the seventh century have been used in the argument for a major English advance in this period (Hoskins 1960: 7–17). Both of these have evoked a great deal of controversy and misspent speculation, to which one hesitates to add. It is wisest to admit at the outset that neither battle can be securely located and the best that can be done for the moment is to get rid of the least likely candidates.

First, *Beandune*. In 614, we read in the *Anglo-Saxon Chronicle*, the West Saxons under Cynegils and Cwichelm met an army of Britons at *Beandune* and defeated it, the British dead numbering over 2,000. That figure seems improbably high and must be viewed with scepticism. The proportion of casualties to the total force involved in a battle of this date, or any date down to early modern times, is unlikely to have been much more than 20 per cent, implying that the British force at *Beandune* numbered some 10,000 men. We may be certain that no such army was assembled. A few hundred warriors, or at most a thousand or so, is a much more likely figure. Where was Beandune? As early as the sixteenth century, the claims of Bindon in Dorset, a lowland ridge near Lulworth Cove, were seriously entertained and they were still supported in the nineteenth century. Twentieth-century historians have generally fought shy of any positive identifications, on good grounds. An exception, however, is Professor W. G. Hoskins, who has identified the site with almost total confidence, and moreover chosen a site well to the west, at Bindon near Axmouth in east Devon. The grounds for this suggestion are claimed to be philological, archaeological and topographical, and in combination they amount to an 'overwhelming' case for Bindon as the site of *Beandune*. Far from being 'overwhelming', the case for Bindon is actually rather weak.

As Hoskins admits (1960: 8), the philological grounds are not conclusive, since the recorded forms of the place-name are late, though they may indeed drive from OE *bean dun* 'hill on which beans grow'. The topographical evidence is no stronger. It is not enough that the Roman road from Dorchester to Exeter ran a short distance to the north, giving an easy approach to Dumnonia. There was another line of approach, the Fosse Way, running in from the north-east from the very area which we know to have been in West Saxon hands in the early seventh century, Wiltshire and northern Somerset. Nor does the presence of two Iron Age hill-forts close to Bindon in any way strengthen Hoskins' argument. Neither site has produced anything to suggest occupation at this date or any other connection with seventh-century warfare. Finally, the archaeological evidence, as has already been argued, does not allow us to assume, with Hoskins, that Dorset was in English hands by 614. Indeed, the Hardown burials apart, it is the *scarcity* of Anglo-Saxon material which is striking, not its presence. The West Saxons, then, were not at hand to crush the British force at Bindon above the Axe. If the archaeological evidence is any guide at all, they were in east Dorset and not in great numbers.

This being so, it may be over-hasty to exclude Bindon in Dorset from consideration. Bindon Hill is only 11 km from Wareham with its undeniable evidence for a literate British enclave, if not more than that, which survived into the late seventh or early eighth century. There was moreover a sizeable earthwork above Lulworth Cove which could have provided a base for a large force of men on the move (Wheeler 1951). In any event *Beandune* is to be placed in this western reach of Wessex and not far to the west on the Axe.

The next engagement recorded in the *Chronicle* is the defeat of the Britons in 658 by Cenwealh at *Peonnum* and their repulse to the River Parrett. Hoskins rejects the old identification of *Peonnum* with Penselwood on the Somerset–Wiltshire border near Zeals on the proper grounds that the name alone is not sufficient to support the hypothesis (Hoskins 1960: 16). But the site he selects, Pinhoe, near Exeter, is supported by nothing more than its name, *Pen* (hill), while if *Peonnum* was fought here a major problem is presented. If the British were defeated close to the walled city of Exeter, what impulse made them flee to the River Parrett 50 km to the east? What disorder of mind, what outbreak of panic would have impelled them to flee towards Wessex and not back into the safety of Exeter's walls or into a fastness farther west? This passage will only make sense if we locate *Peonnum* east or south-east of the Parrett in south Somerset or north Dorset and there are several possible sites for it here, apart from the traditional Penselwood. One of the most attractive is Penn, a prominent hill outside Yeovil, as Mrs K. Barker points out to me. This is in the borderland of Wessex and Dumnonia and close to the Roman road which led from Ilchester to Dorchester, a likely line of approach from north to south by an English force. If put to flight here, the Britons could well have retreated north-east to the Parrett or the Somerset marshes or to Exmoor and the Quantocks beyond.

Three years later in 661 we hear of another battle fought by Cenwealh against the British, at *Posentesbyrig*. Following W. H. Stevenson, Hoskins has accepted that this was Posbury, a small Iron Age fortification on a remote hill-top near Crediton. Anyone who has visited Posbury will question the likelihood that this hill-top, remote from good communications and difficult of access, was the scene of a major clash of arms. Strategically it has nothing to recommend it. It does not command the valley below: it is too isolated for that role. Crediton is the key position in the vale, not Posbury. It is actually unsafe to assume that *Posentesbyrig* lay in Dumnonia at all, for Cenwealh could have faced Britons on his north-western frontier at this time. But even if we allow that it did, there is nothing to support a location above the vale of Crediton, or at any other known site. The Chronicle does not claim a success for Wessex at *Posentesbyrig* (might it perhaps have been a reverse?), so that wherever it was fought the battle probably had no long-term effect on the relations between Saxons and British. More significant by far was the engagement, at an unnamed site, in 682–3 in which the Britons were routed and pushed back to the sea, by Centwine. This could mean either to the Bristol Channel through the lowland of central Devon, or to the English Channel in south Devon. In either event, this English success marked an important stage in the establishment of the supremacy of Wessex over the eastern part of Dumnonia, though a long way short of total control. In 710 the Dumnonian king Geraint was at war with Wessex, five years after his celebrated doctrinal exchange with Aldhelm, and from that time onward the power of Wessex slowly and steadily asserted itself over its western neighbour.

There were sporadic bursts of conflict in the eighth century but there is no sign at this date of a decisive English breakthrough. The *Annales Cambriae* report a British victory in 722 at a place called *Hehil* which was *apud Cornuensis*. This has been identified by some as Hayle in west Cornwall, others with the Camel estuary, earlier called the *Heil*. Both are too far west to be taken seriously and there are better candidates in Hele, Jacobstow or even Hele in the Culm valley. The final phase in the English conquest of the west Welsh came in the ninth century when Ecgbert of Wessex ordered a major attack on Dumnonia in 814 (*Anglo-Saxon Chronicle* E 799). Probably all of Devon and much of Cornwall was absorbed shortly after this. A rebellion by the Cornish in 825 failed when they were defeated by Ecgbert at Gafulford, possibly Galford in west Devon rather than Camelford in Cornwall (*Anglo-Saxon Chronicle* E 815). The British made their final throw in 838, encouraged by the appearance of a large Danish fleet in south-western waters for the first time (*Anglo-Saxon Chronicle* E 828). An alliance was struck with the Danes against Wessex, but again Ecgbert's army was equal to the threat. The king himself hastened to Cornwall and at *Hengestes Dun* (probably Hingston Down near Callington) decisively crushed the strange alliance. This victory marked the end of an independent British kingdom in the far west. We still hear of Cornish kings, like Dumgarth, in the later ninth century (below, p. 295), but they can only have been dependents of the kings of Wessex, reigning as vassals in a conquered land. Dumnonia seems to have remained in this state of a subject province for some time to come, perhaps down to the reign of Athelstan.

The long drawn out contest between Wessex and Dumnonia, as it is sketched for us in the *Chronicle*, is not the unfolding of a determined and expansionist *Westpolitik* carried out by the military might of English kings at the expense of their weaker neighbours. More fundamentally it was a struggle for the possession of land by rival owners, some British, some English, all liable to resort to force. English settlers in the eastern parts of Dumnonia may be expected from the late seventh century onward, the family of Boniface among them, and during the eighth century their numbers will have grown, particularly in the fertile lands of the Exe and the Culm. Disputes were inevitable and on occasion major armies might be called out by rulers to bring matters to an issue. That is the true background to *Beandun* and *Peonnum* and the expansion of Wessex, the struggle for territory and squabbles over land, not the growth of one kingdom at the expense of another [1].

The testimony of place-names supports and greatly expands the archaeological evidence for English settlement in Devon. There are virtually no names which elsewhere in England are associated with Anglo-Saxon settlement before 700, no names connected with Germanic deities such as

Wotan or Thor. A high proportion of names have as their first element a personal name of late (i.e. tenth or eleventh century) date, while others are compounded of two personal names – another late feature. All this points to a very prolonged and gradual process of colonization and naming, extending from about 700 to the Conquest and probably beyond. It may be that English settlement intensified after 800, but it would be wrong to assume, with the editors of the place-name survey for Devon, that the overwhelmingly English nomenclature of the county necessarily means that the influx of English-speaking colonists was so massive that it swamped the British population (Gover, Mawer and Stenton 1941: xix–xx). Over a period of three centuries much can change and many British names may have survived for long after 700 without being recorded. Nor must we fail to note that later history provides many instances of toponymy being transformed by a relatively small landowning group.

It has often been pointed out that there are marked differences between the place-names of north and south Devon. The elements -*cott* and -*worthy* are common in the north and centre, absent in the south. *Hayes* and *hayne* are widespread in the south-east (and in adjoining Dorset), very rare in the north [2]. Colonization from different areas to the east may have played a part here, but the possibility that these differences were the product of settlement at different dates cannot be discounted. The distribution of English names in Cornwall points to marked English influence in the north-east, in the south-east to a lesser extent and, more surprisingly, on Bodmin Moor, though these names may be late arrivals.

Surviving British names are generally scattered over Devon with the occasional small group appearing, as at Trusham, Treable and Dunchideock in Great Haldon, and a cluster of six in Lifton hundred: Breazle, Carley, Dunterton, Kelly, Maindra and Trebick. Occasional names hint at settlements of higher status, for instance Charles on the edge of Exmoor may be derived from *Carn* ('rock') and *lis* ('palace'). The distribution of these Celtic names suggests only random survival of British nomenclature. In the fertile South Hams, a likely attraction for new settlers, there are virtually none. In east Devon there are several (Aunk, Crooke, Duvale, Pinn, Yawl, Hemyock, Dowrish and Whimple, along with several stream-names). A few names in *wealh* ('British'), for example, Walreddon, Walla Brook and Wallover (Cameron 1979–80) and a number of hybrid names applied to hill-forts (Countisbury, Membury and Denbury – the last perhaps referring to Dumnonian inhabitants), complete the picture. A British substratum still existed, but the names of places may not be a sure guide to its scale, especially between 700 and 900.

Athelstan's campaign against the Britons of Cornwall in 936 is usually seen as the last act in the conquest of the lands west of the Tamar. The expedition seems to have been mounted against Cornishmen in revolt, in which they had been joined by other Britons. No details of these operations are recorded. All that we hear concerns Exeter, specifically the expulsion of the remaining British population and the refortification of the city by the king, probably merely refurbishment of the Roman defences. The Cornish were compelled to accept the Tamar as their eastern border as it has remained ever since with only minor deviations. To this period of English overlordship belongs the formal organization of Cornwall into six hundreds of the kind that existed in the Anglo-Saxon kingdoms farther east. The origins of the hundreds is obscure in the extreme (Thomas 1964b), but there is at least a *prima facie* case for regarding these blocks of land as based on earlier divisions of Dumnonia and these in turn may have sprung from tribal organizations of Roman or still earlier date. After Athelstan nothing is heard of warfare between Britons and English in the peninsula. But in the meantime a different threat to the security of the South West had materialized.

The Danish Attacks

From the second quarter of the ninth century, the north-western coasts of Europe came under increasing threat from the sea-borne raids of the Danes (Jones 1968: 204–40). Charlemagne's completion of the protracted task of the conquest of northern Germania brought the Frankish empire into direct contact with the inhabitants of Jutland and the western Baltic islands. His subjugation of the Frisians and the Saxons also meant that Danish raiders and freebooters had a free hand in the North Sea and the English Channel. For a time Charlemagne and his successor Louis the Pious held the northerners in check, but after Louis' death they could be contained no longer. Raids on the Frankish lands began in 834 and in the following year the English shores felt the first descent of the 'heathen men'. The first record of a raid on the South West occurs in the *Anglo-Saxon Chronicle* under the year 851, when the ealdorman Ceorl and a muster of the men of Devon defeated the Danes with great slaughter at a place called *Wicganbeorg*. This is likely to have been near the south coast, as the raiders subsequently retired to Thanet, and the site of Wickaborough only a short distance inland from Tor Bay has a claim as the scene of this engagement.

Nothing more is heard of Danish assaults for twenty-five years, and by that time the character of their onslaught had altered from the rapid thrust of plundering bands to the concerted operations of one or more large hosts. In 876 the army which had been active for a year in Wessex slipped away by a night march from the West Saxon levies and lodged themselves in Exeter. Alfred advanced to the city and, although he was unable to come to grips with the Danes, received hostages from the invaders and extracted solemn oaths from them. In the following year, the host moved north into Mercia. Another English success came in north Devon in 878. A nameless brother of Ivar the Boneless and Halfdan crossed from south Wales with twenty-three ships and beseiged Odda, ealdorman of Devon, and a company of Alfred's thegns at a place which Asser calls *Arx Cynuit* (Asser: 54, 6, 20). This may well be Countisbury Hill above the gorge of the Lyn. The English victory was emphatic, the Danish leader along with 840 men being killed. The boost to Alfred's forces in their Somerset redoubts must have been considerable.

The respite was brief. In 893 Alfred was compelled to take his levies west to Exeter, besieged by one Danish force which had arrived by sea, while a defended place on the north coast of Devon faced a second sea-borne assault. The latter may have been the *burh* at Pilton. These raids were apparently beaten off, and thereafter there were no major attacks until the late tenth century. The next wave of raids began in 981, a particularly severe assault in 988 being foiled by the determined resistance of the Devon thegns, who thereby earned great fame. A more devastating attack followed in 997, when a strong Danish force raided both shores of the Bristol Channel before sailing up the English Channel and into the Tamar estuary. They penetrated as far north as Lydford 'burning and slaughtering everything they met'. They were driven off at Lydford, but they attacked and destroyed the abbey at Tavistock founded barely twenty years before. In 1001 it was on south Devon that the full force of raiding fell, this time with assistance from an English traitor, Pallig, who had broken his allegiance to Ethelred despite being in receipt of wealthy gifts from the king. The Danish ships and their temporary allies sailed up the Teign estuary and destroyed 'Teignton', perhaps Kingsteignton. They then turned their attention to Exeter and moved up the Exe to threaten the city. But they were thwarted by the citizens, even though the invaders defeated a levy of men from Somerset and Devon close by at Pinhoe. After plundering and destroying settlements nearby, they moved off into Wessex. These raids on the southern coast were made easier to mount by the willingness of Norman aristocrats to allow the Danes access to their ports. It was this that brought the English and Norman courts into diplomatic conflict for the first time. The dispute was patched up but the menace in the Channel remained.

The invasion of England by Swein's army in 1003, following the slaughter of Danes in the island by Ethelred's order, brought immediate disaster to the South West. Exeter was betrayed to the Danes by a French servant of Queen Emma who held the *burh* in dower and the place was plundered and destroyed. This marked the opening of the campaigns which were to lead to the absorption of Wessex, and Devon, into the Scandinavian domain. This was finally achieved in the reign of Cnut in 1016.

A marginal note in the Exeter Domesday reports another disturbance which may have occurred about this time or somewhat later. A group of nine manors in south Devon between the estuaries of the Erme and Avon had been devastated by Irish raiders. Seven of the manors had not recovered by 1086, so that it seems reasonable to date this event to the early or middle eleventh century. We are left to wonder whether this was an isolated attack or the most destructive of a series which otherwise went unrecorded.

One relic of Viking visits to the peninsula was recovered by chance from the beach at Goodrington, Torbay, in 1975 (Sykes-Balls 1978–9). This is a gold armlet some 10 cm in diameter, composed of three twisted wires, with a faceted rectangular knob at the ring-junction decorated with punched circles. The object is of almost pure gold, weighing 114.6 grammes. The closest analogies for the Goodrington bracelet come from Scandinavia, closest of all being an armlet from a hoard at Godra Byrummet on the island of Gotland, dated by associated coins to about 1050. The Goodrington example is probably also of this date or a little earlier. There are no comparable objects from Devon and Cornwall, or indeed from southern Britain as a whole.

The slight Scandinavian impress, when compared with south Wales for example, can be gauged from the extreme scarcity of Scandinavian place-names. Lundy is Norse ('Puffin Island'), but there are no certain examples of others in the peninsula. Helford is a possible, but dubious, candidate. Three Anglo-Scandinavian names occur close together in the South Hams, at Grimston, Gripstone and Oldstone. These are probably late in date, perhaps of the eleventh century when such hybrids were common (Gover, Mawer and Stenton 1931: xxvii).

Burhs and Urban Settlement

The origins of the *burh* lay in the defensive measures taken by Alfred and his son Edward in Wessex and by Aethelred and Aethelfleda in Mercia against the menace of the Danish armies. The earliest testimony to the use of local fortifications in a concerted scheme of defence dates from 893, under which year the *Anglo-Saxon Chronicle* informs us that Alfred 'divided his army, so that always half its men were at home, half on war-service, apart from the men who guarded the *burhs*'. The seeds of this scheme may well have been sown fifteen years earlier when the embattled king of Wessex planned his recovery from his fortress in the marshes at Athelney. Sir Frank Stenton's description of the scheme in its developed form still holds good.

> By the early part of the tenth century no village in Sussex, Surrey and Wessex east of the Tamar was distant more than twenty miles (32 km.) from a fortress which formed a unit in a planned scheme of national defence. These fortresses varied widely both in size and design. At Bath, Winchester, Portchester, Chichester and Exeter the plan was probably determined by whatever then remained of the walls of a Roman town or

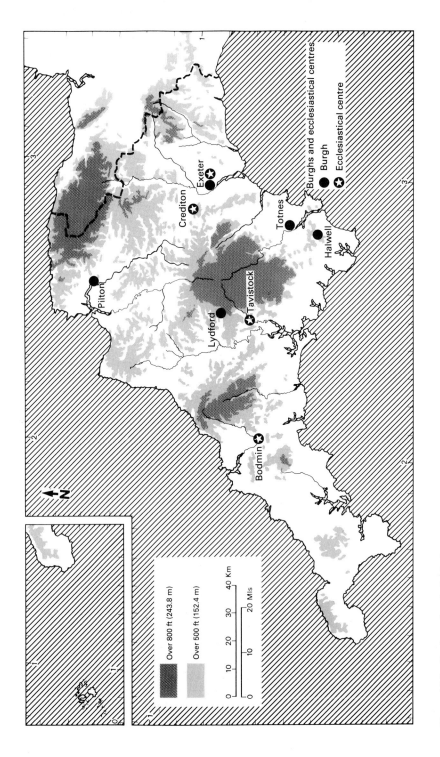

Figure 10.2 *Burhs* and ecclesiastical centres

fort. At Wareham, Wallingford and Cricklade the Saxon fortress consisted of a large rectangular enclosure surrounded by a bank and ditch, and at Lydford in Devon, Christchurch in Hampshire and Burpham, near Arundel, a defensible position was created by a line of earthwork drawn across the neck of a promontory. Each fortress was kept in repair and garrisoned, when necessary, by men of the surrounding country

(Stenton 1947: 261–2).

Four *burhs*, almost certainly all of Alfredian origin, lay in Devon: Exeter, Lydford, Pilton and Halwell. The choice of Exeter, no doubt still girt by its strong Roman defences, needs no further comment. At Lydford, new fortifications were necessary, though the site was well endowed by nature. The site of the *burh* at Halwell is uncertain but it is unlikely to have been at the present village. More probable is that use was made of one of the two presumably Iron Age earthworks in the vicinity, Halwell Camp and Stanborough Camp, both of which are as yet unexcavated. Pilton is the most problematic case. The village which bears this name, north of Barnstaple across the River Yeo, has an obvious attraction, particularly as one version of the Burghal Hidage names the *burh* 'Pilton with Barnstaple'. But there are no visible signs of defences here and the position is not notable for its natural strength. Barnstaple itself is a more obvious site for a fortification and it must quickly have asserted its advantages over Pilton, if indeed that site was ever that of the *burh*.

The *burh* which is likely to reveal most about its lay-out and history is Lydford, the *Hlidan* of the Burghal Hidage. The builders of the *burh* defences chose a wedge-shaped promontory flanked by the gorge of the Lyd on two sides and a narrow valley on the third. The exposed north-western side was defended by a bank 12 m wide and a ditch 200 m in length, with a centrally placed gate. This earthwork almost certainly continued around the edge of the plateau, thus enclosing about 5 ha (12 acres): short lengths of it have been located beneath the castle and the small Norman fortification sited at the south-eastern tip of the promontory. The bank was a complex structure of turf and branches laid over a foundation of larger timbers placed on the old land surface. Within the body of the rampart a number of large squared timbers had been set upright, for what purpose remains obscure.

In the interior considerable areas were parcelled off by boundary ditches and some of the plots were further separated from their neighbours by paths set at right-angles to the main street. Some of the larger pre-Conquest streets still figure in the street-plan of the present village. There was, then, an element of planning, however rudimentary, in the original scheme (largely unpublished: Radford 1970: 94–6). The planting here of a Norman fort and later a castle underlines the strategic significance of the place on the western flank of Dartmoor. Lydford may have held out against the Danish attackers in 997, whereas Tavistock Abbey nearby was destroyed. But when settled times

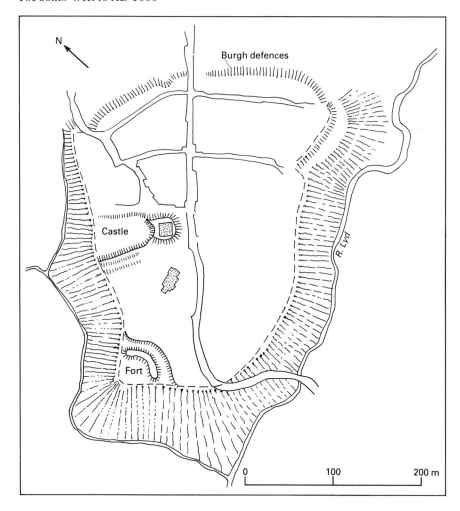

Figure 10.3 The Saxon *burh* at Lydford

returned Lydford made little progress as an urban nucleus and was soon eclipsed by the market town fostered by the great ecclesiastical site of Tavistock.

Exeter in the eleventh century was a wealthy populous city, still protected by its ancient defences, a regional centre which ranked among the greatest cities of England (Allan, Henderson and Higham 1984). At the time of Domesday Book the city paid geld only when other prominent cities did so: London, Winchester and York. Its population cannot be precisely computed from the figure of 399 houses recorded in Domesday Book but 3,000 seems a not unreasonable guess. Already by 1000 Exeter had thus joined the relatively small number of major cities in southern England, a fact which appears the more remarkable when it is recalled that Exeter at that date was the westernmost of English cities (small towns like Lydford, Totnes and Okehampton apart) and that several centuries were to elapse before sizeable urban centres developed in the lands farther west.

Exeter's eminence and prosperity were evidently of recent growth in 1000. There is no sign in the archaeological record of notable advance in urbanism until after the time of Athelstan in the earlier tenth century, and it is not until the eleventh century that the record begins to fill out. Areas occupied before 1000 seem to lie close to the centre of the walled area, about the crossing of the two principal thoroughfares, and structures associated with that occupation are few and modest in scale. A potentially important area within the walls, however, has never been examined archaeologically: the hill of Rougemont and its environs, later occupied by the Norman castle. Construction of that castle in 1068 involved the demolition of many houses, an indication that this elevated ground had been occupied long before.

What is known of the early medieval street-plan does not suggest that it had begun to develop much before the late tenth century at the earliest. Nor does it seem that the origins of the streets lie in a planned layout of the late Saxon period as has been ventured (Biddle and Hill 1971: 82). The Roman street grid had already largely disappeared long before the tenth century and what took its place was a far from orderly series of streets and lanes, few of which are dated at all closely. Some of them at least will have post-dated the Conquest.

The document known as the Athelstan Donation indicates that as early as the early eleventh century it was believed that Athelstan had been concerned to re-establish the monastery at Exeter. On a visit to the city, the king ordered a monastery to be built (or rebuilt) and to the house he gave 26 estates and a share of his collection of relics. This sounds like a refoundation of the old seventh-century monastery, perhaps after a period of decay. Later, in 968, King Edgar established a group of monks in Exeter, though whether in the existing house or in another is uncertain. These monastic foundations need not have been large or wealthy. When Leofric came to Exeter in 1050, he found there only one set of vestments for the mass and five books, a poor showing for four centuries of monastic piety. The Danish attack of 1003 may have been particularly damaging for the monastery and its contents, though other processes may have been at work. It is somewhat surprising that the monastic foundation at so prosperous a place as Exeter was so modest in its achievements, in the eleventh century and later.

The material record from the late Saxon city also suggests only modest prosperity before the tenth century. Small objects are remarkably scarce and of poor quality. A bronze sword-guard found in South Street, Exeter, in 1833 is one of the most interesting, having interlace ornament on its faces which is not far removed from that on certain of the stone monuments (Shortt 1841a, frontispiece no. 5, but almost unrecognizable). On its top it bears the inscription LEOFRIC ME FEC (IT), the name, at least, of the craftsman being

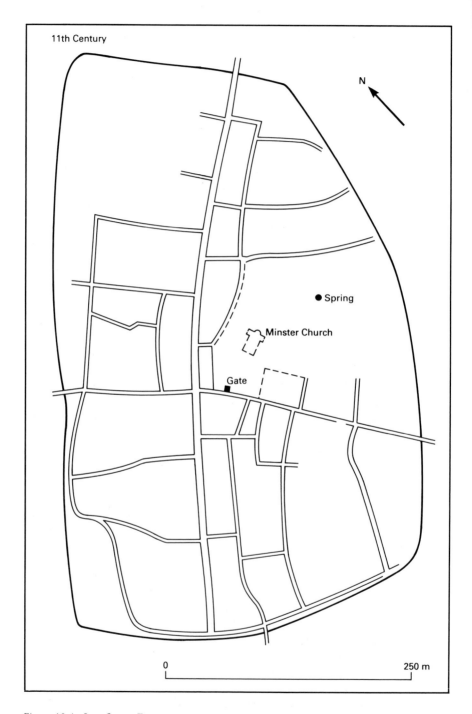

Figure 10.4   Late Saxon Exeter

English. The form of the object and its decoration place it in the tenth century. Somewhat earlier is a gold finger-ring found in a grave in the minster cemetery. This is closest to the Trewhiddle silver rings and may also be of the later ninth century (below, p. 301).

The earliest coinage bearing the mint-name of Exeter, and possibly the earliest coinage struck there, dates to the late reign of Alfred. The reverse type of these issues consists of the first three letters of the mint-name, EXA, arranged vertically in the field. The coins, which are closely matched by contemporary issues struck at Winchester, are extremely rare, only three specimens being known, all from the same pair of dies. Coining at Exeter, as at Winchester, seems not to have continued after the death of Alfred, and in the reign of Edward the Elder and during most of that of Athelstan mint-names do not figure on the coinage, making attribution very difficult. (Indeed, like most of the English mints for much of the tenth century, the coinage of Exeter cannot be securely identified. It is, however, a reasonable assumption that the mint was active from time to time.) A small number of coins of Athelstan, with a small cross as the obverse and reverse type and without a portrait, bear the Exeter signature. Some of these have the legend RAEGENOLD MO [NETA] EAXANIAE CIV [ITAS], and at least one (from a famous hoard found in the Forum at Rome) was struck by the moneyer ABVN at EAX CIVITA. After Athelstan, the mint-names again disappear from the coinage and the south-western mints do not recur until the reign of Edwig (955–9) and the early years of Edgar (959–75). A single coin of Edwig has the mint signature EXA CI [VITAS] and the moneyer's name AETHEL-GAR. Coins of very similar style were struck by two other mints in Devon, Totnes and Barnstaple.

A few years before his death in 975, Edgar instituted a major monetary reform, which involved, among much else, a standardization of the coin-type. A royal portrait henceforward appeared on coins throughout the kingdom and the reverse invariably bore a mint-signature and the moneyer's name, as well as a small cross. The new style was retained under Edward the Martyr (975–8) and in the early years of Ethelred II. The Exeter mint was active in all three reigns, particularly in that of Ethelred II for whom no less than thirty-five moneyers are recorded. Other south-western mints now entered their most prolific phase, the presence of the same moneyer's name at more than one mint suggesting strongly that some of these men were mobile. There is much more to be learnt of all the mints and the chronology of their issues. Exeter, Totnes, Lydford and Barnstaple were probably the most active, and their links with mints farther east, especially Ilchester and Shaftsbury, are well attested. Mints in Cornwall pose greater problems. A unique coin of Ethelred II by the moneyer BRVN, who also appears on Exeter coins, is attributable to Launceston. A small series of coins was issued in the same reign by a mint signing itself GOTHANBYRIG. This has been identified as Castle Gotha near St Austell (above, p. 224) but no early medieval

(a)

(a)

(b)

(b)

Plate 10.1a   Penny of Edward the Confessor, from the Exeter mint.

Plate 10.1b   Penny of William I, from the Exeter mint.

occupation is known there and there is no other foundation for the claim.

It is not surprising that not a single Anglo-Saxon *sceatta* has been found in Devon. Much more difficult to account for is the great scarcity of later Saxon coinage in the county. Why, when Devon lay within the power of English kings, are individual coins so thinly dispersed and coin-hoards entirely absent? A penny of Archbishop Ceolnoth (833–70) from the Deanery Garden, Exeter (now destroyed but probably dating from 833–40), and a denarius of Charles the Bald from Combe Davey on the Blackdowns, struck at Melle in Aquitaine and dating from about 855, seem to be the only recorded pieces of the ninth century (Dolley and Shiel 1981). Even later, finds are scarcely more numerous. Single coins of Aethelred are known from Exeter

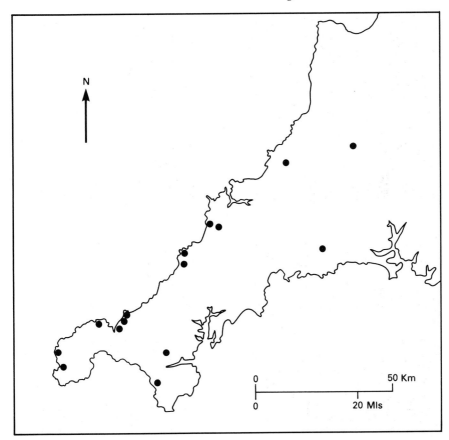

N

Figure 10.5   Distribution of bar-lug pottery

and probably from Lydford, and one of Harthacnut from Plymouth. Given that Exeter was a major mint in the late tenth and early eleventh century, this is an astonishingly modest total. The dispersal of coins by means of trade was evidently not taking place and this state of affairs is in contrast with the rest of southern England (Metcalf 1980: 24).

Similarly undeveloped were centralized crafts, even the simplest such as pottery-making. The most widespread domestic pottery of the later Dark Ages in the west of the region is the material now generally known as bar-lug pottery (earlier 'bar-lip') (Hutchinson 1979). These squat cooking vessels with their flat bases and opposed barred lugs rising above the rim have long been recognized as one component in a *facies* of heavy-duty pottery, found in the western Baltic lands, northern Germany, Friesland and eastern England as well as in Cornwall, in the period from the eighth century to at least the eleventh. The origins of the vessel-type are obscure, but are likely to lie far from Cornwall, possibly in Friesland or northern Germany. It now seems clear that the Cornish version of this widespread pottery type forms a quite distinct strand in the ceramic tradition. There is very little indication that these vessels were made or exported east of the Tamar, though numbers have been recorded in the Isles of Scilly. At present, the greatest concentrations occur on the north Cornish coast, though this is where many of the settlements of this period have been found and this may have distorted the record. The prevalence of bar-lug pottery on some sites is remarkable. At Mawgan Porth, virtually all the pottery associated with the tenth-century settlement, nearly 1,000 sherds in all, was of this kind. In the Gwithian settlement, bar-lug pottery predominated over all other pottery in the later levels, though other grass-marked wares were still present. Clearly, then, it took over all or most of the market in common pottery in Cornwall in the ninth or tenth century and maintained its position of dominance for at least 150 years. At Launceston castle, bar-lug pottery was still in use at the time of the Norman conquest and for a short time thereafter.

The date at which it began is not yet illumined by any such precise evidence. No undoubted association between bar-lug pottery and imported late Roman wares has been reported, so that it cannot be taken back to the sixth or seventh century. The earliest occurrence in a stratified sequence is at Gwithian. Here, as already observed, bar-lug vessels appear in the sequence after other grass-marked wares had been current for some time. For how long is difficult to estimate since absolute dates can rarely be applied to any points in the known archaeological sequences. Since there is no clear indication on chronology from Cornwall, discreet use may be made of the dating of related vessels elsewhere in north-western Europe, though without forgetting that these can provide only a general guide. The bar-lug material from Haithabu (Hübener 1969, 101) does not occur before 800 and may be as late as the later ninth century.

Many communities of the later Saxon period were apparently aceramic. This was certainly true of Exeter down to the tenth century, and even after that pottery was not plentiful (Allan 1984: 13). The forms of the local coarse wares were simple and imports from northern France supplied the only fine wares and those in small quantities. Not until the twelfth century did this situation radically change.

The Church

The seventh and eighth centuries were a formative period for the Church in Britain. That this was so was largely due to the work of Archbishop Theodore of Canterbury (668–90), which extended to pastoral care as well as to theology and Church administration. But the reforms of Theodore and his immediate successors had little or no effect on Cornwall. When the Archbishop addressed himself to those who had been ordained by Celtic bishops and those who did not observe the Catholic Easter, with the warning 'we have no leave to give the Chrism or the Eucharist to those asking it, except they have expressed themselves willing to be in the unity of the Church with us', we need not imagine that this stern advice was received with joy in Dumnonia, Aldhelm, the star pupil of Theodore, when Abbot of Malmesbury wrote in 705 to the Dumnonian king Geraint, to correct British usage in the observance of Easter, again probably without marked success (Bede: V. 18). Five years later Geraint was at war with Wessex which cannot have aided ecclesiastical harmony. Not until the ninth century and Ecgbert's conquest was the western British Church finally brought into line. Some time in the period 833–70, and probably after 850, the Cornish bishop Kenstec from his seat at *Dinnurrin* acknowledged his canonical obedience to Archbishop Ceolnoth. In doing so Kenstec describes his position with deliberate care, a reminder to Canterbury of the long and different tradition of the Church in Dumnonia: 'a see among the people of Cornwall in a monastery which in the British language is called *Dunnurrin*' (Haddan and Stubbs 1871: 674–5). By the later ninth century, then, the rule of Canterbury was acknowledged, however reluctantly. But it is a reasonable guess that some Celtic practices were still upheld. In the manuscript known as the *Lanalet Pontifical*, a tenth-century work now at Rouen but originally compiled for a western English bishop, we find a form of excommunication used by the 'bishop of the monastery of Lanalet', that is, the Cornish minster of St Germans. The book was later in the possession of Lyfing, Bishop of Crediton, before going to Jumieges and finally to Rouen (Doble 1934: 1937).

Ecclesiastical administration was a gradual development at the prompting of the kings of Wessex. In 705 Ine divided Wessex into two bishoprics, centred on Winchester and Sherborne. Later in the eighth century and in the ninth, kings of Wessex granted land in the South West to the abbeys of Sherborne and Glastonbury. The reign of Egbert (802–39) may have marked a critical stage. After his campaigns in the west, further grants of Cornish territory were made to foundations in Wessex. The west Saxon bishops at Sherborne were thus effectively the heads of the Church in Devon and Cornwall. In 884 Alfred gave to Asser 'Exeter and the diocesan territory belonging to it in Devon and Cornwall', which Finberg has reasonably interpreted as a grant of the monastery at Exeter, the endowments of which were to equip Asser to carry out the work of a bishop in Devon and Cornwall within the diocese of Sherborne and under the control of its bishop (Finberg 1953: 116–16). William of Malmesbury, writing in the early twelfth century, tells us that Cornwall and Crediton received their first bishops in 904, but this is based upon a faulty transmission of his source, a version of events in 904 found in the Leofric *Missal*. The separate diocese of Crediton was formed in 909 and to it the

Figure 10.6 The minster church at Exeter

bishop of Sherborne granted his three estates of Lawhitton (around Launceston), Pawton and 'Caellwic'. Athelstan's campaigns in the far South West established a much firmer relationship between the British of Cornwall and Wessex, as William of Maumsbury relates.

> He attacked the British with great force and compelled them to withdraw from Exeter, which hitherto they had inhabited on an equal footing in law with the English. He then fixed the left bank of the Tamar as the boundary of the shire, just as he had made the Wye the boundary for the north British.
>
> (Maumsbury (b): 148.)

That this part of Dumnonia was still regarded as not wholly English in the mid-tenth century is clear from a charter of King Edmund of 944 in which he calls himself 'king of the English and ruler of this province of the Britons'.

The first bishop of Cornwall was Conan, appointed in Athelstan's reign, about 930, but he was most probably not a plenary bishop but a chorepiscopus of the bishop of Crediton. The manumissions recorded in the Bodmin Gospels (below, p. 303) were still being carried out in the presence of the bishop of Crediton in the late tenth century. Only towards the end of that century, in 994, did Cornwall become an entirely separate see. A charter of that year issued by Aethelred afforded a new set of privileges to the new bishop Ealdred on his receipt of a new diocese. The centre of the see was without doubt St German's. A letter of Archbishop Dunstan makes it clear that this was so from the time of the second bishop at least, and thus presumably *ab origine*, and this is further supported by the testimony of Florence of Worcester. The list of early bishops cannot be reconstructed in detail, but the succession is reasonably certain.

Conan	*c.* 930	— 937/55
Daniel	937/55	— 959/63
Comoere	959/63	— 959/63
Wulsige	*c.* 963	— 981/93
Ealdred	994	—1002/18
Burhwold	1002/18	— 1027/31
Lyfing	1027/31	— 1046
Leofric	1046	— 1050

Remains of churches and other major structures are far from plentiful and little is now to be seen above ground of any pre-Norman building. The fragmentary remains of a church have been identified in Exeter, in association with the cemetery which lay immediately to the west of the Norman cathedral (Henderson 1982). This building, over 34 m long and some 10 m wide, may have had a long, narrow nave and chancel, with an apse at the north-east end and a porticus, perhaps with an added tower, against the north wall. More than one phase of building is in evidence in the porticus and the apse, but no firm absolute dates could be obtained from the associated levels. The fact that a building of this size was sited in a cemetery which had been in use for several centuries put it beyond reasonable doubt that this was the late Saxon minster church, surviving in use as the cathedral of Exeter from Leofric's time until the early twelfth century. We do not know when it was constructed, though the scale of the building would appear to preclude a date before about 850. A tenth-century foundation seems more probable.

The cemetery associated with this church has produced one object, a gold ring, which would square with a date of 900 or somewhat later. Several graves further contained deposits of charcoal below the corpse, another feature which is suggestive of a late Saxon date.

None of the medieval churches of Exeter have produced sure evidence of pre-Conquest structures below them or embodied in their fabric. Play is often made with the dedications of churches like St Sidwell and St Pancras in order to advance a claim for late Saxon or pre-Saxon foundation, but none is entirely convincing (Kerslake 1873). That churches other than the minster did exist is reasonably certain, but we do not know where they lay.

Late Saxon churches in Devon at large have been equally elusive. There has been little or no examination beneath Norman structures to determine what their predecessors were like. Two candidates present themselves for such treatment, both in east Devon. One is the cruciform church of Colyton, the plan of which alone hints at a pre-Conquest foundation, to which further support is given by the fine cross (below, p. 299). Equally interesting is the church at Sidbury beneath the Norman chancel of which lies a small stone-walled chamber, 3 m by 2.75 m, entered down a short flight of steps. The walls still stand to a height of nearly 2 m. The chamber was clearly covered in when the Norman rebuilding of the church took place and is thus to be referred to the pre-Conquest period. It is often called a 'crypt', a feature found in only half a dozen Anglo-Saxon churches in all of England. Perhaps more specifically it should be called a hypogeum or relic-chamber, also a rarity in Anglo-Saxon England and better known in Frankish and Carolingian Gaul. A more remote possibility is that it was a mausoleum, cleared of its original contents when rebuilding took place. There are occasional hints of late Saxon details in plan or decorative treatment elsewhere. The church at Dolton near Beaford, for instance, contains a font made from a pre-Conquest cross. But substantial churches in stone were clearly not widespread before the Norman Conquest or immediately after it.

About the beginning of the eighth century and increasingly thereafter, small chapels began to be constructed widely in south-western Britain. The best known lie in Cornwall but others exist on Scilly and presumably also in Devon. These were simple structures, difficult to date by archaeological means and often largely destroyed by subsequent building on the same site. For long the most familiar was that of St Piran on the sands at Perranzabuloe

Plate 10.2 The interior of St Piran's Chapel, Perranzabuloe, Cornwall, showing the main doorway and the altar. The site has now been buried as a protective measure.

(Haslam 1845: 226–30; Tomlin 1982). This was still a visible structure in the sixteenth century, being recorded both by Leland and Camden, but was already then threatened by the blowing sand. It had been engulfed by the eighteenth century, but the site was still known when the Lysons brothers visited this part of Cornwall in 1805. Thirty years later the building was cleared and a plan prepared, though a report of this work was not published until 1877. (On the subsequent history of the building, Tomlin 1982.) The chapel was no more than 10 m in length and 6 m wide, with narrow door openings in the south and east sides and a small window high in the south wall. An altar and table stood against the east wall, hard by the door opening, and over it a small niche was set in the wall. It is not known if this was an original feature. The early nineteenth-century explorers of the chapel noted an immense quantity of human bones lying in the vicinity, clearly derived from a sizeable cemetery. Three graves allegedly containing headless skeletons, were said to have been found beneath the altar in 1835. No goods of any kind appear to have been found in these burials and no instances of stone cists were seemingly encountered. Many of these graves may date from the Middle Ages but the site could already have been used for burial in the early days of the chapel or even before it was built. The date at which the building was erected can only be a matter of guess work. It is reasonably

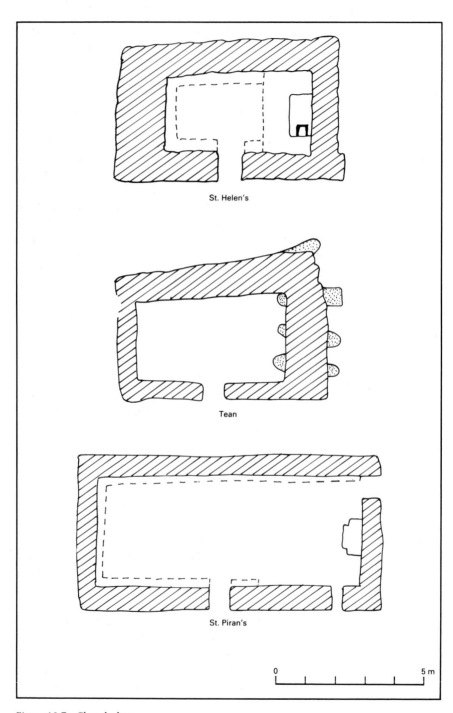

St. Helen's

Tean

St. Piran's

0   5 m

Figure 10.7   Chapel plans

certain to be much later than the lifetime of St Piran himself (in the sixth century?). A date in the 10th century may not be far out. The handsome wheel-headed cross which stands nearby is mentioned in a charter of 960 and is probably to be dated between 900 and 950. The little chapel may have been built not long after the cross went up.

The chapel of St Gothian at Gwithian has also now vanished under blown sand and we must depend on a plan of the mid-nineteenth century (Thomas 1958: 24–6). This shows a nave some 10 m by 5 m and a chancel 4.5 m by 3.8 m the latter probably an addition. A stone altar stood in the chancel but no other furnishings were evident. A large cemetery lay around the chapel and eight graves were found beneath the building itself. At an even greater depth a roughly walled structure was found and below that in turn further burials, the whole sequence suggesting an occupation of centuries. This fascinating site would repay relocation and examination. Several chapels were sited at or over wells and springs. Such is the chapel at Madron near Penzance, a small building (4.5 m by 3 m) with the well-head, fed by a stream, in the south-west corner. Here too a stone altar stood within a tiny chancel, while around the wall ran a stone bench. Rather earlier, probably of the ninth century, is the chapel of St Constantine at St Merryn: indeed this may be the earliest yet known. It too was tiny, only 2.3 m by 1.6 m internally, but with massive walls which curved inward to form a roughly vaulted roof (Williams 1911–12).

The best excavated chapel is that of St Ia at Newton near Camborne. This too was a well chapel, 6 m by 4 m, and perhaps with an upper floor supporting the chapel proper over the well (Thomas 1968a: 74–85). No date can be applied to this unpretentious building, except that it is earlier than the twelfth century, though a cross which Borlase recorded close by is assignable to the tenth century, and that is also the date of the altar-frontal dedicated by Leviut which came from here (below, p. 299).

The siting of chapels often gives some indication of their contemporary significance. One of the most compelling is that at Merther-Uny (Wendron). Here an Iron Age round was adapted for use as an enclosed cemetery about 1000 and a cross with panel ornament erected. It is highly likely that a chapel existed at this date and was later covered by a medieval building. Since the site was not chosen to serve as the centre of a medieval parish, as so often happened, the main environs of a pre-Conquest chapel are here still on display (Thomas 1968a). The little island of Teän, now uninhabited, also possessed a small chapel (measuring 7 m by 4 m) and a cemetery, later than a homestead, which was in use in the fifth and sixth centuries and perhaps until somewhat later. The chapel should therefore date from after 700 and could be a hundred years later. It might have replaced a small structure in timber within which a few graves were laid. The cemetery, in which sixteen graves were identified, was evidently a lay cemetery as young children and perhaps one woman were represented among the remains. Another small stone chapel stood on the eastern summit of St Martins. This was another small rectangular building with a doorway in its south wall. It had, however, been heavily reconstructed and no dating evidence for it was obtained.

The most convincing site of an early oratory chapel lies on St Helen's, or, as it was known in late medieval times, the island of St Elidius. Unfortunately, there is nothing in the hagiographic tradition about this man. The early Christian site on St Helen's was known to Borlase, who sketched the remains of the twelfth-century church. He thought it was the 'most ancient Christian building in all the Isles'. It was not until the Second World War that the site again came to notice, when a fire started by a German incendiary bomb revealed the remains once more. Excavation demonstrated that the first Christian buildings were a rectangular oratory chapel and a round hut. Later, probably in the medieval period, a church was added, and three rectangular buildings used as dwellings. It is possible that from the beginning the site had been bounded by a wall which defined a small precinct. The chapel, which measured 5 m by 2.5 m, was built of massive dry-stone masonry. No special flooring had been provided, the exposed rock serving as paving. At the eastern end, a step running the full width of the building formed a sanctuary-dais and on it a further step supported a stone altar set against the east wall. Between the altar and the north wall lay a stone seat and a low stone bench ran around the entire nave. Four burials, in stone-lined cists, lay at the southern end of the enclosure, undated but probably contemporary with the early use of the site. Datable finds were sparse and the chronology of the early site therefore sketchy. Grass-marked pottery occurred in the earliest levels of the round hut and in one of the rectangular buildings. These sherds point to the eighth or ninth century, though an opening date before 700 is not thereby excluded.

Stone Sculpture

At some date between 800 and 900 the rough-hewn slabs of stone which had hitherto marked sacred sites began to be replaced by monuments of more sophisticated form and refined ornamentation (Langdon 1896). The decorated crosses of Cornwall were to become the finest monuments of this period and even today, when so many have been defaced by centuries of wind and rain or damaged by later reuse, they can be impressive and moving memorials. There seems little doubt that they are in essence a Cornish not a south-western phenomenon. Only a handful are recorded in Devon and there is no reason to believe that they were ever numerous east of the Tamar. The opening date of the series can be fixed only approximately. In south Wales, the earliest of the richly ornamented crosses belong to the ninth century, beginning about 850, and to that period, and more specifically the years 850–900, the early Cornish instances may be assigned on grounds of stylistic affinity. The only monument which can plausibly be linked with an historical personage, the famous Doniert stone near St Cleer, agrees with a late-ninth-century date, King Dumgarth having lost his life by drowning in 878. There are in general obvious similarities with the better-known crosses of Ireland, Scotland and Northumbria as well as Wales, but the precise basis of the relationship between the Cornish examples and the rest is far from clear. Sculptural and other influences on Cornwall at this time came from several quarters and the craftsmen who made these crosses drew their inspiration from a wide variety of sources, including manuscripts and metalwork which might travel far.

No very early (i.e. seventh or eighth century) free-standing crosses are known in the South West, though the addition of the cross motif to existing standing stones appears to signal the growing importance of the symbol after 600. Plain slabs bearing the cross in relief *could* date from the seventh or eighth century, but this has not been demonstrated beyond question. Of more than 400 crosses or fragments known to exist, the most distinctive of Cornwall are those of the 'wheel-headed' type, in which the arms are linked by a continuous curve, a derivation perhaps from the wreath which appears in association with the cross in representational art of the period. The design is found widely in the Mediterranean world, from Coptic Egypt to Spain and southern Gaul. The immediate source for the Cornish examples is most probably Gaul, the agent of transmission being manuscript drawings, small objects such as ivories or pieces of metalwork, or even textiles. William of Malmesbury tells us of copies of the Old and New Testaments, brought from the Continent for sale in Britain (Maumsbury (a): 376–8).

The majority of crosses now stand in churchyards or are housed in churches: no doubt many still occupy their original sites. Others lie in the open country marking routes, church ways (like the cross on Bodmin Moor near the Jamaica Inn), ecclesiastical bounds and isolated memorial sites, like the inscribed pillars of earlier centuries (above, p. 249). As early as 960 a cross on the sands of St Piran could be used as a marker in a land-charter. A few may record leading figures, even kings. The Doniert stone has already been mentioned: its inscription reads DONIERT ROGAVIT PRO ANIMA – Doniert (?Dumgarth) asks for prayers for his soul. An inscription on the cross in Morrab Gardens in Penzance was earlier read as REGIS RICATI CRUX – the cross of King Ricatus. Although it is not entirely certain, this could be the name of a Cornish ruler not otherwise recorded. Chronology is the besetting problem of the crosses, whether individually or in their stylistic groups. From their origins in the ninth century the ornamented stones show little development of any kind for two or three centuries. A group which may be among the earliest are those which bear ornament of panels of punched dots and incised lines, frequently crudely cut and simply arranged. Although they may begin early, these crosses could have continued for many generations and the fact that most of them occur in west Cornwall may suggest a conservative regional school of stone carvers.

The major group of crosses, to which by far the finest belong, are those which bear complex schemes of ornament, earlier somewhat vaguely described as 'Hiberno-Saxon'. These schemes show affinities with those of Anglo-Scandinavian sculpture of the ninth and tenth centuries, the most familiar pattern being the interlace in various forms, the key pattern, the interlaced triquetra, the step pattern and the chain of rings, often in twisted form. These designs occur in a large number of variants and combinations: they are listed here only as an introduction to the grammar of ornament. It is unlikely that a native south-western source was responsible for any of these. Some are ultimately from the heritage of late antiquity, others came from the common stock of motifs used and freely adapted by craftsmen in the barbarian kingdoms of western Europe from the fifth century onward, while a few were inspired by the sculpture of the Scandinavian north. The finest instances of these crosses are those at Cardinham, St Neot, Sancreed, Roseworthy and a fragment at Ludgvan, all to be assigned to the tenth and eleventh century, perhaps to 950–1050. The class is widely spread across Cornwall, the larger number in the west being due to the higher chances of survival there. Those on the southern fringes of Bodmin Moor, at Cardinham, St Neot and Lanivet, may well be the product of the same school of craftsmen. A firmer link between crosses at Sancreed and Roseworthy (now at Lanherne) is provided by inscriptions. Both works have been signed by their sculptor, who appears as RUNHO at Sancreed and as RUHOL at Roseworthy: this is fairly certainly the same man and he was active about the middle of the tenth century. Stylistic links unite a number of crosses in central and north Cornwall. These include Padstow (Prideaux Place), Lanhydrock and Waterpit Down, among others. The last-named was inscribed CRUX IRCUROC, the second word being presumably the name of the dedicator. A few others bear or have borne similar inscriptions and others have probably been removed by weathering.

Among the most interesting are a few with the figure of the crucified Christ. The crosses signed by Runhol bear this scene, as does the broadly contemporary stone in Phillack churchyard. The attitude of Christ is the same in all three, the arms extended and the head viewed directly from the front. Phillack and Roseworthy are further linked by the presence of four round bosses set on the rear face of the cross-head and by the fact that the lower part of Christ's body extends some way down the shaft.

Indicative of the various influences at play in Cornwall in the tenth and eleventh centuries is the occasional appearance of a Scandinavian motif. The side of one of the Sancreed crosses has the undulating curves of a Jellinge-style beast, a tenth-century design in its homeland. To the following century belongs the battered scroll ornament in Ringerike style on the cross on Temple Moor, St Neot and on a fragment at Padstow. There are a few

Figure 10.8   Cornish crosses: Sancreed and Lanherne

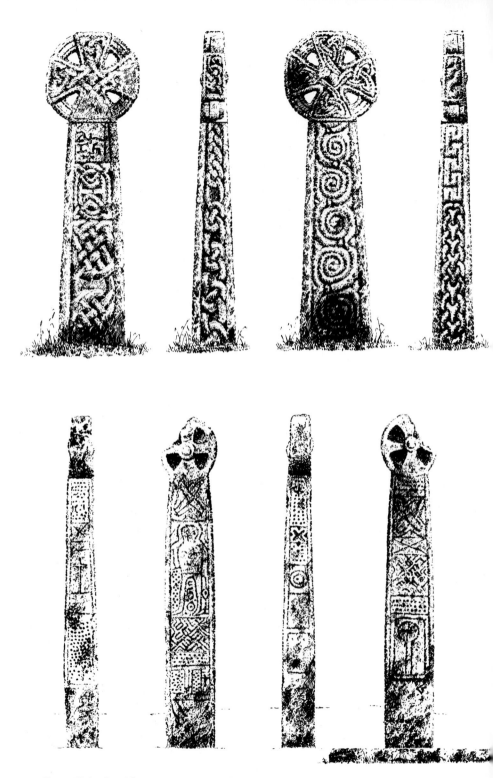

Figure 10.9   Cornish crosses: Lanivet and Cardinham

other traces of Anglo-Scandinavian sculptural influence, chiefly in three hogsback tombstones with interlace. The best of these, in Lanivet churchyard, has a wolf- or dog-like figure crouching at either end of the 'roof'. The others are at St Tudy and St Buryan. All should date to about 1000 or a little later (Langdon 1896: 411–17).

A little church furniture in stone survives from this period. The most remarkable piece is a rectangular altar slab at Camborne, now in the parish church but originally in a chapel of St Ia at Treslothan (Thomas 1968a: 100–1). This is inscribed LEVIUT IUSIT HEC ALTARE PRO ANIMA SUA in majuscule lettering which suggests a date in the mid-tenth century. The ornamented border and the central cross show that the slab was intended to be viewed frontally and is thus identifiable as an altar-frontal. A smaller stone from Treslothan (now in Treslothan church) is similar in form and bears the inscription AEGURED, the dedicator's name. This is more probably a mensa or altar-table. That sculptured slabs were used to adorn more than altars is suggested by a stone at Phillack which shows a crucifixion figure, above the arms of which are two crosses (Thomas 1961: 91–2). There are analogies, admittedly more ambitious, for this type of stone in the roods of Wessex and there is a real possibility that this is the earliest Cornish version of a rood, rather than a memorial slab. It may date from the first half of the eleventh century.

The only cross of Cornish type in Devon stands not far east of the Tamar, at Stentaway near Plymstock. This is a plain wheel-headed cross with an odd, unintelligible inscription or graffito near the base (Masson Phillips 1954). Two decorated stones in Devon are products of the same tenth-century workshop or craftsman. One is now at St Nicholas' Priory in Exeter, though its original siting is unknown, a cross-shaft bearing simple interlace. The other is not a cross but probably a territorial marker. It stands, apparently on its original site, at Copplestone north of Crediton (and gives its name to the village), a 3 m high block of Dartmoor granite with interlace ornament on all its faces. It was already there in 974 when it was mentioned in a charter of King Edgar. A niche later inserted near the top may have contained a small figure. It is interesting that this large block of granite should have been transported 15 km from Dartmoor, while in the granite area itself no sculpted crosses are recorded at all.

Colyton Cross stands apart from the other south-western crosses, though it is broadly contemporary with the monuments at Copplestone and Exeter. It is a fine carving, standing in its restored state a little over 2.2 m high. At the base of the shaft is an acanthus spray and over this a superbly carved panel reaches to the cross head, a scroll design inhabited by bird and animal figures, their forms cleverly absorbed into the pattern in a style reminiscent of Frankish work. For comparable sculpture we must look to Somerset, particularly to pieces at Chew Stoke and Maperton, and all are to be seen as products of the same Wessex workshop. A date in the second half of the tenth century seems appropriate for the lively design of the inhabited scroll, in which there is clear reference to manuscript ornament, as in the borders of Cambridge, Corpus Christi College Ms. 183 and, more generally, in the Lambeth Psalter.

The Monasteries

The English word for a monastery (Latin: *monasterium*) was *mynster*. In the early years of English Christianity the monasteries or minsters were responsible for the pastoral care of communities, under the general charge of bishops, and were thus the forerunners of the parish churches of the Middle Ages. But they served areas which were very much larger than those of the later parishes. By the ninth century the close association between the original meaning of *minster* and monastery had been broken. By then *minster* denoted a body of secular clergy, priests, deacons and men in minor orders, living in a community mainly for economic reasons and not bound, as were monks, by any rule of life. They were for the most part pastors and administrators, or aspirants to those ranks. It is difficult to define what the members of earlier minsters were, since the word *monasterium* covered so many and varied organizations. They may have included secular clergy but most were probably monks. In any event, the early minsters were major centres of pastoral care. In southern Britain as a whole they entered the organization of the Church from the time of Archbishop Theodore in the later seventh century, the very time that Wessex was extending its control over eastern Dumnonia.

The oldest minster in Devon was almost certainly that in Exeter, in which Boniface was educated and which was in existence by at least 675 and probably earlier. The foundation date of the minster at Crediton, according to its charter, was 739. The sites of others can be established, with greater or lesser certitude, on a variety of grounds. Exminster and Axminster still preserve the memory of their status as minsters in their names. Both were royal manors and centres of hundreds. Another minster lay at Braunton in north Devon (another royal manor and hundred-centre), the place being referred to as Brannocminster in a ninth-century document. Yet another royal manor where a minster was established was Plympton, acquired by Edward the Elder from Asser about 900. The pattern of ecclesiastical communities established in royal manors is clear and may be helpful in locating minsters not otherwise attested. Cullompton is a good candidate: a rich church within the royal manor of Silverton. At Colyton, a hundred-centre, in the Axe valley, the pre-Conquest cruciform church and the splendid cross of about 975 are also suggestive of minster status. And the *burhs* of Totnes and Barnstaple are likely sites for minsters, later succeeded by the priories of St Mary and St Mary Magdalene respectively. Whether or not all of the thirty or so hundreds in Devon had a minster is unknowable, but the evidence for a varied, and in part pre-English, pattern of ecclesiastical administration in the west of the county suggests that this was probably not the case (Radford 1975: 5–8).

The greatest monastic foundation of the tenth century was the royal foundation of Edgar at Tavistock in 981 (Finberg 1951). This great Benedictine house was a landowning monastery dependent on the Crown. It lay within the royal demesne of Lifton, administered by Ordulf, brother-in-law to the king. The early supervision of the Abbey lay within his charge. The original endowments were extensive, including twenty properties in Devon, mainly around the fringes of Dartmoor, and in east Cornwall between Bodmin Moor and the Tamar. Destruction by the Danes in 997 had little long-term effect on the fortunes of Tavistock. Indeed the period immediately after the disaster saw it rise to still greater heights under its powerful and wealthy abbot Lyfing whose benefactions were *multa et spectabilia* according to William of Malmesbury. Lyfing was succeeded by Ealdred, later to become archbishop of York. Thus the Abbey was ruled in its first half century by two of the most powerful statesmen of the time and its fame and prosperity were assured.

Portable objects with ecclesiastical links are rare. One group of objects does, however, throw important light upon the wider contacts of southwestern church communities of this date. In 1774, a hoard of precious metal objects and coins was discovered in a streamwork at Trewhiddle, one mile south-west of St Austell (Rashleigh 1789; Wilson and Blunt 1961). Now in the British Museum collection, this hoard remains one of the most significant finds of metalwork of the pre-Conquest period. For the South West at this ill-recorded time, the hoard is doubly important as several of the objects are plainly ecclesiastical. The most remarkable of these are a scourge in silver-plaited chainwork, apparently the only such object surviving from early Christian Europe; a silver chalice, the sole surviving piece of pre-Conquest church plate; a silver mount, probably from the mouth of a drinking-horn; another, smaller, mount; a small silver box; a silver pin with a hollow, fourteen-faceted head; a penannular silver brooch; a buckle, two strap-ends and two belt-loops. Five further objects figure in the original publication of the hoard, but are now missing. They were two silver finger-rings, a small round silver plate pierced by three holes, probably originally attached to the base of the chalice, a small gold ingot, and a small gold bracteate or disc-pendant. The ornament on several of the objects, notably the mounts, strap-ends, box and pin, sits easily within the styles evident on ninth-century metalwork.

Fortunately, the inclusion of a considerable number of coins in the hoard enables a much closer attribution. Out of a total of about 115 pieces, more than 50 were coins of Burgred of Mercia (852–74), and a further 15 were of other Mercian rulers of the later eighth and ninth centuries. The kings of Wessex (Egbert, Aethelwulf, Aethelred I and Alfred) are represented by 18 coins,

Archbishop Ceolnoth of Canterbury by 7. Two pieces came from mints in France, one of Louis the Pious, the other possibly of Pippin. The date of the individual coins thus spans a fairly lengthy period, from the time of Offa in the later eighth century to that of Alfred in the later ninth, suggesting a steady accumulation of money rather than a true cross-section of what was in circulation when the hoard was buried. The date of burial must be deduced from the two coins of Alfred. The mere fact that only two examples of that king's abundant coinage are present here suggests by itself that the deposit as a whole dates from early in the reign. One of the coins is indeed of Alfred's earliest type. The other, however, is more of a problem. It is of Alfred's very common 'small cross' type, not to be dated before 875–80 and possibly as late as 885–90. Unfortunately, this very coin is now missing and there is some doubt as to whether it came from the Trewhiddle hoard in the first case. If it did, then the deposit should be dated to about 890. If it did not, a date of about 875 would seem appropriate.

So important a place in the art of the ninth century is enjoyed by the animal ornament of the Trewhiddle silver-work that it has long been customary to name the style of this period as the 'Trewhiddle style'. Its origins are clearly English with no notable contribution from continental traditions, either Mediterranean or Frankish. Nor is there any trace of borrowing from the Celtic world, despite the general similarity between the ornament of several of the Trewhiddle objects and that of ninth-century Irish metalwork. The hoard can thus be seen as an expression of the dominant cultural position of England during the eighth and earlier ninth centuries, before the onset of the Viking raids. The objects are not therefore at home in Dumnonia where they were eventually buried. How did they come to be where they were found?

It has already been noted that several of the pieces, especially the chalice and the scourge, are ecclesiastical items. All the objects, indeed, could have formed part of the treasury of a church, including the personal adornments and the drinking-horn mounts. The coins also heighten the impression of a treasure which had been accumulated over a lengthy period by a corporate body rather than by an individual owner. A much more difficult question concerns the means by which the treasure came to Trewhiddle. Was this close to the site of the church and did some raid or other emergency enforce removal of the portable treasures to a place of safety? Or is the hoard a cache of loot, derived from one or more communities, farther to the east perhaps, by a Viking raiding party? The later decades of the ninth century were clearly a time when such raids were frequent and Trewhiddle is close to the sea and a landfall in the shelter of St Austell Bay. Wherever these beautiful objects were originally used, they are the most evocative relics of the period when Celtic Cornwall was moving closer to the embrace of Anglo-Saxon Wessex.

One liturgical book survives from the Church of this period in the South West, the Bodmin Gospels (Jenner 1923). This belongs to a well-known class of liturgical text, containing the Gospels appointed to be read at Mass throughout the year. Many such books were produced, especially in the Frankish realms from the earlier ninth century onward, in imitation of late classical manuscripts and, at their finest, rank among the best works of Carolingian and later scriptoria. But there were many which stood at the end of a long line of successive copying and thus contain many errors and imperfections. To this number belongs the Bodmin Gospels.

The book contains 141 leaves, each about 26 cm by 18 cm, and with about 30 lines to the page. It is covered in wooden boards, possibly original, the upper one being sunk to take decorative metal plates and jewels, now vanished. A skin or leather, stained red, still lies over the wooden covers. The book dates from about 900. Apart from the texts of the four Gospels, the volume contains St Jerome's Preface to the Gospels and his Prologue to the Evangelists, the Canons of Eusebius (references to passages which are found in two or more Gospels) and various other summary texts. The lettering is Carolingian minuscule, the initial letters of verses and titles being in red capitals or uncials. The first verse of each Gospel begins with an ornamental capital, but there are no full-page pictures of the Evangelists or other elaborate illuminations. Only red is used and the quality of its application is poor. The text followed is that of St Jerome, though with numerous errors in copying and thus some strange Latin forms. The rite followed is Roman, not Celtic, an important indication that the Roman rite had been adopted in Cornwall by about 900.

The most famous feature of the Bodmin Gospels is not its formal contents but rather a series of later entries, on fly-leaves and in margins (though never on Gospel pages), recording the manumissions of serfs before St Petrock's altar (Jenner 1924). More than 150 names, most of them Celtic, are recorded in this fashion in the period from about 940 to 1050, a major source for personal nomenclature in the period. Thirty-eight of the entries are in Latin, a further 9 in the Wessex dialect of English. Most are bald statements simply recording the manumission. A few, however, are more verbose and include a blessing or a curse on anyone who might subsequently uphold or infringe the act recorded.

The will of one of the bishops of Crediton, Aelfwold (997–1012), survives among the Crawford Charters in the Bodleian Library and gives an unrivalled picture of the possessions of one of these potentates. The Sandford estate was to pass to the minster of Crediton 'as payment for his soul', but for one hide and a plough-team which were to go to one Godric. To the king were bequeathed four horses, four shields, four spears, two helmets and two mail-coats, along with 50 mancuses of gold still owed to the bishop by a creditor, and a sixty-four-oared ship (ready, we are told, but for the rowlocks), the arms and armour a fitting offering for a thegn of the king. There follow individual bequests, of which the most interesting is one of two books, Hrabanus and the Martyrology, to a layman, Ordwulf, who is mentioned immediately after the king and who is probably Ordwulf the uncle of King Aethelred and the founder of Tavistock Abbey. The remaining items say much about the prized possessions of a wealthy churchman (Napier and Stevenson 1895: X).

> To the atheling, 40 mancuses of gold and the wild horses on the land at Ashburton, and two tents; to Aelfwold the monk 20 mancuses of gold and a horse and a tent . . . to his kinsman Wulfgar two tapestries and two seat-coverings and three coats of mail; and to his brother-in-law Godric two coats of mail; and to Edwin the priest five mancuses of gold and his cope . . . [there follow several small bequests to other individuals]
>
> And to Crediton, three service books, a missal, a benedictional and an epistle-book, and a set of Mass-vestments. And on each episcopal estate freedom to every man who was a penal slave or whom he bought with his money. And to Wilton a chalice and a paten of 120 mancuses of gold bar three mancuses. And to his chamberlains, his bed-clothes.

Rural Settlement

The archaeology of rural settlement in the region can scarcely be said to exist at all. No large-scale excavation of any farmstead or village has been undertaken and thorough-going survey of such sites and their field-systems awaits its inception. There is at least one cogent reason why this work has made so little progress as yet. Most of the settlements which were occupied in the pre-Conquest period, a sample of which appear in the Domesday Survey, continued into the Middle Ages and beyond, in many cases down to the present day. Study of their earlier phases will thus never be an easy matter and in most cases can never take place.

Houses in the uplands were constructed in timber and turf, thus leaving little trace behind them. Beneath medieval settlements at Tresmorn, St Gennys and Treworld, Lesnewth in north Cornwall, and on several Dartmoor sites, turf-walled structures often revetted in timber have been recorded. At Tresmorn the sequence of turf buildings was long, beginning perhaps in the ninth or tenth century (Beresford 1971: 57–8). The Treworld houses were narrow, elongated structures, up to 30 m in length and almost certainly of long-house plan, though little can be reconstructed of their internal arrangement (Dudley and Minter 1966). On Dartmoor, at both Hound Tor and Hutholes, small houses with turf walls and sunken floors were found beneath later long-house settlements (Beresford 1979: 112–15). The walls were up to 1.5 m thick and had been faced by wattles. The roofs were probably of turf beneath wattle and thatch. These simple structures seem to have been dwellings, resembling the turf houses still seen in western Ireland. No indication of the stalling of animals has been noted. Some of the larger, and later, houses had timber walls (e.g. Hutholes, house 3, Beresford 1979: 122–4) and occasionally porches. Unfortunately, pottery and other datable artifacts were entirely absent, but these settlements were clearly occupied before 1000 and perhaps as early as the ninth century.

The early medieval settlement of Mawgan Porth lay at the mouth of the Vale of Lanherne overlooking the deep sandy bay of Mawgan Porth itself (Bruce Mitford 1956). The important excavations of 1950–53 on this site have never been published in full, a great loss to the archaeology of Cornwall as no other settlement dating from the period shortly after Cornwall had passed under English domination has yet been excavated on anything like the same scale. Although only part of the site has been examined, building-plans of unusual interest have been obtained, as well as part of a cemetery. The settlement lay on a slope above a small stream only a short distance from the spot where today the stream debouches into the bay. Two separate, but contemporary, groups of stone structures have been disengaged from the enveloping sand, both of them of cellular plan. Another group of buildings lay close by to the south-west and possibly a fourth to the north-east.

The buildings are of exceptional interest as rare representatives of their period and for the details of their plan. The most completely excavated house consisted of four major rooms, all rectangular, set around a central courtyard. The largest chamber, on the west side, was plainly the main dwelling-area. It measured 11 m by 5 m internally. Behind it lay a narrow room, perhaps providing more private accommodation, and leading off this lay a small cupboard or storage space. The plan of the main chamber is in essentials strikingly like that of the later medieval long-houses of the South West and of upland Wales. A timber partition divided the interior into two unequal halves at the point where the longer walls were pierced by opposed openings, this representing the familiar division between byre and living quarters. The byre contained a drain which led out close to the corner of the building. The floor of this end had been scoured and pitted by the trampling of animals. The living quarters beyond the partition were laid out in an orderly fashion. Box-beds enclosed by large slabs of slate lay against the long walls. Smaller spaces bounded by slabs against the south wall may have served as storage-bins. The living-space left free by these structures was further reduced by at least one hearth, a central upright and other minor obstructions, so that it is unlikely that more than four or five persons could easily have been housed in this dwelling. Others may have been accommodated in the rooms across the courtyard, thus enabling an entire family group to be sheltered in this cluster of buildings. The adjacent courtyard structures were similar in plan. Here, too, a dwelling or long-house was the focus of a group of rectangular chambers. The two courtyard-houses appear to be contemporary and to have been abandoned at about the same time.

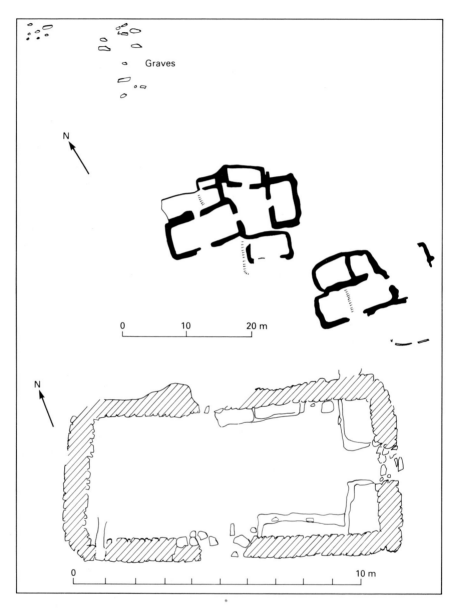

Figure 10.10 Plan of Mawgan Porth settlement and longhouse

Uphill and to the west of the village lay the cemetery, within which twenty-three graves were excavated. The dead had been laid in shallow graves, with their heads to the west. Most had rested in covered cists made of slate slabs on edge. None of the burials had been furnished with any kind of grave-goods. A high proportion of the burials found, almost half, were of infants and young children, probably due to the fact that a part of the area excavated had been specially devoted to burials of the young and not to an outstandingly high rate of infant mortality.

The date of the Mawgan Porth settlement can be estimated only in provisional terms, pending full publication of the material assemblage. A fortunate find from the early excavations here was a penny of Aethelred II, minted at Lydford between 990 and 995. This coin was not securely stratified, but it seems unlikely to have come from a construction deposit or some other early level in the history of the site. More probably, it was lost in the later phases of occupation, or perhaps it had been concealed in the roof whence it was brought down in the final collapse of the structure. In this case it would suggest a broad date for the village in the tenth century and not much later. The evidence of the pottery can at present give no greater precision. Nearly one thousand sherds of bar-lug pottery were recovered but no well-dated imported wares were present. Bar-lug pottery in Cornwall seems on present evidence to date from the later ninth century onward, but it appears to continue with very little outward change until the eleventh century or later. For the present there are no means at our disposal to assist us in sub-dividing the ware and refining its dating. None of the other artifacts from the site is susceptible to dating.

Since so little attention has yet been devoted to the excavation of early medieval settlements, it is impossible to judge how typical Mawgan Porth was of the communities of the far South West. What is most interesting about the buildings in the village is the earliest recorded appearance of the long-house which was to dominate the plans of rural dwellings in the peninsula during the medieval period. Yet at Mawgan Porth in the tenth century the long-house plan was already fully developed and was moreover an integral part of a group of structures around a central courtyard. The implication is that its origins were considerably earlier, perhaps in the centuries immediately following the end of Roman rule, since there are no obvious prototypes among the buildings of the later Roman period. The cellular plan has an obvious precursor in the courtyard-houses of the Iron Age, some of which were certainly occupied in late Roman times, and perhaps later. The hiatus in date between the oval courtyard houses and those at Mawgan Porth may be apparent, not real, since so few of the former have been examined. The advantages of the cellular plan may well have been appreciated until well into the medieval period: indeed it may then have been given new life in the development of the distinctive enclosed farmyards of the South West.

If we look forward in time to the early fourteenth century, to the time when tax assessments give us our first clear impression of the distribution of wealth in southern Britain, we are able to gain some idea of the *relative* prosperity of the South West when compared with regions to the east and north. By the standards of the rest of southern England at this date, Devon and Cornwall were thinly populated and several tracts of country were virtually unoccupied. Certain parts of Devon were more densely settled than the rest of the peninsula, especially the South Hams, the hinterland of Torbay, the valleys of the Exe and the Otter. The wealthiest area was the South Hams, followed by the lower Taw valley and the redlands about the lower Exe. But no part of the entire region approached the recorded wealth of eastern England or the Midlands. Cornwall was a poor land, as it remains today beneath the veneer of the holiday season.

The Domesday place-names of Cornwall are predominantly those of individual farms and small hamlets (Ravenhill 1967). There was only one borough in 1086, Bodmin, and other settlements of any size were rare. The eleventh-century settlements were evenly but never densely spaced in east Cornwall around Bodmin Moor and in the north towards the Devonshire border. Bodmin Moor itself was largely devoid of settlement as were the granite masses to the west of it. In west Cornwall generally, settlement was sparser than in the east, especially along the Atlantic coast and in the Land's End. A few places are mentioned around Mount's Bay and in the Lizard, but most of these were without plough-teams and some had no recorded population.

The scattered distribution of places reveals clearly the nature of the rural pattern of settlement and of the agricultural arrangements which underlay it. It is unlikely that matters had changed fundamentally in the preceding five centuries, and change was to be slow in the following era. One change might be noted here. A large number of the parishes which now exist in Cornwall find no mention in the text of Domesday and indeed are unrecorded until the thirteenth century or later. Several of these (including Penzance, Bude and Fowey) plainly owed their development to the growing importance of sea-borne trade, and many of the other places which first make their appearance well after the Conquest are products of an economy which had not begun to flourish before 1000. In this landscape of scattered holdings it is pointless to look for concentrations of wealth and population. Such centres did not exist. The eleventh-century population was fairly evenly spread in the areas away from the granite uplands, less than a dozen places with more than a hundred inhabitants being recorded. Perhaps less expectedly, plough-teams were also evenly distributed, though with a slight preponderance in east Cornwall around Bodmin Moor. They were surprisingly numerous in the infertile west of Cornwall. Woodland was comparatively limited in its scope and density, partly perhaps because of the inroads of the plough. Most of it lay in the hinterland of the south coast, especially south of Bodmin Moor. Elsewhere underwood is recorded fairly widely, but the uplands, including all of the Land's End and much of the Lizard, were seemingly treeless in the eleventh century. Above all, Cornwall was a land rich in pasture, as today. Nine-tenths of the Domesday settlements were endowed with it, in some cases in abundant measure. And it was mainly sheep that grazed on these moist grasslands, sometimes in flocks of many hundreds. Their wool, however, was probably of poor quality, if the evidence of two centuries is projected back to the eleventh century, and it was not until the fourteenth century that the South West began to contribute to the lucrative export of this commodity.

Like Cornwall, Devon's place-names include a high proportion which are now represented by hamlets and single farms, not villages or parishes, while as many as forty present-day parishes do not appear in Domesday Book at all (Welldon Finn 1967). As it largely is today, Devon in the eleventh century was a land of scattered homesteads and hamlets in a broken landscape. In its total aspect settlement was fairly evenly dispersed, the uplands of Dartmoor and Exmoor excepted. A slightly denser pattern is evident in east Devon, in the South Hams and in the western area of the Culm Measures. Even on the high ground a few settlements had been established by 1086. At Radworthy (Challacombe) at a height of 400 m on Exmoor, for example, there were four people with $1\frac{1}{2}$ plough-teams as well as pastureland, while on the sheltered eastern side of Dartmoor there were a number of holdings up to a height of 320 m. The richest areas, as measured by population, possession of plough-teams and pasture, were clearly the Exe valley, the South Hams, the valleys of Taw and Torridge, and the Culm Measures. Although generally more populous than Cornwall, there were no great concentrations of people in Devon of the eleventh century, even if the recorded population is multiplied by a factor of three or four to arrive at something closer to the actual figure.

Sheep were, naturally, the most numerous livestock, several flocks of many hundreds of animals being recorded, and they were evenly distributed over the county, except for the fringes of Dartmoor. She-goats occur frequently, pigs much less commonly, along with cattle. Horses are recorded in various forms, including 'wild' and 'wood' horses (*equae indomitae* and *equae silvestres*), especially in the Exmoor region. There is no reference to wild or semi-wild horses on Dartmoor (but see the will of Aelfwold, p. 304).

It is instructive to examine the local siting of the thousand or so places which can be identified from Domesday. Thirty-four per cent of these were on spurs or interfluves, 27 per cent in valley-heads, 20 per cent on the sides of valleys and 16 per cent on valley-floors. Very few occur on exposed hill-tops or ridges and on the coast (Ravenhill 1967: 156–7). The high proportion of sitings, over 60 per cent, on interfluvial spurs and valley-heads is obviously significant and should be related to particular forms of land-use. The valley-floors are for the most part narrow and constricted and the sides tend to be steep. Flat or gently sloping ground, suitable for arable is generally found on the spurs and ridges. The favoured site for a farmstead in this type of setting was thus high up on the valley-side, on a spur or in a valley-head. Many such sites are still occupied (for instance in the Taw and Exe valleys), probably continuously from the eleventh century and before, and the present disposition of their land would be comprehensible to the early medieval farmer: meadows on the valley-floor, woodland and rough pasture on the slopes, arable and pasture on the high ground.

What we see in the Domesday Survey is the first written record of an agricultural economy that was already several thousand years old. The eleventh-century peasant and the Bronze Age farmer would each have recognized much of his own narrow world in that of the other. The most remarkable feature of the early history of the South West is the essential continuity which underlay life on the land. The main fabric of that life was to endure until early modern times.

Notes

1. There are interesting analogies with the Marcher society of Anglo-Norman Wales in the twelfth century, as it is outlined for us by Gerald of Wales.
2. There is no real reason, however, to date these place-name forms before the Norman conquest, as Professor K. Cameron points out to me.

Bibliography

Abbreviations

Antiq. Journ.   *The Antiquaries Journal*
Arch. Camb.   *Archaeologia Cambrensis*
Arch. Journ.   *Archaeological Journal*
Arch. Korrespondenzbl.   *Archäologische Korrespondenzblätter*
BAR   *British Archaeological Reports*
B.M. Quarterly   *British Museum Quarterly*
BNJ   *British Numismatic Journal*
B.R.G.K.   *Bericht der Romisch-Germanischen Kommission*
Class. Quart.   *Classical Quarterly*
Cornish Arch.   *Cornish Archaeology*
Eph. Ep.   *Ephemeris Epigraphica*
Geogr. Journ.   *Geographical Journal*
Journ. Arch. Sci.   *Journal of Archaeological Science*
Journ. Brit. Arch. Ass.   *Journal of the British Archaeological Association*
Journ. English Place-Name Soc.   *Journal of the English Place-Name Society*
JRIC   *Journal of the Royal Institution of Cornwall*
Med. Arch.   *Medieval Archaeology*
Num. Chron.   *Numismatic Chronicle*
PDAES   *Proceedings of the Devon Archaeological Exploration Society*
PDAS   *Proceedings of the Devon Archaeological Society*
Phil. Trans. Royal Society   *Philosophical Transactions of the Royal Society*
Procs. Brit. Acad.   *Proceedings of the British Academy*
Procs. Dorset N.H.A. Soc.   *Proceedings of the Dorset Natural History and Archaeological Society*
Procs. Somerset Arch. N.H. Soc.   *Proceedings of the Somerset Archaeological and Natural History Society*
P.S.A.L.   *Proceedings of the Society of Antiquaries of London*
PWCFC   *Proceedings of the West Cornwall Field Club*
TDA   *Transactions of the Devonshire Association*
Trans. Royal Hist. Soc.   *Transactions of the Royal Historical Society*
Trans. Torquay N.H.S.   *Transactions of the Torquay Natural History Society*
Ulster Journ. of Arch.   *Ulster Journal of Archaeology*

Alcock, L. (1969) 'Excavations at South Cadbury Castle. 1968', *Antiq. Journ.* **49**, 30–40.

Alcock, L. (1972) *By South Cadbury Is That Camelot.* London.

Alexander, E. M. M. (1964) 'Father John MacEnery: scientist or charlatan?', *TDA* **96**, 113–46.

Allan, J., Henderson, C. and Higham, R. A. (1984) Saxon Exeter, in J. Haslam (ed.) *Anglo-Saxon Towns in Southern England.* Chichester, pp. 385–414.

Allan, J. P. (1984) *Medieval and post-Medieval Finds from Exeter.* Exeter.

Allen, D. F. (1961) 'The Paul (Penzance) hoard of imitation massilia drachms', *Num. Chron.* **7**, 91–106.

Amory, P. F. S. (1906) 'Supposed currency bars, found near Holne Chase Camp', *TDA* **38**, 370–6.

ApSimon, A. M. and Greenfield, E. (1972) 'Excavation of the Bronze Age and Iron Age settlement at Trevisker Round, St Eval', *PPS* **38**, 302–81.

Arkle, I., Spenser, T. and Lomas, J. (1968) 'The Pilton Long Stone Excavation. 1967', *TDA* **100**, 293–305.

Ashbee, P. (1958) 'The excavation of Tregulland Burrow, Treneglos', *Antiq. Journ.* **38**, 174–96.

Ashbee, P. (1974) *Ancient Scilly.* Newton Abbot.

Ashbee, P. (1976) 'Bant's Carn, St Mary's, Isles of Scilly: An entrance grave restored and reconsidered' *Cornish Arch.* **15**, 11–26.

Ashbee, P. (1982a) 'Mesolithic megaliths? The Scillonian entrance graves: A new view', *Cornish Arch.* **21**, 3–22.

Ashbee, P. (1982b) 'Scilly's Roman Altar', *Cornish Arch.* **21**, 174–6.

Ashbee, P. (1983) 'Halangy Porth, St Mary's, Isles of Scilly, excavations 1975–76', *Cornish Arch.* **22**, 3–46.

Asser, *De rebus gestis Aelfridi.*

Atkinson, D. (1942) *Report on Excavations at Wroxeter, 1923–7.* Oxford.

Balaam, N. *et al.* (1982) 'The Shaugh Moor Project: Fourth Report – environment, context and conclusion', *PPS* **48**, 203–78.

Barber, K. E. (1982) 'Peat-bog stratigraphy as a proxy climate record', pp. 103–13 in Harding, A. (ed.) *Climatic change in later prehistory.* Edinburgh.

Baring-Gould, S. *et al.* (1899) 'Sixth Report of the Dartmoor Exploration Committee', *TDA* **31**, 146–55.

Baring-Gould, S. (1923) *Early Reminiscences.* London.

Barnatt, J. (1982) *Prehistoric Cornwall. The Ceremonial Monuments.* Wellingborough.

Bartrum, P. C. (1966) *Early Welsh Genealogical Tracts.* Cardiff.

Beagrie, N. (1983) 'The St Mawes Ingot', *Cornish Arch.* **22**, 107–11.

Bede, *Historia Ecclesiastica.*

Beresford, G. (1971) 'Tresmorn. St Gennys', *Cornish Arch.* **10**, 55–72.

Beresford, G. (1979) 'Three deserted medieval settlements on Dartmoor', *Med. Arch.* **23**, 98–158.

Biddle, M. and Hill, D. (1971) 'Late Saxon planned towns', *Antiq. Journ.* **51**, 70–85.

Bidwell, P. (1979) *The Legionary Bath-house and Basilica and Forum at Exeter.* Exeter Archaeological Reports, Vol. 1. Exeter.

Bidwell, P. (1980) *Roman Exeter: Fortress and Town.* Exeter.

Bidwell, P., Bridgwater, R. and Silvester, R. J. (1979) 'The Roman Fort at Okehampton, Devon', *Britannia* 10, 255–8.

Blight, J. T. (1856) *Ancient Crosses and other Antiquities in the West of Cornwall.* London and Penzance.

Blight, J. T. (1858) *Ancient Crosses and Other Antiquities in the East of Cornwall.* London.

Blight, J. T. (1861) *A Week at the Land's End.* London.

Boon, G. C. (1974) *Silchester. The Roman Town of Calleva.* Newton Abbot, London.

Borlase, W. (1753) 'Of the great alterations which the Islands of Scilly have undergone since the time of the ancients', *Phil. Transactions of Royal Soc.* 48, 55–67.

Borlase, W. (1754) *Observations on the Antiquities, Historical and Monumental, of the County of Cornwall.* Oxford.

Borlase, W. (1756) *Observations on the Ancient and Present State of the Islands of Scilly.* Oxford.

Borlase, W. (1758) *The Natural History of Cornwall.* Oxford.

Borlase, W. (1769) *Antiquities, Historical and Monumental, of the County of Cornwall* (2nd edn). London.

Borlase, W. C. (1872) *Naenia Cornubiae.* London and Truro.

Bowen, E. G. (1969) *Saints, Seaways and Settlements in the Celtic Lands.* Cardiff.

Bradley, R. (1971) 'Stock-Raising and the Origin of the Hill-Fort on the South Downs', *Antiq. Journ.* 51, 8–29.

Bradley, R. (1978) 'Prehistoric field systems in Britain and north-west Europe – a review of some recent work', *World Archaeology* 9, 265–30.

Bradley, R. (1979) 'The interpretation of later Bronze Age metalwork from British rivers', *International Journ. of Nautical Archaeology*, 8, 3–6.

Bradley, R. (1984) *The Social Foundations of Prehistoric Britain.* London.

Branigan, K. (1972) 'The Surbo Bronzes – some observations', *PPS* 38, 276–85.

Branigan, K. (1977) *Gatcombe Roman Villa.* Oxford.

Branigan, K. (1983) 'A Cypriot Hook-Tang weapon from Devon', *PDAS* 41, 125–8.

Brisbane, M. and Clews, S. (1979) 'The East Moor field systems, Altarnun and North Hill, Bodmin Moor', *Cornish Arch.* 18, 33–55.

Britton, D. (1963) 'Traditions of metal-working in the later Neolithic and Early Bronze Age of Britain', *PPS* 29, 258–325.

Brooks, R. T. (1974) 'The excavation of the Rumps Cliff Castle, St Minver, Cornwall', *Cornish Arch.* 13, 5–50.

Brown, A. P. (1977) 'Late Devensian and Flandrian vegetation history of Bodmin Moor, Cornwall', *Phil Trans. Royal Society* B 276, 251–320.

Brown, P. D. C. (1970) 'A Roman pewter mould from St. Just in Penwith', *Cornish Arch.* 9, 107–10.

Bruce-Mitford, R. L. S. (1956) 'A Dark Age Settlement at Mawgan Porth, Cornwall', in Bruce-Mitford (ed.) *Recent Excavations in Britain.* London, pp. 167–96.

Brunn, W. A. von (1959) *Die Hortfunde der frühen Bronzezeit aus Sachsen-Anhalt, Sachsen und Thüringen.* Berlin.

Bullen, R. A. (1912) *Harlyn Bay and the Discoveries of its Prehistoric Remains.* Harlyn Bay.

Burgess, C. B. (1968) 'The Later Bronze Age in the British Isles and northwestern France', *Arch. Journ.* 125, 1–45.

Burgess, C. B. and Gerloff, S. (1981) *The Dirks and Rapiers of Great Britain and Ireland. Prähistorische Bronzefunde IV*, 7. Munich.

Burl, A. (1976) *The Stone Circles of the British Isles*. London and New York.

Burl, A. (1979) *Prehistoric Stone Circles*. Princes Risborough.

Bushe-Fox, J. P. (1915) *Excavations at Hengistbury Head, Hants, in 1911–12*. London.

Butcher, S. (1978) 'Excavations at Nornour, Isles of Scilly, 1969–73: the pre-Roman Settlement', *Cornish Arch.* **17**, 29–112.

Butler, J. J. (1963) 'Bronze Age connections across the North Sea', *Palaeohistoria* **9**, 1–286.

Camden, W. (1586) *Britannia*. London.

Caesar *De Bello Gallico*.

Cameron, K. (1979–80) 'The meaning and significance of Old English *walh* in English place-names', *Journ. English Place-Name Soc.* **12**, 1–53.

Campbell, J. B. (1977) *The Upper Palaeolithic of Britain*. Oxford.

Campbell, J. B. and Sampson, C. G. (1971) *A New Analysis of Kent's Cavern, Devonshire, England*. Univ. of Oregon Anthrop. Papers, No. 3, Oregon.

Carew, R. (1602) *The Survey of Cornwall*. London.

Caseldine, C. J. (1980) 'Environmental change in Cornwall during the last 13,000 years', *Cornish Arch.* **19**, 3–16.

Caseldine, C. J. and Maguire, D. J. (1981) 'A review of the prehistoric and historic environment on Dartmoor', *PDAS* **39**, 1–16.

Caulfield, S. (1978) 'Neolithic fields: the Irish evidence', in Bowen, H. C. and Fowler, P. J. (eds) *Early Land Allotment*. Oxford, pp. 137–43.

Chadwick, N. K. (1965) 'The colonisation of Brittany from Celtic Britain', *Procs. Brit. Acad.* **51**, 235–300.

Chanter, J. F. (1905) 'Examination of one of the Chapman barrow group'. *TDA* **37**, 93.

Christie, P. M. L. (1960) 'Crig-a-Minnis: a Bronze Age barrow at Liskey, Perranzabuloe, Cornwall', *PPS* **26**, 76–97.

Christie, P. M. L. (1978) 'The excavation of an Iron Age souterrain and settlement at Carn Euny, Sancreed, Cornwall', *PPS* **44**, 309–433.

Clark, E. (1961) *Cornish Fogous*. London.

Clark, J. G. D. (1948) 'Fishing in prehistoric Europe', *Antiq. Journ.* **28**, 45–85.

Clark, J. G. D. (1954) *Star Carr*. Cambridge.

Clark, J. G. D. (1977) 'The economic context of dolmens and passage-graves in Sweden', in V. Markotic (ed.) *Ancient Europe and the Mediterranean*. Warminster, pp. 35–49.

Clark, J. G. D. (1981) *Mesolithic Prelude*. Cambridge.

Clarke, E. M. (1962) *Cornish Fogous*. London.

Clarke, P. J. (1971) 'The Neolithic, Bronze and Iron Age, and Romano-British finds from Mount Batten, Plymouth, 1832–1939', *PDAS* **29**, 137–61.

Collier, W. F. (1877) 'First report of the Committee on Dartmoor', *TDA* **9**, 120–2.

Collis, J. (1979) 'Cranbrook Castle revisited', *PDAS* **37**, 191–4.

Conybeare, J. J. (1823) 'On the Geology of Devon and Cornwall', *Annals of Philosophy* **5**, 184–9.

Coombs, D. (1975) 'Bronze Age weapon hoards in Britain', *Archaeologia Atlantica* **1**, 49–81.

Corney, W. J. (1967) 'A real stone row on Exmoor', *Exmoor Review* **8**, 48–9.

Cotton, M. A. (1958–9) 'Cornish Cliff Castles: a survey', *PWCFC* **2**, 113–21.

Crawford, O. G. S. (1927) 'Lyonesse', *Antiquity* **1**, 5–14.

Croft, Andrew C. K. (1933–6) 'Some remarks on the Giant's Hedge', *JRIC* **24**, 213–28.

Crofts, C. B. (1955) 'Maen Castle, Sennen: the excavation of an Early Iron Age promontory fort', *PWCFC* **1**, 3, 98–108.

Crossing, W. (1906) *Dartmoor and its surroundings*. Plymouth.

Cummins, W. A. (1979) 'Neolithic Stone Axes: distribution and trade in England and Wales', in T. H. McK. Clough and W. A. Cummins (eds) *Stone Axe Studies*. London, 13–22.

Cunliffe, B. (1978) *Hengistbury Head*. London.

Cunliffe, B. (1983) 'Ictis: is it here?', *Oxford Journal of Archaeology* **2**, 123–6.

Cunliffe, B. (1984) 'Relations between Britain and Gaul in the first century BC and early first century AD', in S. Macready and F. H. Thompson (eds) *Cross-Channel Trade between Britain and the Continent*. London, 3–23.

Daniel, G. E. (1950) *The Prehistoric Chamber-tombs in England and Wales*. London.

Daniel, G. E. (1975) *One Hundred and Fifty Years of Archaeology*. London.

Davidson, J. (1833) *The British and Roman Remains in the Vicinity of Axminster in the County of Devon*. Axminster.

Davidson, J. (1835) *The History of Axminster Church in the County of Devon*. Exeter.

Davidson, J. (1843) *The History of Newenham Abbey in the County of Devon*. London.

Davidson, J. (1852) *Bibliotheca Devoniensis*. Exeter.

Davidson, J. (1861) *Notes on the Antiquities of Devonshire which date before the Norman Conquest*. Exeter.

Davies, O. (1935) *Roman Mines in Europe*. Oxford.

Davies, W. (1978) *An Early Welsh Microcosm*. London.

Davies, W. (1979) *The Llandaff Charters*. Aberystwyth.

Davies, W. (1982) *Wales in the Early Middle Ages*. Leicester.

De La Beche, H. T. (1839) *Report on the Geology of Cornwall, Devon and West Somerset*. Geol. Survey, London.

Dennell, R. W. (1976) 'Prehistoric crop cultivation in northern England: a reconsideration', *Antiq. Journ.* **56**, 11–23.

Dickinson, T. M. (1982) 'Fowler's Type G. penannular brooches reconsidered', *Med. Arch.* **26**, 41–68.

Doble, F. H. (1934) *The Lanalet Pontifical*. Bristol.

Doble, F. H. (1937) *Pontificale Lanaletense*.

Dolley, M. and Shiel, N. (1981) 'A Carolingian Denarius with a Devonshire provenance', *BNJ* **50**, 7–11.

Douch, H. L. and Beard, S. W. (1970) 'Excavations at Carvossa, Probus, 1968–70', *Cornish Arch.* **9**, 93–8.

Dudley, D. (1941) 'A late Bronze Age Settlement on Trewey Downs, Zennor', *Arch. Journ.* **98**, 105–30..

Dudley, D. (1956) 'An excavation at Bodrifty, Mulfra, near Penzance', *Arch. Journ.* **113**, 1–32.

Dudley, D. (1967) 'Excavations on Nor'nour in the Isles of Scilly, 1962–6', *Arch. Journ.* **124**, 1–64.

Dudley, D. and Jope, E. M. (1965) 'An Iron Age cist-burial from Trevone', *Cornish Arch.* **4**, 18–23.

Dudley, D. and Minter, E. M. (1966) 'Excavation of a medieval settlement at Treworld, *Cornish Arch.* **5**, 34–58.

Dumville, D. (1977) 'Sub-Roman Britain: History and Legend', *History* **62**, 173–92.

Dunning, G. C. (1959) 'The distribution of socketed axes of Breton type', *Ulster Journ. of Arch.* **22**, 53–5.

Durrance, E. M. and Laming, D. J. C. (eds) (1982) *The Geology of Devon.* Exeter.

Eardley-Wilmot, H. (1983) *Ancient Exmoor.* Dulverton.

Edmonds, E. A., McKeown, M. C. and Williams, M. (1975) *British Regional Geology. South West England. London.*

Emmett, D. D. (1979) 'Stone rows; the traditional view reconsidered', *PDAS* **37**, 94–114.

Eogan, G. and Simmons, I. (1964) 'The excavation of a stone alignment and circle at Cholwichtown, Lee Moor, Devonshire, England', *PPS* **30**, 25–38.

Evans, J. (1860) 'On the Occurrence of flint implements in undisturbed beds of gravel, sand and clay', *Archaeologia* **38**, 280–307.

Evans, Joan (1956) *A History of the Society of Antiquaries.* Oxford.

Evans, E. D., Smith, I. F. and Wallis, I. F. (1972) 'The petrological identification of stone implements from South West England', *PPS* **38**, 235–75.

Evison, V. I. (1968) 'The Anglo-Saxon finds from Hardown Hill', *Procs. Dorset NHA Soc.* **90**, 232–40.

Exley, C. S. and Stone, M. (1966) 'The granitic rocks of South West England', in Hosking and Shrimpton (eds) *Present Views of some aspects of the Geology of Cornwall and Devon.* Penzance, pp. 131–84.

Farley, M. E. and Little, R. I. (1968) 'Oldaport, Modbury: a re-assessment of the fort and harbour', *PDAS* **26**, 31–6.

Field, J. and Miles, H. (1975) 'An Upper Palaeolithic site at Honiton', *PDAS* **33**, 177–82.

Finberg, H. P. R. (1951) *Tavistock Abbey: a Study in the Social and Economic History of Devon.* Cambridge.

Finberg, H. P. R. (1953) 'Sherborne, Glastonbury and the Expansion of Wessex', *Trans. Royal Hist. Soc.* **5** (3), 101–24.

Fleming, A. (1971) 'Territorial Patterns in Bronze Age Wessex', *PPS* **37**, 138–66.

Fleming, A. (1978) 'The prehistoric landscape of Dartmoor, Part 1: South Dartmoor', *PPS* **44**, 97–123.

Fleming, A. (1979) 'The Dartmoor reaves: boundary patterns and behaviour patterns in the second millennium bc', *PDAS* **37**, 115–31.

Fleming, A. (1983) 'The prehistoric landscape of Dartmoor, Part 2: North and East Dartmoor', *PPS* **49**, 195–241.

Fleming, A. (1984) 'The prehistoric landscape of Dartmoor: wider implications', *Landscape History* **6**, 5–19.

Fletcher, M. J., Grinsell, L. V. and Quinnell, N. (1974) 'A long cairn on Butterdon Hill, Ugborough', *PDAS* **32**, 163–5.

Fowler, P. J. (1962) 'A native homestead of the Roman period at Porth Godrevy, Gwithian', *Cornish Arch.* **1**, 17–60.

Fowler, P. J. (1981) *The Agrarian History of England and Wales: Prehistory.* Cambridge.

Fowler, P. J. and Thomas, A. C. (1962) 'Arable fields of the pre-Norman period at Gwithian', *Cornish Arch.* 1, 61–84.

Fowler, P. J. and Thomas, C. (1979) 'Lyonesse Revisited', *Antiquity,* 53, 175–89.

Fox, A. (1948) 'The Broad Down (Farway) necropolis and the Wessex culture in Devon', *PDAES* 4, 1–19.

Fox, A. (1950) 'Two Greek silver coins from Holne, S. Devon', *Antiq. Journ.* 30, 152–5.

Fox, A. (1952a) 'Hill-slope forts and related earthworks in south-west England and South Wales', *Arch. Journ.* 109, 1–22.

Fox, A. (1952b) 'The Castlewich Ringwork', *Antiq. Journ.* 32, 67–70.

Fox, A. (1952c) *Roman Exeter.* Manchester.

Fox, A. (1952d) 'Roman objects from Cadbury Castle', *TDA* 84, 105–14.

Fox, A. (1954) 'Excavations at Kestor, an early Iron Age settlement near Chagford, Devon', *TDA* 86, 21–62.

Fox, A. (1955) 'Some evidence for a Dark Age trading site at Bantham, near Thurlestone, South Devon', *Antiq. Journ.* 35, 55–67.

Fox, A. (1957) 'Excavations on Dean Moor, in the Avon valley, 1954–1956', *TDA* 89, 18–77.

Fox, A. (1959) 'Twenty-fifth Report on the Archaeology and Early History of Devon', *TDA* 91, 168–77 (esp. 170–1).

Fox, A. (1961a) 'Twenty-fifth Report on the Archaeology and Early History of Devon', *TDA* 93, 61–80 (esp. 79–80).

Fox, A. (1961b) 'South-western hill-forts', in S. S. Frere (ed.) *Problems of the Iron Age in S. Britain.* London, pp. 35–60.

Fox, A. (1961c) 'The Iron Age Bowl from Rose Ash, North Devon', *Antiq. Journ.* 41, 186–98.

Fox, A. (1963) 'Neolithic Charcoal from Hembury', *Antiquity* xxxvii, 228–9.

Fox, A. (1964) *South-West England.* London.

Fox, A. (1968) 'Excavations at the South Gate, Exeter 1964–5', *PDAS* 26, 1–20.

Fox, A. (1969) 'The Upton Pyne cemetery', *PDAS* 27, 75–8.

Fox, A. (1973) *South-West England* (2nd edn). Newton Abbot.

Fox, A. and Britton, D. (1969) 'A continental palstave from the ancient field system on Horridge Common', *PPS* 35, 220–28.

Fox, A. and Pollard, S. H. (1973) 'A decorated bronze mirror from an Iron Age settlement at Holcombe, Devon', *Antiq. Journ.* 53, 16–41.

Fox, A., Radford, C. A. R. and Shorter, A. H. (1949–50) 'Report on the excavations at Milber Down, 1937–8', *PDAES* 4, 27–66.

Fox, A. and Ravenhill, W. D. (1959) 'A Roman signal station on Stoke Hill, Exeter', *TDA* 91, 72–82.

Fox, A. and Ravenhill, W. D. (1966) 'Early Roman outposts on the north Devon coast', *PDAS* 24, 3–39.

Fox, A. and Ravenhill, W. D. (1972) 'The Roman fort at Nanstallon, Cornwall', *Britannia* 3, 56–111.

Fox, C. (1938) *The Personality of Britain* (3rd edn). Cardiff.

Fox, C. (1946) *A Find of the Early Iron Age from Llyn Cerrig Bach, Anglesey.* Cardiff.

Fox, C. (1958) *Pattern and Purpose. A Survey of Early Celtic Art in Britain.* Cardiff.

Fox, H. (1972) 'Field systems of east and south Devon. Part I. East Devon', *TDA* 104, 81–135.

Frere, S. S. (1978) *Britannia* (2nd edn). London.

Frere, S. S. (1984) 'British urban defences in earthwork', *Britannia* 15, 63–74.

Galliou, P., Fulford, M. and Clément, M. (1980) 'La diffusion de la céramique a l'éponge dans le nord-ouest de l'empire romain', *Gallia* 38, 265–78.

Galsterer, B. and H. (1975) *Die römischen Steinschriften aus Köln*. Cologne.

Gerloff, S. (1975) *The Early Bronze Age Daggers of Great Britain. Prähistorische Bronzefunde* VI, 2, Munich.

Gilbert, D. (1838) *The Parochial History of Cornwall* (4 vols). London.

Godu, G. and Le Roux, P. (1938) 'Une liste de noms brittoniques du dixième siècle', *Annales de Bretagne* 45, 197–208.

Goodchild, R. G. (1939) *Roman Exeter*. Typescript dissertation in West Country Studies Library, Exeter.

Goodchild, R. G. (1947) 'An antiquary in Devon (W. T. P. Shortt, 1800–1881)', *TDA* 79, 229–55.

Gordon, A. S. R. (1940) 'The excavation of Gurnard's Head, a cliff castle in W. Cornwall', *Arch. Journ.* 97, 96–111.

Gover, J., Mawer, A. and Stenton, F. (1931) *The Place-names of Devon*, Part I. Cambridge.

Gover, J., Mawer, A. and Stenton, F. (1932) *The Place-names of Devon*, Part 2. Cambridge.

Gray, H. St G. (1909) 'The stone circles of East Cornwall', *Archaeologia* 61, 1–60.

Green, H. S. (1984) *Pontnewydd Cave*. Cardiff.

Gregory, K. J. (1969) 'Geomorphology', in F. Barlow (ed.) *Exeter and its Region*. Exeter, pp. 27–42.

Grieg, O. and Rankine, W. F. (1953) 'A Stone Age settlement system near East Week', *PDAES* 5, 8–26.

Griffith, F. M. (1983) 'The identification of four new enclosure sites north of Teignmouth', *PDAS* 41, 63–8.

Grimes, W. F. (1960) *Excavations on Defence Sites, 1939–45*. London.

Grinsell, L. V. (1970) *The Archaeology of Exmoor*. Newton Abbot.

Grinsell, L. V. (1978) 'Dartmoor barrows', *PDAS* 36, 85–180.

Guthrie, A. (1969) 'Excavation of a settlement at Goldherring, Sancreed', *Cornish Arch.* 8, 5–39.

Haddan, A. W. and Stubbs, W. (1869–78) *Councils and Ecclesiastical Documents relating to Great Britain and Ireland* (3 vols). Oxford.

Halliday, F. E. (1953) *Richard Carew of Antony*. London.

Hals, W. (1750) *The Compleat History of Cornwall*.

Hardmeyer, B. and Bürgi, J. (1975) 'Der Goldbecher von Eschenz', *Zeitschrift für Schweizerische Archäologie und Kunstgeschichte* 32, 109–120.

Harris, D. (1979) 'Poldowrian, St Keverne: A Beaker Mound on the Gabbro of the Lizard Peninsula', *Cornish Arch.* 18, 13–32.

Hartley, B. R. (1983) 'The enclosure of Romano-British towns in the second century AD', in Hartley and Wacher (eds) *Rome and her Northern Provinces*. Gloucester, pp. 84–95.

Harvey, J. H. (1969) *William Worcestre, Itineraries*. Oxford.

Haslam, W. (1845) *Perranzabuloe*. London.

Hautumm, W. (1981) *Studien zu Amphoren der spätrömischen und frühbyzantinischen Zeit*. Fulda.

Haverfield, F. (1924) *Romano-British Cornwall, VCH Cornwall*, Part 5. Oxford.

Haverfield, F. and Macdonald, G. (1907) 'The Greek coins from Exeter', *Num. Chron.* 4 (7), 145–55.

Hawkes, C. F. C. (1932) 'The Towednack gold hoard', *MAN* 222, 117.

Hawkes, C. F. C. (1936–7) 'The double axe in prehistoric Europe', *Annual British School at Athens* 37, 141–59.

Hawkes, C. F. C. (ed.) (1955) 'The Crediton hoard', *Inventaria Archaeologia*, Great Britain I, No. 4.

Hawkes, C. F. C. (1977) *Pytheas: Europe and the Greek Explorers*, 8th J. L. Myres Memorial Lecture. Oxford.

Hawkes, C. F. C. (1984) 'Ictis disentangled, and the British tin trade', *Oxford Journal of Archaeology* 3, 211–33.

Hawkes, C. F. C. and Clarke, R. R. (1963) 'Gahlstorf and Caister-on-Sea. Two finds of late Bronze Age Irish gold', in Foster and Alcock (eds) *Culture and Environment*. London, pp. 193–241.

Hawkes, C. F. C. and Smith, M. (1955) 'The Plymstock hoard', *Inventaria Archaeologia*, Great Britain II, No. 9.

Hayes, J. W. (1972) *Late Roman Pottery*. London.

Hayes, J. W. (1980) *A Supplement to Late Roman Pottery*. London.

Hayward, L. C. (1952) 'The Roman villa at Lufton, near Yeovil', *Procs. Somerset Arch. N.H. Soc.* 116, 59–77.

Hebditch, M. and Mellor, J. (1973) 'The forum and basilica of Roman Leicester', *Britannia* 4, 1–83.

Helbaek, H. (1952) 'Early crops in southern England', *PPS* 18, 194–233.

Hencken, H. E. O'N. (1932) *The Archaeology of Cornwall and Scilly*. London.

Hencken, H. E. O'N. (1933a) 'An excavation for HM Office of Works at Chysauster, Cornwall', *Arch.* 83, 237–84.

Hencken, H. E. O'N. (1933b) 'Notes on the megalithic monuments in the Isles of Scilly', *Antiq. Journ.* 13, 13–29.

Henderson, C. (1984) *Archaeology in Exeter, 1983–4*. Exeter.

Henderson, C. G. and Bidwell, P. (1982) 'The Saxon Minster at Exeter', in S. M. Pearce (ed.) *The Early Church in Western Britain and Ireland*. Oxford, 145–76.

Herring, P. J. (1983) 'A long-cairn on Catshole Tor, Altarnun', *Cornish Arch.* 22, 81–3.

Higginbotham, E. (1977) 'Excavations at Woolley Barrows, Morwenstow', *Cornish Arch.* 16, 10–16.

Hooker, J. (*c.* 1600) *Synopsis Chorographical of Devonshire*. [Mss in British Museum.]

Hirst, F. C. (1936) 'Excavations at Porthmeor 1933–5', *JRIC* 24, 1–81.

Hoskins, W. G. (1958) 'History of common land and common rights', in *Report of Royal Commission on Common Land*. London, pp. 149–60.

Hoskins, W. G. (1960) *The Westward Expansion of Wessex*. Occasional Papers No. 13. Leicester University Department of Local History.

Houlder, C. H. (1963) 'A Neolithic settlement on Hazard Hill, Totnes', *PDAES* 21, 2–30.

Hübener, W. (1969) *Absatzgebiete frühgeschichtlicher Topfereien nördlich der Alpen*. Bonn.

Huntingdon, R. and Metcalf, P. (1979) *Celebrations of Death. The Anthropology of Mortuary Ritual*. Cambridge.

Hutchinson, G. (1979) 'The Bar-Lug pottery of Cornwall', *Cornish Arch.* 18, 81–102.

Jacobi, R. M. (1973) 'Aspects of the Mesolithic Age in Great Britain', in S. K. Kozlowski (ed.) *The Mesolithic in Europe*. London, pp. 237–65.

Jacobi, R. M. (1979) 'Early Flandrian hunters in the South-West', *PDAS* 37, 48–93.

Jacobi, R. M. (1980) 'The Upper Palaeolithic of Britain with special reference to Wales', in J. A. Taylor (ed.) *Culture and Environment in Prehistoric Wales*. Oxford, pp. 15–100.

Jarvis, K. (1976) 'Pond Farm Romano-British Site, Exminster', *PDAS* 34, 67–72.

Jarvis, K. and Maxfield, V. (1975) 'The excavation of a first-century Roman farmstead and a late Neolithic settlement, Topsham, Devon', *PDAS* 33, 209–65.

Jefferies, J. S. (1974) 'An excavation at the coastal promontory fort of Embury Beacon, Devon', *PPS* 40, 136–52.

Jenkins, A. (1806) *The History and Description of the City of Exeter and its Environs*. Exeter.

Jenner, H. (1917) 'The Irish immigrations into Cornwall in the late fifth and early sixth centuries', *Reports Royal Cornwall Polytechnic Soc.* N.S.5, 38–85.

Jenner, H. (1918) 'The Royal House of Damnonia', *Reports Royal Cornwall Polytechnic Society*, N.S.4, 1–80.

Jenner, H. (1923) 'The Bodmin Gospels', *JRIC* 21, 113–45.

Jenner, H. (1924) 'The Manumissions in the Bodmin Gospels', *JRIC* 21, 235–60.

Jenner, H. (1929–32) 'The Lannaled Mass of St Germanus in Bodl. Ms. 572', *JRIC* 23, 477–92.

Jensen, J. (1982) *The Prehistory of Denmark*. London.

Johnson, N. (1980) 'The Bolster Bank – a survey', *Cornish Arch.* 19, 77–88.

Johnson, N. and David, A. (1982) 'A mesolithic site on Trevose Head and contemporary geography', *Cornish Arch.* 21, 67–103.

Johnson, N. and Rose, P. (1982) 'Defended settlement in Cornwall – an illustrated discussion', in D. Miles (ed.) *The Romano-British Countryside*. BAR 103, Oxford, 151–208.

Jones, G. (1968) *A History of the Vikings*, Oxford.

Jordanes *Getica*.

Karo, G. (1930) *Die Schachtgräber von Mykenai*. Munich.

Kendrick T. D. (1937) 'The Hameldon Down Pommel', *Antiq. Journ.* 17, 313–14.

Kendrick, T. D. (1950) *British Antiquity*. London.

Kerslake, T. (1873) 'The Celt and the Teuton in Exeter', *Arch. Journ.* 30, 211–25.

Kidson, C. (1964) 'The coasts of South and South West England', in J. A. Steer (ed.) *Field Studies in the British Isles*. London, pp. 26–42.

Kidson, C. (1971) 'The Quaternary history of the coasts of South-West England, with special reference to the Bristol Channel coast', in Gregory and Ravenhill (eds) *Exeter Essays in Geography*. Exeter, pp. 1–22.

Kidson, C. (1977) 'The coast of South-West England', in Kidson and Tooley (eds) *The Quaternary History of the Irish Sea*. Liverpool.

Kirwan, E. (1867–8) 'Memoir of the examination of Three Barrows at Broad Down, Farway, near Honiton', *TDA* 2, 619–49.

Kirwan, E. (1869) 'Notes on the pre-historic archaeology of East Devon, Part II', *TDA* 3, 495–500.

Langdon, A. G. (1896) *Ancient Cornish Crosses*. Truro.

Leeds, E. T. (1926–7) 'Excavations at Chun Castle, Penwith', *Archaeologia* 76, 205–40.

Leland *Itinerary* (ed. L. Toulmin Smith, 5 vols, London, 1907–10).

Liddell, D. M. (1930) 'Report on the excavations at Hembury Fort, Devon, 1930', *PDAES* 1, 1–24.

Liddell, D. M. (1931) 'Report on the excavations at Hembury Fort, Devon', *PDAES* 1, 90–120.

Liddell, D. M. (1932) 'Report on the Excavations at Hembury Fort', *PDAES* I, 162–90.

Liddell, D. M. (1935) 'Report on the excavations at Hembury Fort', *PDAES* 2, 135–75.

Linehan, C. (1983) *Peter Orlando Hutchinson of Sidmouth, Devon.* Sidmouth.

Linton, D. L. (1955) 'The problem of tors', *Georg. Journ.* **121**, 480–7.

Longworth, I. H. (1984) *Collared Urns of the Bronze Age in Great Britain and Ireland.* Cambridge.

Lukis, W. (1885) *The Stone Monuments of the British Isles, Cornwall.* London.

Lysons, S. and D. (1822) *Magna Britannia, Devonshire*, Vol. 6. London.

Macalister, R. A. S. (1945) *Corpus Inscriptionum Insularum Celticarum*, I. Dublin.

Macalister, R. A. S. (1949) *Corpus Inscriptionum Insularum Celticarum*, II. Dublin.

Macalpine Woods, G. (1929) 'A Stone Age site in east Devon', *PDAES* 1, 10–14.

MacEnery, J. *Investigations in Kent's Cavern* [Mss in Torquay Museum].

MacNamara, E. (1972) 'A note on the Aegean sword-hilt in Truro Museum', *Cornish Arch.* 12, 19–24.

Madsen, T. (1978) 'Toftum – Ein neues neolitisches Erdwerk bei Horsens, Ostjutland (Dänemark)', *Arch. Korrespondenzbl.* 8, 1–7.

Maguire, D., Ralph, N. and Fleming, A. (1983) 'Early land use on Dartmoor – palaeobotanical and pedological investigations on Holne Moor', in Jones, M. (ed.) *Integrating the Subsistence Economy*, British Archaeological Reports, International Series no. 181. Oxford, pp. 57–100.

Maltby, E. M. (1980) 'Buried soil features and palaeoenvironmental reconstruction at Colliford, Bodmin Moor', in Sims, P. C. (ed.) *Quaternary Research Association Field Handbook, West Cornwall meeting*, pp. 9–11.

Maltby, M. (1979) *Faunal Studies on Urban Sites: The Animal Bones from Exeter.* Sheffield.

Masson Phillips, E. N. (1954) 'Supplementary notes on the ancient stone crosses of Devon', *TDA* 86, 173–92.

Masson Phillips, E. N. (1965) 'Excavations at Lower Well Farm, Stoke Gabriel', *PDAS* 23, 3–34.

Masson Phillips, E. N. (1966) 'Excavation of a Romano-British Site at Lower Well Farm, Stoke Gabriel', *PDAES* 23, 3–34.

Maumsbury, William of (a) *Gesta Pontificum.*

Maumsbury, William of (b) *Gesta Regum.*

Maxfield, V. A. (1980) 'The Roman Military Occupation of South-West England: Further Light and Fresh Problems', in W. S. Hanson and L. J. G. Keppie (eds) *Roman Frontier Studies XII.* Oxford, 297–310.

Megaw, J. V. S. (1967) 'The Trenoweth collar', *Cornish Arch.* 6, 5–8.

Megaw, J. V. S. (1971) 'Later Iron Age collars from western Britain', *B.M. Quarterly* 35, 145–58.

Megaw, J. V. S. (1976) 'Gwithian, Cornwall: some notes on the evidence for Neolithic and Bronze Age settlement', in Burgess and Miket (eds) *Settlement and Economy in the Third and Second Millennia BC* BAR 33, Oxford, 51–68.

Mercer, R. (1970) 'The excavation of a Bronze Age hut-circle settlement, Stannon Down, St Breward', *Cornish Arch.* 9, 17–46.

Mercer, R. (1980) *Hambledon Hill. A Neolithic Landscape.* Edinburgh.

Mercer, R. (1981) 'Excavations at Carn Brea, Illogan, Cornwall, 1970–73', *Cornish Arch.* 20, 1–204.

Merryfield, D. L. and Moore, P. D. (1974) 'Prehistoric human activity and blanket peat initiation on Exmoor', *Nature* 250, 439–41.

Metcalf, D. M. (1930) 'Continuity and change in English monetary history, I', *BNJ* 50, 20–49.

Metcalf, D. M. (1982) 'Continuity and change in English monetary history, II', *BNJ* 51, 52–90.

Metcalf, D. M. and Walker, D. R. (1976) 'Tin as a minor constituent in two sceattas from the Shakenoak excavations', *Num. Chron.* 7 (6), 228–9.

Miles, H. (1975a) 'Barrows on the St Austell Granite, Cornwall', *Cornish Arch.* 14, 5–81.

(1975b) 'Excavations at Woodbury Castle, East Devon, 1971', *PDAS* 33, 183–208.

Miles, H. (1976) 'Flint Scatters and Prehistoric Settlement in Devon', *PDAS* 34, 3–16.

Miles, H. (1977a) 'The Honeyditches Roman Villa, Seaton, Devon', *Britannia* 8, 107–48.

(1977b) 'Excavations at Killibury Hillfort, Egloshayle, 1965–6', *Cornish Arch.* 16, 89–121.

Miles, H. and Miles, T. (1973) 'Excavations at Trethurgy: Interim Report', *Cornish Arch.* 12, 25–30.

Milles, J. *Mss.* [Materials on Devon Parishes, in Bodleian Library, Oxford.]

Milne, J. G. (1948) *Finds of Greek Coins in the British Isles.* Oxford.

Milne, J. G. and Goodchild, R. (1937) 'The Greek coins from Exeter reconsidered', *Num. Chron.* 5 (17), 139.

Mitchell, S. (1983) 'Cornish Tin, Julius Caesar and the Invasion of Britain', in C. Deroux (ed.) *Studies in Latin Literature and Roman History.* Brussels, 80–99.

Mitford, J. (1963) *The American Way of Death.* New York.

Mold, E. T. (1983) 'Culbone Hill Stones', *Exmoor Review*, 67–9.

Monmouth, Geoffrey of *Historia Regum.*

Montgomerie-Nielsen, E. and Montague, L. A. D. (1933–6) 'Report of the Exeter Excavation Committee 1932–3', *PDAES* 2, 53–109.

Morris, J. (1972) *The Age of Arthur*, London.

Muckelroy, K. (1980) 'Two Bronze Age cargoes in British waters', *Antiquity* 54, 100–9.

Muckelroy, K. (1981) 'Middle Bronze Age trade between Britain and Europe: a maritime perspective', *PPS* 47, 275–98.

Muhly, J. D. (1973) 'Copper and tin: the distribution of mineral resources and the nature of the metal trade in the Bronze Age', *Trans. Connecticut Academy of Arts and Sciences* 43, 155–535.

Napier, A. S. and Stevenson, W. H. (1895) *Anecdota Oxoniensia. The Crawford Collection of Early Charters and Documents now in the Bodleian Library*, Oxford.

Nash-Williams, V. E. (1950) *The Early Christian Monuments of Wales.* Cardiff.

Neal, D. S. (1983) 'Excavations on a settlement at Little Bay, St Martin's, Isles of Scilly', *Cornish Arch.* 22, 47–80.

Needham, S. (1979) 'The extent of foreign influence on Early Bronze Age axe development in southern Britain', in M. Ryan (ed.) *The Origins of Metallurgy in Atlantic Europe*. Dublin, pp. 265–93.

Needham, S. (1980) 'An assemblage of Late Bronze Age metalwork debris from Dainton, Devon', *PPS* 46, 177–216.

Needham, S. (1981) *The Bulford-Helsbury Manufacturing Tradition, British Museum Occasional Papers*, 13. London.

Nennius *Historia Brittonum*.

Norden, J. (*c.* 1610) *Description of Cornwall* (Mss).

Olsen, L. (forthcoming) *Early Monasteries in Cornwall*.

O'Neil, B. St J. (1933) 'The Roman villa at Magor farm, near Camborne, Cornwall', *J. Brit. Arch. Ass.* 39, 116–75.

O'Neil, B. St J. (1952) 'The excavation of Knackyboy cairn, St Martin's, Scilly', *Antiq. Journ.* 32, 21–34.

Orme, A. R. (1960) 'The raised beaches and strandlines of south Devon', *Field Studies* 1, 109–30.

Orme, B. J., Coles, J. M. and Sturdy, C. R. (1979) 'Meare Lake Village West: a report on recent work', *Somerset Levels Papers* 5, 6–17.

Palmer, S. (1977) *Mesolithic Cultures of Britain*. Poole.

Parfitt, E. (1878) 'Archaeological discoveries in Exeter made during April and May 1878', *TDA* 10, 335–48.

Patchett, F. M. (1944) 'Cornish Bronze Age pottery', *Arch. Journ.* 101, 17–49.

Patchett, F. (1951) 'Cornish Bronze Age pottery, Part 2', *Arch. Journ.* 108, 44–65.

Peacock, D. P. S. (1968) 'A petrological study of certain Iron Age pottery from western England', *PPS* 34, 414–27.

Peacock, D. P. S. (1969a) 'Neolithic pottery production in Cornwall', *Antiquity* 43, 145–9.

Peacock, D. P. S. (1969b) 'A contribution to the study of Glastonbury ware from south-western Britain', *Antiq. Journ.* 49, 41–61.

Peacock, D. P. S. (1969c) 'A Romano-British salt-working site at Trebarveth, St Keverne', *Cornish Arch.* 8, 47–65.

Pearce, S. M. (1970) 'Late Roman coinage in south-west Britain', *TDA* 102, 19–34.

Pearce, S. M. (1979) 'The distribution and production of Bronze Age metalwork', *PDAS* 37, 136–45.

Pearce, S. M. (1983) *The Bronze Age Metalwork of South Western Britain*. Oxford.

Pearce, S. M. and Padley, T. (1977) 'The Bronze Age find from Tredarvah', *Cornish Arch.* 16, 25–42.

Pengelly, W. (1870) 'The literature of the caverns near Yealmpton, south Devon', *TDA* 4, 81–104.

Pengelly, W. (1870–1) 'The Ash Hole and Bench Bone caves at Brixham, south Devon', *TDA* 4, 73–80.

Pengelly, W. (1872) 'The literature of the Oreston caverns near Plymouth', *TDA* 5, 249–316.

Pengelly, W. (1873) 'The literature of the caverns at Buckfastleigh, Devonshire', *TDA* 6, 70–2.

Pengelly, W. (1874) 'The Bone cavern discovered in Windmill Hill, Brixham in 1858', *TDA* 6, 775–856.

Petersen, F. F. (1981) *The Excavation of a Bronze Age Cemetery on Knighton Heath, Dorset*, BAR No. 98, Oxford.

Piggott, S. (1954) *Neolithic Cultures of the British Isles*. Cambridge.

Piggott, S. (1957) 'William Camden and the Britannia', *Procs. Brit. Acad.* 37, 199–217.

Piggott, S. (1977) 'A glance at Cornish tin', in V. Markovic (ed.) *Ancient Europe and the Mediterranean*. Warminster, pp. 141–5.

Piggott, S. and Fowler, P. J. (1981) *The Agrarian History of England and Wales, I. 1, Prehistory*. Cambridge.

RCHM (1929) *Roman London*. (Royal Commission on Historical Monuments), London.

Polanyi, K., Arensberg, C. M. and Pearson, H. W. (eds) (1957) *Trade and Market in the Early Empires*. New York.

Pole, W. (1791) *Collections towards a Description of the County of Devon*. London.

Pollard, S. (1966) 'Neolithic and Dark Age settlements on High Peak, Sidmouth', *PDAES* 23, 35–59.

Pollard, S. H. M. (1967) 'Seven prehistoric sites near Honiton. Beaker flint-ring on Burnt Common', *PDAS* 25, 1–18.

Pollard, S. H. M. (1971) 'Flint rings on Farway Hill', *PDAS* 29, 162–80.

Pollard, S. H. M. (1974) 'A Late Iron Age settlement and a Romano-British villa at Holcombe, Devon', *PDAS* 32, 59–162.

Pollard, S. H. M. and Russell, P. (1969) 'Excavation of Round Barrow 248b, Upton Pyne, Exeter', *PDAS* 27, 49–78.

Polwhele, R. (1793–1806) *The History of Devonshire*, 3 vols (1793, 1797 and 1806). London and Exeter.

Pool, P. A. S. (1966) 'The Borlase–Stukeley correspondence', *Cornish Arch.* 5, 11–13.

Pool, P. A. S. (ed.) (1969–72) 'A tour in Cornwall in 1780 by the Rev. John Swete, M.A.', *JRIC* 6, 185–219.

Pool, P. A. S. (1977) 'Cornish drawings by Edward Lhuyd in the British Museum', *Cornish Arch.* 16, 139–42.

Preston-Jones, A. (1984) 'The Excavation of a long-cist Cemetery at Carnanton, St Mawgan, 1943', *Cornish Arch.* 23, 157–78.

Prestwich, J. (1872) 'Report on the exploration of Brixham Cave', *Procs. Royal Society* xx (137), 514–24.

Procopius *Bellum Gothicum*.

Pryce, W. (1778) *Mineralogia Cornubiensis*. London.

Pryce, W. (1790) *Archaeologica Cornu-Britannica*. Sherborne.

Pryor, F. (1980) *Excavation at Fengate, Peterborough, England: The Third Report*. Northampton and Toronto.

Radford, C. A. R. (1935a) 'Tintagel, the Castle and Celtic monastery', *Antiq. Journ.* 15, 401–19.

Radford, C. A. R. (1935b) 'The Hurlers, Cornwall, notes on excavations', *PPS* 1, 134.

Radford, C. A. R. (1937) 'Report of the Exeter Excavation Committee: the Roman site at Topsham', *PDAES* 3, 5–23.

Radford, C. A. R. (1951) 'Report on the excavations at Castle Dore', *JRIC* series I, 1–119.

Radford, C. A. R. (1957–8) 'The chambered tomb at Broadsands, Paignton', *PDAES* 5, 147–68.

Radford, C. A. R. (1962) 'The Celtic monastery in Britain', *Arch. Camb.* 111, 1–24.

Radford, C. A. R. (1970) 'The later pre-Conquest boroughs and their defences', *Med. Arch.* **14**, 83–103.

Radford, C. A. R. (1975) *The Early Christian Inscriptions of Dumnonia.* Truro.

Radford, C. A. R. and Morris, P. (1933–6) 'Report of the Exeter Excavation Committee', *PDAES* **2**, 176–90.

Radford, C. A. R. and Rogers, E. H. (1947) 'The excavations of two barrows at East Putford', *PDAES* **3**, 156–63.

Ragon, M. (1983) *The Space of Death. A Study of Funerary Architecture, Decoration and Urbanism.* Charlottesville.

Rahtz, P. (1968) 'Castle Dore. A reappraisal of the post-Roman Structures', *Cornish Arch.* **10**, 49–54.

Raistrick, A. and Holmes, P. F. (1962) 'Archaeology of Malham Moor', *Field Studies* **1** (4), 73–100.

Rashleigh, P. (1789) 'Account of antiquities discovered in Cornwall, 1774'. *Archaeologia* **9**, 187–8.

Ravenhill, W. L. D. (1965) *Benjamin Donn. A Map of the County of Devon* (in facsimile). Exeter.

Ravenhill, W. L. D. (1967) 'Cornwall', in H. Darby and R. Welldon Finn (eds) *The Domesday Geography of South-west England.* Cambridge.

Ravenhill, W. L. D. (1972) *John Norden's Manuscript Maps of Cornwall and its Nine Hundreds.* Exeter.

Reid Moir, J. (1936) 'Ancient Man in Devon', *PDAES* **2**, 264–82.

Rice Holmes, T. (1907) *Ancient Britain and the Invasions of Julius Caesar.* Oxford.

Richmond, I. A. (1968) *Hod Hill. Volume II*, London.

Risdon, T. (1714) *The Chorographical Description, or Survey, of the County of Devon.* Exeter.

Rivet, A. L. F. and Smith, C. (1979) *The Place-Names of Roman Britain.* London.

Robinson, R. and Greeves, T. A. P. (1981) 'Two unrecorded prehistoric multiple stone rings, Glasscombe, Ugborough, South Dartmoor', *PDAS* **39**, 33–6.

Röder, J. (1951) 'Erdwerk Urmitz: Gesamtplan und Periodenleitung', *Germania* **22**, 187–98.

Roe, D. A. (1981) *The Lower and Middle Palaeolithic Periods in Britain*, London.

Rogers, E. H. (1932) 'The Yelland Stone Row', *PDAES* **1**, 201–2.

Rogers, E. H. (1946) 'The sites at Westward Ho! and Yelland', *PDAES* **3**, 109–35.

Rogers, E. H. (1947) 'The excavation of a barrow on Brownstone Farm', Kingswear, *PDAES* **3**, 164–6.

Rosenfeld, A. (1964) 'Excavations in the Torbryan Caves, Devonshire II. Three Holes Cave', *PDAS* **22**, 3–26.

Rousseau, P. (1978) *Ascetics, Authority and the Church*, Oxford.

Russell, V. (1971) *West Penwith Survey.* Truro.

Russell, V. and Pool, P. A. S. (1964) 'Excavation of a menhir at Try, Gulval', *Cornish Arch.* **3**, 15–25.

St Joseph, J. K. (1958) 'Air Reconnaissance in Britain, 1955–7', *JRS* **48**, 86–101.

Saunders, C. (1972) 'The excavations at Grambla, Wendron, 1972', *Cornish Arch.* **11**, 50–2.

Saunders, A. and Harris, D. (1982) 'Excavation at Castle Gotha, St Austell', *Cornish Arch.* **21**, 109–53.

Scarre, C. (ed.) (1983) *Ancient France. Neolithic Societies and their Landscapes 6000– 2000 bc.* Edinburgh.

Schlette, F. (1964) 'Grabungen auf dem Steinkuhlenberg, Kr. Wernigerode – Ein Beitrag zum Siedlungswesen der Trichterbecherkultur', in P. Grimm (ed.) *Varia Archaeologica.* Berlin, pp. 48–61.

Schuchhardt, C. (1914) *Der Goldfund von Messingwerk bei Eberswalde.* Berlin.

Schwappach, F. (1969) 'Stempelverzierte Keramic von Armorica', in O-H. Frey (ed.) *Marburger Beiträge zur Archaologie der Kelten. Festschrift W. Dehn. Fundberichte aus Hessen,* Beiheft 1. Bonn, pp. 213–87.

Scrivenor, R. C. (1982) *Tin and Related Mineralization of the Dartmoor Granite.* Exeter PhD dissertation.

Sellwood, L. (1983) 'The Mount Batten Celtic Coins', *Oxford Journ. of Archaeology* 2, 199–211.

Severus, Sulpicius *Historia Sacra.*

Shakesby, R. A. and Stephens, N. (1984) 'The Pleistocene gravels of the Axe valley, Devon', *TDA* 116, 77–88.

Shell, C. A. (1979) 'The early exploitation of tin deposits in South-West England', in M. Ryan (ed.) *The Origins of Metallurgy in Atlantic Europe.* Dublin, 251–63.

Shorter, A. H., Ravenhill, W. L. D. and Gregory, K. J. (1969) *South-West England.* London.

Shortt, W. T. P. (1841a) *Sylva Antiqua Iscana.* Exeter.

Shortt, W. T. P. (1841b) *Collectanea curiosa antiqua Dumnonia.* Exeter.

Silvester, R. J. (1979) 'The relationship of first millennium settlement to the upland areas of the south-west', *PDAS* 37, 176–90.

Silvester, R. J. (1980) 'The prehistoric open settlement at Dainton, South Devon,' *PDAS* 38, 17–48.

Silvester, R. J. (1981a) 'An excavation on the post-Roman site at Bantham, S. Devon', *PDAS* 39, 89–118.

Silvester, R. J. (1981b) 'Excavations at Honeyditches Roman Villa, Seaton, in 1978', *PDAS* 39, 37–88.

Simmons, I. G. (ed.) (1964) *Dartmoor Essays.* Exeter.

Simmons, I. G. (1969) 'Environment and Early Man on Dartmoor', *PPS* 35, 203–19.

Simmons, I. G. and Dimbleby, G. W. (1974) 'The possible role of ivy (*hedera helix L*) in the Mesolithic economy of western Europe', *Journ. Arch. Science* 1, 291–6.

Simpson, D. D. A. (1968) 'Food Vessels: associations and chronology', in J. M. Coles and D. D. A. Simpson (eds) *Studies in Ancient Europe.* Leicester, pp. 197–212.

Smith, E. E. (1956) 'Notes on a Series of Flints from Woodbury Common', *PDAES* 5, 117–21.

Smith, G. and Harris, D. (1982) 'The excavation of Mesolithic, Neolithic and Bronze Age settlements at Poldowrian, St Keverne, 1980', *Cornish Arch.* 21, 23–66.

Smith, I. F. (1971) 'Causewayed Enclosures', in D. Simpson (ed.) *Economy and Settlement in Neolithic and Early Bronze Age Britain and Europe.* Leicester, 89–112.

Smith, K. *et al.* (1981) 'The Shaugh Moor Project: Third Report – settlement and environmental investigation', *PPS* 47, 205–73.

Smith, R. A. (1926) 'Two early British bronze bowls', *Antiq. Journ.* 6, 276–83.

Spence Bate, C. (1866) 'On the discovery of a Romano-British cemetery near Plymouth', *Archaeologia* 40, 501–10.

Sprake, C. J. G. (1832) *The Gates and other Antiquities of the City of Exeter.* Exeter.

Startin, W. (1982) 'Halligye Fogou: Excavations in 1981', *Cornish Arch.* **21**. 185–6.

Stenton, F. M. (1947) *Anglo-Saxon England*. Second edn, Oxford.

Stevens, C. E. (1976) 'The Sacred Wood', in J. V. S. Megaw (ed.) *To Illustrate the Monuments*. London, 239–44.

Strabo *Geography*.

Stukeley, W. (1724) *Itinerarium Curiosum*. London.

Sturdy, D. A. (1975) 'Some reindeer economies in prehistoric Europe', in E. S. Higgs (ed.) *Palaeoeconomy*. London, 55–96.

Suetonius *Life of Vespasian*.

Sutcliffe, A. J. (1960) 'Joint Mitnor Cave, Buckfastleigh', *Trans. Torquay NHS* **13**, 3–28.

Sutcliffe, A. J. and Zeuner, F. (1957–8) 'Excavations in the Torbryan Caves, I. Tornewton Cave', *PDAES* 5, 127–46.

Swann, J. S. (1880) 'Notes on the discovery of a Roman villa at Holcombe, Devon', *Archaeologia* **45**, 462–5.

Surete, J. (1792–1802) *Tours in Devon* [Mss in Barnstaple Athenaeum].

Sykes-Balls, H. (1978–9) 'Viking treasure', *Trans. Torquay NHS* **18**, 10–13.

Taylor, J. J. (1970) 'Lunulae reconsidered', *PPS* **36**, 38–81.

Taylor, J. J. (1980) *Bronze Age Goldwork of the British Isles*. Cambridge.

Taylor, S. (ed.) (1983) *The Anglo-Saxon Chronicle: Ms. B. A Collaborative Edition*. Cambridge.

Taylor, T. (1916) *The Celtic Christianity of Cornwall. Divers Sketches and Studies*. London.

Thom, A. (1967) *Megalithic Sites in Britain*. Oxford.

Thom, A. (1971) *Megalithic Lunar Observatories*. Oxford.

Thomas, C. (1958) *Gwithian. Ten Years' Work*. Gwithian.

Thomas, C. (1961) A New pre-Conquest crucifixion stone from west Cornwall, *Antiq. Journ.* **41**, 89–92.

Thomas, C. (1964a) 'The henge at Castilly, Lanivet', *Cornish Arch.* **3**, 3.

Thomas, C. (1964b) 'Settlement-history in Early Cornwall. I. The antiquity of the Hundreds', *Cornish Arch.* **3**, 70–9.

Thomas, C. (1966) 'The character and origins of Roman Dumnonia', in *Rural Settlement in Roman Britain*. London, pp. 74–98.

Thomas, C. (1968a) *The Christian Antiquities of Camborne*. St Austell.

Thomas, C. (1968b) 'Grass-marked pottery in Cornwall', in J. M. Coles and D. D. A. Simpson (eds) *Studies in Ancient Europe*. Leicester, pp. 311–32.

Thomas, C. (1968c) 'Merther-Uny, Wendron', *Cornish Arch.* **7**, 81–2.

Thomas, C. (1971) *The Early Christian Archaeology of Northern Britain*. Oxford.

Thomas, C. (1972) 'The Irish settlements in post-Roman western Britain: a survey of the evidence', *JRIC* N.S. 4, 251–74.

Thomas, C. (1978) 'Hermits on islands or priests in a landscape?', *Cornish Studies* 6, 28–44.

Thomas, C. (1981a) *A Provisional List of Imported Pottery in Post-Roman Western Britain and Ireland*. Redruth.

Thomas, C. (1981b) *Christianity in Roman Britain*. London.

Thomas, C. (1982) 'East and west: Tintagel, medieval imports and the early insular Church', in S. M. Pearce (ed.) *The Early Church in Western Britain and Ireland*. Oxford, pp. 17–34.

Thomas, C. (1985) *Exploration of a Drowned Landscape*. London.

Thomas, C., Fowler, P. J. and Gardner, K. (1969) 'Lundy 1969', *Current Archaeology* **16**, 138–42.

Thomas, R. (1815) *Falmouth Guide*. Falmouth.

Thomas, R. (1827) *History of Falmouth*. Falmouth.

Thompson, E. A. (1968) 'Britonia', in M. W. Barley and R. P. C. Hanson (eds) *Christianity in Britain, 300–700*, Leicester, pp. 201–6.

Thompson, E. A. (1980) 'Procopius on Brittia and Britannia', *Class. Quart.* **30**, 498–507.

Threipland, L. M. (1956) 'An excavation at St. Mawgan-in-Pyder, Cornwall', *Arch. Journ.* **113**, 33–81.

Todd, M. (1975) *The Northern Barbarians*. London.

Todd, M. (1983a) 'Lammana', *Cornish Arch.* **22**, 122–3.

Todd, M. (1983b) 'A Romano-Celtic Silver Brooch from Capton, near Dartmouth', *PDAS* **41**, 130–2.

Todd, M. (1984) 'Excavations at Hembury, Devon, 1980–3: a summary report', *Antiq. Journ.* **64**, 251–68.

Todd, M. (1985) 'The Roman Fort at Bury Barton, Devonshire', *Britannia* **16**, 49–55.

Tode, A. *et al.* (1953) 'Die Untersuchung der paläolitischen Freilandstation von Salzgitter-Lebenstedt', *Eiszeitalter und Gegenwart* **3**, 144–220.

Tomlin, E. W. F. (1982) *In Search of St. Piran*. Padstow.

Tonkin, T. (1702–37) *Materials on Cornish Parishes* [Mss].

Torbrugge, W. (1970–1) 'Vor- und frühgeschichtliche Flussfunde', *BRGK* **51–2**, 1–146.

Tours, Gregory of *Historia Francorum*.

Townsend Hall, R. (*c.* 1864) Mss [Barnstaple Athenaeum].

Turner, J. (1980) 'Chamber cairns, Gidleigh', *PDAS* **38**, 117–19.

von Uslar, R. (1955) 'Der Goldbecher von Fritzdorf bei Bonn', *Germania* **33**, 319–23.

Vachell, E. T. (1964) 'Milber Down. Excavations encroaching on the site of the Romano-British homestead', *PDAES* **22**, 27–30.

Vendryes, J. (1938) 'Une liste de noms bretons', *Etudes celtiques* **3**, 144–54.

Wainwright, G. (1960) 'Three microlithic industries from South-West England and their affinities', *PPS* **26**, 193–202.

Wainwright, G. J. (1980) 'A Pit Burial at Lower Ashmore Farm, Rose Ash, Devon', *PDAS* **38**, 13–16.

Wainwright, G. J., Smith, K. *et al.* (1979) 'The Shaugh Moor Project: First Report', *PPS* **45**, 1–33.

Wainwright, G. J., Smith, K. *et al.* (1980) 'The Shaugh Moor Project: Second Report – the enclosure', *PPS* **46**, 65–122.

Wainwright, G. J., Smith, K. *et al.* (1981) 'The Shaugh Moor Project: Third Report – settlement and environmental investigations', *PPS* **47**, 205–70.

Ward-Perkins, J. B. (1939) 'Iron Age metal horses' bits of the British Isles', *PPS* **5**, 173–92.

Webster, G. (1958) 'The Roman Military Advance under Ostorius Scapula', *Arch. Journ.* **115**, 49–98.

Webster, G. (1979) 'Final Report on the excavations of the Roman Fort at Waddon Hill, Stoke Abbot, 1963–9', *Procs. Dorset NHAS* **101**, 51–90.

Welldon Finn, R. (1967) 'Devon', in H. Darby and R. Welldon Finn (ed.) *The Domesday Geography of South-west England*. Cambridge.

Wells, A. (1978) *The 'Rounds' of West Cornwall*. Exeter MA Diss.

Westcote, T. (1845) *A View of Devonshire in 1630*. Exeter.

Wheeler, R. E. M. (1943) *Maiden Castle, Dorset*. Oxford.

Wheeler, R. E. M. (1953) 'An Early Iron Age Beach-head at Lulworth, Dorset', *Antiq. Journ.* 33, 1–13.

Wheeler, R. E. M. and Richardson, K. M. (1957) *Hill-Forts of Northern France*. Oxford.

Whimster, R. (1977) 'Harlyn Bay Reconsidered', *Cornish Arch.* **16**, 61–88.

Whimster, R. (1981) *Burial Practices in Iron Age Britain*, BAR No. 90. Oxford.

White, D. A. (1982) *The Bronze Age Cremation cemeteries at Simons Ground, Dorset*. Dorchester.

Whittle, A. W. R. (1977) *The Earlier Neolithic of S. England and its Continental Background*. BAR Supplementary Series 35, Oxford.

Whybrow, C. (1967) 'Some multivallate hill-forts on Exmoor', *PDAS* 25, 1–18.

Williams, P. (1911–12) 'Notes on the excavation of the Holy Well of St. Constantine', *PSAL* 2 (24), 96–102.

Williams, S. (1740) 'An attempt to examine the barrows in Cornwall', *Philosophical Transactions* **458**, 465–84.

Willis, L. and Rogers, E. H. (1951) 'Dainton earthworks', *PDAES* 4, 79–101.

Willock, E. H. (1936) 'A Neolithic site on Haldon', *PDAES* 2, 244–63.

Willock, E. H. (1937) 'A further note on Haldon', *PDAES* 3, 33–43.

Wilson, D. M. and Blunt, C. E. (1961) 'The Trewhiddle hoard', *Archaeologia* **98**, 75–122.

Woollacombe, H. (1839) *Some Account of the fortified hills in the county of Devon, whether British, Roman, Anglo-Saxon or Danish* [Mss in Devon and Exeter Institution, Exeter].

Worth, R. H. (1947) 'Prehistoric Tavistock', *TDA* 79, 125–8.

Worth, R. H. (1953) *Dartmoor*. Plymouth.

Worth, R. N. (1870) *A History of the Town and Borough of Devonport*. Plymouth.

Worth, R. N. (1871) *History of Plymouth*. Plymouth.

Worth, R. N. (1874) 'Ancient mining implements of Cornwall', *Arch. Journ.* **31**, 53–60.

Worth, R. N. (1887) 'On the occurrence of human remains in a bone cave at Cattedown', *TDA* 19, 419–37.

Young, A. and Richardson, K. M. (1955) 'Report on the excavations at Blackbury Castle', *PDAES* 5, 43–67.

Index